1977

This book may be kept

TEEN DAYS

Teaching Special Children

McGraw-Hill Series in Special Education

Robert M. Smith, Consulting Editor

Cartwright and Cartwright:
DEVELOPING OBSERVATION SKILLS
Haring and Schiefelbusch:
TEACHING SPECIAL CHILDREN
Ross:
PSYCHOLOGICAL ASPECTS OF LEARNING DISABILITIES AND READING DISORDERS
Smith:
CLINICAL TEACHING: Methods of Instruction for the Retarded
Smith:
INTRODUCTION TO MENTAL RETARDATION
Smith and Neisworth:
THE EXCEPTIONAL CHILD: A Functional Approach
Worell and Nelson:
MANAGING INSTRUCTIONAL PROBLEMS: A Case Study Workbook

Teaching Special Children

Edited by
Norris G. Haring
University of Washington
and
Richard L. Schiefelbusch
University of Kansas

Technical Editor,
ROBERT K. HOYT, Jr.

McGRAW-HILL BOOK COMPANY
New York   St. Louis   San Francisco   Auckland   Düsseldorf
Johannesburg   Kuala Lumpur   London   Mexico   Montreal   New Delhi
Panama   Paris   São Paulo   Singapore   Sydney   Tokyo   Toronto

Teaching Special Children

1234567890 KPKP 798765

This book was set in Times Roman by University Graphics, Inc.
The editors were Stephen D. Dragin and Barry Benjamin;
the cover was designed by Nicholas Krenitsky;
the production supervisor was Dennis J. Conroy.
The drawings were done by ANCO Technical Services.
Kingsport Press, Inc., was printer and binder.

Library of Congress Cataloging in Publication Data
Main entry under title:

Teaching special children.

    (McGraw-Hill series in special education)
    Includes index.
    1.   Handicapped children—Education—Addresses,
essays, lectures. I. Haring, Norris Grover, date
II. Schiefelbusch, Richard L. [DNLM: 1. Education,
Special. LC4015 T253]
LC4015.T32   371.9   75-14251
ISBN 0-07-026430-9

Contents

Foreword

This book was written *by* researchers *for* teachers *about* teaching. It might also be considered a book written *by* teachers *about* research *for* researchers. The content is heavy on *methods*—how-to-do—and *perspectives* of *why, when,* and *what* to do. We hope to help teachers and educational specialists (including researchers) be better measurers and evaluators of children's academic and social behavior while at the same time planning and effecting changes toward desired goals. The book does not set new educational goals. It specifies objectives and methods for achieving long-standing goals.

Our approach is not designed to reduce the creative, humanistic side of teaching. The techniques should help teachers design individualized programs for special children so that the latter can experience "normal" educational activities.

This book is for students and teachers who wish to improve their skills in working with special children. It has a research bias—more specifically an Applied Behavior Analysis (ABA) research bias. The procedures described and the illustrations presented are designed for classroom utilization. The procedures are also applicable for resource teachers, supervisors, consultants, and researchers who work in teaching programs.

Recent advances in teaching and in research about teaching have made it possible to unite the previously separate domains of the teacher and researcher. The separatist era should now be regarded as passé. Teachers now can and do conduct research and researchers can and do teach. Teaching is researchable and research is teachable. The demands of teaching have extended the functional effectiveness of ABA, and ABA has added precision and practical effectiveness to teaching.

This book proposes more than a détente between teaching and research. Teaching and research are rooted in the same functions. All that is required is a common set of behavioral techniques. This book explains and/or illustrates this issue. Beyond the common methods, however, extends a range of required experiences. Each person who works with special children must willingly seek this experience.

This book describes the products of teacher-researcher teams working in instructional settings, usually classrooms, to design and develop improvements in teaching. The improvements are defined as desired changes in the behavior of special children. In other words, a better *method* is determined by a better *product*. Thus the efforts of the teacher, the researcher, the specialist, the parent, the administrator, and the child can and often are shaped by the same recorded events. This conscious system of responding to *shared data* may be one of the most healthy influences in current educational practice.

We wish to extend our thanks to Barbara M. McLean and Sandra S. Grafton for preparing the summaries and discussion questions which contribute significantly to clarifying the issues presented.

The Authors and Editors

Preface

Since *Methods in Special Education** was published in 1967, the field has experienced a revolution. Rapid changes are apparent in instructional strategies and procedures, in the range of instructional environments, and in the range of instructors. The technology of instruction has been influenced especially by behavior modification, which has emerged as a resilient companion to programming and systems planning, individualized curricula, classroom management, and language intervention. The demonstrated effectiveness of the operant model for accelerating behavior, for shaping target behaviors, and for eliminating objectionable behaviors, as described in *Methods in Special Education,* has expanded into a full-scale technology of experimentally planned and behaviorally engineered classrooms, community-oriented instructional programs, and combined professional and paraprofessional instructional programs. The special teacher has become a behavioral engineer who assumes responsibility for planning and developing instructional environments in which precision teaching (Lindsley, 1964), responsive teaching (Hall et al., 1971), or engineered instruction (Hewett, 1972) are employed. These tactics often are taught to other instructional agents such as parents, aides, paraprofessionals, and in-service professionals. A remarkable second- and even third-order effect is achieved, thus economizing and functionalizing the spread of technical expertise.

The increased emphasis on educational planning for special children parallels a decline in categorical groupings, segregated classrooms, and institutionalization. The assumptions now are that all children should be placed

*Haring, N. G., and Schiefelbusch, R. L. (eds.), *Methods in Special Education,* New York, McGraw-Hill, 1967.

in the mainstream of regular class instruction. This objective, of course, places additional demands upon the schools at a time when the cost crunch is forcing them to design larger class groupings and otherwise to reduce the unit costs of instruction. The educational technology described in this book should assist the schools in accommodating to these additional pressures.

We have also seen the emergence of instructional models—models created and validated in an instructional setting prior to a demonstration phase in which the full package is presented to other professionals for subsequent implementation in other schools, communities, and environments. The design built into the instructional model is essentially an environmentally determined technology of instruction. The assumption is that the technology can be taught in situ and that those so taught can extrapolate or translate the methods into a different, but similar, instructional environment.

Included in the disseminable package is a set of instructional objectives, a plan for recording and evaluating behavior, a reinforcement (contingency) system, a schedule of daily events, an environmental design, and a strategy for evaluating and refining procedures as the instructional program evolves.

In this book the authors present a number of instructional models in summarized form and give frequent references to the complete instructional package. The latter may include manuals, workbooks, audiovisual materials (including single concept films), and other multimedia forms.

The variety and extent of these materials suggest that the media expert is fast becoming a part of the instructional technology revolution. He or she aids the educator in designing instructional packages about instructional procedures. Thus the expertise of the media expert is felt in the designing of instructions for students, in-service teachers, parents and paraprofessionals, and educational specialists. The media expert is a recent addition to the technological explosion in special education.

These methodological developments are featured in *Teaching Special Children*. The book reflects a range of new developments in instructional technology, but it does not disregard the basic structure of the field of special education with its popularized terms, its system for individualized instruction for children with handicaps, and its traditional emphasis upon humanism. It should be clearly understood that a technology, at best, is a scientific means to achieve accepted or acceptable ends. Thus the determinations about what are the desirable goals, the end products, and the full-scale nature of society's investment in education must be made by the parents, the friends, and the other constituents of the handicapped. The issues of accountability are also becoming more apparent. It is desirable for educators, including scientists, to remember at all times that they are working to accomplish ends that extend beyond their scientific technologies. At the same time society must determine through its institutionalized channels the nature of its commitment to handicapped individuals. The progress in methods noted in this book is perhaps no greater than, and is probably a reflection of, the progress society has made in providing educational resources for teaching all children.

The book is divided into 10 chapters. The first is an overview and a statement of the rationale of the book. The second is a technological statement of the basic features of a data based system of teaching. Chapters 3, 4, and 5 describe procedures for instructing special children in regular classes and other school settings in the mainstream of education. Chapters 6 and 7 advance a program for instructing children with limited development and with major educational limitations. The role of public education in teaching these children is discussed and prescriptions for teaching are considered in detail. Chapters 8 and 9 provide an in-depth program for teaching language to special children, beginning with early preschool phases of development. Chapter 10 provides a synthesis of procedures for teaching children in a classroom setting. As its title implies, it is an attempt to "put it all together."

The editors wish to acknowledge the skillful, dedicated assistance of Marilyn Barket, Mary Beth Johnston, Kathy Cunningham, Thelma Dillon, Jean Ann Summers, and Leonard Grotta. Also the editorial assistance of Barbara McLean, Sandy Grafton, and especially to Robert K. Hoyt, Jr., who added immeasurably to the quality and form of the content.

Norris G. Haring
Richard L. Schiefelbusch

Chapter 1

Perspectives on Teaching
Special Children

Richard L. Schiefelbusch
Bureau of Child Research, University of Kansas
Norris G. Haring
Experimental Education Unit, Mental Retardation and Child
Development Center, University of Washington

INTRODUCTION

Education is the sustenance of a democratic society. A truly democratic society must provide appropriate education for all its children as well as equal opportunities for all citizens. Countless books have been written about the American educational system, but there have been relatively few children publications about special programs and training models designed for, or about, special children until fairly recently.

In considering the scope of the current educational movement in behalf of special children, we should remember that it stems from a humanistic philosophy. Philanthropic and religious agencies, public and private institutions, private citizens and the media have all contributed to the education of special children. Millions of citizens sincerely believe that special children are entitled to special

1

programs. Without this commitment, special children cannot attain their rightful, productive places in society.

A humanistic philosophy is essential to an educational program for *all* children. However, there are other essentials. For instance, skills and technical expertise must be developed for teaching heterogeneous assemblies of children. Appropriate, individualized educational goals must be established for all children. With good reason, educators sometimes despair that they have neither the wisdom nor the technical resources to discharge their responsibilities. Nevertheless, recent technical progress provides the means for a complete, appropriate system of public education for *all* children.

The focus of this book is upon the special child and the special teacher. The process in which they both participate is called *special teaching*. It is distinguished from *normal* class or *regular* class instruction in order to highlight the functions that make it special. Much of the operational information presented in this book is also appropriate to children and teachers in regular classes. Ideally, special children should learn among their regular class peers, and special instruction should be given by the regular class teacher. Nevertheless, special teaching is sometimes provided in special classes, special settings, and in special arrangements by special teachers.

We dedicate this work to the challenging years ahead. We hope those years will see more cooperative programs in which homes, schools, agencies, and communities all play instrumental roles in guiding special children into productive roles in society.

WHO ARE THE SPECIAL CHILDREN?

Of course, all children are "special"; and a "special," or good, education is prized in all communities of our nation. In the sense in which we use it in this volume, "special" will refer to children with special *needs*. Schools have experienced chronic difficulties in educating certain children. The most common term applied to these children is *exceptional*. It is the approved term for children with marked individual differences. The prevalent system has been to group or categorize children according to disability. Kirk (1972) lists five major deviations: (1) *communication disorders,* including children with (*a*) learning disabilities and (*b*) speech handicaps; (2) *mental deviations,* including children that are (*a*) intellectually gifted and (*b*) mentally retarded; (3) *sensory handicaps,* including children with (*a*) auditory handicaps and (*b*) visual handicaps; (4) *neurologic, orthopedic,* and other *health-impaired* children; and (5) *behavior disorders.*

Critics of disability listings point out that categories with such a heavy loading of physiological and psychological disabilities are not necessarily relevant to education. The critics further suggest that such groupings do not establish bases for educational programming. Instead, the categories may reflect issues of health and administration more than education.

Issues of this nature prompted Reynolds and Balow (1972) to look closely at the categories and variables which characterize the term *exceptional*. They point out two general classes of variables—source variables and decision variables. The traditional variables found within special education—e.g., mental retardation, and vision, hearing, and emotional disturbances—are source variables. They are the sources or indicators of educational problems. Although they may serve to alert us to problems or to potential problems, they do not indicate appropriate educational remediation. The authors suggest that special teachers should stop talking about dysfunctions, deficits, impairments, and disabilities as if these were the starting points in education. They should also discontinue the assumption that recovery from, or remediation of, these disabilities are valid goals for educational programming.

Decision variables (in contrast) relate to the educational environment and are strongly influenced by factors in the child's life. Decisions reached in educational planning should always be positive. They are concerned with teaching and learning and not with recovery from deficits. The educator prevents educational disabilities or educational failures by teaching positive skills and relevant behavior. These in turn relate in a general sense to the child's social and cognitive development.

Quay (1973) divided the source variables into three classifications: process dysfunctions, experience defects, and experience deficits. *Process dysfunctions* include sensory dysfunctions, poor motor coordination, poor short-term memory, inadequate memory span, low intelligence, and other impairments that have an innate psychophysiological basis. *Experience defects* refer to emotional disturbances, inhibitions, fears and anxieties, traumatic experiences, and other features of experience that have apparently done harm to the child. *Experience deficits* result from inadequate experience or training. In this respect the child is assumed to have had inadequate opportunities to learn the behaviors and skills necessary for normal school progress.

The first two categories (process dysfunctions and experience defects) place the exceptionality within the child and in the child's innate or acquired functioning. In contrast, the last category, experience deficit, places the locus of the handicap outside the child. The assumption is that the child has not had sufficient experiences to acquire the desired behaviors.

Quay does not endorse one type of categorization over the others. He favors a consideration blending all three conceptions in an interactive system. He would combine the three categories in one system, assuming that each by itself is unable to handle the diverse bases of the educational handicap. This further implies that educational problems may be the result of the simultaneous occurrence of difficulties resulting from dysfunctions, deficits, and defects.

This rational analysis of the term *exceptional* or *special,* as applied to children in educational programs, probably does not reflect common practice. Special children are most often designated by achievement or other performance tests, by medical diagnosis which specifies sensory or perceptual, neurological or psychological problems, or by some other special analysis based primarily upon neurological impairments, mental retardation classifications, or severe language impairments. The most frequent diagnostic information appearing in school files is information that bears upon the child's psychological adjustment, his intelligence, his conditions of health, or his physiological status. Consequently, such information is responsible for the large numbers of categories and classifications into which special children have been sorted.

In this volume, we wish to encourage a careful analysis of the child's education status and the collection of information upon which educational decisions can be reached. This calls for continual pursuit of educational relevance and analysis of the child's special learning conditions.

Incidence figures on exceptional children have been prepared by a number of agencies. A recent publication by the U.S. Office of Education has established a Maximum Prevalence Estimate for 1971–72. These figures have been reported by Kirk (1972) and Dunn (1973). Approximately 6 million school-age children are listed as handicapped. This figure represents roughly 10 percent of all school children and excludes children with superior cognitive abilities. The largest categories are the speech impaired (3.5%), the mentally retarded (2.3%), the emotionally disturbed (2.0%); those with mild general learning disabilities (1.5%), specific learning disabilities (1.5%), moderate and severe learning disabilities (0.8%), hearing disabilities (0.6%), neuromotor (crippling and health) disabilities (0.5%), and visual disabilities (0.1%) make up the remainder.

These gross estimates do little more than alert schools to the extent of the problem. They do not suggest a philosophy for training nor do they indicate the type of facilities, grouping arrangements, or instructions which should be provided.

CRITICAL ISSUES IN EDUCATING SPECIAL CHILDREN

This is a crucial time for exceptional children and adults. Public awareness of their problems and inequities has increased significantly during the past few years. There is now a major national effort to integrate individuals with special disabilities into the mainstream of community life. This effort contrasts with efforts in the nineteenth century and in earlier years of this century to establish segregated residence centers for the blind, deaf, retarded, epileptic, orphaned, and poor. Such institutions feature primarily protective care to replace the neglect and frequent mistreatment of earlier periods.

Nevertheless, institutions do not provide adequate programs to improve the functioning of impaired individuals. Further, the practice of placing handicapped individuals in special education classes as an alternative to institutionization is now breaking down also, gradually being replaced by noncategorical arrangements for special teaching. Institutional and special class placement may stigmatize many individuals and impair their efforts to live productively in society.

The practice of assigning children to "handicapped" status by intelligence tests, medical diagnosis, or social disadvantages is morally suspect. The practice can be even more damaging than the problems which were originally diagnosed (Jones, 1972).

A critical feature of the problem is that the bulk of the "exceptional" population (at least 90 percent) have relatively mild deviance problems and consequently can adapt to normal education programs. They can participate in regular class instruction and can ultimately assume productive roles in society. Children with mild or moderate disabilities learn and function better among normal peers. Their "exceptionality" thus appears to be only a relatively superficial aspect of their total human resources. They may have been labeled as "deviant" only within the educational environment and may have normal status in the home, the community, or in society in general.

The range of concerns and inequities raised by this brief discussion must be considered in any systematic attempt to teach special children. Prominent in the consideration should be the determination of appropriate life goals and life styles, adequate learning programs and learning environments, and effective methods of instruction. The terms *deinstitutionalization, normalization,* and *noncategorical instruction* require new plans for educating and training special children. The dramatic nature of the problem has been described a number of times by Dunn (1968), Lilly (1971), Quay (1973), and Adelman (1971).

A significant part of the current commitment to teaching special children is a sense of responsibility (accountability) on the part of the professionals. The current point of view is that a good program is one in which the child achieves the learning goals. In other words, responsibility rests with those who plan and execute the teaching program. *Exceptionality* cannot be the explanation for a poor instructional result. Rather than using indecisive diagnostic results to explain that the child cannot learn, the instructor must instead reexamine the effectiveness of the instruction. *Functional* teaching then should be determined by evaluation, and the important thing to be evaluated is the progress of the child.

When placed in such an exposed position, instructors and their administrative planners are forced to design a more functional, explicit approach to education. If educators must assume responsibility for the results of instruction, they must show the variable effects of different modes of instruction. Only in this way can the variable instructional effects be determined and improvements in instruction be highlighted. Providing evaluation which leads to data-oriented instructions for individualized "special" programs is now the challenge facing education. Such efforts should benefit all children. However, the scope of this book is limited to *special children*. Let us hope that instructions can be devised, refined, and demonstrated for all children before society becomes discouraged with failures to achieve "normalization" for all.

Individualized Instruction

Individualization of instruction has been a popular education slogan for a decade. However, many classroom teachers faced with overcrowded conditions and lack of support personnel have not had the curricular programs, procedural expertise, supporting materials, or time and energy to individualize instructional procedures with children who need them most. Regular classroom teachers are often not trained to tailor instructional programs to facilitate remediation of specific response and learning deficits. Consequently, many children are labeled mentally retarded and placed in special classes. Forness (1972) notes that these children are "casualties of the present educational system." The lack of adaptation to each child's differences in rate of acquisition and levels of development, motivation, and readiness is blatantly obvious in the way our schools are run (Holt, 1968; Jackson, 1968; Postman and Weingartner, 1969; Silberman, 1968; Forness and MacMillan, 1972). The causes of failure are more likely related to the inability of the classroom teacher and administrator to design a program that allows the child to progress at his or her own rate rather than the child's innate learning disorder suggested by low performance against an arbitrary statistical norm. Nevertheless, handicapped children (often labeled as learning disabled, perceptually handicapped, educationally handicapped, etc.) can function in a public school classroom without special classes or help from educational specialists. In this undertaking, teachers and specialists need a set of procedures which systematize instruction (Silverman, 1968). The more systematic, precise, and aware the teacher is the more productive the process will be. Through precise educational programs on all levels of public schools, moderately handicapped children and, to some extent, severely handicapped children can succeed in public schools and learn to function independently in society.

Early Intervention and Preschool Education

Severely handicapped children are usually identified shortly after birth or in early childhood as either physically or mentally impaired, or both. They are referred to residential institutions, to special classes in the public school system, or kept out of school altogether. They have noticeable response deficits in language, preacademic and academic performance, in motor and perceptual skills, and in the way they behave socially or attempt to solve social problems. The current trend is for deinstitutionalization and for community-based education and home care. Many parents want to keep their children at home and justifiably insist that these children have the right to an education in their own communities just as other children have.

The popular "wait and see" approach is being replaced by pragmatic programs of infant assessment and diagnosis, and early-intervention programs for children with handicaps. Early assessment and infant programs require a unified community effort involving the medical profession, the educational system, the parents, and the state and local governments. In many instances, critics have been justified in their skepticism that preschool programs do not make a difference in a child's later academic success. Although the early years of a child's life are influential in character formation and development of behavioral patterns, there are many misconceptions about that period. Programs such as Head Start and Follow-Through, as well as early preschool programs for the handicapped and infant stimulation, have shown that systematic instruction in very early childhood around discrimination of information and language and communication skills can facilitate performance for handicapped and disadvantaged populations. When it comes to identifying and planning educational experiences for children known to have developmental disabilities or experiential disadvantages, early assessment and intervention programs are critical (Haring, Hayden, & Allen, 1971).

WHAT IS SPECIAL TEACHING?

There are several current controversies about how to teach special children. They relate to teaching strategies, teaching environments, and supplemental arrangements. Since these controversies strongly influence the articles and books in the field of special education, they should be examined in light of approaches recommended in this book.

Teaching Strategies

Quay (1973) recommends three types of remedial techniques to support special teaching programs. Type I techniques involve a sequence of activities on some (postulated) process level which it is assumed will aid the child's future learning. For instance, it is suggested that gross motor training (e.g., crawling) may improve reading and speaking at a later time. The assumption is that gross developmental processes are essential to later, more complex functioning. If the earlier gross behaviors are not learned under the stimulation of the natural environment, they should be formally taught. A series of such indirect instructions could possibly form the basis for a remedial program for children with lags in educational development.

Type II techniques involve activities of established relevance carried on in the present with the expectation of effects in the future. For instance, form discrimination may be taught now to improve reading at a later date, or auditory discrimination may be taught to improve subsequent speaking skills. Such programs often involve attention, memory, perceptual discrimination, "sequencing," or coordination skills.

Type III techniques involve direct instruction to promote acquisition of the terminal behavior or subaspects of the terminal behavior. The criterion behavior is specified in regard to both the subaspects and the terminal behaviors. Quay points out that

> Type III techniques are "remedial" only in the sense that the child to whom they are applied has not acquired the terminal behavior at the expected time. There is no explicit attempt to "make up" for deficiencies which may have occurred along the way or to "undo" prior adverse experiences. (p.167)

Quay also points out that each of these techniques is rooted in one or more of the three conceptions about the nature and causes of educational exceptionality discussed previously. For instance, Type I activities seem tied to both process dysfunctions and experience defect notions, Type II techniques apply to process dysfunction notions, and Type III techniques to experience deficits. Quay further points out that the validity of Types I and II are more difficult to establish because the linkage between remedial activity and terminal behavior is weak. In contrast, the criteria and the evaluation data employed by Type III proponents tend to be direct and specific. He also points out that

> Type III approaches have, in fact, been used successfully to remediate what appeared to be rather clear-cut process dysfunctions (such as attention and visual perception), experience deficits (such as vocabulary acquisition, verbal expressive skills, and special academic content), and a host of deviant social behavior usually attributed to experience defects. (p.169)

Teaching Environments

The trend to integrate handicapped children into regular classrooms is a reversal of the trend in the 1950s and 1960s that witnessed a tremendous growth in the establishment of special classes for the handicapped. The period of special class placement was accompanied by the administrative convenience of labeling children into categories such as hyperactive, dyslexic, brain-damaged, and emotionally disturbed.

The current view is that all behavior (including exceptional behavior) follows similar behavioral principles. Special class placement reduces the handicapped child's opportunity for intellectual stimulation and normal peer interaction. Many moderately handicapped children can be taught with their non-handicapped peers if their instructional programs are individualized. Seventy-five percent of the children designated as functionally mentally retarded are capable of acquiring basic academic skills, as well as adequate social adjustment if the environment is appropriate (Haring, *Final Report,* 1971).

Lilly (1970) speculates that the special class problem stems from our tendency to analyze exceptionality as a "problem within the child." He urges that we view exceptionality as a psychological construct which was created to make order out of chaotic classroom situations. Lilly proposes that "exceptionality" must be removed from the child and the explanatory construct reexamined. In order to reduce the chaos, we should move from defining *exceptional children* to defining *exceptional environments within the school.*

Lilly places the emphasis upon teaching environments, teaching procedures, and special resources for teaching. He deemphasizes the importance of diagnosing disabilities and exceptionality. He suggests that educators should assume responsibility for planning and implementing instructional programs largely free from the rationalization of "exceptionality" as a construct to explain the limited effectiveness of teaching procedures.

Lilly has defined an *exceptional school situation* as one in which the interaction between a student and a teacher is limited to the extent that *external intervention* is deemed necessary. Most probably this preliminary decision is reached by the teacher in cooperation with a specialist or administrator and, possibly, the parents. In any event, the decision is usually based upon information that explains the child's exceptionality. If the relevant adults (teachers, specialists, school officials, and parents) would examine the alternatives for *external intervention,* they might design better instructional arrangements for the child.

Supplemental Instruction

Supplemental instruction can be provided in several ways:

1 Supplement the instructional technology of the teachers through designed in-service training.
2 Provide the teacher with instructional aids to extend the effects of the instructional plan.
3 Provide specialized, supplemental instruction as an adjunct to the specialized or individualized program designed by the regular teacher.
4 Use more assistance from the home by implementing programs in the home.
5 Develop special instructional environments in which to teach special portions of the curricula.
6 Provide special advisory services to the teacher.
7 Design specialized learning centers in the school through which a child can be cycled to learn critical skills or to supplement the curriculum in specialized ways while continuing the regular program.

These and many other strategies and innovations have been successfully employed to assist teachers of special children. All these possibilities are educational strategies which leave specific decisions to educational planners. An effective solution to the "limited interaction" or to the "exceptional school situation" mentioned by Lilly may emerge from these alternatives. However, as explained in Chapter 5, the educational team may sometimes lack competence to plan and to implement effective educational alternatives. If so, in-service training for teachers, specialists, school officials, and parents should be provided.

Pressure is being applied to our educational system to educate all children in their home communities. Recent legislation in several states requires that all children have an equal opportunity for an education. This issue, with its implications for all school districts, poses substantial challenges. Although some school districts provide comprehensive educational programs for the severely and mildly retarded, most have not made adequate provisions for teaching these special children. Until schools assume this responsibility, the parents of the retarded and the multiply handicapped must educate their children in the home or place them in private or state institutions.

What effect compulsory legislation will have on the schools during the next few years cannot be entirely predicted. Measures most likely to be accelerated are in-service training for teachers, arrangements for resource rooms and resource teachers to assist the regular classroom teachers, team-teaching arrangements, and the placement of mildly handicapped children in regular classrooms. In addition, space must be provided for special classes for severely handicapped children who require special, intensive, individualized instructional programs in group settings apart from regular classrooms.

CRITICAL ROLES IN EDUCATING SPECIAL CHILDREN

The complex task of teaching special children must be shared by teachers, children, specialists, administrators, and parents. Each holds a part of the key to the success of teaching programs. Their roles are mutually dependent and should be examined in relation to the total program.

Role of Teachers

Teachers have traditionally been assigned the most functional role in instructing children of school age. The *regular* and *special* stereotypes have implied that regular teachers should instruct children who can be grouped homogeneously to follow a curricular plan with limited variations. If the variations become extensive, it is assumed that the effectiveness of the instructional plan will suffer. Equally stereotypic has been the assumption that special teachers instruct children who by definition or by diagnosis are excluded from regular classrooms and thus are placed in special classes and taught a special curriculum in a specially designed environment. Both designs, which have been built into certification standards for teachers, include unverified assumptions. Nevertheless, teacher training, instructional programs, classroom designs, segregated classes, and special education models have all been strongly influenced by these assumptions.

Among the questionable assumptions are the following:

1 Special children will be under less pressure and will consequently be better adjusted in special classes.

2 Regular teachers cannot give adequate time and attention to special children without slighting other students.

3 Regular and special children are not compatible classmates in terms of educational goals, social activities, curricula, instructional procedures, or environmental designs.

4 The instructional strategies are best keyed to the etiologic disabilities of the children so that special class groupings offer the most empirical and the most humanistic way to provide equal educational opportunities for special children.

5 Individualized instruction can best be offered in special class arrangements with fewer children who are arranged in homogeneous etiologic groupings and who have special diagnostic information available for educational planning and decision making.

A provocative aspect of the unverified assumptions is that they were developed by nonteachers. We wish to stress in this book that teachers and other educators should be encouraged to determine the most economical and effective way to instruct special children.

Although there may be some validity in these points, at least as the issues are viewed in many educational settings, on the whole the assumptions remain unverified. Conflicting statements also can be made. For instance, many, if not most, special children prefer regular placement. Many regular teachers give effective attention to special children. Most teachers do not alter instructional strategies in accordance with a psychobiological case history. Most often special and regular class children mingle effectively if educational environments are designed to encourage their coparticipation (Iano, 1972).

Role of Children

Children should be assigned more active roles in the process of teaching special children. At first glance this statement may seem circular. How can children be given key roles in teaching children? But children do learn from each other. They learn readily from peer models, and in a structured environment they can record data regarding performances, including their own. In addition, children can instruct other children, play key roles in supporting activities developed by the teacher, and participate in planning and in problem-solving functions. Children who have traditionally played unnecessarily passive and casual classroom roles can be more active in instruction. They will thereby accelerate both their own learning and the learning of their classmates. A number of instructional programs show striking results for pupil-assisted instruction (Whalen and Henker, 1969; Hamblin, 1971; Surratt, Ulrich, and Hawkins, 1970). Children as young as five or six years have learned to instruct, to monitor performance, and to record (chart) data. Both normal and retarded children have served as teacher aides and reliable data recorders. In a period of emphasis upon cost effectiveness, lower unit costs, larger classes, and more heterogeneous groups, the role of children in educating children is expanding.

Role of Specialists

Plans to individualize instruction must take into account the level of functioning for each child. Special curricula, special environments, and special methods of management become essential features of the individualization design. The individual strengths and weaknesses of children call for the primary and second-ary strategies of specialists in auditory training for hearing-impaired children, language training for speech-impaired children, perception training for children with limited vision, special motor training for children with physical impair-ments, and social training for children with inappropriate interpersonal skills.

Specialists in the schools, for the most part, aim to supplement the curricu-lar designs planned for the classroom. The activities of specialists may be set within the classroom *per se,* or in special environments inside or outside the school setting (Sabatino, 1972). In any event, the training should be a part of the regular offering of the school in the sense that all children have special activities.

The most extensive special activities described in this book are the language intervention programs (Chapters 8 and 9). In most phases of this work the specialist is described as a teacher-clinician, meaning that the language instruction can be undertaken by a teaching agent who has special skills. Planning and designing is often done by a language specialist who works with the teacher, but it is the teacher who presides over the language activities in the child's total program.

Role of Parents

Many parents, including parents of severely impaired children, have received valuable instruction prior to their child's enrollment in a formal education program. Many parents have become generalists with extensive knowledge about the child's care, his health, his functioning, and most of all, his personal interests, preferences, fears, and experiences. The information should be put to use in the educational program for the child. The parents should become active members of the instructional team.

The role of the parent continues long after the school phase is completed. The parent is also a liaison agent between school, home, and community. This role becomes increasingly important as the child includes recreational and vocational activities in his daily routines. Finally, the parent is a counselor, a sustainer, and an auxiliary teacher for any formal program of instruction.

In light of these varied and important functions, the parents' role in the teaching program is crucial. Parents should be encouraged to learn Applied Behavior Analysis (ABA) techniques and should be thoroughly instructed about the projects and strategies being developed at school (Wahler, Wenkel, Peterson and Morrison, 1965). The parent and the child must often learn together. In the same sense, teachers and parents are colleagues. Each is a source of support for the other. The same design, of course, should also apply to the administrators and the specialists.

Role of Administrators

Perhaps the most instrumental way administrators directly affect the instruction of children is by acknowledging and encouraging (reinforcing) the best efforts of teachers. A second way is to plan with teachers, specialists, parents, and children so that problems are systematically evaluated and solved. Good decisions improve the work of individuals and teams. The administrator is also a problem solver in designing and supporting a teaching system at various levels, including interschool planning and intraschool concerns. The administrator is also a channel for information and an instrument for the utilization of information that may become a part of the teaching program.

All the above are obvious features of the role of the administrator. Less evident is the role of the administrator in a school system where ABA is a primary strategy for teaching special children. In such cases the administrator should be the coordinator of behavioral projects and the processor of much of the cumulative behavioral data in which each teacher has access to a larger fund of information regarding the effectiveness of explicit teaching strategies. If the information is on file and if it is available in a form that a teacher, a specialist, or a parent can understand, it may not be necessary for the utilizer to do trial-and-error work on the procedure in order to make use of it in the classroom—someone else may already have done that. An important point is that ABA provides data that teachers and others can interpret. There is thus a common language for planning and refining individualized instruction.

BRIEF HISTORY OF APPLIED BEHAVIOR ANALYSIS

Applied Behavior Analysis (ABA) procedures, although of recent origin, have a rich and substantial heritage. Skinner, the founder of operant conditioning, first described the substance of ABA. One of its many contributions was his contention that frequency of responding is a basic scientific datum. Response frequency has become a key measure of ABA technology. Another of Skinner's contributions to today's behavioral technology was to establish functional relationships between independent and dependent variables. He proved that many behaviors are influenced by various reinforcement contingencies.

From that beginning of operant psychology several branches of experimentation developed. Some researchers continued, as did Skinner, to use infrahuman or lower organisms as subjects. Some conducted laboratory experiments with human beings. Others began to work with adults and children in institutions for the psychotic and retarded. Although many researchers have contributed to ABA, this volume concentrates on those known for the development of ABA as it relates to children.

Some of the early work with children using operant procedures was basic research. These studies were conducted in settings not natural to the child's environment. The responses the children were required to emit were not normally in their repertories. The purpose of these studies was to learn about certain conceptual systems rather than about the normal behaviors of children.

One classic study by Azrin and Lindsley (1966) examined the acquisition, extinction, and maintenance of a cooperative behavior. Baer and Sherman (1964) studied the generalized imitations of children. Bijou (1956) studied the performance of children during extinction phases following various fixed-interval schedules. These laboratory studies demonstrated that many of the principles of operant psychology which applied to animals held true with children.

Encouraged by the successes of these laboratory findings, others began to use operant techniques with children in clinical settings. The classic study of this type was by Wolf, Risley, and Mees (1964), who dealt with several behaviors of a young autistic boy in the clinic and the home. Lovaas (Lovaas, Freitag, Kinder, Rubenstein, Schaeffer, & Simmons, 1966; Lovaas, Freitag, Nelson, & Whalen, 1967) used operant procedures in several studies to change various behaviors of schizophrenic youngsters. Several other studies of this type used operant procedures to change, and generally to attenuate, or decrease, the deviant behaviors of children. They had in common the fact that they dealt with one child in a situation where no other children were present.

Operant conditioners then became more venturesome. They entered classrooms. Many applied research studies were conducted to demonstrate that the techniques were successful when used with an individual or a small group within classrooms.

Perhaps the first study of this type was reported by the Zimmermans (1962). They used extinction and positive reinforcement procedures to increase the spelling abilities of one subject and to attenuate the tantrums of another. In 1963 Lloyd Homme and colleagues (Homme, deBaca, Devine, Steinhorst, & Rickert), reported that the Premack principle was an effective strategy for controlling a wide range of nursery school behaviors.

The work of Harris, Wolf, and Baer (1964) and others at the Developmental Psychology Laboratory at the University of Washington is noteworthy for this extension of operant principles to group situations. They demonstrated in a series of studies how isolated play, crying, climbing, and other nursery school behaviors were amenable to change by manipulating the contingent praise of teachers.

Several other researchers demonstrated how these principles could be used in classrooms with one or more children to attenuate certain troublesome behaviors. O'Leary and his colleagues (O'Leary, Kaufman, Kass, & Drabman, 1970) did such work, as did Becker and his fellow workers (Becker, Madsen, Arnold, & Thomas, 1967). The favored targets of these researchers were children who talked out or left their seats.

Many of these researchers used the term *behavior modification* to describe their methodology. They had taken the vital features of operant conditioning— identification of an observable response, measurement of that response over a period of time, involvement of reinforcement contingencies to affect the frequency of that response—and adapted them to problems of classrooms.

Along with studies which proved that operant or behavior modification techniques can effectively control troublesome behaviors, some researchers also sought to demonstrate that the techniques could change the attending behaviors of pupils. Several investigators have demonstrated that teacher praise is associated with pupil attention; i.e., when teacher praise is arranged contingent on the attention of pupils, the amount of time they pay attention is increased. Hall and his colleagues clearly demonstrated in several settings that teacher attention can alter the attending or studying behaviors of youngsters (Hall, Lund, & Jackson, 1968; Cossairt, Hall, & Hopkins, 1973).

Several researchers using ABA techniques investigated various academic behaviors of children. One of the earliest attempts to obtain academic measures was the work conducted by Birnbrauer, Wolf, Kidder, and Tague (1965) at the Rainier School in Buckley, Washington. In their programmed learning classroom those investigators reported that measures in reading, writing, and arithmetic could be obtained continuously. Arthur Staats and his group conducted several studies which related to the effects of reinforcement contingencies on various reading behaviors (Staats & Butterfield, 1965; Staats, Finley, Minke, & Wolf, 1964; Staats, Staats, Schultz, & Wolf, 1962).

So the technology evolved from operant conditioning in laboratories concerned with conceptual systems to behavior modification which dealt with troublesome or attending behaviors in the classrooms. Perhaps the best known of these researchers is Ogden Lindsley, who developed precision teaching emphasizing the measurement of a wider range of classroom behaviors, including academic skills.

A BEHAVIORAL MODEL FOR INSTRUCTION

To qualify as a model, a teaching program must present a systematic, replicable set of teaching functions. This book proposes a model based upon Applied Behavior Analysis (ABA). The explicitness and the instrumental nature of the system depend upon the recording of specific behaviors, immediate feedback of data resulting from the teaching events, and the arrangement or rearrangement of conditions to accelerate learning.

Procedures for recording events and the data feedback are presented in Chapter 2 Evaluation and Measurement. The arrangements for accelerating learning conditions are developed throughout the book. For instance, Chapter 3 focuses upon the functions of classroom management for learning and upon direct teaching, including systematic planning and motivational issues. The functions of organized learning (curriculum) are discussed in Chapter 4. The functional arrangements for learning are developed in each of the remaining chapters. Chapter 5 extends the explicit techniques to classrooms and community settings. Chapters 6 and 7 develop functional materials and conditions for teaching severely limited children, and Chapters 8 and 9 explain the functional conditions for teaching language. Finally Chapter 10 "puts it all together."

The sections that follow in Chapter 1 provide an overview of the content of the book. The content includes measurement, behavior management, individualized curriculum, and systems planning. Each of these areas bears out the wide applicability of the ABA emphasis, and together they characterize the direct teaching procedures recommended.

Measurement and Evaluation

Recent developments in measurement and evaluation technology have led to the formation of measurement procedures which allow the teacher to assess directly pupil performance in the tasks being taught on a daily basis. This may be the most significant aspect of the behavioral emphasis in education. Measurement procedures provide continuous information for making decisions about instructional approaches for individual children. In addition, the performance measure is sensitive to small increments of learning. Considerable attention is devoted to this topic in Chapter 3; however, the other authors make specialized application of measurement as an implicit part of their teaching system. For instance, Haring and Gentry (Chapter 3) present measurement as a prominent part of their management strategy and also as a means for determining behavioral objectives and pupil performance in their *direct instructional* system. Likewise, Lovitt (Chapter 4) demonstrates daily measurement in curriculum research. The explicitness of the measurement procedures in Chapters 3 and 4 are matched by the emphases in Chapters 5 through 10. Each emphasizes daily event recording and the utilization of the data for planning, refining, and maintaining the effectiveness of the teaching program.

Since the measurement and evaluation functions are critically important in teaching special children, perhaps a short analysis of the functions is appropriate in this overview section. Since this discussion must indeed be brief, however, the reader should extend his grasp of measurement and evaluation by checking the first three sections of Chapter 2 (Introduction, Behavior, and Basic Approaches to Assessment), Assessment of Pupil Performance in Chapter 3, Development of Behavioral Targets and Procedures for Evaluating Them in Chapter 7, General Analysis of a Language Program in Chapter 8, and the Data Management section of Chapter 10. Other measurement and evaluation information is available in the book, but these sections contribute to a general understanding of the rationale and the general procedures for recording and using explicit behavioral data.

In the process of teaching, measurement begins with the first evaluation of the child's behavior when first seen. This starting point, or baseline, is used for objectively recording a child's present level of functioning, for planning, including the setting of teaching objectives, and for comparison with subsequent behavioral levels. (This point is brought out explicitly in Chapter 8 in assessing language.) The initial behavioral level is usually charted on a graph. The two primary variables are time and frequency. On the graph, time is expressed as units along the horizontal line (abscissa) and frequency as units on the vertical line (ordinate). By plotting frequency of occurrences of a behavior and connecting the plotted points, it is possible to draw a line illustrating behavioral change. These issues are explained in detail in Chapter 2.

In order to handle complex events, White and Liberty break behavior change into physical and temporal dimensions and explain how to determine *critical effect* (the most important change in the behavior as a result of the procedures). Critical effects can simply be counted and plotted. Of course, initial evaluations can be undertaken in a number of ways depending upon the kind of target behavior the teacher is interested in assessing. Each of the following chapters have something special to contribute to this issue.

Once the initial behavioral levels have been determined, the instructional goals are tentatively set and an instructional program is designed. In order to facilitate the teaching program, data which express the child's progress are plotted daily. Probes are frequently used to determine special dimensions of progress. Haring and Gentry (Chapter 3) provide a detailed account of probing procedures, i.e., procedures to sample small segments of behavior in order to assess progress.

Continuous event recording, including the probes, can be used to determine the relationship of the child's progress to the actual procedures used in teaching the child. For instance, the type of reinforcement and the schedule of reinforcement can be checked as a relationship between the dependent variables (the child's responses) and the independent variables (the teaching procedures).

In order to determine these relationships with greater certainty, an experimental design can be easily employed. These are discussed and illustrated in Chapter 5. The three most common designs are the reversal design, the multiple baseline design, and the changing criterion design. Each design has special advantages and can be used according to the purposes of the teacher.

As explained by White and Liberty in Chapter 2, change is a most important condition to measure. The major purpose of performance measurement is to provide a base against which another measurement may be compared, and through which the growth of a child may be observed. Procedures in Chapter 2 for accomplishing this objective provide a strong contrast to the summative or end-of-instruction measures that are routinely used in measuring pupil performances. These measures include group, normative data and standardized educational measures which are only indirectly related to actual instructional performance. Furthermore, these educational tests are usually given infrequently— usually at the beginning and/or the end of a school term. The view expressed in this book (see White and Liberty's Introduction) is that continuous event recording is more sensitive to increments of learning and provides functional information for frequent adjustments in teaching procedures.

Behavior Management

The process of reinforcement (contingency management) is one of the primary aims of classroom teaching. Following the stimulus-response-reinforcement (S^D-R-S^R) paradigm, a stimulus is anything in the environment that serves to evoke a response, and a response is specific *observable* behavior. Reinforcement is the presentation of a desirable or rewarding consequence for a response—a consequence which increases the probability that the same type of response will be made to the same stimuli in later instances. The reinforcement component of the paradigm is the key to successful behavior modification. Appropriate contingency arrangements bring behavior under the control of the reinforcer. For instance, if a child is reinforced by receiving free time for answering a series of math problems correctly, chances are that the child will either maintain or improve the performance contingent on the free time.

Reinforcement Principles

Reinforcement is a procedure through which a given behavior is increased or maintained. There are two distinct forms of reinforcement: positive and negative. *Positive reinforcement* is the contingent presentation of a stimulus that increases or maintains a behavior. *Negative reinforcement* is the contingent removal of an aversive stimulus to increase or maintain a behavior. Many of the problems encountered in classroom situations can be handled by using reinforcement procedures to increase the frequency of behaviors that already exist. There are several types of reinforcers as well as several methods of reinforcement that can be systematically delivered.

Positive Reinforcement When a teacher is interested in increasing low-rate behaviors such as task completion, various academic skills, group participation, etc., effective positive reinforcers must be found. Positive reinforcement is the presentation of a pleasant event after a response, which increases the probability that response will recur. The teacher may influence the probability of a child's responding to a task or the accuracy and efficiency of the child's performance by providing rewarding conditions in the classroom.

Positive reinforcement can be generally categorized as primary reinforcement, social reinforcement, high-strength activities, and token reinforcement. *Primary reinforcement* is the process of presenting a stimulus that meets a basic life need, such as food, water, and clothing. Many researchers have utilized primary reinforcement to teach language, physical, and social skills to children with severe behavior disorders. Primary reinforcement can be scheduled into the classroom structure in the form of snacks, milk breaks, and lunch on a contingent basis. Small parties can be given to a class contingent upon the student's attaining a specific goal. If primary reinforcers are used in the classroom, the teacher must be aware of the critical nature of timing their delivery. If an event is to be reinforcing, it must be a direct consequence of a response. Effects of reinforcement too long delayed are weakened. This is true for all types of reinforcement.

Social Reinforcement Social reinforcement is more useful in achieving student behavioral change than is primary reinforcement because of the impracticality of primary reinforcers in the classroom. Traditional forms of reinforcement such as grades on papers or assignments provide an example of social reinforcement. Social reinforcement is a form of conditioned reinforcement, that is, a presented stimulus, object, or event that (through frequent pairing with another stimulus already possessing reinforcing properties) has itself acquired reinforcing value. Conditioned reinforcers develop as the individual interacts with the environment. Social reinforcement in the form of praise, smiles, and compliments replace earlier, more primary reinforcers such as feeding and touching. The frequent pairing of primary reinforcement with praise or attention causes verbal and social events to become reinforcing by themselves.

With some children, social reinforcers fail to become strong, are not applied to a wide variety of responses, and generalized reinforcers do not develop. When this occurs, the child usually has a variety of behaviors at low levels of development which are resistant to effective reinforcement. Such socially deficient children have extremely limited repertoires of social responses, and the environment exerts very little control over the child's behavior. Teachers often overlook the fact that some children grow up without experiencing typical combinations of primary and conditioned reinforcers. In such cases shaping procedures can be implemented. With a child who makes few appropriate responses that can be reinforced, it is necessary first to evoke behavior which roughly approximates the appropriate behavior and then shape it through a series of approximations until the final appropriate behavior becomes conditioned. Shaping must be planned carefully, beginning with identifying the terminal behavior and specifying the successive approximations to be reinforced.

Reinforcing inappropriate behavior is a major problem encountered by the classroom teacher. Every teacher must realize that a child's responses to teacher behavior are consequences of the teacher's behavior. The responses a teacher makes to a pupil's behavior are the result of the teacher's history of conditioning. To be aware of the influence that a child's behavior has on the teacher, he or she must be aware of avoiding a "coercive cycle" (Patterson & Reid, 1970). A teacher who responds to Sally's giggling by saying "stop that giggling and get back to work" will likely use the same response the next time the situation occurs if Sally actually stops giggling and goes to work. Actually, the behavior that is being reinforced and maintained is giggling behavior rather than working behavior, because it is giggling to which the teacher attends. Once Sally stops giggling, the teacher stops paying attention to her. Because the giggling behavior is being reinforced by teacher attention, Sally will probably emit giggling behavior in the future if teacher attention is rewarding to her. To compound the problem, the teacher's conditioned response to Sally's giggling may result in other children giggling.

A great amount of classroom research has been done that demonstrates the use of various social reinforcers in increasing students' good behavior. The teacher's main objective in using reinforcement is to become established as a positive reinforcer for each child. If positive reinforcement has little effect in maintaining the child's appropriate behavior, environmental conditions must be rearranged so that social behavior becomes a positive reinforcer for the child. If teacher attention, either positive or negative, to inappropriate behavior maintains the rate of that behavior, the teacher must withhold or withdraw attention from that behavior and redirect it to other behaviors that need to be strengthened. Far too many children do not respond satisfactorily to "normal" classroom conditions and demands (being able to sit quietly, to attend to work, to complete an assignment accurately, to follow directions, etc.). The stimuli fail to reinforce the appropriate behaviors, and, most unfortunately for the pupils' learning careers, the teacher never becomes a social reinforcer. These children are not reinforced by coming to school or by responding to academic materials, and if the teacher continues the same patterns for reinforcement, their skill development and academic progress will remain relatively slow. To strengthen rates of response to instructional cues, the teacher must systematically identify and apply reinforcing consequences and plan the classroom environment so that each child can plan the natural consequences to maintain appropriate academic, social, and verbal behavior.

High-Strength Activities   One of the most effective procedures in designing a reinforcing classroom environment is the application of the *Premack
principle*. After extensive laboratory studies, Premack was able to demonstrate
that the behaviors one actually engages in may be used to reinforce behavior
that occurs rather less frequently. Applying the principle to the classroom,
Homme et al. (1963) showed that using access to high-frequency behaviors,
such as running and screaming, could be made contingent on performance of
low-frequency behaviors, such as academic tasks.

There is nothing new about this practice. Lovaas calls it a practice as old as
child rearing (1968). When a mother says ''Before you go fishing, you must mow
the lawn'' or a teacher schedules a rock 'n' roll party contingent on the pupils'
meeting a group criterion level, they are employing the Premack principle. For
each child in any classroom some activities are naturally reinforcing and others
are not. One child may find arithmetic, gym, and art reinforcing but may abhor
reading and spelling. Another child may be initially reinforced only by sailing
plastic boats in the sink, while nothing else in the environment appears to be
reinforcing. Consequently, the classroom must be arranged to accommodate a
wide range of activities and possibilities. Dividing the classroom into high- and
low-strength areas is one method that has been found successful (Homme et al.,
1963; Haring & Kunzelmann, 1966). Academic tasks are usually done in the low-
strength areas where stationary desks or carrells are provided. Desks should be
well stocked with whatever materials the child might need as part of learning
readiness-for-task procedures. The high-strength areas should be arranged for
independent, free-time use by the children. Everything should be accessible to
them, including equipment and supplies for planned activities and working on
projects.

Token Reinforcement   Token reinforcement is another special case of
conditioned reinforcement. With token reinforcement, the child is given some
small item or marks as a reinforcing consequence for a specific response or
pattern of responses. Regardless of what form they take, token reinforcers are
exchangeable at a later time for another reinforcing item or activity.

However, token systems are often used in haphazard ways. Teachers who
decide to use a token system should be aware of the consequences. Token
reinforcement may be the most flexible reinforcement plan to adopt in the
classroom. Various kinds of tokens are easily dispensed and easily become
conditioned reinforcers. Token systems allow for the individual needs of all the
children, but also provide control for satiation and deprivation. A child given
only extra gym or art after performing to criterion will soon be satiated by these
reinforcers, even if those events are reinforcing for a time. Successful token
systems provide for diverse opportunities that allow the child to choose what to
do at the moment rather than engage in a specific event. Thus, the tokens remain
strong reinforcers.

The token system can be incorporated with the use of high-strength activities. The teacher and the students are thus able to work out extensive lists of activities, events, and conditions having potential as reinforcers in the classroom. The high-strength area can be gradually developed to provide for all the children's needs and equipped with games, toys, puzzles, records, etc. The extent to which a token system is effective is dependent on the back-up items and activities available. Delivery of tokens can be combined with individual attention and praise so that social reinforcement is generalized from the token reinforcement schedule.

Reinforcement systems are acknowledged in each of the learning programs described in this book. However, some of the applications are especially noteworthy. For instance, Haring and Gentry use reinforcement to enhance classroom management; Lovitt employs reinforcement to facilitate task completion; Hall, Copeland, and Clark motivate for improved class attendance, appropriate behavior, higher achievement scores, and so on; Spradlin and Spradlin advocate primary reinforcers for low-functioning children; Schiefelbusch, Ruder, and Bricker recommend reinforcers as part of a language "maintenance" system; and Hopkins et al. explain procedures for praising students as a feature of classroom management.

The applications, of course, are only instrumental parts of teaching systems. They do not represent teaching experiments or systems. Nevertheless, reinforcement technology is a prominent feature of a larger behavioral design for teaching.

Stimulus Control Principles

Although *reinforcement* is given the greater emphasis in discussions of the behavioral paradigm, *stimulus* functions are also important in designing and generalizing learning tasks.

A *stimulus* is any physical event or object in the environment that is related to the person's (child's) behavior. Stimuli might refer to objects like doors, windows, other people, parts of one's own body, clothing, and so on. The term could include vocal sounds, words, sighs, and laughter; it could include visual configurations such as words on a page, colors, length, and width. The term might also refer to a broader context, such as an entire room, although we will usually then speak of the "stimulus situation."

> Stimulus control . . . deals with how people learn to behave in ways that are appropriate for the stimulus situation that they are in. It will include distinguishing between different situations (discrimination), lumping basically similar situations together in general categories (concept formation), procedures for teaching discrimination and concept formation (fading) and communication (verbal behavior). In general, this covers what might be called a behavioral approach to intellectual behavior. (Miller, p.217)

Stimulus control functions are utilized in individualized curriculum activities (Chapter 4), in planning for teaching the severely retarded (Chapter 7), and in teaching language (Chapter 9). Spradlin and Spradlin (Chapter 7) are especially cogent in discussing three procedures for stimulus control, i.e., stimulus shift, stimulus modes, and imitation shifts. Each procedure fits into a process for teaching new responses.

Individualized Curriculum

Curriculum technology provides methods for determining what and how to teach, how to arrange and sequence material, what program cues to use, and how drill and practice are best utilized in the teaching-learning system. Application of principles of programming provide teachers with a precise system for arranging cues, specifying instructional objectives, and sequencing information. The precise arrangement of instructional programs and the constant analysis of the child's performance to determine the rearrangement and refinement of specific programs constitutes the critical interaction of the learner and the teaching system. Using this approach, it is possible to achieve efficient programming for each child on an individual basis. Chapters 3, 4, 6, 7, 9, and 10 provide detailed discussions of individualized curricular programs.

Each of the chapters presents a distinctive approach to the process of individualization. Lovitt in Chapter 4 gives a detailed account of his procedures for designing appropriate teaching units in arithmetic, reading, spelling, writing, and verbal behaviors. Lovitt explains in detail how to combine method and curriculum. His information is directed to teachers who must adapt curriculum units and to devise methods for special children.

Spradlin and Spradlin (Chapter 7) present a program for severely retarded children based upon self-help skills, toilet training, cleanliness training, dressing skills, self-feeding, social skills, and perceptual and motor skills. They, too, describe procedures for teaching substantive areas appropriate to special children. However, in their teaching, the individualization process leads to a nonacademic curriculum.

Bricker, Ruder, and Smith (Chapter 9) teach much younger children; their curriculum is focused largely upon psycholinguistic content. They describe, as do other authors, how definitive teaching procedures can be used to complete a curricular sequence. Again a synthesis of structure and function are combined into a curricular system.

In "Putting it all Together" (Chapter 10), Hopkins discusses a curriculum that includes mathematics, reading, spelling, composition, writing (penmanship), and science. Hopkins strives for simplicity and motivation in all phases of his curricular designs. He seems to favor close interaction between teacher and student in designing all phases of the learning experience.

Perhaps Lovitt provides the keynote explanations for each of the curricular presentations. "Curriculum . . . refers to many learning activities . . . such as reading, writing, arithmetic, penmanship and spelling . . . and also includes the many teaching procedures which assist in the development of academic skills. Some of these procedures are modeling, feedback, reinforcement contingencies, and verbal directions."

Systems Planning

The teaching-learning system has definite beginning and ending points, specific goals and objectives, and flexible modes of operation (systematic instructional procedures) that take the learner's skills and behavioral repertory into consideration (Haring, 1971).

The Process of Analysis   Systems analysis can be utilized for analysis alone, or to analyze and modify an operation. One goal of analyzing or studying a system might be simply to understand, or to satisfy curiosity—as one might study the solar system. A more utilitarian goal is the understanding and evaluation of changes needed to improve a system by manipulating problem elements systematically rather than in a haphazard manner. The process of systems analysis requires identification of all the component parts of an existing system and determining their relationships or dependencies.

In contrast, when systems analysis is considered as a means of *solving a problem,* the problem is considered as a whole, then analysis and synthesis take place. In analysis, elements are *separated* to examine their relationships; in synthesis, elements are *combined* to create a system. After examining a problem, one may set goals for its solution. For instance, if a student cannot read, a short-range goal is to devise a system for teaching him to read. The long-range goal is, of course, that the student will read. After the integration of elements to achieve a goal, the next concern is to determine ways of making goal achievement most efficient.

The steps taken in systems analysis include definition of the problem, collection of information relative to the problem, synthesis of a solution, implementation of the solution, evaluation of the solution, and provision of feedback. Feedback can consist of data that facilitate decisions or decisions based on the analysis of data.

In many instances, the *initial definition* of the problem is relatively imprecise; for example, Tom cannot read. The second step, collection of information, can be stated in the form of a task analysis; for instance, "What skills essential to reading are missing from Tom's repertory?" An analysis of his skills may show that he knows the names of most of the letters but can differentiate the sounds of only some of them. He is capable of making still fewer vowel sounds in response to a visual cue and has only a very small sight vocabulary. After such assessment or diagnosis one must specify for each skill or subskill to be acquired the behavior that is to be exhibited, the conditions under which the behavior is to occur, and the criteria for acceptable behavior (Mager, 1962). Additionally, it will be necessary to determine the sequence of skill development through which the pupil will progress.

When the problem has been defined more precisely, it is necessary to determine what *further information* will help the solution. Or, once the dependent variable (the skill to be learned) is known, one may ask what independent variables can be used to modify it, and what the constraints are on these variables. Independent variables that influence learning occur in the following categories: the pupil's individuality, the conditions preceding the pupil's performance, the characteristics of the required response, and the conditions following performance.

After one considers as many combinations of the above variables as possible, in order to arrive at the best solution, the third step in systems analysis—*synthesis of a solution*—is approached. Many limits and constraints determining what must and what must not be done will be imposed on the potential solution. One consideration in establishing theoretical options and limits is their impact on organizational and practical issues. For instance, it must be determined whether or not the materials that call for the appropriate response are available and whether the people and cues are the most desirable ones. Is there enough time to provide the appropriate feedback? What reinforcers are available, and what effect will their use have on other children? In many cases the existing constraints will eliminate some possible solutions, perhaps even some of the more desirable alternatives. Regardless, one seeks an alternative that best achieves the solution with attainable or available resources.

When a strategy has been synthesized to meet the problem, the fourth step, *implementation,* can be initiated. Upon its completion, the strategy and its effects upon the child can be evaluated.

This fifth step, *evaluation,* is necessary in order to know if, or how well, the objective was satisfied. This information is useful in determining alternative action in the event of a failure, or in deciding how to approach the next objective. Evaluation can also improve the system. When information on the system's output is returned it is called *feedback*. Since the purpose of feedback is to improve the system, it may take place at any temporal point in the system's evolution and/or between any of its developmental stages, i.e., defining the problem, studying the problem, synthesizing a solution, implementing the solution, and evaluating the solution.

The quality of the analysis is limited by the amount of data available. For instance, if only posttest scores are available, all that can be determined is how well the objective was met. If an item analysis of the posttest scores is available, it may be possible to see with greater clarity what procedures are not effective. If daily or frequent data are available, it may be possible to determine why the system was not effective, and to make some judgment about the system's efficiency for the student. When data are accumulated daily, the teacher can watch a student's performance closely and make adjustments sooner.

Systematic Instructional Procedures   The synthesis of behavioral and systems technology makes possible the development of a set of procedures by which a classroom teacher, with the aid of trained administrators and resource personnel can provide individualized instruction for each child based on his or her current performance levels and reliable predictions of the child's progress. These systematic instructional procedures consider the classroom organization, the scheduling of reinforcement, control and management of behavior, direct and daily measurement, selection and sequencing of materials for the individual student, and so on. The development of a set of standard procedures that are flexible and applicable is a further impetus in providing quality education for every child in our society. Systematic instructional procedures attempt to ensure naturally reinforcing behavioral patterns between teachers and students. Although these may not be the best ways of changing behavior and providing an environment that unfolds the child's learning process, these procedures represent a synthesis of the most effective and efficient presently available process of intervening with behavior and designing individualized instructional programs. This is an important point if we are to provide vital learning experiences for children, both handicapped and nonhandicapped, in public schools. Our procedures and instructional methods must be flexible enough to create an information flow which improves interpersonal exchanges; such exchanges are the essential reinforcing elements of the teaching-learning process.

The utilization of systems planning is most apparent in Chapter 3. Haring and Gentry provide a section on Systematic Instructional Procedures: The Instructional Hierarchy. In this section they draw together the systematic approaches they use in the Experimental Educational Unit at the University of Washington. Many of these were initially designed by O. R. Lindsley and colleagues and are commonly identified as precision teaching.

Lent and McLean, in Chapter 6, also make functional use of systems planning in designing and adapting materials and procedures for teaching retarded citizens. Bricker, Ruder, and Vincent-Smith, in Chapter 9, use systems analysis in planning a language program for preschool children. Each uses the procedures to plan, to develop, and to evaluate the effectiveness of their instructional system.

STANDARD INSTRUCTIONAL PROCEDURES

Professional educators are exploring the possibility that there may be procedures basic to instruction upon which all seasoned and successful teachers agree. The search for basic principles of learning has a long history in American psychology, beginning perhaps with Thorndike and leading to research in learning theory. Five components of instruction may form the basis for building a standard set of teaching procedures which will help teachers become more efficient in managing academic and social behavioral change in the classroom. The growing technology of teaching is simply a more precise way of tailoring instruction for the individual child.

In considering standard instructional procedures we asked ourselves, "What do teachers do that is basic to instruction?" The first component nearly always agreed upon is that the teacher must discover what responses the individual has which relate to what is going to be taught. Thus, an initial assessment of performance is the first step in successful instruction. The second step is to state clearly the objectives of instruction. The best method for accomplishing this is to begin with global goals, breaking these down into specific objectives, and finally establishing short-term aims within those objectives. The third basic component is to provide a formative system to measure student performance. Seeing changes on daily and weekly bases serves to reinforce student progress and to supply data which point to changes in the parts of the system that are not working. The fourth component is to specify a criterion level of performance so the student and teacher both know when objectives are met. The final component is to provide motivation beyond the actual instructional process, either by using environmental events or special privileges for work completed.

These components are "essential teaching functions" that can become standard operating procedures. The procedures eliminate guesswork and miscommunication between student and teacher when the teacher is assessing the child's level of performance, and they lead to designing a program that builds on existing responses.

SUMMARY

This volume is not an attempt to defend an old ideology or to present a new one. Educational problems will not be resolved by the formulation of a new ideology, a new epistemology, or a philosophical treatise. Needed are classroom procedures and organization structures validated by research. Those tools will allow teachers to design programs to meet individual needs, evaluate progress on a daily basis, and intervene and remediate emotional and behavioral problems, and facilitate learning. The purpose of this volume is to present ways to use the most contemporary refinements in educational science, including the skills of applying behavioral principles in educating children on an individual basis. This is possible only if educators are guided by a set of psychological and scientific principles based on behavioral and developmental objectives.

Technology can assist this process by:

1 Individualizing instruction and providing the child with means for independent learning.

2 Condensing vast amounts of information and sequencing it into a manageable flow.

3 Providing techniques for slicing and arranging curriculum and instructional procedures to teach a child with a serious learning problem.

This volume is organized into categories critical to changing behavior, measuring that change, using the measurement of performance as the basis for making decisions about refinements of instructional procedures that involve arrangements of the environment and curriculum, and methods for maintaining and generalizing behavior changes.

In a specialized (but functional manner), White and Liberty develop and illustrate the bases for classroom evaluation and measurement. Each of the other chapters also includes some contextual explanation of those procedures, but none so comprehensively. For this reason Chapter 2 makes a contribution to each of the other chapters and to the overall plan for teaching special children.

Chapter 2 makes an especially coherent case for continuous event recording, for measuring change (in contrast to static events), and for evaluating the effects of change relative to critical effects and to both low and high rate events.

Other chapters extend the second and offer further validation for its viewpoint. For instance, Gentry and Haring (Chapter 3) discuss measurement for instructional management, planning and decision making, and long-term evaluation. Chapter 3 also gives a functional description of measurement probes and their value in providing data relevant to sequencing learning steps and maintenance of learning effects.

The primary purpose of Chapter 3 is to delineate the procedures for planning and for management. These procedures have received extensive testing in the classrooms at the University of Washington's Experimental Education Unit (EEU) and represent a thorough approach to the procedures of teaching special children. The focus is upon teaching children with deviance problems in both special and regular class arrangements. This material is a natural extension of Chapter 2 and serves also to introduce the more intensive teaching procedures developed in Chapter 4.

Lovitt's emphasis upon curriculum planning, individualization, and teaching in Chapter 4 provides a number of effective instructions for teaching children with learning disabilities. The procedures and examples cover reading, arithmetic, spelling, and communication (penmanship, cursive writing, creative writing, typing, and increased verbal behaviors). Information from Chapter 4 applies to the other chapters. Points of special relevance include evaluation and measurement (Chapter 2), planning (Chapter 3), language instruction (Chapter 8) and (Chapter 9).

In Chapter 5, Hall, Copeland, and Clark describe procedures they have used with teachers, parents, administrators, and specialists to record and manage the behavior of special children in a range of community settings. Consequently, their emphasis is upon how to teach the procedures to achieve the extended effects recommended by Haring and Gentry in their management section. With nominal adjustments, the teaching procedures would apply to each of the designs developed in other parts of the book. The content of Chapter 5 is also in agreement with teacher-training methods recommended at the end of Chapter 10.

Chapters 6 and 7 are methodologically compatible with the rest of the book, but because the authors refer more specifically to moderately and severely retarded children, they treat a number of issues that other chapters overlook. For instance, Lent and McLean (Chapter 6) emphasize the technology which enables the educator to select target behaviors, implement systematic training, and to determine the precise dimensions of accountability. These procedures can have great impact in an area of special teaching that has been largely neglected or deemphasized. The chapter also provides a commendable design for curriculum development for "trainable" children.

In Chapter 7, the Spradlins provide a realistic analysis of the issues that must be faced in providing educational programs for severely retarded children. They cover a number of critical problems created by extreme behavioral deficits. These include the need for altered curricula, changes in evaluation procedures, and radically new teaching procedures. The last must be designed to include parents and others who can provide extensions of the instructional environment.

This last point is also emphasized as a feature of language training in Chapters 8 and 9. The moderate to severe deficits described in Chapters 6 and 7 must be evaluated in relation to expectations and established environmental functions. The severely retarded must develop a range of personal and social skills in order to function as members of society. The aim, then, is to teach behaviors that can move trainees toward a normal status. Language, of course, is a prominent part of this design.

Chapters 8 and 9 together provide an extensive overview of the language-training-program design and an intensive presentation of an illustrative language program for infants and small children. The emphasis is upon early language-training activities but the design for language training at all levels is explained.

A major condition of the language chapters is the combining of cognitive and behavioral modes. The resulting procedures include a systematic design for teaching language structures and functions to all children regardless of their levels of functioning.

Chapter 10 explains teaching procedures by describing the methods used in Super School, a classroom of selected heterogeneous children from grades 3 and 4. The methods are presented simply, the philosophy of the authors being that a method need not be complicated to be effective. They believe that a sound but simple procedure allows for natural, creative adjustments, individualization, and provides much of the functional skill of teaching.

However, the primary purpose of the chapter is not to advocate a reduction in technical complexity. The intent is to illustrate how a classroom program can be effectively planned and maintained. In describing their procedures simply and briefly they establish the orientations for teaching special children, leaving to earlier chapters the more extensive task of explaining the detailed methods for measurement, evaluation, and data management (Chapter 2), for classroom management (Chapter 3), for curriculum design and adjustment (Chapter 4), and for teaching the procedures to other instructional agents (Chapter 5).

Since Hopkins and Conard do not teach moderately or severely retarded children like those described in Chapters 6 and 7, they do not cover many of the issues brought out in detail in that section of the book. Nevertheless, there is a comfortable, compatible treatment of issues in more specialized methods and materials that are developed in these chapters. In like manner, the language sections (Chapters 8 and 9) are also supported in Chapter 10 (and in Chapter 4) in regard to social and reading functions.

The important issue to consider in Chapter 10 and other chapters is that most functions of teaching are brought out more than once; but, in each context, they are explained in relation to the operations being developed. In this way the application functions are considered along with the functional principles. Chapter

10 thus illustrates the motif of the book by illustrating the applications and the natural bases for other applications which precede it.

As authors, we have tried to identify the issues of instruction and pinpoint the controlled and measured experiences with which to answer important educational questions. We are optimistic about achieving the gains made possible through the growth of behavioral science and technology. This volume shows how behavioral technology can be applied in centers and schools for handicapped children as well as in regular classrooms and resource rooms. It is intended for counselors, administrators, school psychologists, clinicians, and regular and special classroom teachers, and for applied researchers working regularly in actual classroom situations. No procedures, strategies, or materials are discussed that have not already been applied to learning environments.

CHAPTER 1 DISCUSSION TOPICS
Perspectives on Teaching Special Children

Objective This chapter establishes the thesis that *educators* must be provided the means and methods to determine the most economical and effective ways to instruct special children.

Exercises The following memos reside in a folder in Wintergate School in North Bend, Nebraska.

Date: April 1, 1973
Subject: Ronald Rightson
From: Sarah Spring, second grade teacher
To: Harold Hazzit, school psychologist
I want to bring Ronald Rightson's performance to your attention because of the disruptive behavior he has been causing in my classroom. I feel that Ronald is the instigator of most of the trouble that I have with my second grade. He is inattentive, will not do his seat work, and incites the other children to such tricks as making inappropriate noises, throwing things, and getting out of their seats without permission. I have examined Ronald's school record and am aware that he is classified as emotionally disturbed and an underachiever. Knowing this helps me understand Ronald but does not solve the problems that he causes in my room. I fear that my other students are all falling behind in their progress and will not reach the points that they should have by the end of the year if these incidents continue. Would you please examine Ronald and help me with this difficult problem?

Date: April 13, 1973
Subject: Ronald Rightson
From: Dr. Harold Hazzit
To: Ms. Spring
I have given Ronald Rightson the MMPI and the Stanford Binet. His record and the tests show that he is an emotionally disturbed child, probably marginally brain-damaged, whose problems have resulted in the retardation of his mental growth and development.

He scored 75 on the Binet that I gave him. The MMPI shows deviant personality construction with a strong tendency toward aggressive acting-out behavior. Probably the best thing for Ronald would be placement in a special education facility with family counseling.

Date: April 14, 1973
Subject: Ronald Rightson
From: Ms. Spring
To: Vice Principal Headman
The School Psychologist recommends that Ronny Rightson be placed in a special education facility and that he have family counseling. As you know, my classroom was intended to be for normal children only. I am not trained in special education or in counseling. Where can we find the right kind of help for Ronny?

Date: April 17, 1973
Subject: Ronald Rightson
From: Mr. Headman
To: Sarah Spring
As you undoubtedly are aware, we do not have a special education classroom in our school system. While we do have children in our system who have problems, we feel that these must be dealt with by our teachers. A teacher must be flexible enough to cope with most of these problems herself—and with the help of the school psychologist and nurse. However, if you feel it will help you, I will be happy to drop around some time when you are working with Ronald and take a look myself. Keep me informed.

The following questions are appropriate for small-group discussion after each person has read Chapter 1, "Perspectives on Teaching Special Children." A report on findings from each group would serve to measure comprehension of the basic definitions and attitudes presented in the chapter.

1 Is Ronald a "special" child? Is he an "exceptional" child?
2 Is the information about Ronald in Wintergate School's files useful? If yes, how would you use the information? And what other information would you seek?
3 Which of the assumptions found in the Teaching Environments section do Ms. Spring, Mr. Headman, and Dr. Hazzit ascribe to? What definitions would they give to the words "economical" and "effective" in terms of instruction for Ronald?

Behavioral Assessment and Precise Educational Measurement

Owen R. White and Kathleen A. Liberty
Experimental Education Unit, Mental Retardation and Child
Development Center, University of Washington

INTRODUCTION

The purpose of education is to shape the skills, behaviors, and knowledge each person needs for independent action in his or her adult life. Education has had several thousand years of trial-and-error experience in this endeavor. Each new student has added to the storehouse of information. Each teacher has left behind a slightly better curriculum, more effective materials, and improved techniques. Education has come of age. Or has it?

Actually, the records teachers share are all too often stored only in their minds. The audience is limited and details are embellished with each retelling. Did all the things we remember really happen just that way? Are the facts written down?

The truth is that the words of those that have gone before are all too often vague, abstract, or distorted by the passage of time.

Yet, the real problem frequently lies not in communication but in the collection of the basic behavioral information. Without guidelines, observations of children and the world in which they move are often shaded by what we think we *should* see, or perhaps, by unusual and dramatic sidelights to the performance of the child which have nothing to do with learning per se. Decisions based upon such information are subject to grave errors. Programs in which a child grows are altered. Programs which doom a child to eventual failure are continued. And so it goes.

It is the purpose of *measurement* in education to collect facts which accurately describe the behavior and changes in the behavior of each pupil. Assessments realistically plot the course of each child's growth and aid in making decisions regarding how that growth may be enhanced. Further measurement defines the effects of each change we make to discover the combination of of events that actually helps the individual child to learn. Or so it *should* go.

There are many forms and types of measurement. Each has been designed to address some particular question and to provide direction in the decision-making process. Unfortunately, all variations which might prove useful to the educator cannot be covered here. In order to narrow the field, this chapter emphasizes four things: First, discussions center on the needs and resources of the classroom teacher. Most of the information pertains equally well to parents, specialists, counselors, administrators, and other educators. Secondly, examples and reviews of specific procedures are taken from experiences with handicapped children. Because of the similarities between the so-called handicapped child and normal children, the same basic procedures apply in any case. Third, procedures applicable to the individualization of instruction are treated in far greater depth than procedures designed to assess groups. Without precise individual measurements, group measurements are meaningless. Individualization of instruction has therefore received increased attention in recent years. Finally, we concentrate on issues in measurement and assessment which are relatively new and about which less is published elsewhere. Information concerning other, more widely published measurement and assessment procedures is referenced briefly.

The chapter is divided into several major sections. Each works through one or more basic issues of measurement and assessment and reaches some conclusions. The conclusions reached or implied by each section provide the framework for the sections to follow. Most of the measurement procedures employed in other chapters are covered to some extent here, but the reader may notice that not all those chapters follow the same guidelines. The reader should realize, however, that the procedures employed by the authors of this text were designed to be applied in special research situations or to answer special questions. They are, without exception, valid for these purposes. The material presented here, on the other hand, is designed to provide a *general* framework of measurement and assessment, applicable in a wide variety of situations. To begin, we turn now to what must always be the focus of our attention—the behavior of children.

BEHAVIOR

Seeing Is Believing

Educators, psychologists, counselors, and specialists of all sorts have built an intricate world of labels. Children no longer cry, they are emotionally disturbed. A girl no longer has problems with long *e*'s, she is borderline retarded. A student can no longer be bored, he must have a short attention span. It is easy to create polysyllabic names which transform each behavior into signposts for trauma, retardation, or mental disease. With the attachment of the label the trap closes. Whether or not behaviors persist or fade away, it is a simple matter to discover new signs of disorder from whatever behaviors remain. The child cries? She must be emotionally disturbed! She has stopped crying? *Worse,* now she is repressing her hostilities! What might be normal or even better than average in the eyes of some can be reduced to disaster by an ignorant person who commands the right vocabulary. In addition, the label often becomes the "cause" of behaviors. ("She can't read *because* she is retarded.") Superficial labeling removes the teacher from the position of accountability for what the child does or does not learn. ("I couldn't teach her to read; she's retarded.") We reach a point where we need no longer believe what we see—we can see what we believe. It is all in knowing where to look.

In order to avoid this transgression in assessment, educators must take care to believe what they see, and not the other way around. The object of measurement, the target for assessment, must be *observable behavior.* The test for observability is a simple one: Can other persons see the same behavior at the same time? Do they all agree as to when the behavior did or did not occur. Do they agree on how many times it occurred and agree on the force or intensity with which it occurred? In short, do all concerned persons see the same thing? If so, then the behavior is observable. The measurement of that behavior is likely to be accurate. If not, then the target behavior must be redefined, rechecked, and revised.

These rules are common to all measurement and assessment. Even persons interested in "intrapsychic" behaviors (i.e., things that go on in the mind) must agree on which observable behaviors are indications of which "inner" behaviors. Without this agreement, measurements and assessments are worthless. Further, if observable behaviors are indicators of unobservable behaviors, then they must remain consistent. We must avoid the "crying equals emotional disturbance," and later, "not crying equals emotional disturbance" type of error. Regardless of how the child behaves, we cannot leave him to circle endlessly in a trap of labels with no way out.

Since all measurement must be of observable behaviors, many persons are dropping the notion of labels and indicators altogether and classifying the targets of measurements in simple terms of what was measured—the observable behaviors. One does not measure "frustration," but rather records sighs, head-scratches, hits on the table, and threats of quitting. One does not measure "decoding," but notes words read orally, sentences repeated, sounds said, or comprehension questions answered.

Seeing Change

It is not enough to see behavior. As educators we must see *change* in behaviors. A description of an observable behavior must include a description of the part of the behavior to be changed.

Change in behavior may take many forms. A *topographical* change involves the muscular or skeletal part of the behavior. An answer may be either oral or written (using different muscles). A hand may be raised or lowered (using a different sequence of the same muscles).

Behavior may change in *force*. Does a child whisper, or shout? When writing, is the pencil mark so light that the words are illegible, or is the mark made with such force that the pencil lead breaks. In each case the general topography (i.e., the muscles and sequence of muscle actions) remains about the same, but the energy or force is changed.

Behaviors with the same force may still vary in *locus*—their direction or target. Does the child shout at the teacher, or at one of his peers? Is the answer written at the base of the problem, or on an answer sheet? In order to change locus, some part of the topography must also change. Have you ever tried to look at a different part of a room without moving a muscle?

These first three types of changes are usually classed under the general heading of "physical." They all deal with the behavior itself. Behavior does not occur in a vacuum, however, behavior occurs in time. There are three "temporal" dimensions of behavior which must also be considered:

First, the *duration* of a behavior may change. A shout may last for two seconds, or drag on for a whole minute. A child might take five minutes to read a short story, or an hour. The behaviors are more-or-less the same, but they take different amounts of time to complete.

Second, the *latency* between a behavior and some event may change. That is, the delay between some stimulus, or cue, and the time when a behavior is finally emitted may get longer or shorter. A child, for example, who comes to his mother within a minute when called is considerably different than one who takes 30 minutes to arrive after the first call. They both arrive, so the behaviors per se are the same, but the relationship between the behavior and some other event in the environment (in this case, calling) changes.

Lastly, the *frequency,* or *rate,* of a behavior, the number of times a behavior occurs within a specified period of time, may change. Words may be read orally at 10 words per minute or 100 words per minute. In each case the behaviors (words read) remain the same, but are occurring more or less rapidly. The change is not between the behavior and the general environment, but rather between two or more instances of the same behavior. In this sense, behavior may create part of its own environment.

Some dimensions of behavior are found in summary form in Table 2-1, along with notes on the information and data collection requirements implied by each.

Table 2-1 Dimensions of Observable Behavior Change

Dimension	Type of change	Definition	Example	How measured
Physical	Topographical	Change in the muscular or skeletal aspect of the behavior	Pointing to each word as it is read; running a finger down the page as it is read	Observation; record which parts of the body are used in what sequences
	Force	Change in force with which the behavior is performed	Hitting a ball into left field; hitting a ball over the fence	Dynometer (special equipment)
	Locus	Change in the object or person at which the behavior is directed	Writing a word on the blackboard; writing a word on a spelling test sheet	Observation; record contact or direction each time the behavior occurs
Temporal	Duration	Change in the length of time the behavior lasts	Reading orally for one minute; reading orally for ten minutes	Observation; record start and stop time for each behavior (stopwatch usually required)
	Latency	Change in the length of time between the stimulus and the occurrence of the behavior	Answering question immediately after it is asked; answering question five minutes after it is asked	Observation; record time from end of stimulus to initiation of behavior (stopwatch usually required)
	Frequency, or rate	Change in the number of behaviors which occur during a specified time period	Counting five objects in one minute; counting ten objects in one minute	Observation; record count of behaviors during time period (stopwatch may be required, but not usually)

The list of dimensions could go on forever, but for practical purposes, those covered here may be considered basic and the most frequently used. For a further listing, consult the *Glossary of Behavioral Terminology* (White, 1971a).

Critical Effect

Precise descriptions of behavior may be difficult to write. To complicate matters further, changes in behavior may be produced in more than one dimension at a time. When teaching a crippled child how to walk, for example, changes may occur in the topography of walking (i.e., the sequence of muscles used), the force exerted by the muscles, and the frequency with which steps are taken. A complete description of the behavior and behavior changes would be long and complicated. The measurement of those changes would be equally difficult.

Fortunately, there is an alternative. We may describe behavior in terms of *critical effect,* that is, the most important change which the behavior produces in the environment of the child. In walking, the most important change (critical effect) is moving the child from one place to another. Improvement in walking may be measured in terms of the number of times the child is able to achieve that critical effect. How many times can the child walk from point *A* to point *B,* in say, ten minutes? As the child improves, the steps may get larger, the force of the strides more powerful, and the frequency of placing one foot in front of the other may increase. Put them all together, and you get the critical effect of movement from point *A* to point *B* and back more and more frequently in ten minutes. Measurement need not be of a variety of behavioral dimensions, but simply a count of the number of times the critical effect is achieved.

Most behavioral descriptions are expressed in terms of critical effect (e.g., "words read orally" does not discuss the muscles, only the result). Still, we must be careful to include in the behavioral description or critical effect any important information about the other dimensions of behavior. If it is important for a child to respond to a question within one minute (latency), then the behavior description should be "responds to question orally within one minute following the question."

In summary, the target of measurement must be an observable behavior. To describe the behavior, one may describe each of the relevant dimensions (Table 2-1), or its critical effect. If some aspect of behavior is particularly important, it must be included as part of that critical effect.

BASIC APPROACHES TO ASSESSMENT

In order to select an assessment strategy of the greatest value, the educator must consider at least three things: the number of learners involved in the assessment, the criteria against which the adequacy of the behavioral change will be measured, and the frequency with which data must be collected.

Assessment Targets—Groups or Individuals?

Although each child is an individual, groups of children are also important. When an educator is introduced to a learner, there may be no information available for planning an "individualized" program. Although the student has individual characteristics, the educator will be forced to look for similarities between that child and others taught in the past. On the basis of past successes and failures, a new program may then be selected that has a reasonable chance for success.

The main concern in initial program selection should be the creation of a curriculum and learning environment which maximizes the probability of success for *all* children. Although individual differences must be recognized, it is impractical for the head of a math department, the principal of a school, or the supervisor of a district to examine in detail each record of each student. Group summaries (including statements of "highs," "lows," and "variances") must usually suffice. Similarly, the researcher who is interested in finding out "what is best for what *type* of child" must work with and analyze data on several such children. Otherwise he cannot generalize his findings to the children he was unable to test. Since formal research often requires a certain amount of disruption in the ongoing educational process, and since much is written elsewhere concerning such strategies (e.g., Senter, 1969; Winer, 1962; Glass & Stanley, 1972; Kirk, 1969), that subject will not be pursued further in this chapter.

Once an initial program has been selected for a child (based perhaps on group data), the teacher's emphasis in assessment should turn to the individual. The remainder of this chapter will concentrate on the collection and analysis of individual data, therefore, rather than the assessment of groups. After an individual's data are used to refine and improve his program, of course, it should be added to the group data to help select the appropriate program for the next child.

Assessment Referents—Norms or Criteria?

Progress data must be compared or judged against some standard of success or failure. Without some evaluation standard, the information will have no clear meaning.

Until recently, the most common standard was the *norm*, or average level of performance. The performances of individuals were compared against the average, or "normal," performance of their peers. At one time this method of comparison was vital to the educational system because not all children or young adults could be served by available educational resources. Only the "fittest" were allowed to continue up the educational ladder. To determine the relative prowess of each child, he was compared against those with whom he was competing.

Now the question is not who will be served, but *how?* Not who will advance, but *when* is each child ready? The question, "which are most capable," is no longer meaningful. They all could be capable. But what is "capable?" To answer that question, a new standard was developed—the *criterion*. Instead of being compared to his peers, a child is compared against some predetermined standard which states what is necessary for the child to "succeed." If the goal is "life," then certainly one of the criteria should be "breathing." It is likely that all children in a classroom meet that criterion. If the goal is "being parents," then one of the criteria would certainly be "passing through puberty," but it is unlikely that any child in a preschool class has yet attained that criterion. Unlike the norm-referenced test (where roughly half the children must be below the norm, and half above), the criterion-referenced test does not measure one child's performance against another's, but only whether or not the child in question has actually attained specified levels of competence.

Unfortunately, criteria in use today are frequently the result of armchair revelation. Someone simply leaned back and "logically" or "rationally" conjured up the most desirable level of performance for a particular skill or behavior. Such criteria are always debatable and are dependent solely upon a potentially capricious logic system.

Ideally, criteria should define the minimum acceptable performance level which (1) facilitates learning in the next step of a sequential task ladder and/or (2) is required for maintenance in, or improvement of the environment of the learner. For example, the rate of oral reading at the first level of a series which ensures equal or improved rates of reading when the child moves on, or that rate of oral reading which ensures that a high school student will be able to find employment. Criteria defined in this manner must be determined empirically— by trying different criteria and finding out which ones work, or by examining "real world" situations to find the "natural" criteria.

In the first case, that is, trying different criteria, there are two alternatives. First, all children in a reading series may be moved on to the next level on some arbitrary date. This is a common practice. The performances of the children are then examined to determine which children improved in the next level, and which did not.[1] By working backward and finding out what performances those improved readers had in the first level, the minimum acceptable level (criterion) for advancement[2] may be determined. Since the first group of children to be analyzed in this manner may have characteristics somewhat different from those that follow, one should not assume that criteria derived in this manner will apply equally in all cases. Analysis of the usefulness of criteria should continue with each new group.

The second method of criteria-setting based on the success or failure of children in each succeeding curriculum step involves setting artificial or arbitrary criteria for advancement. Instead of moving all children to the next level on the same day, each is advanced to the next level whenever individual performances reach a preset "aim." Children are *not* often advanced at the same point in time. After all children have advanced, the data are examined to determine how many children succeeded in the next step. If a large proportion did *not* succeed, then the "aim" is set higher for the next group. This is frequently a point of some confusion. If children fail, people are prone to lower aims to make the criteria

---

[1]The criteria for "success" or "improvement" are sometimes difficult in themselves to set. Usually they include statements of rate (speed) of both correct and error responses, and the amount of daily or weekly growth. More will be said of this in a later section.
[2]A statistical technique, called "discriminate analysis" may be employed in the operation of matching later improvement with past performance levels (see, for example, Anderson & Bancroft, 1955; Dwyer, 1951; Kendall, 1957; and Roa, 1972), but even relatively unsophisticated approaches to the process are often quite successful.

easier to reach. Such changes are purely artificial, however, and do not actually reflect increased competence in the child. The idea presented here is to *raise* the criteria for *earlier* steps in a learning sequence; based on the assumption that if we work to increase a child's competence at those lower-level tasks, his chances for success on higher level tasks will increase. If virtually all children succeed in the next step, the aim for the previous step is left the same (and renamed a "criterion"), or perhaps even lowered to determine if lower aims (taking, presumably, less time to reach) are just as effective in building the child's skills. This technique should be used whenever the proper criterion level has been estimated through the application of the first method discussed above.

Finally, criteria may be established by determining the actual working requirements in the next level of learning or employment. For example, the reading load of a college freshman can be determined from the usual class load and amount of time available for study. From that information, required reading rates can be determined and set as criteria for "college-bound" high school students.

Regardless of the method employed, the determination of criteria can be a slow process, and criteria must frequently be updated because of changes in curriculum or increases in requirements. Nevertheless, criteria *can* be determined by the classroom teacher. With the utilization of standard procedures, data-sharing among teachers, administrators, specialists, parents, and researchers, we can speed the process considerably. Empirically derived criteria, in which considerable faith may be placed, are well worth the price. Instead of merely discriminating between children, as norm-referenced tests are designed to do, they help the student achieve successful learning experiences. For these reasons, criterion-referenced analyses are the primary basis for the following discussions of assessment. For a more detailed discussion of both the norm-referenced and criterion-referenced measurement and assessment, the reader is referred to DeCecco's book (1968), *The Psychology of Learning and Instruction: Educational Psychology*.

Frequency of Assessment

All educational measurement should assess change. A child may make immediate gains, gradual gains, or no gain through any given segment of his educational experience.

For many, the only concern is whether or not a child attains preset criteria. It matters not, in these cases, whether a child learned all the material in the first few hours or days of instruction, acquired the material throughout the course, or even if the child came into the situation with all of the required skills at the start and made *no* further progress—as long as he has the skills which were to be taught. It is necessary, therefore, only to test the children at the conclusion of the course. This approach is called a *posttest-only,* or *test-after,* strategy. This approach does not provide the information necessary to adjust programs to meet the needs of individual children, to avoid wasting the time of the more or less skilled members of the group, or even to make efficient revisions

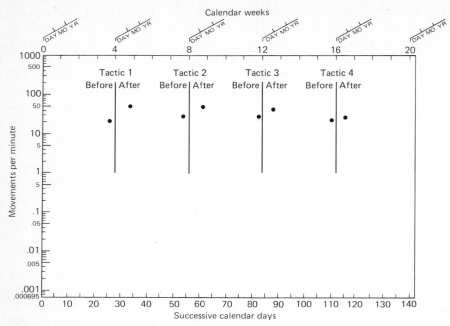

Figure 2-1 *(Courtesy of J. T. Spaulding and M. Waechter).*

in the curriculum for succeeding groups. For purposes of these discussions, therefore, the posttest-only method is unacceptable. There may be cases when such tactics are the only ones feasible (e.g., when screening for employment), but in the classroom designed for individualized instruction, especially of handicapped children, they must be avoided.

The *pretest-posttest,* or *before-after,* approach to assessment resolves some of the problems in the posttest-only method by assessing the children at the beginning of a course or section of the curriculum, as well as after the material or skills are to have been learned. The pretest provides some information for the individualization of instruction and some means by which the adequacy of the course may be evaluated in terms of student *gains* instead of simply the final level of student performance. Attempts at individualization still cannot be assessed or revised until the end of the course, and this prohibits any sound revision of programs during the course of instruction. Further, attempts at the analysis of student gains may still be misleading.

Examine Figure 2-1. Assume that the data represent four different tactics for teaching a student math facts. The object of the analysis is to determine which tactic produces the largest change and, therefore, should be tried first with future students. Rank the tactics in order of effectiveness (one equals the most effective, four equals the least effective). Consider only the difference or gain between the "before test" and the "after test" for each tactic—do not consider just the final, or "after," rates.

Most people, including the authors in the absence of additional information, would rank the tactics in exactly the order they are presented. Tactic one appears to have produced the greatest change, then tactic two, three, and finally tactic four appears to have produced the least change.

Now look at Figure 2-2. The data are from exactly the same sources, but now we can see that an assessment was made for five days before the tactics were tried and for five days after each tactic was started. The last data point in each phase (i.e., the periods before and after the change) are the same data points that were shown in Figure 1-2. Note that changes are found not only between the last data points in each phase. Changes are occurring almost daily. In tactics one and three, the data indicate that the child was getting better even before the new tactics were introduced. In tactic two, apparently no progress was being made before introducing the change in programs; and in tactic four, the child apparently was getting worse before the teacher tried the new approach. The lines drawn through the data summarize the daily progress. The dotted lines in the "after" portion of the data indicate where we might have expected the child to go if we had simply left the program alone. Those lines allow us to examine where the child is in contrast to where he *would have gone* and how he is now changing in comparison to how he was changing.

The difference between the prediction (dotted line) and the child's actual performance (solid line) is greatest after the use of tactic *four*. Since the lines are moving apart in those data, we can assume that the benefits of the new program

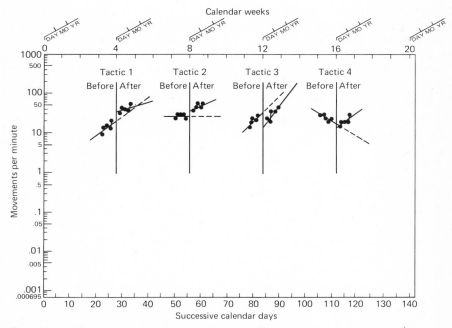

Figure 2-2   *(Courtesy of J. T. Spaulding and M. Waechter).*

would even increase further if we leave it in effect. The next greatest difference was produced by tactic two—the change is from no progress to some progress. In tactics one and three, however, where the child was already making some progress before the change, the change did not seem to enhance the growth as well. If we rank the results of the new programs now, one would have to say that tactic four produced the most favorable change, then tactic two, then tactic three, and least of all, tactic one. What appeared to be the best approach, now appears to be the worst, and vice versa!

Progress assessment is only possible when data are collected on several days throughout each program. Daily assessments of this sort are the only means by which a teacher can remain truly reactive to the needs of the student and timely in the program decisions required by individualized instruction. For those reasons, *continuous* or *daily measurement* and assessment techniques will be emphasized in the sections to follow.

ASSESSMENT DATA

The variety of data collected in education is exceeded only by the number of analytic treatments which may be used with the data. Unfortunately, educators often make an arbitrary selection. Other criteria are simply too abstract and mathematical. Given the parameters outlined in earlier sections, however, the problem becomes more manageable. First, data which are amenable only to groups of subjects may be eliminated because of our previously stated concern for individuals. Secondly, data which measure the performance of students at only one time may be eliminated, since it has been suggested that measuring *change* (over time) is more important. Third, data which fail to relate directly to observable behavior or its critical effects may be eliminated. We are left with a great deal, but far less than the total. As we continue with our discussion about data, the educator should continually bear in mind these most important criteria: "Given *this* child, *this* situation, and *this* goal, do these data and procedures provide the information necessary to plan and revise the most effective program for behavior change?"

Yes or No?

There are many ways to change behavior. Measuring many of those changes requires sophisticated equipment and/or a great deal of time, but many aspects of behavior have relatively little meaning in the context of even the most immediate behavioral or educational objectives. Whenever possible, it is wiser to attempt the specification of a behavior's critical effect, rather than its particular topography, locus, or latency. If one or more of the smaller aspects of behavior are particularly important to the situation (e.g., a child should respond to a question within one minute), then those aspects must be included as part of the critical effect.

Once a critical effect has been defined, all the aspects of behavior that are necessary to achieve that critical effect may be assessed with simple yes or no statements. "Yes, the critical effect was achieved," or, "No, the critical effect was not achieved." An educator may occasionally encounter certain situations where other data are required. For example, in at least one research article (Walker et al., 1968), it was found that with one child the most critical variable was not whether or not the child was out of his seat, but the *duration* of out-of-seat behavior. Still, variations of the simple yes/no statement form the basis for the vast majority of essential educational assessment, so the remainder of this chapter will concentrate almost exclusively on that form of data.

Checklists

Yes/no statements are used most simply in the form of checklists. The critical effects or criteria for a section of the program or curriculum are merely listed on a piece of paper. As each of the critical effects is achieved, it is checked off. When all items (or some predetermined proportion of the items) have been checked, the child is considered to have passed that section of the program.

Checklists are a valid form of measurement for behaviors which are essentially permanent. That is, once the behavior has been displayed, it is not likely to be dropped from the repertory of the subject. For example: When a child learns to stand up, he is unlikely to lose that skill unless he has an illness or an accident. If standing-up behavior per se is of some concern, it can be adequately assessed by a checklist.

The types of behavior which are amenable to checklist assessment may be increased with the specification of additional criteria for success. Perhaps, for example, standing up is *not* sufficient in itself, but rather, standing for a period of five minutes is required. In that case, the five-minute criterion could be added to the checklist, and when competence at that level is demonstrated, the behavior is checked off. Similarly, "reads orally at a rate of 120 words per minute" could be placed on a checklist. When the criteria for behaviors on a checklist begin to increase, however, additional data (e.g., duration or rate) must be collected in order to be able to make a yes/no statement. Checklists will still offer advantages if there is reason to believe that most of the behaviors are, in fact, in the repertory of the child being assessed. If other data must be collected, at least the collection of data on existing behavior will be carried on for only one or a few days, but if more time is needed in order to attain criteria, and to be checked off the list, it may be best to view the *other* data (e.g., rate or duration) as the primary assessment information, and the checklist merely a way to keep track of what projects to embark upon next.

Finally, checklists are essentially "posttest only" assessments. The behavior is tested, and possibly checked off, only after there has been some opportunity for it to be learned. If the behaviors on the list represent very small steps in the sequence of learning (e.g., where one step is "adding one and one together and stating orally the correct answer of two," and the next step is "adding one and two together . . ."), then the checkmarks will be made frequently enough to provide information for appropriate program changes. If, on the other hand, the skills listed are relatively complex and require some time to acquire (e.g., "can write correct answers to four-term addition problems with carrying"), then the information provided by the checklist is not likely to assist daily program review and revision.

Checklists in Time

The most common checklist for research and detailed classroom assessment is the *time-ruled checklist*. The same behaviors are assessed over and over again according to some preset schedule (i.e., time-rule). If the teacher wants to know what types of social behaviors a child emits when playing with his peers, for example, there are several options for collecting the information.

The teacher may sit quietly and write down everything that happens while the children play. The results might look something like this:

1 John comes into the room,
2 All three peers look up,
3 John says, "Hi,"
4 Two of the peers say, "Hi,"
5 John goes to the peer that did *not* say "Hi,"
6 The peer turns away,
7 John touches the peer and says, "You're stupid,"
8 The peer. . . .

Complete information can be collected in this manner *if* the teacher can move her hands rapidly enough to write down everything that happens, and *if* she does not miss something when looking down to write. Such recordings tend to cause writer's cramp, however, and may be subject to a bias (e.g., the teacher may be looking for negative remarks, and emphasize them out of proportion to their actual occurrence). Narrative information is also difficult to analyze. Changes in behavior from day-to-day, even though fully described, must be ferreted out from the irrelevant descriptions.

Despite these drawbacks, narratives may serve to identify behaviors of concern. Once those behaviors are determined, they could then be abstracted or drawn out of the narrative and placed in a checklist. The narrative above would yield a list of behaviors very similar to the numbered lines. Line 7, however, would become two listed statements, since it contains two different behaviors ("touching," and "saying").

The checklist can be made more flexible if separate codes describe behaviors, the person emitting the behavior, and the person or persons to whom the behavior is directed. For example, let J = John, P1, P2, and P3 = the three peers, and G = greet (i.e., in this case, "Hi"). When an interaction occurs, the teacher first records (or checks) the code for the person emitting the behavior, then the code for the behavior, and finally the code for the locus (direction or target) of the behavior. Line 3 from the narrative above would be: "J/G/P1, P2, P3." Line 4 would be "P1, P2/G/J." Using the same codes (note the absence of P3 in line four's code, though), two different interactions were recorded.

Using a checklist and coding system sharply reduces the teacher's writing task. The teacher need only check the behavior codes as behaviors occur. Further, because there is likely to be greater consistency in the codes from day-to-day than with narration, comparisons are easier; but this is true only if great care is taken to define the meaning of each code so that each day it appears it means that the same behavior or interaction occurred.

If each behavior or interaction on the list is checked or coded only once during any given day, a great deal of information is lost. If negative comments are coded on two successive days, one will still not know if the negative comments followed the same behavior of the peers on both days. That information might be contained in a narrative, but it would be lost on a sheet where all possible behaviors are simply listed and checked off, regardless of the order in which they occurred. This problem brings us to the third option—the time-ruled checklist.

If several checklists (or spaces in which codes may be written) are listed on the same sheet of paper, the teacher can code the first interaction in the first space, the second interaction in the second space, and so on. At the end of the observation time, a running documentary of the interactions will have been recorded in sequence. One problem still remains. For example, if a child plays alone for 30 minutes, and then with a peer for 2 minutes on one day; and on the next day he plays alone for only 4 minutes, and then with the peer for 20 minutes, there has been a change in behavior, but the codes would look the same (i.e., the code for "play alone," then the code for "play with peer"). The problem arises because a new code is not written down until the interaction or behavior changes. To avoid this problem, researchers and observers usually move from one space to the next after a certain period of time—regardless of change or no-change in the behaviors or interactions being coded. If the intervals for change were set at one minute, for example, then "play alone" would have been coded in 30 successive boxes the first day, and only 4 successive boxes on the second day. Moving from one checklist box to the next is time-ruled, thus the name *time-ruled checklist*.

Depending upon the number of behaviors listed (potential codes), and the number of behaviors that actually occur, the observer may or may not have time to code everything happening in any given interval. To reduce confusion and hesitation, observers usually set up a hierarchy or priority list of behaviors to rank the behavior codes in order of importance. If two behaviors occur at once, only the higher priority behavior is coded. If the same behavior occurs more than once in the same interval (i.e., during the time when only one box is being coded), it is still counted only once. This helps avoid differences between two days' data which may be due only to the ability of the observer to code faster on one day than the other. Because of these two limitations, coding intervals are usually set as small as possible (around 6 to 10 seconds) so that the probability is low that too many important behaviors will occur during any given interval. As behaviors occur with more or less frequency, there is a greater chance of coding them in more than one box. Finally, in order to ensure that the observer is watching the behavior for the same period of time during each interval (and not looking down more or less often to code), many researchers set up two intervals—one for observation, one for coding (e.g., look for 10 seconds, code for 5 seconds, look for 10 seconds). The coding interval is set so that virtually any code can be written in the time allowed. Observers are instructed not to look up before that interval is over, even if they finish ahead of time.

The primary advantage to time-ruled checklists over other forms of data collection and measurement is that they allow the observer to monitor several behaviors at once in the context of those things which occurred naturally before and after each behavior was emitted.

The interpretation of time-rule checklist data can sometimes be tricky. Special consideration must be given to the effects of code hierarchies and the size of interval chosen. Careful observer-reliability data are essential to make sure everything is going as planned. For these reasons the time-ruled checklist is not often used by teachers. Researchers usually use such lists only as long as necessary to determine which behaviors or interactions should be monitored in other, simpler, and more direct ways. For a more detailed discussion of such measurement devices, the reader is referred to *Behavioral Observation and Frequency Data: Problems in Scoring, Analysis, and Interpretation* (Jones, 1973).

"Yes, Yes, a Thousand Times Yes"

In the most rudimentary form of checklist, the behavior is counted only once. In the time-ruled checklist, the behavior is coded only once in any given interval, but at least the number of intervals containing its code can be more than one. In the first case, the only information available to the teacher amounts to an all-or-nothing proposition. Unless the behaviors which are checked are quite small (so that several new behaviors are checked each day) the statements provide little information for daily programming and revision. In the second case, there are difficulties in setting-up, using, and interpreting a time-ruled checklist. In most cases, therefore, the teacher should select a single behavioral target, provide many opportunities for it to occur in the same day, and then simply count the number of times that it occurred.

If a behavior may occur a maximum of three times during a day, then the possible counts are zero, one, two, or three. *Change* in behavior from day to day could be noted between any combination of those values (e.g., from one-to-three, from two-to-zero). The higher the possible behavior count, the greater the number of changes that can be noted. Because change is the most important part of learning (indeed, if it is not all of learning), behaviors should be selected that provide the greatest possible range of change statements from day-to-day. That does not mean that the behavior *will* change. But if it does change, however slightly, there is a good possibility of *seeing* that change. Take, for example, a child who is reading two short stories a day which average about 500 words each. In order to see a change in the number of short stories read, the child will have to jump from two stories to three stories (a 50% increase), or from two stories to one (a 50% decrease). That is a large step in just one day. If *words* were being counted, however, then between the two stories he reads 1,000 words in just one day. To show an increase, he needs to read only 1,001 words the next day—an increase of just one-tenth of one percent! Counting words allows smaller changes to be measured than counting stories.

As a rule of thumb, the teacher should select behaviors and set up conditions to allow a child to emit at least 10 behaviors. That does not necessarily mean that the child *will* emit those 10 behaviors, only that it is likely or possible. If counts of 10 or more are the rule, rather than the exception, then we can measure changes with as little as a 10% increase or decrease in behavior. In order to achieve this goal, the teacher may find it necessary to increase the number of opportunities for the behavior to occur (e.g., provide math fact sheets with more problems; have the child drink plenty of fluids to increase the frequency of bathroom behaviors), or select smaller units of behavior to count (e.g., *words* instead of *stories; hits* instead of *fights*).

In summary, the basic unit of measurement most useful to the teacher is the yes or no statement of critical effect. In order to observe change in behavior from day-to-day, however, regularly occurring behaviors should be selected. By counting and comparing the number of times a behavior occurs each day, the teacher knows if the behavior is increasing or decreasing. Appropriate decisions can then be made as to whether the program should be changed or left the same.

In order to see small changes in behavior, it is best to select behaviors or situations which allow at least 10 examples to occur. In most situations, redefining the target behavior, offering more problems or practice material, or watching the behavior for longer periods of time will allow the teacher to observe the behavior 10 times. This may, of course, be impossible in some situations (e.g., when out-of-seat behavior happens only once or twice a day).

Standardizing the Counts

When comparisons are made between two or more situations, confusion may result. For example, if a child reads 300 words correctly one day, and 50 words correctly the next day, it appears that he is regressing. On the other hand, if 12 minutes were allowed for reading on that first day, and only 1 minute on the second, then the same child actually changed from (300 divided by 12 =) 25 words *per minute* on the first day to (50 divided by 1 =) 50 words *per minute* on the second day. Now it appears that he is getting better! The difference lies not only in how many behaviors occur, but in the opportunities to behave.

All tests or measurement situations designed to assess a behavior should be exactly the same. Comparisons between results are then simple, direct, and valid. Standardized tests attempt to approximate that ideal world, but they have several drawbacks.

First, there are simply no standardized tests available for many behaviors. Secondly, standardized tests usually require considerable time to administer, making them difficult to use in daily assessment and good program monitoring and revision. Third, even in cases where a standardized test is short enough for daily administration, repeated exposure to the test destroys the type of standard measurement situation in which the test was designed to be administered. That is, the child is not supposed to have such frequent practice in taking the test. The teacher is thus faced with the task of assessing behaviors in nonstandard situations, and then somehow making comparisons with standardized results. The task is not as impossible as it may seem. In most cases the teacher must examine only three things—the freedom to respond, the opportunities to respond, and the time to respond.

Freedom

The first question a teacher should ask when comparing two behavior counts is whether or not the child was as free to respond in one situation as he was in the other. Was anything pacing, prompting, or inhibiting the child differently in one situation than the other? For example, if on one day a child's word list is presented in the form of flash cards at the rate of one word every five seconds, and on the next day the same cards are presented at the rate of one every ten seconds, then any change in the number of behaviors counted may be due only to the difference in the pace of those two situations. Similarly, out-of-seat behavior data taken on a day when a child is free to move in and out of his seat cannot be compared with a day when the child was literally tied with rope to his chair. Behavior may occur or fail to occur simply because of constraints in the environment. In such cases, the counts reflect the world around the child, not change or learning in the child.

It is best to create situations in which the child is free from external (physical) constraints while responding. Machines or flash cards held by the teacher should be replaced by typed lists or open books. Only when the child is free to respond at his or her *own* pace can the educator assess the effectiveness of program variables (e.g., newer reading materials, better types of cues, free time given for improved performances) in terms of changes and learning they produce in the child. If constraints do exist, then they should be recognized, described, and kept as consistent as possible from day to day.

Opportunity

Opportunities to respond may run out. If a child who is capable of reading 100 different words is given a list with only 20, then he will be unable to show his teacher the extent of his reading ability. If on the next day he is given a list of 30 words, the same child will still be able to read them all. Comparing the two counts (20 on the first day, 30 on the next) implies that the child has improved when it is really the situation which has changed to allow the child more opportunities to show the teacher what he can really do. The same mistake can be made in the other direction. A child may look like he's getting worse if he answers 10 questions correctly on Monday, and only 5 questions correctly on Tuesday. We may find, though, that on Monday, he was asked 20 questions (answering one-half of them correctly), and on Tuesday he was asked only five questions (answering them *all* correctly). What at first looks like a poorer performance suddenly becomes a tremendous improvement.

It is best to allow the same number of opportunities to respond each day. If that is not possible or not desirable, *percentages* may be calculated to keep the number of behaviors counted in perspective to the number of opportunities to behave. To calculate percentage, simply divide the behavior count by the number of opportunities (i.e., the total *possible* behavior count), and multiply by 100.

$$\text{Percentage} = 100 \times (\text{behavior count} \div \text{total possible count})$$

If only correct responses are counted, then the percentage is called "percentage correct." Dividing the "error count" by the total possible will yield "percentage error." In most situations, since responses are either correct or errors (i.e., there are no "omissions" or other possible ways to count the behavior), the correct and error percentages will be opposites of one another. If the correct percentage is equal to 80, then the error percentage must be equal to $100 - 80 = 20$.

If one of the percentages goes up, the other must go down by an equal amount. Thus, it is necessary to record only one or the other. If more than two types of behavior counts are kept (e.g., if "errors" are broken down into "omissions," "substitutions," "mispronunciations," and so on), then separate data should be kept on each of the different counts and percentages.

Going back to the examples given at the beginning of this section, if a child read 20 out of 20 words correctly, or 30 out of 30 words correctly, he was 100% correct. The use of percentages places each count in direct relationship to the number of opportunities to behave. 10 out of 20 questions (50%) is obviously inferior to 5 out of 5 questions (100%), demonstrating correctly the growth in accuracy from one day to the next. If accuracy is the prime concern in an educational situation, then percentage data is one way of equalizing or standardizing behavior counts from day to day or across different situations.

Time

Accuracy is only one dimension of a behavioral performance. Another dimension of behavioral change is equally important—*fluency*. Assume, for example, that the progress of two children in a special class is being reviewed by a committee. The committee is to decide if the children are ready for a regular class. Both children are about 97% accurate in reading words orally in the book used by the regular class, and both have comprehension scores above 85%. The scores for both children have remained essentially the same for several weeks. It appears that they have reached a "plateau" of growth in the special class. Assuming that the information about both children is equally encouraging on other academic skills, in social development, and in other areas of concern, both children should be transferred to the regular class. The committee then begins to examine the measurement situations. First, were the conditions of measurement such that each child was free to respond under similar conditions for each day the behaviors were counted? Yes. Every day each child read to the teacher orally, alone, away from the rest of the children. The books were always the same (i.e., essentially the same reading level), and the prompts, cues, corrections, and praises of the teacher were carefully controlled so that the measurements reflected the child's behavior, not that of the teacher. How about the opportunities to respond? Each day one story was read. The stories were roughly the same length, but might have varied as much as 50 or 75 words in length from day-to-day, averaging about 700 words total. Since percentages were calculated, however, the small differences in opportunity to respond were always taken into account. The committee is likely to decide that both children have reached a normal level of performance and have stopped growing in the special class. "But," the teacher says, "the children are as different as night and day!" The committee neglected to enquire about the *time* each child took to reach the level of accuracy reported, and to read the stories each day.

One child takes about six minutes each day to read a story 700 words in length. The other child takes 14 minutes to read the same story (quite a time burden for any teacher, even in a small special class). Even though the second child has approximately the same accuracy level as the first, he would have great difficulty keeping up with the children in a regular class. To demonstrate these differences, we must somehow account for time in our statements of performance. Using the same basic logic used in the calculation of percentages, we can divide the behavior count by the number of minutes over which that count was taken. The result is called the *rate* or *frequency* of responding.

Rate or *frequency* = (behavior count) ÷ (number of minutes spent counting)

In the cases above, one child would have a rate of (700 behaviors/6 minutes =) approximately 117 words read *per minute,* and the other child would have a rate of (700 behaviors/14 minutes =) 50 words *per minute.* In the same amount of time, the first child will read twice as much material as the second child. The second child would have difficulty in a regular class.

Now, what about that "plateau"? Have both children really stopped growing in the special class? Using rate instead of percentage to describe their progress, we may find that although the second child is only reading about 50 words per minute now, a few short weeks ago he read just 30 words per minute. Each day his rates have been improving. If his program is continued, his rate will be over 100 words per minute in about three weeks. If the program is changed, his progress may stop.

The fluency or frequency of responding is important in almost every behavior. Almost all children get out of their seats from time-to-time, but it is the one who does so once or twice each minute who is the problem. As with percentages, the differences in count which are due to differences in situations (here, the amount of time spent observing), may be eliminated *if* we always watch a child for the same period of time. For ease in comparison across different situations, we can divide the behavior count by the time to make the units or counts of comparison "standard." Where percentage data attended primarily to accuracy, rates or frequency data will attend primarily to fluency or the number of times a behavior is likely to occur in each minute of observation. Note, however, that the collection of rates on error responses as well as correct responses will reflect both speed and accuracy; but correct and error percentages cannot reflect speed.

Record Floors

Results possible in one situation may be impossible in another; For example, when we tried to compare 10 questions answered correctly with 5 questions answered correctly. In the second case, only 5 questions were asked. How could 10 questions be answered? We solved the problem by dividing each count by the number of opportunities to behave. What would have happened, however, if *no* change in accuracy had been achieved by the child. He was 50% accurate on the first day, which means that he answered 10 out of 20 questions correctly. If he were still 50% accurate on the second day, how many of the five questions should he have answered correctly? Half of five is 2½. How can a child answer 2½ questions correctly? By giving a partial answer? By answering one part of a two-part question? No, if behavior counts are to be simple and accurate, then they should reflect all or nothing. Either he does or does not achieve the critical effect. There are no half behaviors. If that is the case, then a child who is asked five questions cannot demonstrate 50% accuracy. The child will either answer two questions correctly (40% accuracy), or three questions correctly (60% accuracy). When compared against the first day's data (50%), the child *must* look like he improved or got worse. A no-change statement is impossible because the score achieved on the first day cannot be achieved under the conditions of the second day.

All information based on counts of "whole numbers" (i.e., one, two, three, . . .) will have "gaps" or holes in the sequence of possible scores. It is due simply to the fact that the counts themselves have gaps (nothing exists between one and two, between two and three, and so on). If a quiz has five questions that are each counted as "all-correct," or "all-incorrect," then the possible counts would be 0, 1, 2, 3, 4, or 5. Let us assume that the quiz was timed for exactly 10 minutes. The child had no less and no more time to work. The possible percentage scores are found by dividing each possible correct count by the total number of items:

$$\frac{0}{5} = 0\%$$
$$\frac{1}{5} = 20\%$$
$$\frac{2}{5} = 40\%$$
$$\frac{3}{5} = 60\%$$
$$\frac{4}{5} = 80\%$$
$$\frac{5}{5} = 100\%$$

No other scores are possible. The rates which could be achieved would be found by dividing each possible count by the time, 10 minutes:

$^0\!/_{10}$ = 0 per minute
$^1_{\ 10}$ = 1 per minutes (that is, $^1\!/_{10}$ of a behavior each minute, which is the same as one behavior each ten minutes)
$^2\!/_{10}$ = .2 per minute (one behavior each 5 minutes)
$^3\!/_{10}$ = .3 per minute (one behavior each 3.3 minutes)
$^4\!/_{10}$ = .4 per minute (one behavior each 2.5 minutes)
$^5\!/_{10}$ = .5 per minute (one behavior each 2 minutes)

If the actual performance level of a child falls below any one of the possible (measurable) rates or percentages, then it must be recorded as the next lowest rate or percentage that *can* be measured. If, for example, a child completes the first two problems on the quiz and is one-half finished with the third, his performance count is 2.5. Since the answer to the third question was not written down, however, the teacher is only able to record a count of 2. His percentage score may really be ($^{2.5}\!/_5$ =) 50%, but is recorded as only ($^2\!/_5$ =) 40%. His "real" rate may be ($^{2.5}\!/_{10}$ =) 0.25 responses per minute, but is only measurable as ($^2\!/_{10}$ =) 0.20 responses per minute.

The gaps between possible scores are all the same size for any given number of items or minutes. With 5 items all percentage gaps are 20%, and with 10 minutes, all the rate gaps are 0.10 responses per minute. The lowest score possible in each case, other than zero, is also equal to the size of these gaps. The lowest nonzero percentage that can be recorded here is 20%, and the lowest nonzero rate that can be recorded when observing for 10 minutes is 0.10 responses per minute. These lowest possible values are called *record floors*. They define the lowest rate or percentage score (other than zero) which may be measured in any given situation, and the least amount of change which must occur in a child's behavior before it can be noticed (i.e., "bridge the gap" from one possible score to the next).

Imagine the following test. A child is placed in front of a small building with five stories. As in Europe, the street-level story will be labeled *ground,* or *zero;* the next story (one level up) will be called the first story, and so on, up to the *fifth story,* which is five levels above the street. There are no stairs in the building, but there are holes leading from each story to the one above and the one below. The test is to see how many of the stories the child is able to climb using a stepladder. The problem is that the stepladder is magic and will disappear after 10 minutes. The clock begins, and the child picks up the ladder outside of the *zero* floor. He enters and begins to work. He fumbles, finally sets up the ladder, and starts to climb. He *almost* reaches the first floor, when the ladder begins to fade. The ladder disappears just as he reaches for the first floor. He falls. Since each floor is padded, he is not hurt, but comes to rest on ground zero where he started. The tester comes, checks, and sees him standing there no higher than when he started. Score: 0%, 0 floors per minute. Does that mean that he did not climb at all? No, only that his performance was below the *record floor* (the first floor). On the second day the child is more organized, and before the ladder disappears he is about one-third of the way up the ladder to the third floor. Still, when the support is gone, he falls back to the second floor. Score: 40% (two floors out of five), 0.20 floors per minute. Does that mean that he only climbed two floors? No, only that the second floor was the highest point we could measure when the time ran out.

It should be pretty obvious that the record floor, which reflects the size of the gaps in our measurement system, can really be a limiting factor in assessing the performance of the child. The lower the floor, the smaller the gaps. Since the record floor is calculated as one divided by either time (for rate) or total possible count (for percentage), the way to lower the floor is simply to record the behavior for longer periods of time or to provide more possible opportunities to behave. If, for example, the same building were divided into ten floors (admittedly, with low ceilings), then the lowest possible nonzero score the child would be able to achieve would be ($\frac{1}{10}$ =) 10%, not 20%. If the time allowed for the test were further increased to 20 minutes, then the lowest possible nonzero rate would be 0.05, not 0.10 floors per minute. In either case, it is likely that the performance of the child on the first day would have been recorded as something other than zero and that the measure of success for the second day would more accurately reflect his actual achievement. Record floors are indicators of the sensitivity with which we are able to assess a performance. Comparisons between situations where different record floors exist may show change only because what is possible in one case is impossible in another.

Record Ceilings

Every building has a highest possible point—a point beyond which a child cannot climb, not because he has run out of strength or time, but because that was the way the building was constructed. Tests have the same limitations.

On a five-item quiz, taken in 10 minutes, the child cannot achieve a rate greater than 0.2 questions per minute. That does not mean that he cannot solve the problems with greater fluency, only that if he does, we will not be able to measure it. Ceilings like that often slow children down. They could go faster, but what's the use? To allow children room to grow, it is best to set up situations where they will never quite be able to take advantage of all the opportunities they have to behave (questions, problems, or whatever). If a child is able to read 80 words a minute, then give him a story with 200 words, and time him for a minute. If you want him to finish the story, then fine. Still, he is assessed (for fluency) only during that first minute. As he approaches the greatest measurable rate (200), give him even longer stories. Many persons think that children are frustrated by never reaching the limit. The truth is that most children are delighted to have the extra space to challenge their abilities to learn and to grow. They get their satisfaction by seeing the possibility for *improvement* from day-to-day, instead of simply finishing, just like the day before, and the day before.

In percentages, the problem of ceilings is more complicated. If a child answers each question attempted correctly, then he has attained 100% accuracy *regardless* of the number of questions asked. The ceiling is always within reach. Indeed, in most cases, we want that ceiling to be within reach. One could provide a number of problems which are well beyond the level of the child's ability, or provide more questions than he could possibly complete and count all questions which were omitted as errors. But both of those alternatives are too artificial and depend too much on how the test was constructed rather than measuring how the child is performing. For example, one teacher could provide a child with 100 items, only 50 of which the child completes. Counting all uncompleted items as errors (even though such omissions are really the absence of behavior), the child receives a score of 50%. On a different day, the test could be constructed with only 75 problems. If the same 50 items were completed, the child would achieve a score of roughly 67%. It looks as if the child improved, but really only the test changed. In the final analysis, percentage data are likely to have a fixed and definite ceiling.

The Effects of Ceilings and Floors

Some of the effects of ceilings and floors have already been discussed. The concepts are important, however, and bear review. First, the record floor is the lowest measurable nonzero level of performance in any given measurement situation. If the performance of the child falls below the record floor, then it will be recorded simply as zero. Because such measurements may not actually reflect "no behavior," but merely that the conditions were such that no behavior was *counted,* rates or percentages which fall below the record floor are often called "no counts," instead of "zero."

Secondly, the size of the record floor also defines the size of the gaps between each of the other measurable levels of performance. If a child is observed for two minutes, then the record floor is ($\frac{1}{2}$ =) 0.50 behaviors per minute. Only rates which are multiples of that floor may be measured ($1 \times 0.5 = 0.5$; $2 \times .5 = 1.0$; $3 \times .5 = 1.5$; etc.). If the actual level of performance falls between any of these points, then it will be recorded as the next lowest level. A child actually reading at a rate of 8.25 words per minute will be measured as reading only eight words per minute. Even though the *absolute* size of an error (as defined by the record floor) will be the same size anywhere along the measurement scale, one should note that the higher the counts, the less the *relative error* in measurement. An error of 0.25 words per minute in measurement with a count of eight is equal to a ($^{0.25}/_8$ =) 0.031, or roughly 3%. An error of 0.25 words per minute with a count of 80 is only ($^{0.25}/_{80}$ =) 0.0031, or $\frac{3}{10}$ths of 1 percent. The relative error in measurement may be reduced, therefore, by setting up situations in which the behavior may occur many times.

Third, because different record floors will produce different gaps in the possible measurement scale, the rates or percentages which are possible in one instance may not be possible in another. In comparing two rates or percentages when the record floors are different, what may appear to be a change in the child may only be a change in the floor. This does not mean that conversion to percentages or rates will not assist the evaluator in making comparisons across different situations, only that some care must be taken when the results of the comparison are close.

Finally, the floor and the ceiling represent the absolute limits of the measurement scale. Performances which fall above or below these limits are lost. If a child's performances bounce right along the floor or ceiling, then we really cannot say what the child *is* doing, only what he is *not* doing (i.e., he is not performing within the limits of our measurements). Strictly speaking, that is not very helpful. If a child is performing on the floor or ceiling, the teacher should lower the floor, or raise the ceiling to "find the performance," and start measuring the child. Furthermore, as a child's performance approaches a floor or ceiling, it is likely to change even before it reaches the limit. Some children slow down, others speed up. Once they have reached the limit, they may bounce back from it, not because they cannot maintain the improved performance, but simply because there is nothing left to do. When setting the floor and ceiling, therefore, it is best to set them as far away from the expected performance levels as possible to give the child room to grow.

TALKING ABOUT CHANGE

Education should not stand still. The big product should be change. Our discussion about general approaches to assessment, data types, and data standardization was meant to provide a base for the discussion of how measurements may be compared, and through which the growth of a child may be observed. It matters not where a child *is,* it only matters how fast he is growing. If there is growth—rapid, steady, continuous change—then any goal can be reached.

The assessment of change has never been given as much attention as the procedures to obtain a single measure of performance. Too many persons assume that if a single measurement is precisely taken, then simple repetitions of that measurement will make behavior changes obvious. There are several alternatives for describing change and reaching conclusions about their relative importance, however, each of which should be carefully considered. The reader should note, however, that any rules of thumb which are offered in the discussion which follows are likely to fail from time to time. The reader should look at each new situation carefully and determine its individual requirements for the most precise approach to assessment.

Absolute and Relative Change

If a child has increased his reading rate from 10 words per minute to 15 words per minute, there are at least two ways to describe that change. First, we may state in *absolute* terms how many more words he is able to read in a minute now than he was able to read before. To determine this value, subtract one score from the other: $15 - 10 = 5$, showing that the child is able to read five more words per minute. The program appears to be helping the child to grow.

After several weeks the teacher may make an assessment to determine if the program is maintaining its effectiveness. The teacher notes that in the present week the child changed from 60 to 75 words per minute, in contrast to the much earlier change of 10 to 15. Figuring the absolute change as before ($75 - 60 = 15$), it looks as if the program is actually improving in its power to help the child grow. No need to worry about *that* child, so she sets his work aside and begins to devise change plans for less-fortunate children. But that is an erroneous conclusion. There are different ways of looking at change. Some are more accurate or representative than others under some circumstances.

Relative differences or changes can be found by dividing the larger performance measure by the smaller and labeling the change as × (times) or ÷ (divide), to indicate whether there was an increase or a decrease in performance. Using the first week's data for the child described above, the relative change would be $15 ÷ 10 = × 1.50$. The × indicates that the change was up. Instead of simply saying that the child increased by five words, we can say that his second reading rate is 1.50 times greater than his first. By making such change statements we keep the size of the change in proportion to the original performance. To illustrate this point, look again at the most recent assessment of the reading performances of the child above. During the last week, he changed from 60 words per minute to 75 words per minute. In relative terms, the change would be $75 ÷ 60 = × 1.25$. Using relative change statements it appears as if the most recent change (× 1.25) is less than the child's first week's change (× 1.50). Why? Because being able to read 15 more words when you start at 60 is a smaller proportionate increase than being able to read 5 more words when you start at only 10.

So, which way should the change statement be made? Using one method (the absolute change), the teacher will conclude that the program is increasing in ability to help the child grow. Using the other method (relative change), the teacher could conclude that the program effectiveness is decreasing. Should she leave the program alone, or should she change it? In most cases, the relative change statement should form the basis for program decisions. This is especially true when the continued effectiveness of programs is being assessed over long periods. Relative change statements are "fair to the little guy." Children with low rates of performance do not have to make huge steps (in absolute terms) to show that a program is working when their programs are first started, they need only make good gains in proportion to where they start. Conversely, we expect our programs to produce the same proportional increases later in their programs when they achieve high rates of performance. Children with higher rates of behavior must strive to make much larger absolute gains in order to have their program look as effective as it did when their performances were much lower. The next question of course should be "is that possible?" The answer is "yes."

If a program is well-designed, broken down into appropriately sized units, is well-sequenced, and provides motivation and feedback, children will grow in increasingly larger absolute steps and consistent proportional (relative) steps. A limit will eventually be reached, and the performance of the child will level off. The limit may be imposed by the program (e.g., there are no more words to read in the time available), the child (i.e., he has reached the physical limits of his abilities), or motivational variables (e.g., there is simply no good reason to read faster). In any event, the program should be changed at that point. Even here, proportional statements of change are an asset. With absolute change statements, the progress of children usually appears to taper off. It is difficult to decide when progress has slowed down enough to warrant a change in the program. With proportional or relative change statements, however, the point where a ceiling or limit is approached is usually marked by a quick drop in relative progress statements. The point where a program should be changed is in most cases much more apparent.

Relative change may also be calculated as a *percentage*. There are several variations of percentage-change statements. The most common and easiest to interpret is calculated by subtracting the first value (e.g., the first performance measure taken) from the second or most recent value (e.g., the second or last performance measure taken), divide by the first value, and multiply by 100. Using the same data examined earlier, a change from 10 to 15 words per minute in reading would result in the following increase: $[15 - 10) \div 10] \times 100 = +50\%$. The child increased his performance 50% between the first and second assessments. That is, the size of the change was equal to one-half (50%) of his starting rate.

Percentage statements of change are "directional"; however, changes of the same size, but in opposite directions (one up, the other down), will look different. Looking at the data above, going from 10 to 15 resulted in a percentage change statement of 50%. Going from 15 to 10, on the other hand, would result in a percentage change statement of $[(10 - 15) \div 15] \times 100 = -33\%$. It looks smaller going down. Looking at the times/divide statements we find that in either case the values look the same ($\times 1.50$, $\div 1.50$). Going up, or going down by the same amount produces the same sort of statement, but with a different label ($\times$, or $\div$). It is sometimes easier to detect similar but opposite changes with times/divide statements. For that reason alone, they are recommended over percentage-change statements.

SEEING CHANGE

To make timely alterations in a child's program, the teacher must measure the performance of the child as frequently as possible. For most behaviors that means short, daily practices or probes. It would be foolish to assume that any teacher could remember all the information those measurements will provide. It must be written down.

Figure 2-3 shows part of a commonly used *data record sheet*. It provides space for recording the minutes over which the behavior was counted, the counts (for both correct and error performances), correct and error rates (counts divided by time), the rate record floor (one divided by the time), and the rate record ceiling, if there is one. Additional space is provided for comments which help the teacher remember special events or conditions that could affect the future interpretation of the data. One line is allowed for each day of the week. This

		Time observed	Rate Correct	Rate Error	Rate Correct	Rate Error	Rate floor	Rate ceiling	Comments
__ / __ / __ day mo yr	Sun.								
	Mon.								
	Tue.								
	Wed.								
	Thur.								
	Fri.								
	Sat.								
__ / __ / __ day mo yr	Sun.								
	Mon.								
	Tue.								
	Wed.								
	Thur.								
	Fri.								
	Sat.								
__ / __ / __ day mo yr	Sun.								
	Mon.								
	Tue.								

Project number ( )
page ___ of ___
Data Record Sheet

Project names _____

Figure 2-3

eliminates writing in the date each day. The blank lines where data are not collected will serve as quick reminders of the days that were skipped. *Note:* Too many blank lines waste both paper and the student's time: assess the child *frequently!* Modifications of the form can be made to fit special circumstances (e.g., if data are never collected on the weekends, or the assessment time will always be the same).

Although the data record sheet contains all the information necessary to perform an adequate assessment of change, the interpretation of a list of numbers can be difficult. Children rarely go steadily up or down in their rates. There are always little backslides and an occasional day when rates make an unexpected jump. It is important for the teacher to see each change by itself, but even more important that all the little ups and downs fit into some coherent image of the child's overall growth. Is he getting better, or only having an occasional good day? To provide a better perspective of the daily changes, the teacher should make a chart or graph of the data.

With a little practice, six to ten different charts can be updated in only one minute. Children themselves (even in kindergarten) can keep their own charts, providing a little added incentive for their work. Special charts and charting practices are discussed in other chapters, but at this point it will be helpful to review a few basic considerations.

The type of chart selected can make the difference between seeing change and seeing only a pretty line. When selecting a chart, the array of alternatives is staggering. They vary from 100-to-a-tablet "quadrarule" to "rockets-to-the-moon." The teacher should select a single chart that will be usable in most situations. Without such a standard, comparisons between one behavior and another, one child and his peers, one year to the next, will be difficult. Without those comparisons, a wealth of information which may be useful in the development of a better program for individual children and better curriculums for all children will be jeopardized. Let us turn first to the consideration of scales—the rules by which the horizontal and vertical lines of the chart are drawn. Although a chart may have any number of scales, those useful in the classroom normally require no more than two—one to describe when the information was collected, and one to describe the assessed level of performance.

The first scale, marked horizontally along the bottom of the chart, is usually easiest to select. Generally, only two alternatives are considered. First, a scale may mark off each day of the calendar. Each day is represented by a vertical line on the chart.[3] When information is collected on the performance of a child, it is charted on the line corresponding to the day on which it was collected. If no information is collected on a given day, then that line is left blank. The second alternative is to simply label the vertical lines as "trials." Each time the performance of the child is measured, the results are charted on the next vertical line. If three measurements are made on one day, then three successive vertical lines are used. If no information is collected on any given day, then no blanks are left. The next time information is collected, the next line is used.

Charting by calendar days has the advantage of showing graphically when the behavior was measured, and when it was not. It indicates if a child's performance increases or decreases following vacations, weekends, and other days when practice was not afforded in the classroom. In certain cases (e.g., most academic behaviors), calendar day charting will also present a more accurate picture of a child's growth pattern. In the absence of other criteria, however, the choice between a scale marked off in terms of calendar days or one marked off in trials will be based primarily on whatever practical implications one or the other holds for the classroom in question.

The second scale, which is marked on the left side of the chart, is somewhat more difficult to select. Because of conclusions reached in the preceding sections, we will limit our discussions to those alternatives which may be used to indicate rates of responding. That is, the lines or hash-marks on this scale indicate how many behaviors were counted during each minute of observation. Some potential controversy is thus avoided, but one major decision must still be made. There are two ways to space between the lines.

The first method is based on the *equal-interval* rule. Each line (indicating

---

[3]Vertical lines are usually left off charts when they are published, as are the horizontal lines. The places where the lines cross the bottom and left side of the chart are marked with dashes to indicate where the lines would be. The data on the chart stand out much better. In any event, charts used in the classroom have all the lines present.

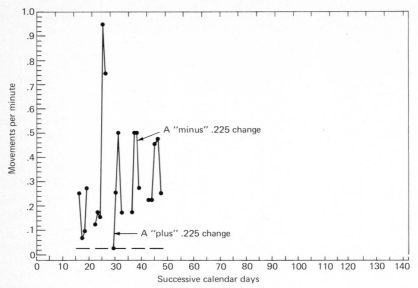

Figure 2-4

some possible rate) is the same distance from the line below (the next lowest rate) as it is from the line above (the next highest rate). This spacing resembles a common ruler. Since all lines are equally spaced, adding or subtracting the same number from any two lines will result in changes which appear to be the same size. Figure 2-4 provides an example. Two changes are pointed out—one from a rate of .025 to .25 (a "plus" .225 change), and the other from a rate of .50 to .275 (a "minus" change). They appear to be the same size, even though they occur at different points on the scale.

The second method of line spacing is based on a *logarithmic* or *equal-ratio* rule. Here, each line is *not* the same distance from the line below and the line above. The lines get closer together as the rates they represent increase. Eventually the lines become so close, that not all lines are drawn. For example, all lines from one to ten may be drawn (1,2,3, . . . 10), but then the lines start jumping by "tens" in value (10, 20, 30, . . .) until 100 is reached. Then the lines increase in value by 100, and so on. This type of chart shows changes differently. Instead of making all equal plus or minus changes look the same, all *times* or *divide* changes of the same size look the same. Figure 2-5, using the same data shown in Figure 2-4 demonstrates the point. In addition to the two changes pointed out in Figure 2-4, two more changes are noted—one from a rate of 0.10 to a rate of 0.25, and the other from 0.20 to 0.50—both proportionate changes of *times* and *divide* 2.50 respectively. They look the same size, while the equal plus and minus changes no longer look the same.

Choosing between these alternatives can involve procedures which are rather complicated and mathematical. Readers interested in a detailed discussion of those issues should examine data transformations (e.g., Winer, 1962). Two considerations in particular will be sufficient for our purposes here. First, in the discussion of how behavior change should be described, it was concluded that *times* and *divide* statements are generally more informative. It would follow, then, that the chart selected should accurately represent that sort of change. Furthermore, certain studies (e.g., White, 1972; Stevens and Savin, 1962) indicate that ratio charts are usually more accurate in their representation of the way behavior changes. They should provide a better base for program decisions. Secondly, ratio charts allow a wide range of behavior rates to be depicted on the same chart. In Figure 2-5, any behavior which occurs between a rate of 0.000695 (one behavior in 24 hours) and a rate of 1,000 behaviors in one minute could be charted on the same chart. Because of this wide range, virtually all behaviors that might interest the teacher may be charted in one, standard, easily compared format. Given both considerations, it is recommended that the ratio chart be employed. After a period of familiarization, such a chart is no more difficult to use or understand, and offers many advantages. There may be times when another chart will be more mathematically appropriate. Those times will be relatively rare, however; and it usually takes a mathematician or statistician to determine the best chart for the unique characteristics of the data. In the remaining sections of this chapter, therefore, a standard chart based on ratio rules will be used.

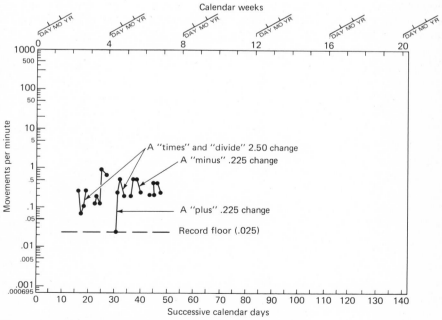

Figure 2-5 *(Courtesy of J. T. Spaulding and M. Waechter).*

SUMMARIZING THE DATA

The best way to illustrate how a child is doing is to display progress data on a chart to show how the child changes from day to day and week to week. There are times when a chart is not available, however, and a simple list of all the performance measures would take too long or be too complicated to understand. In these situations, it is necessary to summarize the data with one or two numbers which represent all the individual performance measures recorded. Two methods of doing this are frequently employed in the classroom.

The *mean* is the most common approach to data summarization. All the scores or rates are added together. The total is then divided by the number of values added. If, for example, a fifth-grade girl had rates of 120, 110, 115, 130, and 5 for her week's reading practices, then the mean would be $(120 + 110 + 115 + 130 + 5) \div 5$ (the number of scores) = 96. Note that in this example the mean, 96, is lower than four out of the five scores the girl achieved in her practices. If someone were to use the mean as a "best guess" for how the child was doing, they would be underestimating the actual performances 80% of the time. Why? The mean is greatly influenced by "deviant" or "unusual" values. The greater the difference between one score and the majority of other scores, the greater its influence will be in determining the mean. In some situations, such as comparing large groups, this is desirable. When summarizing the performances of a single child, however, the mean can often be misleading. If a child is sick on one day, as was the case with the fifth grader above, then the performance of that one day will affect our entire impression of the child's level of skill and ability.

The *median,* or *middle,* as it is sometimes called, takes a different approach to summarizing information. Rather than taking the "weights" of each measure, adding them up, and then describing their "average weight," the median simply finds and describes the middle value. Fifty percent of the performance measures will fall on or above the median, and fifty percent on or below the median. For our little girl's reading scores, the median would be 120. Two data points fall above that value (125 and 130), and two values fall below (110 and 5). The summary statement (the median, in this case), as a best guess of the child's reading level, more accurately reflects what the child is actually doing on most days.

The mean tries to balance the effects of high and low data points like a teeter-totter. If there was one very low day below the mean, then there will have to be many "moderately high" days above the mean to balance the effect of that low value. The median treats all days as if they were equally important. The only balance for which the median strives is one where the *number* of data points is equalized above and below its value. Changing the extreme scores (as long as they do not cross the median) will not influence the median. But changing extreme scores can drastically affect the mean.

Since educators are interested in a child's usual or consistent performance, the median is recommended. To determine the median:

Steps:
1. Number of data points = 7
2. 7 divided by 2 = 3.5
3. 3.5 + .5 = 4, so the median is the 4th lowest rate.

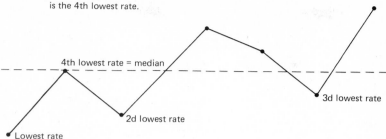

4th lowest rate = median

2d lowest rate

3d lowest rate

Lowest rate

Figure 2-6

1 Find the total number of values to be summarized and divide by two.
2 Add 0.5 to the answer found in step 1.
3 If the answer to step 2 is even (no fraction), then the median will be found by counting up from the lowest score (or down from the highest) until that number is reached. If, for example, there were seven values, then $7 \div 2 = 3.5$, add $0.5 = 4$, so the fourth data point from the bottom will be the median. If the answer to step 2 is a fractional number, then the median will be between the next lowest value and the next highest value. For example, with 10 data points, $10 \div 2 = 5$, add $0.5 = 5.5$, so the median is between the fifth and sixth value from the bottom or top. Figures 2-6 and 2-7 demonstrate these procedures.

When calculating the median, data points with the same values are still counted separately. If the three lowest data points in Figure 2-6 were all the same rates, for example, they would still be counted as one, two, and three. Similarly,

Steps:
1. Number of data points = 10
2. 10 divided by 2 = 5
3. 5 + .5 = 5.5, so the median is *between* the 5th and 6th lowest rates.

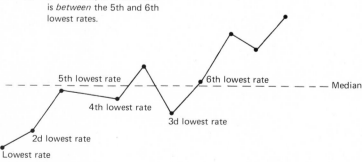

5th lowest rate

6th lowest rate

Median

4th lowest rate

3d lowest rate

2d lowest rate

Lowest rate

Figure 2-7

when two or more values near the center of the data set have the same value, it is possible for them all to be the median. In extreme cases, where all data points have the same value, then all data points will be the "median."

SUMMARIZING THE CHANGE IN DATA

In the previous section two methods were discussed for finding a single number to describe a set of performance measures. Instead of listing all five of the girl's rates, we calculated her average (median) performance for that week to be 120 words per minute. Over relatively short periods of time, or in cases where no progress is being made, such summaries are adequate. Most children are growing, however, and no single number can describe both where a child is and how fast he is getting somewhere else.

We could calculate a series of medians, one for each week. By charting all those medians, we would get a picture of the child's average performance each week and how that average is changing from week to week. Depending upon the number of weeks recorded, however, we might not be any better off than if we simply looked at *all* the data on a chart. What is needed is some way of taking into account the values of each performance measure without losing track of their order or sequence over days and weeks. A number of methods have been developed to do just that. They enable us to find a line passing through the data to describe how the average performance is increasing or decreasing with each new day.

The lines we draw through the data may be straight or curved. They may even bend and twist around, up and down, any number of times. Too much twisting, however, may make the summary difficult to understand. By drawing straight lines, we make the simplest possible statement about the progress of the child. It is also much easier to use a straight line for predicting how a child will do in the weeks to come. All we need do is place a ruler or straightedge along the line on the chart and extend it over the weeks for which we want predictions.

Even limiting ourselves to a concern for straight lines only, there are many alternatives for finding the line we want. Some of the methods are based on the properties of the mean. They will, therefore, emphasize those unusual days. The effects of those days can be even more drastic in deciding how steep the line of progress will be than when determining the simple mean. To take an extreme example, assume that a child was ill on Monday and was able to read only 20 words a minute in her practice. On Tuesday, Wednesday, Thursday, and Friday, she felt better and read exactly 100 words per minute each day. Most people would say that the child was making no progress. Rates of exactly 100 for four days in a row looks like a plateau. Indeed, the rates are so consistent, that one might ask if there is a ceiling holding the child back. In any event, they would disregard the first day's data as too unusual and representing too small a segment of the whole week. Using a mean-based method of finding a line of progress, however, results in an estimate that the child is progressing at a rate of $\times 9.52$ words per minute gained per week. That would mean that each week was 9.52

times better than the week before. At the end of the next week, according to this statistic, the child should be reading at a rate of 1,307.66 words per minute. Even if a slightly more conservative approach to the application of mean-based solutions were taken, the prediction would still be that the child would be reading 228 words per minute by the next Friday. Growth that fast is certainly possible, but looking at the data in question, it is a bit unlikely.

Fortunately, a number of methods have been developed (e.g., White, 1971*a*, 1971*b*, 1972*a*, 1972*b*; Koenig, 1972) which allow us to find a line of progress based on the properties of the median. Although the method that produces a line most like a median is too laborious to use in the classroom (see White, 1972*b*), two other methods can be used to describe the progress of a child and to predict the child's future performance. One method is a simple extension of the first, so both may be learned at once. The first method is the *quarter-intersect* (Koenig, 1972), and is the fastest method available for finding a line of progress. The second method, called the *split-middle,* begins exactly in the same manner as the quarter-intersect. In fact, the same slope (steepness) of the line of progress will result. The only difference between the two methods is that with the split-middle the line may be raised or lowered slightly on the chart (but keeping the slope the same) until the data are more evenly divided above and below the line as should be the case with a median. If all that is necessary is a statement of how fast a child is changing, then either technique will do. For the most precise statement of where the child is now, or will be in the next week or so, the split middle will be the more appropriate choice. Figures 2-8 through 2-14 illustrate the calculation of each line.

When the line of progress is put on a chart, we have a picture of a child's progress. A way must be devised to describe how steeply the line is moving up or down the chart with each succeeding week. The simplest way, if a chart is available, is to find the value of the line on one day, and compare it to the value of the line one week later.

To avoid as much guesswork as possible, begin by finding a data point which falls on the line. The value of that day's rate will be known exactly (if good records have been kept), and since that rate falls on the line, the value of the line

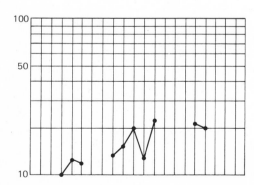

Figure 2-8 Step 1: Count the number of data points you wish to summarize. In this case there are 10.

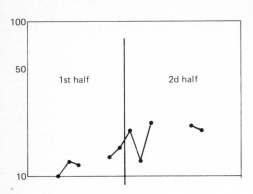

Figure 2-9 Step 2: Divide the data points into two equal groups by drawing a *vertical* line through the data. Hereafter, these groups will be called the first and second halves. With practice you should be able to keep the two halves separate "in your head" without actually drawing the line. For now, however, the line is recommended. This line represents the "median day" for the entire data set. If there are an even number of data points, then the median day will fall between two of the data points (as is the case here). If there are an odd number of data points, then the median day will fall on one of the data points.

will be known also. In Figure 2-11, the first data point falls on the line and has a value of 10 behaviors per minute. Moving ahead seven days (one week), the data point for that day does not fall on the line, so we must estimate as well as we can what the value of the line is at that point. Looking at other data points with approximately the same level as the point of the line in question will sometimes help. The performance of the child on the day before, for example, was just a little lower than the rate we are trying to estimate. On that day the child reached a rate of 15 behaviors per minute. The value of the line for the next day, therefore, is estimated to be about 16 behaviors per minute. So, in one week the child gained in performance from a rate of 10 behaviors per minute to a rate of 16 behaviors per minute. Using the method of calculating relative gains, we find that the slope, or steepness of the line is $16 \div 10 = \times 1.6$ (note the use of the $\times$ to indicate that the line is going up with each succeeding week). We can now say that the child is progressing at a rate of $\times 1.6$ per week; that is, each week's

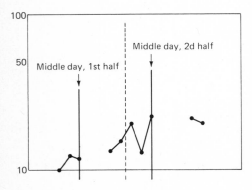

Figure 2-10 Step 3: Split each half of the data in half again with two more *vertical* lines. Since there is an *odd* number of data points in each half (5), the dividing line will not fall *between* two data points (like it did when the phase was divided in half the first time), but rather, the dividing line will fall *on* a data point. In this case, with five data points, the middle day of each half will be the third data point when counting from left to right. Draw a vertical line through that middle day in each half. As a check on the work up to now, one can count the number of data points in each section. *Discounting* (i.e., *not* counting) any data points *on* any dividing line, there should be the same number of data points in each section. In this case there are two in each section, so the divisions have been made correctly.

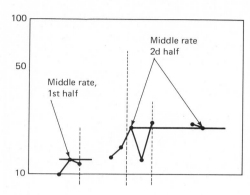

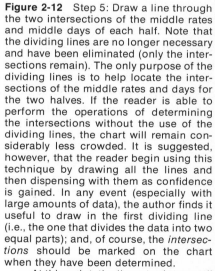

Figure 2-11 Step 4: Find the middle, or median, *rates* for the first and second halves. Data points falling on *vertical* (day) middle lines in each half *will* be counted (e.g., the third day in each half, even though it falls on the middle day for those halves, *will* be considered when finding the middle rate). Any data point falling on the first vertical line drawn (which divided the original data into two parts) will *not* be counted when finding the middle or median rates. Draw a horizontal line from the middle rate in each half to the line representing the middle day in each half. Note that there are two "middle rates" in the second half. This does not change the fact that those values represent the middle rate—the line simply goes through both of them. It is even possible (though not likely with rates other than zero) that all rates in some project are the same; and, therefore, that all rates are the "middle" rate.

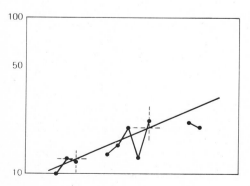

Figure 2-12 Step 5: Draw a line through the two intersections of the middle rates and middle days of each half. Note that the dividing lines are no longer necessary and have been eliminated (only the intersections remain). The only purpose of the dividing lines is to help locate the intersections of the middle rates and days for the two halves. If the reader is able to perform the operations of determining the intersections without the use of the dividing lines, the chart will remain considerably less crowded. It is suggested, however, that the reader begin using this technique by drawing all the lines and then dispensing with them as confidence is gained. In any event (especially with large amounts of data), the author finds it useful to draw in the first dividing line (i.e., the one that divides the data into two equal parts); and, of course, the *intersections* should be marked on the chart when they have been determined.

At this point, the "quarter-intersect" line has been found. If the analyst stops here, a good "picture" of the student's average week-to-week progress is given by the line drawn in this step. The line might be a little high or low overall, however, and to get the best estimate of the student's *magnitude* (level) of responding, one more step should be completed.

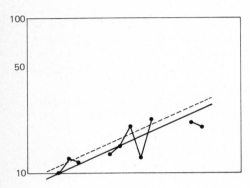

Figure 2-13 Step 6 (optional): If, as in this case, the line drawn in step 5 (represented here by the dotted line) does not "split the data in half," then it might be moved up or down until it does. In this case the original line had only three data points above it and seven data points below it. Moving it down to the position represented by the solid line, we end up with four data points above the line of progress and four data points below it (with two falling on the line). Make sure that when the line is moved, it is kept parallel to the original.

If this step is taken, then the "split-middle" line has been calculated. The slope (steepness) of the line is the same, but its magnitude (how high or low it is on the chart) is slightly different than with the "quarter-intersect" line. The "picture" one gets of the progress is the same, therefore, but a better estimate can now be made as to how high or low the student is for any day along the line.

average performance is 1.6 times greater than the week before. A relative-gain statement was used here because the chart employed was of the ratio type. With an equal interval chart, the formula for absolute gains is more appropriate. Lines of progress drawn on interval charts are likely to be somewhat less accurate than lines on ratio charts (see White, 1971a, 1972a).

To complete our description of the child's performance, we should indicate where the child started and where he ended up. One way would be to simply indicate the first and last rates achieved by the child; but any single performance measurement may be in error and may not adequately represent just how a child is doing at any particular point. For example, would you like to represent the

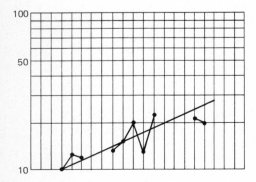

Figure 2-14 Step 7 (for either the quarter-intersect or the split-middle): Look at the finished product. If possible, remove all lines that were drawn to help determine the final line of progress or "celeration line." The final line represents a summary of how the student is generally progressing ("growing") from day to day. By extending this line across future, as yet uncharted days, one is able to predict with reasonable accuracy where a student will be; and when, if ever, the student will reach the aim set for him. If it looks like it will take the student too long to reach the aim, then the program should be changed. This way failure might be *prevented,* rather than being corrected after it occurs.

little girl's reading performances discussed earlier as starting with a rate of 5, when her median performance is over 100? Since the line of progress is very much like a moving median, it is usually better to indicate the value of the *line* at the beginning of the data and at the end. On the first day in Figure 2-13, the value of the line is 10. We know that because the data point for that day falls on the line and we can simply check our records. On the last day that a performance measure was taken, the line has a value of about 26. This value must be estimated, since no data point actually falls on the line at that point. A complete description of the child's average performances and progress would be that he "started at a rate of 10 behaviors per minute, progressed at a rate of × 1.60 behaviors per minute per week, and ended with a rate of 26 behaviors per minute." In simple notation, this is usually written as (10, × 1.60, 26).

One word of caution before moving on to a discussion of how the line of progress is used to make educational decisions. Nothing is ever perfect. The line of progress, calculated as indicated in this section, will prove a useful and generally accurate tool. At times it will be in error. Look at the results of your calculations carefully. If they do not appear reasonable, then attempt to collect more performance measures, and try again. As a rule of thumb, lines based on less than five performance samples will not be very accurate. Lines based on seven samples will be adequate for most purposes, and with nine to eleven performance samples, the teacher can be quite confident that errors will be few and far between. With more than eleven days of data, the increase in accuracy is not great. It might be wise, therefore, to use only the last eleven days' data so that the estimate of progress is based primarily on the most recent performances of the child. For a more detailed examination of the accuracy of the split-middle line of progress, see *The "Split-Middle": A "Quickie" Method of Trend Estimation* (White, 1971*b*) and *The Prediction of Human Performances in the Single Case: An Examination of Four Techniques* (White, 1971*a*).

Using the Line of Progress

As a Summary of How a Child or Client is Progressing   Such summaries are considerably more precise and informative than the subjective or poorly constructed estimates of progress generally made. Precise statements concerning the rate of a child's growth results in a higher level of meaningful communication between professionals, paraprofessionals, parents, and all other persons concerned with the child's education.

As a Means of Deciding Who Needs Help   Given that it is the purpose of a teacher, counselor, or similar practitioner to produce and facilitate change in the behavior of those persons for whom he or she is responsible, the ability to accurately and precisely determine and express progress (systematic change) in behavior should bring to bear greater attention on this critical function. One should be in a better position to precisely identify those most in need of assistance (i.e., those who are changing the least and have the lowest line of progress). It should be noted that if the philosophy of "help those that are changing the least" is carried to its logical conclusion, then those with whom the teacher spends the greatest time may no longer be those who are at the "bottom" of the class on any given day. It is very often the case that children at the low end of the class are, in fact, progressing nicely, while some children at the top of the class have stopped improving altogether. The teacher would be obligated to work with that "top" student, even if only to arrange additional materials to challenge his abilities.

As a Means of Describing the Effects of Program or Curriculum Changes   A set of data with lines of progress provides a teacher with a continuous and precise record of the effects of his or her efforts. Over time, then, one might expect a gradual refinement of general tactics and strategies employed by the teacher.

As a Means of Estimating If and When a Student Will Reach an Aim   Aside from the economic allocation of the teacher's time on the basis of the relative need of one child versus another, the line of progress can be used to assess the individual needs of a child relative to his own aims or goals. By placing a star on a child's chart to represent the performance level desired and the date by which that aim should be met, the teacher only needs to extend the child's line of progress out to that date to see if he is likely to meet or exceed that aim. If the line passes over the star (i.e., reaches the criterion performance prior to the desired date), then the program can be left alone. Indeed, perhaps the prediction indicates that additional materials should be prepared to take advantage of the fact that the child is making better-than-expected progress. If, on the other hand, the line of progress passes below the star (i.e., indicates that the child will reach the desired performance level much later than expected), then the program can be changed then—*before* the child actually fails. The implications of avoiding failure are tremendous. This use of the line of progress, above all others, is by far the most important.

IN CONCLUSION

This chapter was intended to provide a general understanding of the purposes, procedures, and alternatives for precise educational measurement and assessment. Although a number of specific tactics have been discussed, a greater number have been omitted. If the material reviewed is overly complicated, that is an unfortunate by-product of the authors' desire to provide the reader with a broad base of information with which to begin the design of his or her own measurement and assessment system. Be assured that precise measurement and assessment need *not* be a complicated or tiring chore. Indeed, aside from its position as a critical element of the educational process, it is also a source of tremendous satisfaction. To see children grow, and to know that the growth is *real,* is a wonderful thing.

CHAPTER 2 DISCUSSION TOPICS

Behavioral Assessment and Precise Educational Measurement

Objective This chapter provides general discussion of recent issues on the needs and methods of precise educational measurement and assessment with which the reader can begin the design of his individual measurement and assessment system. The chapter does the following:

1 Provides a general framework of measurement and assessment applicable in a wide variety of situations.
2 Concerns the reader with the selection of basic measurement strategies.
3 Presents the types of data most appropriate to the educational situations.
4 Presents methods of recording and charting the results of measurement.
5 Presents the general approaches to assessment in terms of the targets (group or individuals), the criteria, and the frequency of assessment.
6 Stress the major purpose of performance measurement as the observation of the growth of the child.

These questions could be used for written assignments, class or small-group discussions, or as study questions for longer papers.

Exercises Several last-term junior high students have deficits in a specific area of study. Select the area of study (one that you are knowledgeable in) and assume the role of the teacher facing this situation.

1 Pinpoint the behavior to be assessed.
2 Set a minimum acceptable performance level for these students.
3 Suggest the criterion and the means of measuring it that will best help the students meet this minimum performance.
4 Suggest alternative criteria which could be used and possible methods of updating them.
5 Suggest the best assessment target—individual or group—and discuss the potential of each type of assessment target.
6 Suggest two specific kinds of checklists that could be used for collecting the desired data and explain their use and information gathered.
7 Design a method of recording and charting the results of your measurement.
8 Write an answer to a parent's query about the progress of her child during a six-week grading period that includes information gathered in the activities above.

Direct and Individualized Instructional Procedures

Norris G. Haring
Experimental Education Unit, Child Development and Mental Retardation
Center, University of Washington

N. Dale Gentry
Experimental Education Unit, Child Development and Mental Retardation
Center, University of Washington.

INTRODUCTION

Introducing children with learning disabilities or behavior problems into a regular classroom requires individualized planning. Such planning takes time outside the regular school day. During the school day the teacher must engage in many time-consuming tasks such as monitoring oral reading, checking answers on work sheets, and recording performance data. If teachers are to succeed in the regular classroom placement of moderately handicapped children, local district administrators must recognize this problem and provide assistance through parent volunteers, high school and peer tutors, and college students in practicum training.

Regular classroom teachers further must have information and skills to develop and implement individualized instructional procedures. This chapter includes procedures to make individualized instruction a reality in the lives of more teachers and children throughout the country.

Group-based instruction, in whatever form, assumes that children can be selected to start at the same place in a curricular sequence, progress at the same or similar rates, profit from the same teaching procedures, and learn similar material. Unfortunately, most children bring different entry skills, progress at different rates, and finish with different amounts of knowledge and levels of proficiency. On the other hand, individualized instruction, which does not make the same assumptions, is frequently difficult to implement and usually requires enormous expenditures of teacher time and energy.

Although we are still far from developing a comprehensive set of instructional procedures flexible enough to be applicable in every teaching situation, there are basic procedures and guidelines which teachers can use to individualize instruction.

Advances in teaching technology have added precision to the education of the moderately handicapped child through systematic arrangement of instructional procedures, cues, and special curriculum. New educational technology allows teachers to successfully integrate moderately handicapped children into regular classrooms (Christopolos & Renz, 1969). When teachers apply open-classroom concepts, the children are able to move freely from area to area, from basic skills work to free-time arts and crafts and to language and communication centers. The smooth application of high- and low-strength areas and mutual contracting for learning makes comprehensive learning and behavior management systems a delight. At the same time, many classrooms in the country have not changed. Somehow the advances in educational and behavioral technology have been ignored, and many teachers and districts are depriving many children of the opportunity for accelerated learning.

MANAGEMENT FOR EFFECTIVE INSTRUCTION

It is the teacher's responsibility to change children's behavior. Change is demonstrated by children learning to perform basic math facts, to read aloud, to solve equations, to recite a poem, or developing social skills such as learning to play a group game, follow an adult direction, or refrain from hitting a peer. However, teachers are responsible for changing only a fraction of the thousands of behaviors children emit, and they are left with decisions for determining which ones to alter. Fortunately, most of us agree on general priorities for behavioral change. Those areas in which there is broad general agreement include (1) language and communication skills, (2) preacademic behaviors, (3) academic behaviors, (4) social competencies, (5) physical and "mental" fitness, (6) vocational competence, and (7) leisure-time and recreational activities. Even so, the number of potential educational targets is monumental, and the more conscientious and precise a teacher is, the greater the number of specific child behaviors to be managed.

The conscientious teacher will face a dilemma in organizing to achieve the desired change.

Teachers usually teach about thirty youngsters, each of whom is likely to have numerous academic and several social behaviors which should be modified. This problem is compounded by the fact that there may be a wide range of differences among children. The problem is further complicated by the great number of educational practices and the wide variety of instructional procedures teachers have inherited. When we consider the wide range of behaviors, pupils, and educational variables with which teachers must deal on a daily basis, it is no wonder they frequently feel harried and weary at the end of a day, sometimes wondering if they have made any progress.

The overwhelming complexity of the task confronting teachers provides an explanation for the failure of education to effectively implement individualized instruction. However, with effective management, *individually tailored programs* are feasible and practical. They have been successfully implemented in an increasing number of regular and special classroom settings throughout the country.

Management versus Operations in Individualizing Instruction

In the administration of instruction, a distinction should be made between management and operations approaches. Operation is achieving an objective through one's own efforts. Management is defined as achieving an objective through the use of resources and the efforts of others. In operation, one directly engages in tasks designed to achieve an objective. The only way an individual can increase performance is through expending more of his or her own time and energy on the tasks involved. Because of this, improvement through an operation is limited by the time an individual has and the efficiency with which he or she completes the tasks. However, with a management approach one can achieve many objectives by increasing the amount of time, effort, and resources applied to a problem through coordinating the efforts of others. Management rather than operation is required in the instructional process. As long as teachers use an operations approach, they will be frustrated because of the amount of time that they can spend on an almost infinite amount of work to be achieved. By using a management approach teachers can multiply the results of their own behavioral expenditures.

In a management system, the person responsible for management must have individuals to whom responsiblity can be delegated. In many classrooms, the only individuals a teacher has are those children who are being taught. In this case, the children themselves occupy a role in the management of their learning. This also teaches children to be agents in managing their own education. In other cases, the teachers will have teacher aides, secretaries, and volunteers who can assist in management.

Dimensions of Instructional Management

A management approach involves (1) identifying the general goals which one wishes to achieve, (2) specifying these goals in terms of enabling objectives which lead to achievement of the goal, (3) identifying the activities and necessary resources to achieve the specified objectives, (4) delegating responsibility for those activities to reach the objectives, and (5) systematically inspecting progress toward objectives.

General Goals   A teacher's primary goal is to provide conditions which lead to effective pupil learning. But some goals relate to activities which are not direct instructional activities. Such a goal might be to conduct effectively those classroom administrative and organizational activities necessary to classroom operation, for example taking daily lunch count and reporting pupil attendance. Even though such activities seem trivial compared to direct instructional practices, they must be completed so direct instruction can occur. A third goal is to communicate with other persons who are important in a child's life. Parents, other teachers, and support personnel are all individuals with whom the teacher must communicate in order to provide the best conditions for a child's learning. A fourth goal which is not a direct instructional activity is recording, summarizing, and reporting individual pupil progress. Measurement activities which are not direct instruction are important because they provide systematic information which contributes to the child's learning process. To prevent such activities from consuming a disproportionate amount of time, they should be handled in a systematic fashion.

Enabling Objectives   Refining general goals into enabling objectives is an important management step. Objectives must clearly identify intended outcomes and must be written simply enough to make them usable. The general goal of providing an effective instructional process can be stated through enabling objectives: (1) to assess each child for placement in reading, arithmetic, spelling, and handwriting by the third week of the school year; (2) to establish long-range objectives for each child, i.e., where the child will be at the end of the school year in each specified subject area; (3) to establish immediate objectives which are a first step toward long-range objectives; (4) to write a systematic instructional materials, instructional procedures, reinforcement conditions, and evaluation procedures; (5) to obtain performance data on each child in each area at least three times per week; and (6) to use the obtained performance data to determine when to advance to new learning objectives or to provide alternate instructional procedures.

The general goal of efficiently conducting classroom administrative activities might lead to enabling activities such as to collect attendance, lunch count, and milk money within ten minutes each day.

Activities and Necessary Resources   The next major step is to delineate the activities and identify the resources needed to achieve a specific objective. In order to assess pupil performance for placement in a math sequence, a teacher might decide to administer and score a series of increasingly difficult one-minute arithmetic probes to each youngster in class. The resources needed include sufficient probes for each youngster, a watch or clock for timing the pupils, pencils for the children to write with, and answer sheets for correcting. The level of detail depends on the needs of the situation and the temperament of the teacher.

Delegating Responsibility   Delegation of responsibility comes naturally to some teachers. Others have to work hard at delegating tasks. In preparing to administer a series of math probes the authors have observed teachers in the same school engage in very different practices. One teacher constructed a series of probes, typed them on ditto masters, ran them off on a duplicating machine, collated and stapled them, and placed them on the children's desks and was ready one Monday morning to administer the probes. A second teacher selected probes from an existing sequence several weeks ahead and had the clerical staff type, duplicate, collate, and staple them. Then on the selected Monday morning the teacher had one of the children pass them out. Both teachers had achieved the same objective, but at very different levels of personal time and energy. Delegation of tasks may require a rather large expenditure of time at first. However, great savings of effort and time are seen on subsequent assignments.

The development of competent personnel is necessary in a management approach. It is surprising how many routine teacher tasks children can learn to perform to free the teacher for more essential tasks.

Inspecting Progress   One key to effective management and delegation is inspection of progress. The teacher mentioned in a preceding paragraph (who delegated responsibility for completing the probe sequence) dropped in the office occasionally just to "see how things are going." Such casual inspections ensured that the probes were ready on time, and gave him a chance to clarify instructions.

The systematic management of an instructional setting requires deliberation and planning. Most teachers cannot remember all the objectives, activities, and schedules of events in a classroom, much less implement a systematic plan from memory.

Decision Making

When teachers do not recognize that much of their behavior as managers is the selection of alternatives, their decision-making behavior is likely to be inconsistent and based on impulse or emotion rather than on systematic considerations of the consequences.

Since educators are concerned with changing behaviors, the decisions teachers make should increase the probability of achieving behavior change. For example, if one youngster hits another youngster, a teacher might see two alternatives: (1) scold the child or (2) momentarily remove him from the situation in which the hitting occurred. The teacher might then consider the potential consequences of scolding the child. She might decide that scolding would not alter the probability of hitting behavior in the future as much as would momentarily removing the child from the situation. In this case, selecting the alternative of removing the child from the situation might be the desired decision because it reduces the probability of the child's hitting in the future. This leads to a second consideration about decision making. The only basis by which we can eventually determine the actual consequence of different decisions is to collect data on the effectiveness of alternatives in dealing with behavior. In fact, the only way we can determine empirically whether removing a youngster from a situation is more likely to decrease hitting behavior than scolding is to collect data on each alternative. Once data have been collected on different occasions with different children, we can identify the alternatives with a higher probability of working. However, the effectiveness of such alternatives must be verified when applied to other children.

Whenever possible, decision points should be anticipated ahead of time and principles or rules formed for decision making. Consider the youngster who has a history of hitting other youngsters. The teacher might make a simple rule that if Johnny strikes another child then x will happen. For example, Johnny might be removed for two minutes. A decision point has been anticipated and a rule formulated for the action to follow in that situation. The same principles apply to academic performance. Suppose a youngster were to score less than 50 percent on a criterion test on math facts. Obvious alternatives are to allow the pupil to go on to new material or require additional practice on the material which is not yet mastered. The rule might be that if a youngster has achieved less than a certain criterion performance, then learning will continue on the currently assigned material.

The "goodness" of a decision can only be determined by its effect; for example, if the goal is to reduce a youngster's hitting behavior, the effectiveness of that decision is determined by whether the youngster hits less frequently. The first application of an intervention does not always change a youngster's behavior. Therefore, the same intervention must be adhered to consistently for several days in order to determine what effect the intervention has on the individual child. An effective teacher will formulate alternatives that he or she will follow if a child behaves in a given way. Teachers must adhere to these alternatives consistently.

Rules will take the form of an "if . . . then" statement. If Johnny does x, then I will do y. "If Mike stands up and disrupts the class, then I will do x. If Sally reaches criterion performance on a task, then I will do y." The teacher can anticipate many of the decisions that he or she will be required to make. However, considering numbers of children and the infinite combinations of behaviors that children can engage in, events will occur for which the teacher has not formulated rules. In such situations the teacher should consider what effect his or her actions will have on the future behavior of the child.

In cases where a child becomes violently angry or has a seizure, the teacher must make a quick decision and take immediate action. In the case of physical threat by a youngster, the first step is to reduce the probability that either the youngster or someone else will be injured. The next step is to take action which will reduce the probability that the youngster will engage in that behavior in the future. In the event of some health emergency the teacher must take steps to reduce the possibility of further physical injury or danger and summon the appropriate medical assistance.

Fortunately, most decisions a teacher makes involve instructional activities. A daily record of pupil performance provides a good source of information to determine the efficacy of instructional decisions and to help refine the decision-making process. In many schools teachers hold the option for making 90 percent of the instructional decisions. Furthermore, teachers who recognize that much of their behavior is decision making are likely to better appreciate the effectiveness of those decisions in achieving educational goals for children. Teachers can specify and automate the instructional process to give some of the responsibility for decision making directly to children.

Measurement: The Focus of Instructional Management

Teachers have an almost limitless number of specific events they may manipulate to enhance the probability that children will learn. These events fall into only a few classes of activities. Teachers may (1) alter the setting in which the child is working, (2) select from a variety of curricular materials, (3) implement different instructional procedures, and (4) arrange consequences according to pupil performance. A major problem is the evaluation of the efficacy of combinations of events from these various instructional events and conditions. Events which are found to be effective will be continued. Those which are found to be ineffective will be discontinued or replaced.

Teachers have always had measurement methods. Periodically obtained raw scores and percentage statements on assignments and exams have long been part of the teacher's repertory. Letter grades based on these scores and the subjective interpretation of other performances have been extensively used to evaluate and report pupil progress. Standardized tests given on a yearly basis have been used to evaluate individual and group performance. In recent years, anecdotal and other narrative reports have often supplemented or replaced numerical descriptions of academic performance. Even more recently, daily measures of the frequency of correct and error responses have been used to determine instructional effectiveness.

The specific use to be made of information gathered on pupil performance should serve as a guide to the type of data to be obtained. All data are collected to make decisions. The scope of magnitude, and the immediacy or frequency of decisions are the two basic dimensions which should be considered in determining the type of data to collect. Some decisions, such as determining the effectiveness of a selected curriculum series on the overall performance of an entire class in a school system, are major decisions. Evaluating the effectiveness of a flashcard drill on a pupil's acquisition of addition facts leads to a decision of a much smaller scope. The data collected in each instance might be quite different. In the first case, data are needed to allow a comparison of the effect of using the adopted series over not using it. In the case of learning addition facts, the teacher may need information on whether a child has achieved or is progressing toward specified criteria performance levels. The frequency and immediacy of the decisions is a related issue. It would not be reasonable, for example, to evaluate the effectiveness of an entire text in a few days or even a few weeks. On the other hand, it does not take more than a few days, at the most, to evaluate a flash-card drill.

Teachers have historically given regular classroom assignments and administered weekly or periodic quizzes. The raw scores or percentage scores obtained from such quizzes are based on overt pupil performance. The reporting units, i.e., percent correct, are based on a uniform scale. Because the content and difficulty levels of such exams are likely to vary from testing to testing, they are not always as indicative of pupil progress as they are of differences in the content and difficulty of the course and tests. Also, such tests are given so infrequently that they are not very useful for altering conditions to improve pupil learning. Letter grades based on percent scores, and frequently including teacher judgments about effort, are even less useful for making instructional decisions.

Achievement tests, which are used by many schools to supplement other forms of measurement, are not useful for direct instructional decision making. They are usually given annually. They are constructed to sample very broad information, so they usually do not measure the content of a course. In fact, knowledgeable persons become concerned if they know a teacher has taught to an achievement test. The resulting data are referenced to normative groups, and not to levels of performance. Achievement tests were not designed for use as a formative tool for the day-to-day instructional decisions.

The measurement procedures described in Chapter 2 by White and Liberty on precise daily measurement have been used extensively by the authors and other school personnel in the Pacific Northwest. They meet the conditions described for evaluation of performance in subsequent portions of this chapter.

Motivation through Classroom Management

Premack Principle   An effective technique for motivating pupil performance in systematic classroom management is the Premack principle (Premack, 1959). Becker, Englemann, and Thomas (1971) refer to the Premack principle as "Grandma's rule"; i.e., If you do what I want you to do, you get to do what you want to do. "If you mow the lawn, then you can go swimming." In more scientific terms: Making a high-frequency behavior contingent upon a lower-frequency behavior will likely increase the rate of occurrence of the lower-frequency behavior.

The classic application of the Premack principle was by Lloyd Homme and his colleagues (1963) to manage the disruptive behavior of preschool children. Several experimental programs have been developed using various combinations of token reinforcement, high-strength activities according to "Grandma's rule," and social reinforcement from the teacher.

The program at EEU has used low- and high-strength areas involving the

Premack principle (Haring & Kunzelmann, 1966; Haring & Phillips, 1972). The classroom is divided into specific areas. One area is designated as low-strength and is usually reserved for academic tasks. It is equipped with desks, language and communication areas, and tables for group activities. In contrast, a high-strength area containing science, arts and crafts, and social activities areas can be used for free time.

Contingent Free Time Using Grandma's rule and the high- and low-strength areas to motivate student academic performance, the teacher makes free time contingent upon performance of academic tasks. Teachers sometimes use naturally occurring events in the classroom to reinforce academic behavior. Other teachers have used stars, marks on the board, and other means to signify a child has performed well on certain tasks. Other investigators (O'Leary & Becker, 1967; Birnbrauer, Wolf, Kidder, & Tague, 1965; and Wolf, Giles, & Hall, 1968) have used tokens which are exchangeable for items of back-up reinforcement. Combining token systems with free-time contingencies provides powerful motivational tools. Lovitt, Guppy, and Blattner (1969) were able to show that free time functioned as a reinforcer in improving spelling accuracy of fourth graders. Homme et al. (1968; 1970) demonstrated the effectiveness of contingent access to a play area in reinforcing the academic learning of a variety of emotionally disturbed children.

The Behavior Game Tactics which are successful with individual students have also been applied in group situations. One example of this is the "behavior game" (Billingsley and Smelser, 1974) to modify disruptive behavior of entire classrooms. Behavior games operate along principles of learning which reflect the notion that behavior is a function of the environment (Swenson and Billingsley, 1973). The behavior game structures the classroom environment so desirable behaviors are rewarded and undesirable behaviors go unrewarded. Whether the game is "won" in the sense that pupils can gain rewards or "lost" in that rewards are withheld is determined by the behavior of the entire class.

Rewards or punishments are typically shared by all. In the behavior game employing reward, for example, a teacher might explain to the pupils that for each five minutes that talk-outs do not occur the entire class will receive one point. A free-time period at the end of the day depends upon the group's having earned a minimum number of points. This Behavior Game may be used alone or in conjunction with another which involves punishment. Punishment often becomes a necessary alternative tactic if reinforcement does not reduce disruptive behavior. The use of punishment is seen when the teacher gives "bad behavior marks" for undesirable behaviors. For each mark accumulated, the maximum time available for a valued activity such as recess or free time is reduced by some specified number of minutes.

Sufficient research has now been conducted to draw the following general conclusions about behavior games and their application in classroom management:

    1   Behavior games can be operated at low cost and energy and using conditions occurring naturally in the classroom as effective rewards or punishments.

    2   Classroom teachers can employ behavior games without much technical assistance. Formal training in behavior modification is not necessary.

    3   Effective group behavior games tend to be associated with increased opportunities for teacher-approved behavior. As fewer situations occur that require verbal or physical reprimands, the teacher is freer to deliver social reinforcement during pupil-contact time.

    4   Group behavior games may act to improve learning conditions by diminishing disruptions that previously interfered with the educational process.

DIRECT INSTRUCTIONAL PROCEDURES

There are a number of important steps to follow in the process of providing direct and individualized instruction. These include (1) assessing pupil performance, (2) setting goals, objectives, and aims, (3) systematic planning of instructional or management programs, (4) selecting or preparing suitable instructional materials, (5) specifying instructional procedures, (6) arranging motivational factors, and (7) evaluating pupil progress.

Assessment of Pupil Performance

Of the three types of assessment tests used extensively, normative tests, diagnostic tests, and criterion tests, we are primarily interested in criterion tests.

    A normative assessment measures a pupil against a larger reference group. In the past, psychologists have administered intelligence, achievement, and personality measures and recommended placement in programs. For example, a pupil who scored two standard deviations below the mean on intelligence and achievement tests, with no major personality deviations, might be placed in a classroom for the mentally retarded. The assumption is that placement in such a setting will provide instructional practices that will benefit the younster. Regardless of the actual validity of such an assumption, the level of precision for such assessment and placement is very gross.

    However, by considering the results of both intelligence and achievement tests the same professionals have attempted to formulate goals consistent with a child's ability and level of achievement. Such assessment helps establish very global goals but is not a definitive statement of capabilities and achievements. A low score on an intelligence measure does not mean that the child cannot or will not increase his performance in the future.

    Diagnostic tests are more useful in formulating goals and objectives for a given youngster because this type of assessment tells where a child is in terms of a general construction of skills. For example, a diagnostic reading test may reveal that a pupil has a large sight vocabulary but is deficient in phonic skills. Another measure may indicate that a pupil has progressed only to a specified performance level on certain motor coordination tasks. Diagnostic tests of this sort usually indicate a child's level of performance in some developmental or task area. Since diagnostic tests present a wide range of task difficulty, the teacher is able to make an analysis of the errors that a pupil makes, place the youngster in suitable curriculum, and provide instruction designed to remediate the deficiencies uncovered by the diagnostic test. For example, a teacher might present a pupil with readers from three different levels of a reading series and monitor the pupil's accuracy and fluency in each of the readers. The pupil would be placed in the reader commensurate with his or her reading ability. In addition, the teacher might note the errors a pupil made and provide instruction for those errors.

Efforts to use diagnostic tests to determine causes has led to preoccupation with processes occurring within an individual to the exclusion of manipulable factors. A reading deficit thus may lead to a search for neurologic or perceptual deficiencies upon which the reading deficit is based. However, external causes of reading failure are also possible. The assignment of causes, whether internal or external, must always be an inferential process, since it is impossible to replicate an individual's previous history and organic state. There is a type of assessment which is more useful. If a youngster demonstrates a low rate of acquisition under one set of instructional conditions and a high rate of acquisition under another set of instructional conditions, the reason for different rates should be considered in designing new learning situations for the individual. Determining acquisition rates requires the repeated measures discussed by White and Liberty in Chapter 2 of this volume.

Criterion-referenced assessment not only describes an individual's general level of performance but also states that performance in relation to success criteria. Thus, it gives not only the current performance level, but also how far a pupil must progress to achieve some specified level of achievement. One knows both where the pupil is starting and where he or she is going. Criterion assessment also requires specifying an instructional or curricular sequence of objectives. A sequence of objectives can be specified to establish which objectives the individual has already achieved and which ones require additional practice.

Probing Procedures   The probing process takes a relatively brief sample of a pupil's performance on a standard task under standard conditions. The data from such a probe can then be used to make evaluations of the effectiveness of the instructional procedures.

Probe materials consist of small, internally consistent units of learning. For example, a probe might consist of all the basic addition facts, such as problems with sums of zero to three. Such a probe controls the uniformity of materials to which pupils respond. Addition facts, for example, constitute problems of approximately the same length. Probe materials also control the uniformity of response. In other words, to each fact which the pupil must write an answer, there is either a one- or two-digit answer. Probing procedures also help control the conditions and the amount of time under which a child performs. Probes are generally given in the same manner each day, at the same time of day, and in the same relationship to instruction. In other words, they are always given after, before, or in the middle of the instructional period. They are also given for the same amount of time; for example, a one- or two-minute timing. Because both the materials and procedures are uniform from day to day, any changes in performance reflect changes in academic growth. The data can then be used to evaluate pupil progress and the efficacy of whatever instructional procedures are being used.

In order to prevent children from simply memorizing the answer or sequence of answers to probe materials, alternate forms are constructed in which problems of the same class are varied. Measures can be taken on the same materials, but pupils cannot simply memorize a sequence of answers. It is also advisable to provide more work than a youngster can perform on a probing task so that a ceiling will not limit that pupil's performance. For example, if a one-minute timing is being given on addition facts, the teacher should provide more problems than the pupil can work in one minute.

Using probing procedures with direct daily measurement has several advantages over more traditional evaluation. First, the teacher is able to construct measurement units or probes which correspond to the actual instructional objectives used in the classroom. Second, probes provide uniform measurement for individual pupils within each learning step. Third, a display of data taken from probes helps pupils see daily progress. Fourth, controlled probes enable a classroom teacher to collect performance data on specified learning tasks.

Preparation   Several preliminary steps are necessary before a teacher begins to use probing procedures. The first step is to identify a sequence of tasks to be taught. Arithmetic might be sequenced into rote counting, counting objects, addition, subtraction, multiplication, and division processes. Each of these general tasks would be further refined into its component parts. Addition processes, for example, might be subdivided into basic facts, two-column problems without carrying, two-column problems with carrying, multiple-column problems without carrying, etc. (see Figure 3-1).

Probe sheets help determine pupil performance competency. Information obtained from probes is useful only if it is quickly available to the teacher and pupil. When constructing probes it is useful to make scoring keys at the same time. Counting correct and error answers can be facilitated by arranging a constant number of problems in each row. The number of problems completed is simply a multiple of the number of problems per row times the number of rows completed. Figure 3-2 gives an example of a probe sheet used at the EEU.

A probe is a brief sample of a child's performance on a given task. Therefore, children will perform for short uniform timings. At the EEU we recommend one-minute timings unless there is a specific reason to use shorter or longer timings. We have also used thirty seconds, two minutes, four minutes, five minutes, and ten minutes.

Sufficient problems should be included on a probe sheet so that no pupil will finish in the allotted time. If a pupil finishes before the timing is completed, the upper performance rate is limited, and it is impossible to measure daily improvement.

Arithmetic Sequence and Task Slices

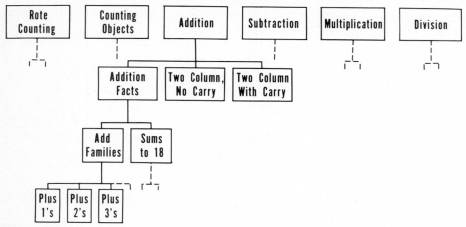

Figure 3-1 Example of task sequencing and slicing.

Children may not be as capable as we assume on very basic skills. In the case of the arithmetic probes, the basic response necessary for completing math problems is writing numerals. It is important to measure pupil competence in rote numeral writing, since that may affect performance on higher level tasks. Similarly, writing letters is a basic response for spelling and writing tasks. Saying sounds, letters, and words are prerequisite to oral reading. Tentative proficiency rates have been determined for each of these basic responses.

Rates (answers per minute) of correct and error performance are sensitive measures of pupil progress. Teachers desire both accurate and fluent responding. One method of determining rates is to find the typical performance for pupils of a given age or grade level. For the math problems under discussion we might select 40 digits per minute or greater for the correct criterion and 2 or fewer errors per minute for the error criterion.

If probes were presented only once or twice they would acquire some of the same limitations as infrequently administered tests. We could not be certain how well a score represented the usual performance, nor would the data obtained be frequent enough to be useful for making decisions about the pupil's instructional program. Probes, therefore, should be presented frequently, preferably each day.

A variety of influences can confound the information gained from probes. One of these influences is the amount of time a child performs. Typists know that their typing rates will vary with one-, five-, and twenty-minute timings. The same variation can occur with children performing academic tasks. This source of confusion can be reduced by using the same length of timing each day.

After administering, correcting, and securing a correct and error count on a probe, it is important to convert the data to responses per minute. This is done by dividing the number of responses completed by the number of minutes in the timing. For example, 50 correct responses in two minutes is 25 responses per minute (50 ÷ 2 = 25). For one-minute timings no conversion is necessary. The correct and error counts are also the number of responses per minute. For ten-minute timings simply move the decimal one place to the left.

Probes provide data to aid in making instructional decisions. However, data presented in rows and columns are difficult to interpret. It is essential to chart data so the teacher (and pupil) can observe the relationship among different days' performances. Figure 3-3 is part of the "standard behavior chart" distributed by Behavior Research Company, Kansas City, Kansas. It allows correct and error data to be displayed in close proximity and in a proportional relationship (i.e., one can read the ratio of correct to error answers). Percent of improvement each week can be determined directly from the chart.

Probing as Assessment   Probing procedures are somewhat different in assessing a pupil's placement in an instructional program and in monitoring progress within a program to determine when proficiency performance has been achieved.

Name: _____

Date: _____

Say Letters (random)   Time: _____ I minute _____

Count: _____

g l y w o q o h m z c f h o l b x e t q

p a b d u y e n z d i u w q n b x t p w

p l a e r u f k v n x w d g s z l p e t

p l h k j u n b v c x z a s d f h k l r

p t u r w q b h d l j z a t y u f l j e

s t e h j l s e y p m c v h b a d f t p

z m g t p o w r s a k g l d b m r q t u

y o f j s f p e w m j c z s p l i q w n

p l s t u h a n j i f r e y l d v b o e

l i p j m c f r h w a x t u i f v c o p

j l d t z i o w r e q p u g f k d l s a

p i t g k s v n x m z t p o u i e l g y

o l s t n w i j g y r c d f p a j l r e

k b r u e p w s b h u i m d f v p t y u

Figure 3-2 "Say Letter Names" probe sheet.

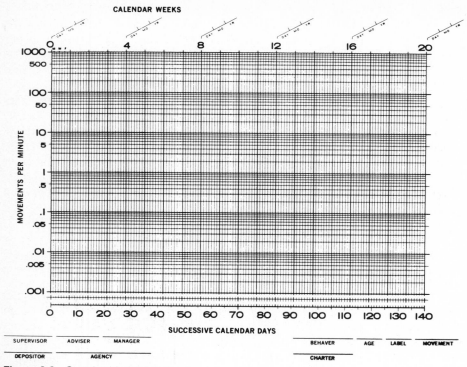

Figure 3-3 Standard behavior sheet.

It would be extremely cumbersome to ask a pupil to perform all math tasks to determine the entry point in an instructional sequence. Therefore, a few probe sheets are selected from a wide variety of tasks to secure performance data. On these selected sheets the data will be in three groups: those tasks on which the youngster readily meets proficiency criteria; those tasks on which the youngster makes errors on most items; and those tasks on which the youngster passes some items and errs on some items. The teacher can then select additional probe sheets for tasks near the child's point of transition from failure to competency. Of course, if the teacher is already familiar with the range of tasks the child has previously performed, that information can be used to guide the initial selection of probe sheets.

Suppose we wished to assess a pupil's entry point in the math sequence previously described. For initial data the probe sheets might consist of the following movement cycles:

1 Write numerals
2 Count objects (dots)
3 Addition facts
4 Subtraction facts

5   Multiplication facts
6   Division facts

If a pupil met criteria on the first three tasks, erred on all items of the last three tasks, and completed only a few items correctly on the subtraction task, additional probe sheets could be selected from the more complex addition tasks. By using such a funneling process it is possible to focus on a pupil's precise entry point for the arithmetic program.

A limitation of traditional test data is that the score obtained at a single testing may not represent a child's usual performance. Data obtained using probing procedures also indicate that a single day's performance can be misleading. Each probe should be presented for a minimum of five days to obtain a reliable median score. In five days a pupil's rate of progress can also be determined, a factor that is sometimes very important in planning an instructional program. Once probe data are collected and analyzed, the child should be entered in a teaching sequence just higher than the last task on which proficiency was met.

An Example of Probing Procedures   Probing procedures are used to obtain part of the intake information collected on children before they enroll at the Experimental Education Unit. The EEU teachers need performance data on children's basic academic skills before they can plan more detailed assessment and establish instructional objectives. Those tasks on which the staff decided they would need pupil performance data include:

1   Saying letter names by reciting the alphabet
2   Saying numbers by counting forward from one
3   Saying letter names from a visual cue when the letters of the alphabet are presented sequentially
4   Saying letter names from a visual cue when the letters of the alphabet are presented in random order
5   Saying the sounds of letters from a visual cue when the letters are presented in a random order
6   Saying the sounds of blends, digraphs, and diphthongs from a visual cue when the letter combinations are presented
7   Saying numbers from a visual cue when the numerals are presented in random order
8   Printing lower case letters with a visual model present
9   Printing capital letters with a visual model present
10   Writing cursive letters, lower-case, with a visual model present
11   Writing cursive letters, capitals, with a visual model present
12   Writing digits with a visual model present when the numbers are presented in a random order
13   Saying words from a reader designated by grade level which the referring teacher has selected for a pupil
14   Writing digits to basic addition facts when the facts are presented in a random order

15 Writing digits to advanced addition problems when the problems are presented visually

16 Writing digits to subtraction facts when the facts are presented visually

17 Writing digits to advanced subtraction problems when the problems are presented visually

18 Writing digits to multiplication facts when the facts are presented visually

19 Writing digits to advanced multiplication problems when the problems are presented visually

20 Writing digits to division facts when the facts are presented visually

21 Writing digits to advanced division problems when the problems are presented visually

Each of the tasks is presented to the pupil on a probe sheet such as the one for printing lower-case letters shown in Figure 3-4.

The pupil is presented with the probe and given instructions. For example, on the "printing" probe displayed in Figure 3-4, the pupil is instructed, "Please print these letters (examiner points to letter) on the lines beneath them (examiner points to line beneath letter). Are you ready? Please begin." The examiner times

ACADEMIC ASSESSMENT BATTERY

Experimental Education Unit
Child Development and
Mental Retardation Center
University of Washington

Write Letters: Print (Small)
#27

Name:_____
Date:_____
Correct:_____Error:_____
Omissions:_____

a b c d e f g h i j

k l m n o p q r s t

u v w x y z a b c d

e f g h i j k l m n

o p q r s t u v w x

Figure 3-4 Probe sheet used to present task of printing lower-case letters to pupils.

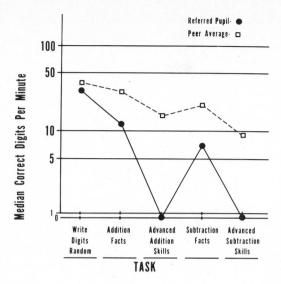

Figure 3-5 Median correct digits per minute for referred pupils and two peers on selected arithmetic tasks.

the pupil for one minute, then says, "Thank you," and proceeds to the next probe. The timing is made as unobtrusive as possible. The standard length of timing is to obtain uniform performance conditions, not to exert pressure on the pupil.

The probes are given for five consecutive days to help ensure that reliable data are obtained and to observe performance trends. Children who improve appreciably during the five-day period are likely to require different programming than children whose performance remains stable or deteriorates.

If probes are to be used for precise assessment or for daily monitoring of pupil performance, they must be constructed on tasks which are more finely sequenced than the intake sequence described above. Suppose on the sequence of intake tasks it was found that a pupil was proficient at saying numbers, writing digits, and performing addition facts, but could not perform advanced addition tasks. A sequence of advanced addition skills could be constructed and the pupil's performance probed on each skill until the exact skill requiring instruction is found. Thereafter, the appropriate probe would be presented daily to evaluate the pupil's progress on that task.

The use of probing procedures and the obtained data can be shown by considering representative data for Bert, a pupil referred to the EEU, and comparable data on his peers (see Figure 3-5). Bert's correct scores for selected arithmetic tasks are shown by dots (.) and the average correct scores for his peers is shown with boxes (□). Bert approximates his peers' performance on writing digits in a random sequence; however, his score on addition and subtraction facts is about one-third that of his peers. On advanced addition and subtraction tasks Bert scored zero, compared to 15 and 9 correct digits per minute on addition and subtraction tasks for his peers.

Bert's peers, whose data are shown in Figure 3-5, were selected because the referring teacher considered their academic performance acceptable. We suspect that if Bert performed at a level comparable to his peers, the teacher would also be satisfied with Bert's performance. The peers' scores, then, are preliminary criteria which Bert should meet before he returns to his classroom.

Establishing Instructional Goals, Objectives, and Aims

We have emphasized that education and society have defined broad educational goals. A goal is a statement of long-range directions and is usually presented in general terms. An objective is a much more specific statement, may be derived from a general goal, and includes three essential characteristics: a statement of a pupil response, a description of the conditions under which the response is to occur, and a statement of the criteria for acceptable performance (Mager, 1972; Wheeler and Fox, 1972). Aims are statements of performance criteria which indicate a desired frequency or rate of performance, such as desired rates of correct and error words per minute when reading orally (Haughton, 1972). It is essential to develop precise instructional objectives for both the learner and the curriculum used for instruction. Only when teachers know precisely what it is that children are to learn will they be able to arrange effectively the learning environment to support that learning. Teachers can determine accurately when children have achieved desired instructional outcomes only if those outcomes are stated clearly and precisely. Curricular materials are selected to teach children information or skills which are part of their learning objectives. It is reasonable to expect that the objectives which the material is intended to teach will coincide with the learning objectives the teacher has established.

Within the established goals, teachers will have some freedom in specifying instructional objectives. However, our social and educational institutions have established broad parameters which are further narrowed by school district philosophy and policy. There may be areas of concern in which districts have not formulated general or specific policy. Teachers formulate general goals and specific objectives in these areas. Districts will have identified general goals and specific objectives but may have inadequately specified their details. For example, if a district has indicated that physical fitness is a goal, but has not defined behaviors indicative of physical fitness, a physical education teacher may have the freedom to specify such behaviors. Or if oral reading were a behavior specified as important by a district but the criteria for performance were not stated, a teacher would likely have the freedom to do so. Finally, where individual differences exist in pupils that do not fall within district guidelines, teachers are usually expected to deal with those differences. In practice, teachers have considerable freedom to specify and formulate objectives.

It is useful for teachers to specify both long-range and immediate instructional objectives. Long-range objectives should not be confused with general goals. For example, if a teacher knows that at the end of a school year a child must be able to read 100 words per minute and answer comprehension questions at 80 percent accuracy in a fourth-grade reader, that knowledge will guide the teacher in selecting the scope of instructional activities during the year. Or if a teacher knows that a handicapped teen-ager will be working in an environment where a variety of safety signs will have to be recognized, then the teacher can arrange for the child to learn to read those signs instead of other reading materials which may be less useful.

Longer-range objectives can assist teachers in formulating immediate objectives. If the youngster who must read at fourth-grade level within a year is deficient in second- and third-grade sight vocabulary or basic phonic skills, the teacher may set immediate instructional objectives which lead to accomplishment of the longer-range objective. An immediate objective, for example, might be to learn a selected list of sight words at 100 percent accuracy within a specified time interval.

Establishing the conditions under which performance will occur and the criteria for acceptable performance are tasks which should be taken rather seriously. For example, it may be important to specify the number of new items to be included in a specific learning objective, since this may have considerable influence on how a youngster performs on the task or how rapidly new knowledge is acquired. Similarly, the criteria for acceptable performance can be very significant. It may seem desirable for a child to learn math facts to 100 percent accuracy, but the child may not actually retain that knowledge unless the facts are learned both to 100 percent accuracy, and to a correct performance rate of at least 30 facts per minute.

Long-range Objectives   Long-range objectives may be selected by defining the task which a child should perform at a given time. One approach is to accept a district's, school's, or teacher's statements about tasks which children must perform each year. If the district expects children to read a selected fourth-grade text at the beginning of the fourth grade, then the task is at least partially defined by the selected reader. A second approach is to identify where a child should be in a task hierarchy. When using a commercial program with a clearly stated sequence of objectives, the teacher can select the point in the sequence where a child should be at any given time. A third approach is to determine what task a child needs to perform in the future and require its completion. For example, one might want a child to tell any selected time on a circular face clock at the end of a six-month interval. A fourth approach would be to accept some "normative" task as an objective, i.e., tasks that most children perform at a given time. An example of this might be for a child to tie his or her own shoes by the time the child enters kindergarten.

Long-term objectives for children at the EEU are selected by considering what tasks a child needs to perform in order to return successfully to a classroom in the referring district. Children must perform tasks in basic academic areas. Teachers in the referring district should specify the instructional sequence or curricular series, as well as the grade level in the sequence or series, on which children must perform by the time they return to the school district. Referring teachers are also sometimes able to specify performance criteria or aims which

RETURN PLACEMENT OBJECTIVES

SUBJECT	MATERIAL	PUPIL PERFORMANCE	PERFORMANCE CRITERIA				Desired Achieve. Date
			Grade or Material Level	Working Time	Response Criteria		
					Correct	Error	
Reading	Lippincott Readers	Say words orally	Book D	Ten minutes	65 words per minute correct	1 word per minute error	2/8/74
Reading	Sullivan Program Reading	Write answers	Book 4	Ten minutes	5 answers per minute correct	0 answers per minute error	2/8/74
Math	Sullivan Program Math BRL	Write digits to presented problems	Book 27	Ten minutes	10 digits per minute correct	1 digit per minute error	2/8/74
Spelling	Buchanan Spelling	Write answers	Book 8	Until task complete	100% correct		2/8/74

Figure 3-6   Long-range objectives for one pupil referred to the EEU.

children should achieve in specified materials and at designated grade levels. When they are not, the EEU staff helps establish aims by referring to data collected on similar children. Figure 3-6 shows some long-range objectives established for one pupil referred to the EEU.

A second way EEU staff determine long-range objectives is to present the previously discussed intake-probing sequence to referred pupils and to selected peers who are performing acceptably. The peer performance is then used to define the criteria which the referred pupil must achieve before returning to the referring district classroom. See Figure 3-7 for an example of return placement objectives derived by this procedure.

Immediate Objectives   Immediate objectives should be selected to provide initial steps toward longer-range objectives. For example, a teacher at the EEU decided to teach division to a pupil. The sequence of immediate objectives shown in Figure 3-8 was selected for this pupil, partly because the sequence was readily available as a commercial program, and because the instructional sequence was acceptable to the teacher. An alternate sequence of divison objectives could have been selected by constructing a sequence or using a sequence formulated by a different textbook publisher. It also might have been necessary to segment the division problems into more refined categories. Such refinement was not necessary in this case, since the pupil made adequate educational progress by working in the programmed text on the objectives specified.

Aims Educators using direct and daily measurement of pupil progress find that accuracy is not the only important dimension of pupil performance. Fluency, or speed, of correct responding is also important to academic proficiency. More fluent (faster) performance results in greater retention and better generalization, and may facilitate performance on subsequent, more difficult tasks. This does not mean that children should perform at extremely high rates. However, moderate rates are necessary for proficiency. Research designs to assess appropriate aims are difficult to formulate, and some disagreement exists about what constitutes proficiency. Haughton (1972), for example, suggests 80 correct digits per minute on most arithmetic computation skills, whereas Ellis (1973) suggests a minimum of 30 correct digits per minute. On the phonic skill of saying letter sounds, Henderson (1971) advises an aim of 100

RETURN PLACEMENT OBJECTIVES FOR ON ACADEMIC ASSESSMENT BATTERY

PROBE	Intake Assessment Score		Return Placement Objective	
	Date:		Date:	
	C	E	C	E
Say Letters	274	3	278	1.13
Say Numbers	67	5	133.5	0
Say Letters Order	82	0	49.65	0
Say Letters Random	35	5	89.38	.75
Say Sounds	25	9	60.75	4.25
Say Sounds Multiple	12	5	60.63	4.88
Say Numbers Random	49	2	84.88	2.25
Write Letters Print, Small	22	2	35.75	.75
Write Letters Print, Capital	22	2	27.5	.75
Write Letters Cursive, Small	6.5	6	——	——
Write Letters Cursive, Capital	4.0	7	——	——
Write Numbers Random	29	1	37.88	1.13
Say Words	8	17.5	58.13	7.5
Addition, Facts	11	0	29.25	0
Addition, Skills	0	0	15.13	.88
Subtraction, Facts	7.5	2.0	24.88	.38
Subtraction, Skills	0	0	9	2

Figure 3-7 Return placement objectives derived from peer-performance scores.

SEQUENCE OF IMMEDIATE OBJECTIVES

Instructional Content	Instructional Material	Grade or Material Level	Pupil Performance	Performance Criteria			
				Time Duration	Performance Aim Correct	Error	Desired Achievement Date
Division Probe 1 digit divisor 1-2 digit dividend 1 digit quotient no remainder	Sullivan Programmed Mathemtics Behavioral Research Laboratories	Book 27 First half	Write digits in answer	5 minutes	30 digits per minute correct	0 digits per minute error	18 Jan. 74
Division Probe 1 digit divisor 1-3 digit dividend 1 digit quotient no remainder	,,	Book 27 Second half	,,	,,	,,	,,	1 Feb. 74
Division Probe 1 digit divisor 1-4 digit dividend 1-3 digit quotient no remainder	,,	Book 28 First half	,,	,,	,,	,,	13 Feb. 74
Division Probe 1 digit divisor 2-5 digit dividend 1-5 digit quotient no remainder	,,	Book 28 Third quarter	,,	,,	,,	,,	22 Feb. 74
Division Probe 1 digit divisor 1-2 digit dividend 1-2 digit quotient with fractional remainder	,,	Book 28 Last quarter	,,	,,	,,	,,	5 Mar. 74

Figure 3-8 Sequence of immediate objectives selected for a pupil at the Experimental Education Unit.

sounds per minute, Starlin (1971) suggests 40 per minute, and Ellis (1973) indicates 30 per minute as a minimum rate. Specialists in different curricular areas have also suggested grade-level guidelines for oral reading rates.

A teacher should select aims, or desired rates, which can either be substantiated with data or with considerable experience which indicates that such rates are indicative of proficient performance. The reader who is interested in considering aims might start by referring to Haughton (1972), Starlin and Starlin (1973a, b, c,), Starlin (1971), and McCracken (1971).

Systematic Classroom Planning

Systematic planning requires writing down a teaching plan which considers all the environmental events relevant to pupil learning. Systematic planning of pupil programs has several advantages over cursory or unsystematic planning, even though the initial cost in teacher time may be greater. A well-specified planning format can ensure a systematic and orderly consideration of elements of instructional importance and reduce the probability of overlooking some important component. By establishing a systematic plan and adhering to it the teacher is better equipped to evaluate both the influence of specific instructional components and the efficacy of the total plan. A written plan is a permanent record of the conditions under which a child or children performed. Finally, such a plan allows other educators to implement the same instructional plan or to replicate the plan with the same or other children.

Writing a Systematic Plan   A systematic plan should include the following elements:

Instructional objectives: Immediate instructional objectives should be stated so the teacher can assess progress.

Setting: Elements of the setting which may affect pupil performance include the number of other children present during instruction, a child's location and position in the classroom, the time of day the program is presented, and the general noise level of the classroom.

Curriculum: Aspects of curriculum include: the type of material (such as programmed or conventional), the content of the program, the format of the display, the type of display, whether the program is commercial or teacher-made, the title of the materials, the author, the publisher, the book or material number, and the grade level or level of difficulty of the material.

Instructional procedures: Procedural considerations relate to the presentation of instruction or to the teaching methods used with pupils. They include such elements as who or what will present the material, how the material will be presented, how many examples will be presented, what type of special teaching tactics might be used (such as manipulating cuisinaire rods), how many practice problems a pupil will perform, what instructions are given, what material the pupil is told to work, and how long a pupil is told to perform.

Observable behavior: The observable behavior the pupil will engage in to show that the material is actually being learned should be specified. The units of behavior to be counted should be indicated. For example, on math problems, will each digit be counted or only each complete answer?

Evaluation: Ongoing evaluation should be a part of the total teaching plan. Evaluation is planned along with the instructional process procedures. The following areas should be considered for formulating evaluation precedures: What type of data will be collected? What behavior will be monitored? Who will count and time performances? What data collection tools and procedures will be used? How will data be displayed and used? Who will be responsible for displaying and utilizing data? What decisions are to be made from the data? What are the decision-making rules to be employed? Who will be responsible for ensuring that those data are used for decision making?

Behavior consequents: Behavior consequents should be as systematically planned as instructional procedures. There are several distinct classes of consequents: correction of work performed; social approval (such as teacher praise); point or token reinforcement followed by back-up reinforcers; primary reinforcers such as food-contingency contracts; and consequents of higher-level reinforcement such as the opportunity to advance to new learning tasks.

In addition to specifying the consequents of the behavior, the teacher should specify their relationship to pupil performance. For example, if a pupil is on a point system to earn free time, then it is important to state the number or rate of responses which earns points. Such relationships are usually stated as the ratio of

PLAN SHEET

Pupil _____ Date _____ Room _____   Aim: Correct Rate _____

Supervisor _____ Advisor _____ Teacher _____   Error Rate _____

Target Date _____

Curriculum and Setting	Instructional Procedures	Correct Performance			Error Performance		
		Pupil Behavior	Contingency	Consequences	Pupil Behavior	Contingency	Consequences

Figure 3-9   Plan sheet used at the EEU.

responses to points; e.g., 50:1. Sometimes, however, rate contingencies are specified, such as 50 words per minute correct earn 5 points.

The plan sheet currently used at the Experimental Education Unit, University of Washington, includes most of the elements presented above. Figure 3-9 is an example. The terminology on the sheet has been modified for this text. The plan sheet is used to describe the conditions and procedures employed with a pupil, including those areas described above. Data-recording procedures are generally described in the column entitled "Pupil Behavior."

An example of a plan sheet written for a spelling program is presented in Figure 3-10. It should be noted that the presented plan is only one component of the total spelling program. It is also noteworthy that the presented plan is a "common" plan, applicable to many pupils. Specific planning details can simply be completed for individual needs. Data obtained on individual pupils will indicate if the plan is effective for each individual. If a teacher has pupils for whom the plan does not result in regular improvement an alternate plan must be written.

Selecting Curriculum for Instruction

Instructional materials must have the same content as the learning objectives the teacher has selected. This is difficult to achieve. Education has not provided teachers with precise and comprehensive information regarding learning objectives in different subject matter areas. Teachers have been left to select or devise their own objectives, a task so large that teachers rarely have either the time or expertise to complete it. Most textbooks have ambiguous objectives. It has been difficult to relate textual materials to the objectives the teacher selects. In those cases where objectives have been well specified (such as in programmed learning materials), they have not always coincided with teacher-selected objectives.

Another desirable characteristic of instructional materials is that they break a learning task into small, sequential steps. Traditional textbooks have frequently provided a potpourri of steps and sequences that can only be satisfactorily achieved by a majority of the pupils. Programmed textbooks have provided a much clearer delineation of tasks and their sequences. However, most programmed texts have been linear. They provide the same sequence of tasks for each person and do not allow rapidly learning pupils to bypass unnecessary frames, or they require slow-learning pupils to repeat frames. Rarely have curricular materials been produced which have broken learning tasks into small sequential steps to allow the learner to advance through the task according to individual pupil mastery of each step.

It is generally desirable for instructional materials to provide overt or active responding on the part of the pupil. Research has not been decisive in favor of

PLAN SHEET

Plan Sheet Number____ of ___ Pupil _____ Completed by _____ Date _____

Room _____ Supervisor _____ Advisor _____ Manager _____

CURRICULUM and SETTING	INSTRUCTIONAL PROCEDURES	CORRECT PERFORMANCE			ERROR PERFORMANCE		
		Pupil Behavior	Contingency	Consequences	Pupil Behavior	Contingency	Consequences
Teacher made spelling program	Teacher presents list of ten words to the pupil.	Pupil hears words on language master card and writes correct word	1:1	Manager marks each word correctly spelled with a 'C'	Pupil hears word on language master card and writes incorrect word	1:1	Manager marks 'X' for incorrect spelling. Pupil is instructed to write word correctly in a sentence.
Teacher selects ten words from spelling text and makes word list.	Teacher asks pupil to read the words to the teacher , to assure pupil knows words.	Teacher corrects	100% : 1 Correct	Pupil receives star at top of paper if words are 100% correct			
Book _____ Level _____ Pages _____	Teacher asks pupil to record each word on a language master card	Pupil counts number correct					
Words selected	Pupil is insructed to listen to each word on languge master and write it correctly	Pupil charts Correct	2 days at 100% :1 Correct	After second consecutive day at 100% correct pupil receives new word list			
1. _____ 2. _____ 3. _____ 4. _____ 5. _____ 6. _____ 7. _____ 8. _____ 9. _____ 10. _____	Pupil is insructed to raise hand for teacher contact when all ten words are spelled	Desired performance equals 100% Correct					
Date begun Time of day							

Figure 3-10 Plan sheet sample written for a spelling program.

overt responding, but there are a number of reasons for requiring it. It is only through overt performance that the teacher can actually observe that pupils have reached their learning objectives. When pupils perform overtly it is possible to complete an analysis of errors, which can lead to remediation. It is possible to reinforce overt responses, thus assuring that a pupil is actually working on desired learning tasks. When overt responses are not required, it is virtually impossible to be sure whether a pupil is actually studying prescribed material or simply staring at a book.

Pupils should not be "locked" in terms of overt responding. In other words, the curriculum or machines or teachers should not control the presentation of material so the pupils' response rates are restricted. In basic academic skills, proficiency appears to be partially related to speed or fluency, which implies a free response rate. On more complex tasks, it is pointless to waste pupil time waiting for the next instructional item. It is frustrating to many pupils to have to wait for instruction.

Curricular materials should provide easy and immediate correction and feedback. One of the strongest arguments in favor of programmed materials has been their immediate correction and feedback. With many other materials, however, it is also possible to procure or construct answer keys that pupils themselves can use to correct their performance. Besides enhancing pupil learning and self-management, provision of pupil-correction procedures relieves teachers of potentially time-consuming tasks and allows them additional time to manage pupils' learning environments.

Good instructional materials must allow individualization of pupil performance. This means that pupils may respond individually, that they are placed in materials at their own level, and that they advance to subsequent task levels when they have demonstrated proficiency on the current task.

Instructional materials should specify the prerequisite knowledge required to enter the program. On some tasks the prerequisite skills are readily apparent. For example, it is clear that complex addition tasks require knowledge of basic facts and numeral recognition. However, it is not always evident what reading level is required for a social studies assignment.

Instructional materials should be clear and consistently presented. The format should not lead to errors that are irrelevant to or outside of the desired learning task.

Other features characterize good instructional materials. The most important criterion is whether or not the materials allow pupils to achieve specified learning objectives. Until further research verifies the exact characteristics of "good" instructional materials, we must rely on those characteristics which have a partially empirical and logical base.

The sequencing of instructional tasks must be logical. One important component of task sequencing is "task slicing." Figure 3-11 illustrates different levels of "slicing" for addition families. For some pupils presentation and instruction on all families, i.e., level 1, will be adequate. Tasks for children with demonstrated learning deficits may need to be "sliced" into smaller components.

Levels of 'Slicing' For Addition Families

LEVEL 1	LEVEL 2	LEVEL 3	LEVEL 4
Addition Families Second addend is 0 to 9	Second addend is 0 to 3	Second addend is 0 or 1	Second addend is 0
			" " " 1
		Second addend is 2 or 3	" " " 2
			" " " 3
	Second addend is 4 to 6	Second addend is 4 or 5	" " " 4
			" " " 5
		Second addend is 5 or 6	" " " 5
			" " " 6
	Second addend is 7 to 9	Second addend is 7 or 8	" " " 7
			" " " 8
		Second addend is 8 or 9	" " " 8
			" " " 9

Figure 3-11 An illustration of slicing an academic task into successively smaller units of instruction.

Sequencing and slicing academic tasks is a tedious and time-consuming venture. Educational organizations and commercial companies have invested heavily in "sequencing objectives." Although teachers are well-advised to review existing sequences before generating their own, even if a teacher obtains a suitable sequence from an external source, much modification and slicing may be required before the sequence is usable.

The selection of instructional objectives and materials has been less precise than the previous discussion might indicate. Teachers who select their own task sequence have two alternatives for procuring instructional materials. First, they may construct their own teaching materials. This is common in basic skills, where teachers construct work sheets based on a task sequence that most suits them. Second, teachers may select from published texts, duplicating books, pages, or segments of materials which coincide with their task sequence, to build files of materials to match their instructional sequences.

Teachers may choose to follow the sequences selected by the author of an instructional program. When the teacher does this, it is important to inspect the program to ensure that the publisher's sequence of objectives actually coincides with the sequence the material covers. In evaluating pupil performance beyond commercially produced tests, the teacher is well-advised to construct small tests, or probes, which cover the content of the objectives included in the text. For example, the EEU teaching staff has constructed a series of probes which covers the content of each book in a programmed math series published by Sullivan and associates. Figure 3-12 shows an example of such probes. These probes can be

BRL MATH   NAME _____
BOOK 15
TEST 2-A   DATE _____

```
  ( )           ( )           ( )           ( )
   16           324            27           257
 +  7          +37           +16          +336


  ( )           ( )           ( )           ( )
  173            48           247           508
 +  8          +37          +127          +489


  ( )           ( )           ( )           ( )
    9           364            47           106
 +54          +227           + 8          +389


  ( )           ( )           ( )           ( )
  267            15           327           153
 +214          +17          +569          +128


  ( )           ( )           ( )           ( )
   29           437             5           258
 +47          +427           +29          +627
```

Figure 3-12   Math-fact drill sheet.

used to measure pupil performance on a daily basis on the material covered in the text. Hence, a pupil could pass a probe before working in a section of a text, while completing a section, or after completing the section of the text. Whenever a pupil demonstrates proficiency on the probe, he is ready to advance to the next instructional objective. The teacher may move the pupil on regardless of the amount of the text actually completed. If the pupil fails to achieve criterion performance on the probe, even after completing the textual material, the teacher knows that additional instruction is necessary.

Systematic Instructional Procedures: The Instructional Hierarchy

Teachers have few systematic guidelines for instructional procedures. The selection of procedures has been unsystematic and random. Their efficacy with individual pupils has been difficult to assess. On the other hand, procedures have sometimes been so rigidly prescribed, such as with espoused teaching methods, that teacher flexibility in altering instructional procedures for individual differences in pupil performance has been severely restricted. An adequate conceptualization of the types of teaching procedures available to teachers should provide guidance for systematizing the selection of procedures and should increase the repertory of alternatives a teacher has for specific instructional tactics.

There are actually four classes of instructional procedures teachers may employ: (1) demonstration and/or modeling, (2) drill, (3) practice, and (4) application. For example, music instruction can demonstrate how a scale or musical selection sounds when played correctly. Drill would be the rote repetition of a series of musical notes. Practice would be the use of the notes in a repetitive series of scales. Application would be the use of the notes in new or novel pieces. Drill of a skill to one level might constitute practice on a simpler or subordinate skill. Therefore, the conceptualization of whether an instructional activity constitutes drill, practice, or application depends on the particular instructional unit.

The use of demonstration, drill, practice, and application usually follows in that order. In other words, after a task is demonstrated correctly, drill on the specified task will usually precede practice on that task. When a skill is acquired through drill, the pupil is ready to practice the skill in more complex material. When proficiency has been achieved at the practice level, the pupil is ready to apply the newly learned skill in a novel context in more advanced material. The use of instruction procedures out of such a sequence can lead to failure of pupils to make adequate progress on many learning tasks.

The actual, or "hard-core," components of instruction can be arranged in an instructional hierarchy that begins with the most basic, preparatory task and moves to more complex levels. The instructional hierarchy is a learning-based model adapted from principles of behavior focusing on academic behaviors. The

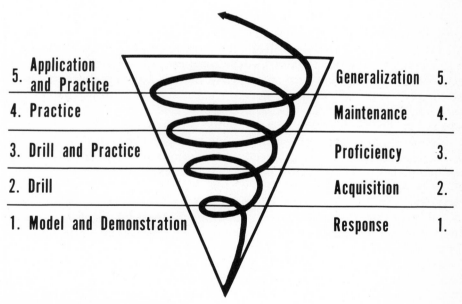

Figure 3-13 Instructional hierarchy.

emphasis is on teacher behaviors and teacher-child relationships. The content of nearly all learning-based operant models is the activity of a person in relationship to the environment (Kanfer, 1972).

Implementing the measurement and assessment methodology described by White and Liberty in this text necessitates awareness and control of teacher behavior. Planning and organization must lead to teacher-awareness of behavior which facilitates student behavioral change and contributes to the reinforcing nature of the environment.

The teaching-learning process is a helical or spiral loop that includes the elements of feedback (learning), feedforward (performance,) and reinforcement. The teaching-learning system is characterized by several features. It has definite beginning and ending points, specific goals and objectives, and flexible modes of operation (systematic instructional procedures) that takes the learning skills and behavioral repertory into consideration (Haring and Phillips, 1972).

Figure 3-13 illustrates the cybernetic nature of the instructional hierarchy. The behavior (or process) of the hierarchy depends on feedback information (learning) and the feedforward of information (performance) after the informational input (stimuli) is processed against the existing bias. What this does is emphasize the problem-solving nature of the teaching-learning process and its systems counterpart, the instructional hierarchy.

Model and Demonstration   In remedial situations focusing on specific academic or perceptual deficits, initial contact between teacher and child is usually achieved through the use of a model. Modeling techniques can be used to set the occasion for a response using some type of media or three-dimensional model that is easily perceived by the child. If a child has difficulty in sensory reception or in decoding input information, the model should be made more basic. Examples of models are flash cards for word or number drills, color shapes for form and color discrimination, and a tape recording of vowel sounds.

Two types of modeling are available to the teacher. One involves actual display of desired performance, live or mediated, and is called *perceptual modeling* (McDonald, 1972). The second is symbolic. A *symbolic model* uses language or descriptive phrases to describe an expected task or response. Instructions on how to perform a skill is one example. Children with academic handicaps or sensory deficits may need to receive information to directly engage their functioning perceptual apparatus. When direct information is presented, the child does not have to interpret either oral or written descriptions that are often confusing.

The next step is *demonstration,* or showing the child the required response using the model. To provide the child with the exact response allows imitation of the task and begins the process of close approximations that make up the drill phase. When teaching a complex task, the demonstration may be only a "cue" rather than the complete task. This is done because demonstrating the whole task would be too much input and could result in frustration. The teacher should "slice" tasks into as many steps or approximations as necessary for the child to master the skill.

Smith (1973) demonstrated that modeling is an efficient means of obtaining response acquisition. She found that a demonstration-plus-permanent-model technique of teaching computational math increased performance. This consisted of presenting the child with a completed math problem of a specific class and a demonstration of how to compute it. However, Smith (1973) notes that using a model as a referent is not applicable in all curriculum areas, especially ones which require verbal responses.

Information from probes and performance data can be used in designing models and planning representation of novel tasks. Construction of probe sheets and sequencing of materials will naturally provide concrete models that can be demonstrated quickly and easily. All information pertaining to modeling and demonstration should be recorded on the plan sheet so a clear record is available.

Drill and Practice   Drill exercises give the pupil a chance to approximate the model by repetition. Drill exercises assist in the acquisition of new information or behavior not previously in the child's repertory. Smith's (1973) research verified that there are at least two kinds of learning stages: acquisition and proficiency. Specific interventions and remedial tactics are necessary depending on whether the learning problem is one of acquisition or one of bringing the child to proficiency.

Providing systematic drill allows a child to advance at an increased rate toward proficiency on basic academic skills. The failure to provide sufficient drill (or repetitive practice) in antecedent learning does not allow for adequate mastery of basic academic skills necessary for success on sequentially related tasks (Ausubel, 1969). Since bringing a child to performance proficiency or criterion is the main focus of remediation, slicing the response requirements into readily accessible segments and providing systematic drill is essential. Eaton and Feldman (1973) found that teacher-administered flash-card drills were more influential in increasing the correct rate on basic addition facts for a nine-year-old girl than were drills that were self-administered by the pupil.

Research at EEU continues on antecedent and concurrent events in the instructional process (Gentry, Gardebring, & Eaton, 1973; Eaton, 1972; Gentry, Kohnstamm, & Eaton, 1973). Data are accumulating to substantiate the role of drill exercises in basic acquisition. However, the literature related to instruction often fails to precisely define drill and also does not differentiate drill from practice.

Drill   These exercises elicit imitative responses to a model or a demonstration of a specific skill. The targeted skill is repeated until acquisition, or 100-percent correct response, is achieved. Practice provides the child with a more complex application of the acquired information that will bring about maintenance of the response. What constitutes drill on one level may constitute practice on another level. Drill on a series of c-v-c phonetically regular words, for example, might constitute practice for specific vowel sounds. Another example of drill that is a prerequisite to practice is reading to a criterion level on drills on short vowel sound before practicing words using the sounds. Practice usually consists of applying skills in novel situations in which the parameters of response are greater than in drill. Maintenance of an acquired skill or bit of information is ensured through practice.

Application   When proficiency, or desired rate, is reached, the child can generalize the skill to higher levels. *Application* of newly acquired skills needs to be achieved through transferring information to novel situations. If a child who experienced difficulty with vowel sounds achieved a criterion rate in a basal reader, situations should be provided where the child may read outside a structured instructional situation so the new skill begins to generalize in other reading areas. Application provides an opportunity to use a learned behavior in a problem-solving situation. This should be done with minimal teacher cues about correct performance. Although most educators agree that providing for application opportunities in regular classroom settings is necessary for prediction and correction of a child's performance in the "real world," few know how such opportunities are included in the curriculum.

The use of instructional texts constitutes a teaching procedure. However, using texts without considering additional instructional procedures has at least two major dangers. Few textbooks provide the exact amount of drill, practice, and application that is appropriate for each individual. Although some pupils will receive approximately the amount of instruction they need, others will receive too much or too little. Secondly, textbooks frequently move children too rapidly to the application components of instruction, without adequate preparation at the drill and practice levels.

The systematic use of instructional procedures will ordinarily lead a teacher to provide initial drill on an activity. Such drill need not be unimaginatively conceived and applied. Specific drill procedures include repeated performances on a work sheet, the use of flash cards, presentation of material on the language master, manipulation of beads or rods, and selecting multiple-choice answers. It is important to establish criterion levels of performance so that both teacher and learner have an indication of when a youngster is ready to move from drill to practice. Practice may utilize the same procedures as drill or may incorporate more complex tasks with less redundance. Finally, the application of the skill in new learning is important. For example, the use of newly acquired reading skills to enjoy a story or to acquire new information provides natural positive reinforcement for engaging in preliminary drill and practice exercises. The teacher should be careful to arrange sequences of drill, practice, and application in small units so the learner will move through the complete cycle to the frequent application of newly learned skills. Much of the need for extrinsic reinforcement will be reduced by following this procedure.

Feedback   The central functional concept in cybernetics is feedback. Feedback information serves to guide action and correct errors (Haring & Phillips, 1972). Feedback alerts the individual to the particular cues to which one must respond. Through feedback, the child learns how to overcome the tendency to push the wrong typewriter key or to confuse the letter *b* with the letter *d*. In this way we respond to stimuli that provide further information about the pattern of response necessary and whether or not responses are correct. Another way we use feedback information is to evaluate our behavior in order to know the outcome of an action. Gaining information about the consequences of one's behavior (that is, reinforcement from outside) makes learning and performance a reinforcing event in itself. Some psychologists believe that the phenomenon of reinforcement should be subsumed under the concept of feedback (Haring & Phillips, 1972). It is not our primary intent to discuss the parameters of feedback, but to show the concepts in the instructional hierarchy.

Immediate corrective feedback or knowledge of results is important in instruction. However, Smith (1973) found as the result of several research projects that feedback tactics were not successful in increasing computational performance. Other researchers (Conlon, Hall, & Hanley, 1972; Hillman, 1970; and McKenzie, Egner, Knight, Perelman, Schneider, & Garvin, 1970) successfully used corrective feedback techniques to influence computational behavior. In fact the Hillman study (1970) used a paper-correction tactic almost identical to the correct and incorrect notation used in Smith's study. Hillman found this tactic was a positive factor in increasing performance, but Smith's data did not show this to be true. In both acquisition and proficiency situations, Smith (1973) found the influence of feedback tactics to be limited. However, feedback has not been universally defined.

Information-measurement theory equates the measure of information with the measure of uncertainty (Pribram, 1971). Feedback, in this sense, would be an internal or brain function, not measurable in the sense of knowledge or results. Feedback, in Pribram's sense (1971), is the ability of the brain to organize information in the process of learning. More research needs to be done to provide data to advance a definition of feedback. The cybernetic and information theory definitions of feedback must be made applicable to teaching-learning systems. The function of short-term and long-term memory play important roles that have not been made clear.

After feedback, the concept of the feedback loop needs to be considered in relationship to the teaching-learning system. The spiral in Figure 3-12 represents the feedback loop that functions in the instructional process. Nearly all activities can be broken down into a *feedback loop*. The loop is similar to step-by-step progression in programmed instruction (Haring & Phillips, 1972). The following example of teaching a child to write the letter *A* illustrates this.

> A child, holding a pencil at about a 45-degree angle, starts a mark at the bottom of a line . . . moves pencil upward to next line at a slant of about 45 degrees . . . brings pencil down at approximately a 45-degree slant from first line . . . places crossline midway between the two slanting lines. (Haring & Phillips, 1972, p. 103)

The calibration of movement cycles (described by White and Liberty, this volume) is a means of breaking down academic behaviors so they can be programmed into the feedback loop. This is as important a skill for a teacher as is the sequencing of the learning task or the ability to "slice" or break-down a skill into more accessible steps.

Motivating Pupil Performance

Most teachers see children as having high or low motivation depending on their overall productivity. The ideal state of motivation leads a child to perform whether or not he receives praise or material reward. The notion of extrinsic reinforcement has been viewed as manipulative. In any event, considering motivation as a generalized, internal condition, one child may be motivated and another unmotivated, depending on how briskly teachers proceed on learning tasks. Teachers often try to enliven instruction to arouse student interest and to sustain their motivation. Techniques include animated lectures, audiovisual materials, novel presentations, and classroom discussions.

A pupil is motivated if a task is promptly completed after an instruction is given, if it is worked on consistently, if minimal teacher supervision is asked for and received, and if a reasonable amount of production results. An additional dimension is the quality of work. There are other peripheral components of motivation, such as appearing to be very interested in the assigned activity. A pupil who asks many questions, who approaches the teacher for advice on an assignment, and who is good-natured about a school task is more motivated than a child who appears to be totally disinterested.

Research based on performance data (Ferritor, Buckholdt, Hamblin, & Smith, 1972) indicates that motivation is reasonably specific to a given task and it is largely dependent upon the consequences which follow an individual's performance. An individual who works consistently at a task, who responds at a reasonably high rate, and who ends up with a large amount of work accomplished is motivated. Motivated performance can be generated and maintained on most tasks simply by providing appropriate reinforcement contingent upon the desired behavior. Ferster and Skinner (1957) and Hall (1971) have discussed these principles at length in other works. Applied behavior analysis is one of the most effective tools available to both regular and special teachers to motivate learning in both normal and handicapped children.

Evaluation of Pupil Performance

One of the most important teaching tasks is the evaluation of pupil performance in the total teaching plan. The collection of pupil performance data and the use of data for assessing pupil progress are the most essential elements of individualized instruction. Evaluation of pupil performance can take two forms. Data may be obtained frequently enough to make a continuous or ongoing assessment of a pupil's progress. Second, data can describe the outcome of an instructional intervention once the instruction is completed. The first type of data is formative (Bloom, Hastings, & Madaus, 1971), and the second type corresponds to summative data.

Formative Use of Data   The formative use of data consists of evaluating whether pupils have been appropriately placed, determining whether they are progressing adequately toward their objectives or aims, and deciding when they have reached their specified performance criteria. The entire evaluative process depends on knowing precisely the criteria for placement in an instructional sequence, what the aims or other performance criteria are within the sequence, and what rate of progress a pupil is expected to maintain enroute to an objective within the sequence.

The first step in evaluating performance is to establish placement criteria. Once placement criteria are established, it is a simple matter to check a pupil's initial performance data against the entry criteria. A teacher might use a child's oral reading performance to determine where, in a series of readers, a child should be placed. Hansen and Lovitt (1974) administered different-level readers (in the Lippincott series) to their pupils. They placed pupils in the highest-level reader in which the pupil scored 45 to 64 words per minute correct, with 4 to 8 errors per minute, and where the score on comprehension questions was 50 to 75 percent correct. Starlin and Starlin (1973c) set the instructional level for beginning reading pupils on oral reading tasks at 30 to 49 words per minute correct with 3 to 7 errors per minute. The preceding criteria indicate that it is possible to determine objective placements. Once such criteria are determined, it is a simple matter for a teacher to compare a pupil's daily data with the selected placement criteria. If the pupil does not meet the criteria, then the teacher should secure pupil data in other level materials until the appropriate placement is determined. Placement criteria may be determined by referring to the guidelines proposed by Starlin and Starlin (1973a, b, c), those proposed by McCracken (1971), and to research such as that conducted by Lovitt and Hansen (in press). One would use the probing procedures discussed earlier to assess a pupil's initial performance on selected grade-level materials and to make appropriate placements.

A second use of data in evaluating pupil progress is to determine when pupils have reached their performance criteria for a given objective. On basic skills, such as learning computational math processes, phonics skills, sight vocabulary, and given reading materials to proficiency, there are four ways to determine criteria.

Many informal reading inventories list the number of words per minute that children should be able to read at different grade levels, as well as the percent of correct performance. For those who prefer, aims can simply be stated as the number of required correct *and* error answers per minute.

A second way to determine aims is by comparison with the performance of competent peers. For example, if the best reader in a second-grade class read at 80 correct words per minute, with about 2 errors per minute, then perhaps a teacher would select aims which are comparable for less-proficient peers. One should be cautious in using such an approach, since typical performance may not necessarily be proficient performance.

A third way to determine aims is to assess the effect of different performance rates on subsequent learning tasks. Suppose a child learned addition facts with sums to 3 at 20 correct answers per minute, and on addition facts with sums to 4, 5, etc., it took progressively longer to achieve the same rate of performance. The teacher would have some evidence that the low rate of performance on the simpler tasks impeded acquisition of more complex performance. The teacher might wish to establish higher performance levels and see if the child's rate of progress improved. This design is complex and requires repeated measurement with many pupils over a period of time, but it may be one of the more fruitful ways to study proficiency performance.

A fourth way to determine aims is through "ratio analysis." Suppose an adult can write numbers at 120 digits per minute and can perform addition problems at 60 digits per minute. A teacher might decide that a youngster who can write 80 digits per minute should be able to write answers to the same math problems at 40 digits per minute. The formula for such "ratio analysis" is

$$\frac{\text{Adult write number rate}}{\text{Adult computation rate}} : \frac{\text{child write number rate}}{\text{child computation rate}}$$

Given any three of the four bits of information, the teacher is able to determine the fourth bit.

There are advantages and disadvantages to each of the four procedures. Experience with teachers at the EEU and in public schools indicates that teachers tend to underestimate their pupils.

However, once performance aims have been established, teachers have relatively straightforward criteria for advancing pupils to subsequent tasks. The teacher simply decides on how many days the pupil must achieve the proficiency criteria (Eaton & Swenson, 1973), then implements the decision. A teacher may set a pupil's oral reading aim at 100 words per minute correct with three or fewer errors for two consecutive days. When the pupil achieved two days at the proposed criteria, the teacher would advance the pupil to a new task.

Even after they have established criteria for initial performance levels and for advancing to new tasks, teachers are still faced with decisions about adequacy of pupil progress from the initial performance level toward the specified aim. For example, if a child's correct and error performance remained constant from day to day, the teacher would conclude that the pupil was not improving, and would alter the instructional plan. Determining adequacy of progress enroute to objectives consists of deciding the minimum amount of progress that will be acceptable each day. Because pupil performance is somewhat variable, one day's low performance, for example, should not cause major revisions in the pupil's instructional program.

Summative Use of Data   The summative use of data consists of describing performance characteristics over an entire instructional condition and comparing the effectiveness of that intervention with other instructional interventions. The comparison of instructional interventions can be either with individual children or with groups of children. One might want to determine which interventions were most effective for a given pupil. In this case it would be advantageous to review the data for that pupil for a large number of interventions. Or one might want to determine interventions which were most effective with large numbers of pupils. This would require an analysis of data obtained with different individuals. Generally, the initial performance level, trend of progress, and ending performance level provide usable data for summative evaluation.

CONCLUSION

Direct and individualized instructional techniques offer both special and regular classroom teachers a set of procedures to enhance instructional management. Recent advances in behavioral and educational technology have led to the development of systematic assessment, instructional, and evaluative techniques that allow teachers to individualize pupil process and to economize teacher time. Direct instruction is the direct measurement of a pupil's performance on a learning task and the accompanying arrangement of instructional programs and procedures for each child.

Instructional management involves five steps: (1) the identification of the general goals the teacher desired the child to achieve, (2) specification of these goals in terms of enabling objectives which will lead to achievement of the goal, (3) identification of the activities and necessary resources to achieve the specified objectives, (4) delegation of responsibility for engaging in activites to reach the objectives, and (5) systematic inspection of progress toward objectives. These are actually the planning stages of instruction. Direct and individualized instruction necessitates comprehensive planning and programming. A teacher who plans both wisely and flexibly can save time and energy in the classroom.

The process of direct and individualized instruction includes the following steps: (1) assessing pupil performance; (2) setting goals, objectives, and aims; (3) systematic planning of instructional or management programs; (4) selecting or preparing suitable instructional materials; (5) specifying instructional procedures; (6) arranging motivational factors; and (7) evaluating pupil progress. The first four of these steps focus on planning and collecting data on current performance levels for each child in the classroom as means of specifying individual objectives and program needs.

Assessment procedures take three forms: (1) assessment to formulate goals and objectives; (2) assessment to place children in a specific curricular or instructional sequence; and (3) assessment to determine manipulable "causes" of deficient performance. Probing is one proven means of assessment. The probing process is the practice of taking brief samples of pupil performance on standard tasks under standard conditions. Such procedures enable the teacher to have specific performance data which are relevant to planning both basic instruction and remedial intervention. Probe information is useful in setting long-term objectives, immediate objectives, aims or desired rates. In this way instruction is sequenced into steps for each child according to the ability of the child to perform at his or her own rate.

By using probe data and having set goals, objectives, and aims the teacher is able to write systematic plans. These plans, recorded on plan sheets, enable the teacher to have information on what was attempted in the act of instruction so modifications can be made if necessary or a successful tactic can be replicated.

The selection of curricular materials is perhaps one of the teacher's most difficult decision points. We have presented a format that can be useful in selecting curricular material. One of the greatest gaps in education is the amorphous nature of textbooks and instructional materials in general.

The actual process of teaching can be conceptualized as an *instructional hierarchy*. The four steps in this process are (1) demonstration and/or modeling; (2) drill; (3) practice, and (4) application. These "hard-core" components of instruction begin with the most basic, preparatory task and then move to more complex levels of the instructional process.

The initial thrust of behavioral research was done on ways to motivate pupil performance. We have suggested a number of ways that the classroom environment and the naturally occurring contingencies of reinforcement can be used to motivate pupil performance including both academic and social behaviors.

Finally we have suggested some ways in which performance may be evaluated. The use of direct and daily measurement gives the teacher a usable technology to both evaluate and modify pupil performance.

The need for individualized planning and procedures cannot be overemphasized. This chapter begins to bring forth procedures that have proven to be effective in the search for direct and individualized instruction. We hope that the future will see these procedures used on a wider scale throughout the nation.

CHAPTER 3 DISCUSSION TOPICS
Direct and Individualized Instructional Procedures

Objective   This chapter presents the student with a formula (which combines practices and discoveries in behavioral and educational technology) for constructing systematic assessment, instructional, and evaluative techniques which allow teachers to provide efficient individual instruction and efficient classroom management.

Exercises   Reread the case history entries for Ronald Rightson which follow Chapter 1. Suppose that Haring and Gentry were consultants to Mr. Hazzit *and* the North Bend educators. They would, first of all, contend that Ronald could (and should) be allowed to remain in Ms. Spring's classroom. They would need to immediately and forcefully back up their contention with convincing discussion of the logic of integration of moderately handicapped and normal children in classroom settings; providing in-service training for Ms. Spring and for Mr. Hazzit in areas of instructional "operation" and instructional "management."

1   Make a topic outline of points to be covered in the first part of the hypothetical presentation Haring and Gentry must make to Mr. Hazzit and Ms.

Spring—and, ideally, all the other *teaching and nonteaching* personnel in North Bend. If you use sources other than this chapter, indicate what they are. Haring and Gentry would undoubtedly quote their own works as well as the works of others. Educators are accustomed to relying on the added credibility of citations when they are suggesting a rather dramatic change in the life-style and tradition of a school or school/community.

2   Read the mini-situations described as exercises at the close of Chapter 10. What decisions would the participants make? What information were the decisions based on? Was the information adequate? Was the decision appropriate for the information? Then fabricate your own, similar list of situations—pretending that the teachers of North Bend are attending their first in-service session with Haring and Gentry and that they have been asked to make a list of management-problem situations and operations-problem situations from their own "real-life" classrooms.

3   In groups of three, select one "best" situation from your compilation. Still in your role as an instructional manager (decision-maker) in the North Bend school system, now reconsider the Haring and Gentry listing of important steps to follow in providing direct and individualized instruction. Using your chosen situation, expand it in enough detail so that you can, in your group, have enough realer-than-life fiction to deal with all six enabling objectives. In other words, prescribe for your pupil in your particular situation (1) an assessment procedure; (2) a long-range learning objective; (3) an immediate objective; (4) a systematic instructional plan (and be careful to include specifics in terms of materials, teaching techniques, reinforcement conditions, and evaluation measures); (5) a data-collection plan; and (6) a method of using the data for feedback pertaining to *all* the other five items.

Chapter 4

Applied Behavior Analysis Techniques and Curriculum Research: Implications for Instruction*

Thomas C. Lovitt
Experimental Education Unit, Mental Retardation and Child
Development Center, University of Washington

INTRODUCTION

This chapter concerns curriculum research my associates and I have conducted with elementary-school-age children during the past six years using Applied Behavior Analysis (*ABA*) techniques.

Curriculum, as used in this report, refers to the many learning activities of elementary-school-age children, such as reading, writing, arithmetic, penmanship, and spelling. Curriculum also includes the many teaching procedures that assist in the development of academic skills. Some of these procedures are modeling, feedback, reinforcement contingencies, and verbal directions used in the Applied Behavior Analysis approach.

*Gratitude is expressed to the following researchers who managed the investigations reported here. Karen Curtiss, Mary Kirkwood, Marie Eaton, Cindy Thompson, Colleen Blankenship, Cheryl Hansen, Debby Smith, James Smith, Mary Hurlbut, and Tal Guppy.

CHARACTERISTICS OF APPLIED BEHAVIOR ANALYSIS

Several applied behavior analysts, in attempts to explain the system, have identified various components. One of the most widely quoted explanations is by Baer, Wolf, and Risley (1968). They describe *ABA* as applied, behavioral, analytical, technological, and conceptually systematic.

In our *ABA* curriculum research, we characterize this system as comprising five ingredients: *direct measurement, daily measurement, replicable teaching procedures, individual analysis,* and *experimental control.*

Direct Measurement

When *ABA* techniques are used, the behavior of concern is measured directly. If the researcher is concerned with the pupil's ability to add facts of the class 2 + 2 = [ ], or to read words from a Ginn reader, those behaviors are measured. When *ABA* techniques are employed, the same behavior scheduled for teaching is measured. Such measurement is more direct than methods such as normative tests, which measure behaviors that are not of immediate concern.

Daily Measurement

The behavior of concern is measured very frequently in *ABA*. If, for instance, the pinpointed behavior is the pupil's ability to add facts of the class 2 + 2 = [ ], he is given the opportunity to perform that skill for several days during a baseline. The reason for using data from several days of measurement is to level out days when the pupil performs very poorly with his better days. In some teaching and research, the pre-posttest methodology is used. A test is given before treatment and another is given after treatment. Progress is based on a comparison of the two scores. Judgments or decisions derived from such limited data could be pernicious and the consequences for some children could be disastrous.

Replicable Teaching Procedures

Another important feature of *ABA* is that the procedures used to generate the research data are adequately described. In most instances they are explained in enough detail that other interested researchers could replicate the studies. By contrast, other types of research sometimes explain procedures rather casually. For example, one Brand X research study that used a phonics training program as an intervention simply said that "daily phonics drills were conducted." It would be impossible for an interested teacher or researcher to replicate these investigations. In *ABA* research, if a phonics treatment were used, the reader would be given the amount of time used for instruction, which phonics elements were stressed, how they were presented, what the nature of the pupils' responses were, and what type of feedback or reinforcement was provided.

Individual Analysis

The very heart of the *ABA* technology is that the data from individuals are presented. In fact, some have referred to this methodology as the *single-subject method*. In an *ABA* study, if data are obtained on five subjects, a graph of each subject's performance is shown. All the idiosyncratic behavioral patterns become obvious. Although the general effects on all five could be the same, no two graphs of pupil performance would be exactly alike.

Other research systems report the data of groups—experimental and control. A mean score may explain the performance of a group while the average score may represent the score of no one subject. It may appear that the group effect was positive, when in fact the treatment was very significant for some, ineffective for others, and had a slightly negative effect on others. However, when averaged, the composite effect is positive. It is sad that in education, where bromides professing individual differences are so abundant, so much educational research is only group-relevant.

Experimental Control

In every research study, regardless of the methodology, the researcher is obligated to prove that the effects on the dependent variable were attributed to the manipulated or scheduled independent variable. He must establish a functional relationship.

This is extremely important. If researchers recommend that method C be used by all reading teachers because the researchers found that it improved certain reading skills, they must be certain that variable C and nothing else caused the improvement.

In order to substantiate their claims, Brand X researchers may resort to statistical control. Their typical research method is to form control and experimental groups, give a pretest, provide a treatment for the experimental group and no treatment or a placebo for the control group, then give a posttest at the end of treatment. The pre- and posttest data of the two groups are then statistically analyzed and the winner announced. The significance of the conquest depends upon which probability level is achieved: 0.05, 0.01, 0.001.

In contrast, the *ABA* researcher uses experimental control to establish relationships between the independent and dependent variables. More specifically, he uses replication.

The ABA design is a favored form of replication. During the first A phase, no treatment is arranged. Then a treatment is scheduled throughout the B condition. Then the treatment is removed. If the behavior changed during the B phase and changed back to its original level in the return to the A phase, a functional relationship had been demonstrated. There are several other replication techniques available to the *ABA* researcher, such as the multiple baseline and crossover designs.

SETTING AND STUDENTS

Most of the research presented here was conducted in the Curriculum Research Classroom of the Experimental Education Unit (EEU) over a period of several years with learning-disabled children.

The EEU, directed by Norris G. Haring, has been in operation since 1965. It is part of the Child Development and Mental Retardation Center, University of Washington. It is committed to Applied Behavior Analysis. All the important pupil behaviors are identified and measured daily, and these data are used to make various educational and administrative decisions.

The Curriculum Research Classroom is smaller than the other classes at the EEU and smaller than the usual public school classroom. The staff includes the author, a head teacher, a research assistant, and a few graduate students.

For the past several years we have chosen, as a research population, elementary-school-age children, ages eight to twelve, who have been identified as learning-disabled. Each year we have had six or seven children in the classroom.

Before entering our class, these children attend either regular or special classes. Of the 35 children who have been in this class, 14 came from special classes. We have had only two girls in this classroom. Their IQ scores (for whatever that is worth) have been in the normal range: from 80 to 115. Academically, the children were achieving below their peers in reading, some by as much as three years. Most of the children had related language arts deficits and were relatively poor in spelling, composition, and penmanship. About half of them were below average in arithmetic.

With few exceptions, the children were socially quite normal. They could carry on conversations about their homes, pets, hobbies, and sports as skillfully as most other children their age. Few had behavior problems, but many were *referred* because of behavior problems in addition to their academic deficits.

These children were as healthy as their non-EEU peers. Although they were absent a few days because of tonsil infections, colds, and flu, their absentee rate was no higher than would be expected of other children their age. A normal proportion of these children wore eye glasses. None wore a hearing aid, and none were physically disabled. Of the 35, about 6 were on some form of medication while in our class.

Only two or three of the children displayed mild articulation problems. One pupil's speech was somewhat garbled because of articulation, and rate differences.

They were from middle- to upper-middle-class homes. The occupations of their fathers included university football coach, Boeing engineer, physician, high school teacher, and construction worker.

Each year we began with a different group of children. The pupils stayed in our class for four academic quarters. They then returned to their original school systems. Most of them have now gone back into regular classes, although some were placed one or two grades below their age peers.

RESEARCH

This research is explained by subject matter area: reading, arithmetic, spelling, communication, and pupil management. Many studies described here have been published in various educational or Applied Behavior Analysis journals. The complete articles are not included. Each project is condensed. Enough information is provided so that interested teachers may apply some of the findings or techniques in their classes, and curriculum researchers may replicate certain of the procedures. For those who would like to read the entire reports, references are included (see footnotes 1 through 13).

There has always been a research implementation gap. Researchers have traditionally bemoaned the fact teachers have not applied research findings. There are many reasons for this lack of rapprochement between researchers and teachers, but the primary reason is that many teachers and researchers have generalization problems.

When some teachers read research they are unable to extract elements to implement in their classes. They tend to view generalization as an all-or-nothing proposition. If they cannot incorporate everything used by the researcher, they will not accept any of it.

Similarly, many researchers, when describing their investigations, tend to convey the idea that their study should be generalized lock, stock, and barrel. Rarely do they suggest that some teachers in specific situations may use certain of their techniques or findings.

This chapter is an attempt to respond to this dilemma. Following each research summary there is a brief section entitled ''To the Teacher.'' Those sections contain features from the research that teachers might consider using in their classes. These are specific recommendations pertaining to materials, instructional techniques, measurement, performance analysis, performance objectives, and learning principles.

Reading Research

Effects of Phonics Instruction on Oral Reading[1]   Perhaps no other aspect of reading instruction has generated more debate and confusion than has phonics training. Some reading experts have stated categorically that pupils must have an extremely good phonics background before formal reading instruction commences. They argue that unless the pupil has systematic part-word training, he will lack certain word-attack skills and will not become a proficient reader. Other reading experts do not agree that phonics skills transfer to other, more complex reading behaviors. They maintain that the English language is so irregular that it is fruitless to teach phonics rules and generalizations. They recommend that reading instruction be more direct, that pupils be taught words rather than word elements.

As with most controversies, extremists are rare in reference to the whole-part-word argument. Most teachers have taken moderate approaches. They see merit in teaching certain phonics generalities along with certain exceptions and some whole words. Nevertheless, even though most reading teachers do not take radical positions on this issue, the controversy persists.

The research described here was designed to bring data from an *ABA* approach to bear on this topic. We sought to answer two questions: (1) if the phonics skills of a pupil are improved, will his ability to read orally increase, and (2) if his phonics skills improve, will concurrent gains be noted more in a phonics- or a nonphonics-designed reader?

The subject was a ten-year-old boy. He had been described as dyslexic. Daily behavioral measures were obtained in seven areas: five phonics skills and two in oral reading. The five phonics skills emphasized medial vowels, consonant blends, sound blending, translocation of letters, and digraph-diphthongs. Oral reading was from a Lippincott and a Ginn reader. The former book was designed primarily on phonics principles, the latter on the whole-word method.

To assess the boy's performance in the phonics areas, five word sheets were constructed. The medial vowel sheet contained a list of 20 three- or four-letter words. Each word contained a short medial vowel. The consonant list was made up of 20 words, each beginning with a different consonant blend. The sound-blending list contained 20 consonant-vowel-consonant words. The translocation list comprised 25 words containing potentially transposable letter combinations (*flit, clap, spot*). The digraph-diphthong sheet was made up of 26 sets of words. Each set featured a different combination, e.g., *ee* or *ay*.

A correct response for the medial vowel and consonant blend tasks was the accurate writing of only the vowel or the blend. A correct response for the sound blending, translocations, and digraph-diphthong tasks was the correct spelling of the entire word. A correct oral reading response was the correct pronunciation of a word. Omissions, substitutions, and additions were errors.

Correct and incorrect rate scores were obtained in each of the seven tasks. To obtain these rates the teacher timed each performance, e.g., medial vowels, and counted the number of correct and incorrect responses. She then divided the number correct and the number wrong by the time required to complete each task.

An AB (baseline and intervention) design was used for this research. During the baseline period the pupil was given feedback on his phonics performance. After he responded to the five sheets, the teacher corrected his papers, pointed out errors and told him the correct responses. Meanwhile, throughout this baseline phase, no instruction was offered as he read orally from the two books. If he erred on certain words, the teacher merely asked him to continue reading.

In the next condition, a 10-minute instructional period was arranged prior to obtaining the seven measures. This instruction was based on the Slingerland teaching procedures which emphasized multisensory instruction. Some instructional time was devoted to each of the five phonics elements. No instruction was focused on oral reading. Reliability checks were made during both conditions of the study for each measured behavior. These checks pertained to timing, accuracy of marking the responses, and general procedures.

Three important findings came from this study: (1) when phonics skills were precisely defined and when instruction was directed toward them, those skills were improved; (2) when phonics skills improved, so did oral reading rate

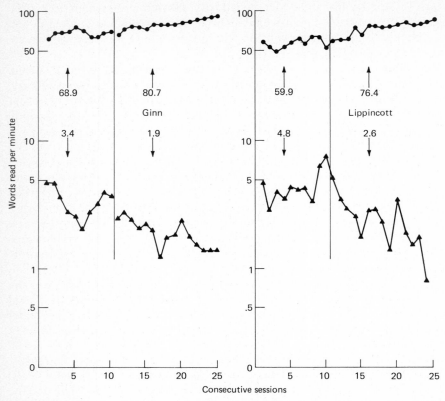

Figure 4-1 Correct and incorrect rates throughout two phases as the boy read from a Ginn and Lippincott text. The numerals indicate correct and incorrect rate medians.

(correct rates increased, incorrect rates decreased); and (3) more improvement was noted as the pupil read from the phonics reader than from the nonphonics reader.

Figure 4-1 illustrates the changes in oral reading rates across the two conditions for both readers. The data from the whole-word book are on the left portion of the figure, and from the phonics book on the right. The vertical lines separate baseline and instructional phases.

One way to compare the data from both books is to contrast median scores. The correct-rate median gains were greater for Lippincott than for Ginn. Likewise, the incorrect-rate median gains were greater for Lippincott. Another way to compare the data is to contrast trends. An inspection of the correct rates across conditions in the Ginn reader reveals that the trend of those data was only slightly more acute during the intervention than in the baseline phase. By comparison, the differences in the trends of the correct-rate data in the Lippincott text are greater. When incorrect-rate data across conditions are studied, the trends in the Ginn book are about the same. However, when the errors in Lippincott are analyzed, the trend of the intervention phase was downward, whereas the trend of the baseline phase was upward.

To the Teacher   There are at least three points from this study the teacher might consider. One is to carefully define instructional procedures. In this project, Slingerland techniques were precisely defined and consistently used.

Another point is that pupils should be required to respond to the same material during a project. Daily, throughout this study the pupils responded to five identical word lists. Had those materials varied from one day to the next, the teacher would not have known which particular words were learned and would, therefore, not have known whether her instructional technique was effective.

A third point is that in order to monitor the development of advanced skills such as "creative writing" or "reading," several subskills related to that major skill must be measured. In this report seven measures were obtained daily, five in phonics, two in oral reading.

Comparison of Measurement that is Direct and Daily with Achievement Test Scores[2]   Perhaps the most widely used technique for evaluating pupil progress is the achievement test. In many school systems an achievement test is given at the beginning and the end of the year to measure such skills as reading, spelling, and arithmetic.

These scores are used to document teacher competency and to make placement decisions about whether to assign students to special or regular classes, high or low reading groups, or to one grade or another. At other times they are used to report pupil progress to teachers, administrators, or parents.

The two important evaluative dimensions that are void when achievement tests are used are direct and daily measurement. The achievement test often measures a behavior that is only indirectly related to the behavior of concern. Achievement tests provide infrequent measures of performance because they are given only once or twice a year.

Although we had criticized achievement tests for some years and had strongly recommended that they be replaced by direct and daily measures, we had no data on how disparate the two systems were in regard to describing performance. Two years ago, therefore, we examined the comparative efficacy of achievement tests and direct and daily measurements.

At the beginning and the end of the year we gave our pupils the *Metropolitan Achievement Test* (MAT) and the *Wide-Range Achievement Test* (WRAT). Throughout the year we also obtained direct and daily data from the children in reading, writing, spelling, and arithmetic. At the end of the year we compared the reading subtest achievement test scores with the reading data obtained from direct and daily measurement. Several differences between the two measurement systems became evident.

The achievement test scores did not agree among themselves. The fall tests disagreed more than one-half grade level for three of six children. The most discrepant scores were on a pupil who received a 2.4 rating on one test and 4.4 on the other. The scores of the two tests in the spring disagreed four out of six times. The widest differences for a pupil on the two tests were 4.0 and 8.7.

In regard to placement, we compared the actual initial placement of pupils when direct and daily measurement procedures were used with their fall achievement test scores. Using our method of placement we required each child to read several days from a number of readers representing different grade levels. We graphed correct and incorrect rate performances as they read. After several days we analyzed the data and selected initial readers for the children based on their relative performance. Only three of the six placements, according to direct and daily measurement, agreed within one-half grade level with an achievement test score. A comparison of the book level they were actually reading in at the end of the year with their spring achievement test scores revealed concurrence between an achievement test and actual placement four out of six times.

In regard to the data about pupil growth throughout the year, all pupils gained in MAT scores. Their spring scores were all higher than their fall scores. According to the WRAT, however, there was no growth for two pupils and a deterioration for another. Direct and daily measurement data indicated improvement in all children. Furthermore, this improvement was indicated in three ways: their correct rates increased from fall to spring, their incorrect rates went down, and they read from more difficult material in the spring than in the fall. Achievement tests provided only a grade-level difference score as a measure of improvement.

A final advantage of direct and daily measurement over achievement test measurement must be emphasized. When the former system is used, a teacher can see from one day to the next whether progress is being made. If the data indicate the child is not improving, a different teaching routine can be scheduled immediately. By contrast, if a teacher waits until spring to discover whether or not her teaching was effective, she does not have time to redesign her instruction to keep the pupil from failing.

To the Teacher   This project clearly points out the advantages of using direct measures over achievement tests. Pupil scores on achievement tests are not always correlated with their classroom performances. The comparison also shows what can happen when performance is measured infrequently. Since all behaviors are variable, any educational decision made from one or two samples may be detrimental to the child.

Teachers should place students according to their daily performance with classroom materials and should use direct and daily procedures to communicate progress to parents and teachers. This study further suggests that teachers should use pupil data to evaluate all instructional techniques intended to improve reading.

Another aspect of this study which merits consideration deals with communication. Many teachers, particularly special education teachers, use direct and daily measurement data to communicate children's growth to their parents. They find this method of communication far superior to other styles because of its objectivity and individuality.

A final note from this study pertains to the widespread practice of using achievement tests to evaluate performance contracts and teacher performance. Many teachers have been critical of achievement tests used for these purposes. Unfortunately, when asked for alternative evaluation strategies, many are unable to respond. Direct and daily measurement should be seriously considered as a replacement for achievement tests.

Effects of Various Reinforcement Contingencies on Oral Reading Rate[3]   In each of three studies the effects of a reinforcement contingency were investigated. In two, the contingency was arranged for correct responses and in one, the contingency was arranged for errors. The reinforcer was leisure time. Pupils, during certain conditions, were able to earn minutes of free time. Correct and incorrect rate data were gathered. Incorrect responses were additions, omissions, and substitutions.

The studies shared other common features. As the pupils read, some feedback was provided. If a word was mispronounced or left out, the word was pronounced by the teacher. Comprehension data were obtained in all the studies in addition to the oral reading data. Reliability checks were also obtained. A second observer monitored some of the sessions and checked the teacher's timing, counting, and general procedures. A final common feature in all the projects was that each pupil read daily from two readers. One reader was the experimental text, the other a control. In the conditions where a reinforcement contingency was scheduled, it was associated with only the experimental text. No interventions were scheduled for the control reader.

In Study 1 an eleven-year-old boy read orally for five minutes each day from two readers. The experimental reader was a Bank Street text. The control reader was a library book, *Encyclopedia Brown Saves the Day.*

This project used an AB design. During the first condition neither instruction nor reinforcement contingencies were in effect. Only a type of feedback was used. Throughout the second condition a reinforcement contingency was arranged. The requirements were that if, after the five-minute reading period, his correct rate was equal to or exceeded 50 words per minute, he was granted points on a 25:1 ratio (for each 25 points he earned one minute).

When his performances in the two conditions were compared, it was revealed that, on the average, his correct rate improved by about twelve words per minute from first to second condtion, while his incorrect rate was reduced about one word per minute. His reading rates throughout both conditions in the control reader were stable, hence unaffected by the contingency.

In the second project the pupil was a nine-year-old boy. He read daily from a Bank Street and a Merrill reader. The former text was the experimental book; the latter, the control book. The project used an AB design. The first period was the baseline. During the second condition a contingency was arranged for the experimental text. The contingency focused on errors and involved a withdrawal of points. Each day the pupil was given, noncontingently, 15 points. The points were then taken away on a 2:1 ratio, for every two errors one point was withdrawn. At the end of the reading session the remaining points were redeemable for minutes of free time.

This project revealed that the student's incorrect rate improved from one condition to the next. However, his correct rate across conditions was unaffected. His rates in the control text were unchanged across conditions.

In Study 3 the pupil was an eleven-year-old girl. The two readers were from the Macmillan and Laidlaw series. The Macmillan book served as the experimental reader.

This experiment comprised four phases. An *ABA* design was used. In the first and third conditions, feedback was provided as the girl read. Neither instruction nor reinforcement contingencies were arranged. Throughout conditions two and four, a 30:1 ratio for correct responses was scheduled. For each 30 correctly read words, one point was given.

The results indicated that the girl's reading performance was better throughout the conditions of reinforcement than in those phases performed without contingencies. In Conditions 2 and 4 her correct rates were higher and her incorrect rates lower than during Conditions 1 and 3. Her correct and incorrect rates, as she read from the control reader, were stable throughout all conditions.

Improvement was noted in all three studies as a result of the reinforcement contingencies. In Study 1 the contingency applied to correct responses. In Study 2 the contingency was arranged for errors. In Study 1 correct rates were influenced more than incorrect rates. In Study 2 errors were influenced more.

To the Teacher   Many procedural features from this study could be used by teachers. First, the time for reading instruction was only about 15 minutes per day per child. When good material is used, when the ongoing reading procedures are satisfactory, and when effective teaching techniques are used, pupils thrive, even though the reading periods are short. This should be encouraging to teachers who have several children in their classes, and yet who want to individualize their programs.

Another consideration is the use of two readers. Classroom teachers may not be as concerned with the control feature of the second reader as we were. However, a teacher might want to use two readers for generalization purposes. She could have a pupil read from two texts and arrange some teaching technique such as drilling on errors for only one reader. By obtaining data from both readers the teacher could determine whether the technique influenced the reader it was associated with and whether the effects transferred to the other reader.

Teachers should note the various ways contingencies were arranged. Pupils can be given something or they can lose something depending on their performance. They could gain points for correct responding and lose for errors. Reinforcement systems have further flexibility since the gain and loss ratios can be adjusted. A pupil could gain points on a 5:1 ratio (one point for five correct responses), or the ratio could be set at 500:1. The possibilities are infinite.

Another dimension of the reinforcement system is the great variety of events which may be gained or lost. Such events in the past have included points, minutes of free time, models, classroom privileges, and recess.

Effects of Previewing on Oral Reading[4]   This experiment dealt with noncontingent interventions. These noncontingent events were three types of previewing: oral, silent, and teacher previewing.

Various forms of previewing have been used for years by teachers of reading. Publishers have recommended this approach as a method for teaching fluency. In spite of the widespread use and support of this technique, little research has been conducted on the topic.

In two studies that used three types of previewing the general procedures were the same. The pupil read orally for two minutes daily. Feedback regarding mispronounced or omitted words was provided. In both studies reliability checks were taken on timing, accurate monitoring of responses, and general operating procedures.

In Study 1, the pupil was a ten-year old boy. He read from a Lippincott reader each day. This project consisted of five conditions and used an ABA design. Throughout Conditions 1, 3, and 5, only feedback was scheduled.

During the previewing conditions the pupil was requested to read the material twice. The first reading was considered practice, the second the "real" performance. Throughout the first reading the pupil was coached on difficult words. This was not the case when he read a second time. Only the data from the second reading were graphed.

These data indicated that oral previewing had substantial effects on correct rate. Although his incorrect rate maintained across the various conditions, his correct rates, during previewing conditions, were nearly double those rates when previewing was not used.

In Study 2, two types of previewing were used—silent previewing and teacher previewing. The subject in this study was nine years old. He read each day from a Lippincott text.

This study used an ABA design for both types of previewing. During the first condition, only the feedback procedures previously described were in effect. Throughout the second phase, silent previewing was scheduled. Prior to reading the story orally, the boy read it silently. As he did so, he could ask the teacher to explain unknown words. In the third condition the previewing technique was not included. These data indicated that the technique greatly influenced correct rates and mildly influenced incorrect rates.

The next part of the study investigated the teacher previewing technique. Following the baseline phase, which was the final condition of the first part of the study, the teacher read to the pupil the material that he subsequently read orally. Throughout the next condition no previewing was used. In the final, or fifth, condition, previewing was again instituted.

The data from the final three conditions indicated that, although incorrect rates were not affected across conditions, correct rates were substantially altered. During the teacher previewing condition the pupil's correct rate was nearly double that during nonpreviewing conditions.

To the Teacher   In this report, all types of previewing were effective. Their greatest effects, however, were on correct rates. Incorrect rates were not significantly improved.

Therefore, if a pupil's incorrect rate is too high and the teacher wants to reduce it, she should perhaps select a tactic other than previewing. She might choose to drill the pupil (following each reading assignment) on his errors, or she might concentrate on one error pattern of the pupil. However, if the teacher's goal is to improve a pupil's fluency—his correct rate—one of the types of previewing used here could be appropriate.

We have investigated other types of previewing. One allowed the pupil to listen to a tape recording of the story he was to read. In another project we recorded on language master cards phrases from the story the pupil would subsequently read. After he listened to the phrases he read the complete story. All these previewing techniques have generally been effective in increasing fluency.

Relationship of Oral Reading and Comprehension   In the two previous studies the major concern was the measurement and development of oral reading. In this study, although oral reading was again of primary concern, equal emphasis was upon silent reading and answering comprehension questions.

This study ran for three quarters. Four measures were obtained daily. The measures pertained to oral reading, answering comprehension questions from orally read material, silent reading, and answering questions from material read silently. Throughout the first two quarters the pupils read orally from a Lippincott reader and silently from a Ginn text. The two readers were matched for reading difficulty. That is, as the pupil read orally from the two texts for a few days, his rates in both texts were about the same.

Each day the pupil read 500 words orally in a Lippincott reader, then answered 30 comprehension questions. As the pupil read, the teacher corrected missing and mispronounced words. The pupil then read 500 words silently in a Ginn reader and answered 30 comprehension questions. No feedback was provided for silent reading. The comprehension questions were of three types: interpretation, recall, and sequencing.

Following a baseline period where neither instruction nor reinforcement contingencies were in effect, the class was split into two groups. With one group a contingency was scheduled for oral reading rate. For the other, the contingency was arranged for the comprehension of orally read material.

The contingency was based on progress and focused on errors. In oral reading a projected trend was drawn on the graph. If on any day a pupil's oral reading rate was lower than that slope, he had to practice the words he missed. Each error was embedded in a phrase, and for several minutes he practiced reading those phrases. In comprehension, a similar projected trend was drawn. Any day a pupil's comprehension score was below the line, he had to redo the questions he had answered incorrectly.

A crossover design was used for this research. During the first quarter the contingency was in effect for some pupils for oral reading, and for other pupils for comprehension. Throughout the winter quarter the project was conducted again. The only difference was that the groups were alternated. Those who were in the oral contingency group in the fall were placed in the comprehension group.

The project was run a third time in the spring quarter. At that time the reading texts were switched. Lippincott became the silent reader and Ginn the oral reader. During that quarter both contingencies were alternately arranged for all pupils. If, during the first part of the quarter a pupil was in the group where the contingency was on oral reading, he was transferred to the group where the contingency was on comprehension in the second half of the quarter.

Reliability checks were scheduled through the year. These checks focused on timing, accurate counting of responses, and general procedures.

Several findings resulted: (1) when the contingency was arranged for oral reading, that performance improved; (2) when the contingency was arranged for oral reading comprehension, that performance improved; (3) when the contingency was arranged for oral reading, oral reading comprehension was unaffected, silent reading and silent reading comprehension improved; and (4) when the contingency was arranged for oral reading comprehension, oral reading improved, silent reading and silent reading comprehension improved. The biggest gains were those indicated by points 1 and 2.

To the Teacher   Throughout this project the pupils read 500 words orally and silently each day. This is a reasonable amount. The pupils were generally attentive and they read enough material to cover a complete story or a large portion of a story.

Other projects discussed in this section were scheduled by time. The pupil read two or five minutes each day. Whether the teacher prefers that pupils read a fixed number of words or for a certain period of time each day, she should settle on one method or the other. If the situation is not stabilized in amount or time, the data from one day to the next will not be comparable. Some teachers may be dissatisfied with both options because they want children to read complete stories. One way to schedule uniform times or amounts and also allow pupils to finish their stories is to have them read beyond the point of timing. If, for example, the teacher requires the pupil to read for five minutes and at the end of that time a half-page remains of the story, she could make a mark at the five-minute point, and let him continue reading until a logical conclusion is reached. The data from the five-minute reading could be recorded to provide the teacher with a reliable measure of the same unit of reading each day.

Teachers could also consider the instructional technique used and the way it was scheduled. First, the instruction for oral reading required the pupils to rehearse their erred words embedded in phrases. The procedure for teaching comprehension merely required the pupils to correct their incorrect answers. Second, instruction for oral reading or answering comprehension questions was scheduled only when the pupils' performance was unsatisfactory. If their performance was adequate, they received no instruction.

A final point to be considered from this project is that teaching should be focused on the behavior of concern. In this project the greatest oral reading and comprehension gains occurred when a teaching technique was directed toward those behaviors. Although generalizations sometimes occur, as noted in the first reading project, the teacher should still direct her attention to the immediate behavior of concern, rather than at a related skill.

Arithmetic Research

Using an Antecedent Event to Facilitate Subtraction[5]   In the early days of behavior modification and Applied Behavior Analysis, behaviors were altered almost exclusively by reinforcement contingencies. Reinforcers such as tokens, praise, or candies were always presented after the designated behavior occurred. They were referred to as subsequent events. Many subsequent events have been shown to function as reinforcers. Some reinforcement theorists have boasted that if they can find a reinforcer for a given individual they can teach him several skills. Reinforcers are no doubt here to stay.

However, behaviors are altered in other ways. Events that come before the behavior occurs are also influential. Certain antecedent events have long been used by teachers and parents to instruct children. Many of those events (previewing, modeling, and verbal instructions) are reported in this book.

The experiment described here was one of the initial Applied Behavior Analysis research efforts that investigated the effect of an event other than a reinforcement contingency. The experiment was comprised of three studies, each used an ABA design. The pupil in the experiment was an eleven-year-old boy.

Study 1 included three conditions. Throughout the study the boy was required to perform 20 problems of the type $[\ ] - 2 = 6$. In the baseline phase he received no teaching, feedback, or reinforcement. When he finished 20 problems, he was thanked and sent on to another academic activity.

During the second condition, he was required to verbalize each problem before he wrote the answer. He said, for instance, "Some number minus two equals six." He then wrote the answer. The teacher monitored his behavior during this phase and occasionally reminded him to verbalize each response. During a third phase he was asked to refrain from verbalizing the problems and answers.

The data from this study indicated that his performance was far superior in the condition where verbalization was required than during the baseline phase when no verbalization was required. Further, his performance maintained, even improved, in the final condition when verbalization was no longer practiced.

Two other studies like the first were carried out. In the second, problems of the type [ ] $- 20 = 40$ were used. The problems in the third study were like $4 - 3 = 9 - [ ]$. Each study comprised three phases. During the first, no verbalization was required. The pupil verbalized each problem and answer throughout Phase 2; then, in the final phase, he no longer verbalized.

The results of these studies were identical to those of Study 1. During the baseline phase his correct rate and accuracy were low, then much improved in the second phase. In the final condition the behavior of subtracting was maintained, despite the removal of the cue.

To the Teacher   The experiment demonstrated that a technique that has been used for years by teachers and parents can be effective. Many teachers have encouraged their pupils to think before they make a response. More importantly, this experiment demonstrated the scope of Applied Behavior Analysis techniques. Clearly, all the teaching variables used by teachers for years—modeling, various aids, and mnemonic systems—can be evaluated within the Applied Behavior Analysis framework. These events can as easily be subjected to analysis as the many reinforcement variables that have for so long been monitored by this system.

This project, like several others, emphasized the use of consistent materials. If a teacher wishes to teach a specific skill, he or she must define that skill, then provide the pupil with proper materials. Teachers are often frustrated in their attempts to teach specific arithmetic skills from commercial texts. The items in some texts vary considerably from one page to another. Teachers who wish to teach pupils to be proficient with specific skills are, therefore, forced to construct their own arithmetic sheets. When it is necessary to prepare supplementary materials, the teacher should first define a specific class of problems to teach (e.g., addition problems where the addends are from 0 to 9 and the sums from 0 to 18). Next, several sheets with problems of this type should be made. The same number of problems should be on each sheet. The teacher may also want to use all different problems on a sheet and different arrangements of problems from one day to the next.

The sequencing of phases in this report merits some consideration. Each project in this report consisted of three phases. During Phase 1—baseline—it was confirmed that the pupil needed assistance. During Phase 2—when the verbalization technique was scheduled—he improved. During Phase 3—when the technique was removed—his behavior was maintained. This arrangement of phases should be the most popular teaching design. It allows the teacher to ascertain the effects of her teaching technique (Phase 2), and to view how well the pupil's behavior maintains when the technique is taken away (Phase 3).

Another feature is a warning: "Don't allow a teaching technique to be used too long." In this project, although the pupil reacted favorably when the technique was scheduled, he improved even more when the technique was removed. Although the teaching technique was initially necessary, had it been left in too long, subsequent growth would have been inhibited.

Use of Modeling to Influence Acquisition of Arithmetic Skills[6] The instructional technique in this study is perhaps the oldest and most widely used technique available—showing and telling someone how to do do something. Teachers often help pupils compute certain types of arithmetic problems. They go to the chalkboard and demonstrate how a problem should be solved. As they go through the steps of the problems, they verbalize the process. Sometimes the sample problem is left on the board while the children complete their assignment.

This experiment comprised three studies. Throughout, ABA designs were used. In Studies 1 and 2 the intervention was the demonstration of a problem, then leaving that sample as a model for the pupil to consult. In Study 3 components of that technique were investigated. Reliability checks were obtained on timing, accuracy of marking responses, and general procedures.

In Study 1 the pupils were assigned different types of problems. Some were presented problems like $470 \times 249 = [\ ]$, others, multiplication problems like $22 \times 13 = [\ ]$ and $8 \times 0 = [\ ]$. During the baseline phase the pupils received no instruction, feedback, or reinforcement. They worked for two minutes each day on the sheets.

Throughout the intervention condition the modeling technique was used. The pupils were shown how to do a problem of the assigned type and that model was left on their sheet. They could refer to the model at any time. The data throughout this condition revealed that rapid acquisition occurred for all pupils. Furthermore, throughout the intervention phase their scores were nearly all perfect. In the final condition, when the modeling intervention was removed, their scores, with few exceptions, remained high.

Throughout Study 2 the pupils were assigned different problems than those used in the first study. Again baseline data were taken. Their performances were generally zero throughout this period. Next, a feedback intervention was arranged. Following the completion of an assignment the teacher marked each pupil response as correct or incorrect. This checked paper was handed back to the pupil. Since the students could not do many of the problems, most of their responses were marked as errors. None of the pupils progressed during this condition, although the procedure was in effect for about seven days.

In the third phase, the same modeling technique used in Study 1 was scheduled. The results of that period were as impressive as those in Study 1. Effects were immediate and lasting. When the intervention was withdrawn, the accuracy of the pupils continued to be good.

In Study 3, elements of the modeling intervention were used. Throughout this study different problems were again assigned. As in the other two studies, the pupils worked two minutes each day on the problems. In the first phase no teaching was scheduled. During the intervention phase the model alone was used for some of the pupils. The sample problem was placed on their work sheets, but they were not shown how to perform the problems. For other children, during the intervention period, only the demonstration was provided. The teacher showed them how to do a sample problem, then took away the model. The pupils were unable to refer to the sample as they worked.

The results of these efforts indicated mixed success. For some pupils this partial technique was effective, for others it was not. Since the total technique—demonstration and permanent model—required about two minutes of instructional time, it was recommended that the whole intervention be used.

To the Teacher   A number of features from this investigation reinforce notions presented in others. This report illustrates again how arithmetic problems of certain types can be taught as a group. For another, this report also used a maintenance phase to indicate whether a certain level of performance would maintain once instruction was removed.

Effective teaching techniques are not always complex. The one used here—modeling—consisted of only a few elements and took only a few seconds to administer. In fact, some children, as indicated by the last experiment in this report, were able to learn new information when only a part of the modeling technique was used.

Teaching procedures should be as simple as possible. There are two reasons for using only the mildest and briefest remediation procedure. One, if a procedure takes more time than necessary, both teacher and pupil time are wasted. Two, if a complex procedure is used to effect change, an inordinate amount of time may be spent weaning the pupil from the procedure. Teachers, like physicians, should prescribe only enough treatment to cure the problem. If more is prescribed, immunities may build up.

The important message from this project is that once a skill has been specified for instruction, and a legitimate technique such as modeling is arranged, the acquisition of that skill can be sudden. In this project, once the teacher showed the pupils how to do the problems, they invariably complied. Their acquisition of the skill was not gradual over a period of days, but immediate.

Proficiency Techniques and Arithmetic[7]   With some pupils, for certain types of problems, the basic concern is for proficiency, not acquisition. Some pupils are able to compute certain problems, but they require so much time to arrive at the answers that they are not proficient.

In order to use computation skills in everyday situations, a person must be somewhat facile. If he is required to make change, he must do so within a reasonable time. If someone buys a commodity from him worth $15 and gives him $20, he must rapidly calculate how much change he must return. The customer would be unimpressed if the merchant took 10 or 15 minutes to complete such a transaction.

In this series of studies several interventions were scheduled to assist pupils in becoming proficient with certain arithmetic facts. In most instances, ABA designs were used. In every study, reliability measures were obtained.

In order to establish proficiency measures, we obtained data from public school pupils the same age as ours as they worked on several types of problems. We then calculated the correct rates of these pupils for the various classes of problems. Next, for all classes of problems, the correct rate scores were ranked. We selected the seventy-fifth percentile score for each class as the desired rate. To be proficient, our pupils had to score at or above that score.

During Study 1 a baseline period was scheduled. Throughout the intervention period a verbal instruction was programmed. Each day, prior to the arithmetic assignment, the pupil was instructed to "go faster."

The correct rates of all children improved during this phase. Most of the pupils obtained rates that were proficient. When the instruction was no longer scheduled throughout the third phase, their correct rates continued to be satisfactory.

In the next study, following a baseline phase, contingent toy models were arranged. Throughout this intervention phase a 4:1 ratio was scheduled. For each four correct responses one point was granted. Models were purchased for 50 to 75 points. All the children's correct rates improved when this contingency was arranged, but not as much as when the simple instruction was used. Some of the pupil's scores reached proficiency. When the intervention was removed, the correct rates of the pupils generally maintained.

In the next study three types of feedback were investigated. Following a baseline phase, a type of feedback was arranged. The three types of feedback were (1) indicate correct and incorrect problems on the pupil's paper; (2) inform him of yesterday's and today's correct rate; (3) tell him the day's rate and the desired rate.

The results from these feedback studies were very unimpressive. Only small gains were noted for a few children. When the interventions were removed, some rates actually fell below baseline level.

The final intervention in this series of studies was a combination of the two most successful proficiency techniques. The intervention comprised the instruction to "go faster" and the toy-model contingency. Following another baseline, this intervention was arranged. During the intervention phase, prior to responding to the problems, the pupil was given the instruction. Then, following the session, he was granted points redeemable for models on a 4:1 ratio.

The results of this study were the most impressive. All pupils' correct rates improved more than they had when either the instruction or the model intervention was used. In every case proficiency rates were reached.

To the Teacher An important feature of this project concerns the distinction between acquisition and proficiency. One reason to develop such a discrimination is that the goals for either are different. Generally, the objective of acquisition projects is accuracy; whereas the objective of proficiency projects is increased speed.

A further reason for distinguishing between the two types of performance is that certain instructional techniques are better suited for one aspect of performance than the other. When the concern is to assist pupils to acquire certain behaviors, some of the instructional procedures might be modeling, various manipulative aids, and drill. If the concern is to develop proficiency, it might be useful to tell the pupil what is expected, and to use reinforcement contingencies.

This project again noted the positive effects of simple teaching. When the pupils were told to "go faster," they did. In fact, the effects of simple instructions were even more influential than contingent models. When instructions are clearly and consistently stated, pupils will often comply.

It must be pointed out, however, that the best effects on math performance were noted when the two procedures were combined. Although no more instruction should be used than is necessary, two established procedures may need to be combined in order to obtain immediate and impressive proficiency gains.

Teachers should be on the lookout for not only those procedures that are generally effective but also those that are generally ineffective. Three types of feedback were used in this study, and the performances of only a few children were minimally influenced. In the preceding study a type of feedback was not effective in an acquisition situation.

To us, these results were surprising, for there is abundant literature about feedback which generally acclaims its benefits. It is possible that our pupils had poor experiences with feedback and generalized from that. It is also possible that the types of feedback we used would be effective in other academic areas or that other types of feedback would be more effective in math. These considerations notwithstanding, teachers should carefully evaluate their feedback techniques.

Withdrawal of Positive Reinforcement[8]   The primary difficulty of the pupil in this study was not acquisition. She could solve rather complex computational problems. Neither was her difficulty one of obtaining proficiency. Her correct rates for most basic facts matched those of her peers.

This young lady's performance was erratic. Some days, when asked to perform certain subtraction problems, she was very accurate. On other days, she erred on all the problems. Occasionally her responses to a row of problems would simply be a series of numbers, like 21, 22, 23. She was apparently not motivated to perform consistently.

This young lady was assigned three pages of arithmetic problems daily. Each page contained 25 problems of a different class. The Class 1 (C1) problems were like $18 - 9 = [\ ]$. C2 problems were of the class $24 - 6 = [\ ]$; borrowing was required. C3 problems were like $34-16 = [\ ]$; again borrowing was required. For each class of problems several sheets of different problems were developed. Thus, the pupil worked on different figures from day to day. Reliability checks, pertaining to items previously mentioned, were obtained throughout the study.

The design of the study was a multiple baseline. Throughout the first phase, which ran for six days, no instruction, feedback, or reinforcement was scheduled. When the pupil had responded to the problems on the three sheets, she submitted her papers to the teacher. No further interaction took place. Her

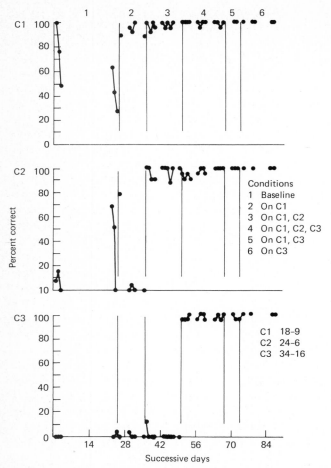

Figure 4-2 Percent correct scores for the three arithmetic sheets throughout the study. The data reveal her scores on C¹ and C² were erratic during baseline. The withdrawal technique was successively effective on each sheet of problems.

performance during this period was variable. Her scores on two of the three sheets were high one day and low the next (see Figure 4-2).

Throughout the second condition of this project a withdrawal contingency went into effect. For each error she made on the C1 sheet, one minute of recess time was taken away. The data from this phase revealed that her scores on C1 were high, but her scores on the other two sheets remained low.

During the next phase the same withdrawal contingency was associated with the C2 problems, in addition to the C1 items. In the next condition the contingency was arranged for all three sheets. Throughout those phases the results were impressive. Successively, as the contingency was arranged, the girl's performance improved.

During the next two conditions, the contingency was removed, first from the C2 sheet, then from C1. In the final phase the contingency was in effect for only the C3 sheet. As indicated in the figure, her accuracy on all the sheets remained high, even when the contingency was removed.

In this project, instructions were not used; for in the past she had been asked to "be more accurate" and "work faster." She was not responsive to comments alone. Neither in this project were other commonly used instructional techniques, like feedback, modeling, or teaching aides, used. She knew how to solve the problems and did so when she wanted to. Hers was a motivational problem, since she saw no reason for performing the problems. To effect that change she was deprived of recess time contingent on errors.

That the girl was sensitive to the withdrawal contingency was indicated in two ways by her response pattern. First, she reacted immediately. The day the contingency was scheduled, her performance improved greatly. Second, this immediate accuracy was noted on only the contingency sheet. When the point-removal technique was arranged for C1, only performance on that sheet improved, not on the other two.

It was somewhat encouraging when her accuracy continued to be high during the final two phases. When the contingency was removed from the C1 and C2 sheets, her performance did not collapse. Something other than the withdrawal contingency was maintaining her behavior.

To the Teacher   The simplest effective techniques possible should be used to change behavior. When artificial arrangements are used to induce favorable change, teaching is not finished even though the target behavior improves. When an artificial technique is used to stimulate progress, once progress is noted, the teaching situation must continue until the pupil can perform the behavior under natural conditions. This is not to say that artificial circumstances should never be arranged. If the goal is to teach something and that skill does not develop naturally, synthetic aids, sometimes in the form of reinforcement contingencies, must be used.

Furthermore, reinforcement contingencies should be the initial teaching technique when the teacher knows the pupil can perform the task but will not. If the teacher has every reason to believe a pupil is capable of performing a task (perhaps he demonstrated this ability in the past), the teacher should not use teaching strategies like modeling or instructions. If the pupil is not motivated to perform the task, he probably will not change until the motivational atmosphere is changed. Rather than engaging in a quixotic search for an effective teaching technique, the teacher should change the motivational system by arranging a contingency.

In selecting a contingency the teacher has the choice of *giving* the pupil something contingent on a specified behavior or *taking* something away. In this project, minutes of recess were taken away for incorrect answers. It could have been arranged so that additional minutes were given for correct answers. Another possibility is to use both, to give something for correct answers and take away something for incorrect answers. Whether the event is given, taken away, or both, it should be something of value to the pupil.

Various Types of Story Problems The preceding projects in this section dealt with computational problems. There are other important components of the mathematics curriculum. One of the major elements of a complete math program in the elementary grades is story problems.

Most teachers agree that pupils must know how to use the computation skills they have acquired and that story problems provide an opportunity to use those skills in a realistic way.

Most elementary teachers also agree that it is one thing to teach children to develop computation skills and quite another to teach the skills needed in solving story problems. Some teachers believe that the reading levels of math texts are beyond those of their pupils' reading texts. In a comparison study we found that this was not necessarily the case. When matched by grade level—readers and math texts—some children actually read better from certain math texts than from their assigned readers.

With that information we designed an investigation to identify which elements of story problems *were* most troublesome. Our first step was to study the story-problem formats from three commercial arithmetic texts. We then constructed several problems for a number of format types.

Our plan was first to offer pupils problems of a very simple type, then to present problems that included more format variation. The problems were changed from one class to the next by either adding one more element or changing one feature of each problem. Most of the classes of problems represented a specific format found in commercial arithmetic books. Using such a plan, advancing pupils from one class of problems to the next, we planned to detect which elements were most troublesome.

Before the pupils were given the story problems, we tested them to be certain they knew the 32 words used in the first class and could compute the facts used in those problems. Once this was determined, we proceeded with the study, using problems similar to the following: "John had 2 apples. Tom gave him 4 apples. How many apples did John have then?" All problems used the same proper nouns, only the noun *apples,* and were made up of three sentences.

Rather than describe the other classes of problems, I shall note some of the format modifications. In one class we added a lead sentence that was not necessary for solving the problems: "John liked apples." In another class we put in a sentence that had misleading information. If the problem dealt with apples, some information about another category, plus an irrelevent numeral, was included.

In some classes a variety of nouns were used. Initially only the noun *apples* was used. Later, the proper nouns were expanded. Initially, only John and Tom were used. In some problems the numerals were presented in two different ways (David had *four* burros. He was given 2 burros). In another class, blanks were included. Ordinarily they had not been used.

The thirteenth class was a potpourri. Problems from all the preceding classes were presented on the same sheets. When a student had reached criterion for all 13 classes, he was assigned (over a period of days) 85 problems taken verbatim from three elementary arithmetic books. These problems were mixed both in terms of format and process. One problem that contained four sentences and required addition was followed by another problem that required subtraction and included irrelevant information.

Each day the pupils were given three sheets of problems from a class: one addition, one subtraction, and one combination addition-subtraction. There were five problems on each page, and several sheets were made for each format. The pupils responded to different problems from day to day. When these problems were presented to the pupils, they initially received no feedback. This baseline ran for six days. If at the end of that time their scores were perfect for three consecutive days on all three sheets, they were advanced to the next class of problems. If, however, their last three scores were not perfect, a teaching technique was arranged. Following the completion of an assignment, the pupil was required to read aloud each incorrectly solved problem. Two other teaching techniques were devised and successively used if the first technique proved ineffective.

This strategy of moving from one class to another only when three successive 100 percent days were noted on all sheets was adhered to throughout the study. Reliability checks were obtained as the students performed each class of problems.

Our children had little difficulty advancing through the 13 classes. Correct rate and accuracy scores were lowest for most of the pupils when they began the class with the misleading information. Furthermore, most pupils had difficulty with problems which included an irrelevant lead sentence, a blank, and numerals presented in two ways. However, when the pupils were required to respond to the mixture of problems on class 13 and the 85 problems from the math texts, they committed very few errors.

Throughout this study about 40 percent of the errors were operational (adding rather than subtracting) and 40 percent computational (e.g., $4 + 3 = 8$). More errors were made on the combination sheets than on those where only addition or subtraction were required.

When the first instructional technique was required, it was generally effective. There were few instances when the other two techniques were used.

In order to respond with consistent accuracy to the story problems in commercial texts, the pupil must develop several skills. Certainly he must have the requisite computation and word-calling behaviors. Beyond those skills, he must be prepared to write his answer following or sometimes within the problem, to discriminate between necessary and irrelevant data, to classify and group nouns, and finally to make dozens of discriminations between various cues and foils from one problem to the next.

Our project was successful. After the pupils had responded correctly to our 13 classes of contrived problems, they were quite able to solve the multidifferential problems from the commercial texts.

To the Teacher   One important feature of this study was the necessity to design materials. The story problems in all the commercial books we investigated varied considerably. Furthermore, most books contained few story problems. If teachers want to teach story problems they should first identify the types of problems and then generate several problems of each type.

This study represented one strategy for teaching story problems, that of assisting pupils in developing competencies with first one specific type of problem, then another. When pupils were able to compute problems of one type at a time, they were assigned problems of all classes. This instructional strategy could apply to subjects other than story problems, that is, teaching one class of problems at a time, then teaching pupils to solve problems of many types together. In spelling, for example, words that contained one phonic element could be taught, then other types. Finally, words of many classes could be simultaneously presented.

By contrast, another teaching strategy is to present problems or items of several classes at the same time. If the pupil does not discriminate between types, certain types may be removed from the program until he discriminates from among those left. In this study, the pupils could have initially been offered story problems from 12 different classes. If they could not solve problems of certain types—if certain types were confusing—those problems could be pulled out of the program. Problems of other classes could also be removed until a pupil's performance was satisfactory. Once that point was reached, certain problem types could be gradually put back into the program. An instructional technique could then be focused on the newly introduced problems.

Another feature of this study that deserves some consideration is the practice of analyzing errors. In this project errors were categorized as operational or computational. Had some students committed several errors of one type, specific remediation for that form of error would have been arranged. Regardless of the program—reading, penmanship, computation, story problems—the teacher must do more than count correct and incorrect responses. The child's style of responding must be analyzed. If the child's pattern of responding is studied, clues for subsequent remediation may become apparent.

Spelling Research

A Free-time Contingency with Fourth Graders[9]   One study reported in this chapter that was not conducted in the research classroom was carried out in a regular fourth grade. Perhaps the most significant feature of this investigation was the demonstration that leisure time can serve as an effective reinforcer for most of the members of a class.

The study took place in a class of 32 pupils. The project was conducted entirely by the classroom teacher. The teacher administered the spelling program, calculated and graphed the pupils' scores, and managed the contingency system. In order to arrange leisure time as a contingent reinforcer the classroom was modified.

This study used a simple AB design. During the baseline phase of the study, spelling was administered in a very traditional manner. On Monday the new words were introduced and the children read a story containing those words. On Wednesday a trial test was given. On Thursday they completed some workbook exercises pertaining to the words and wrote each word several times. On Friday the final test was given. Each pupil's Friday score was graphed as a correct percentage score.

During the next phase the pupils were presented the new list of words and were given the same type spelling assignments as before. The pupils were simply required to hand in their work. No specific time was scheduled for the completion of these activities as there had been during the first phase. The major difference between this condition and the former was that spelling tests were given four days a week, rather than only one.

During this phase the pupils were through with spelling for the week when they received a 100 percent score. If on Tuesday, the day of the first test, a pupil scored 100 percent and he had handed in the assignments, he was free during the time of the subsequent spelling tests to engage in a number of leisure-time pursuits. He could read a comic book, work on a puzzle, draw pictures. The pupils continued taking the test until results were perfect, or through Friday.

Throughout this phase the teacher recorded the pupil's score as 100 percent if he returned a perfect paper on Tuesday, Wednesday, Thursday, or Friday; otherwise, if the pupil never achieved 100 percent, his Friday score was recorded. Furthermore, the teacher recorded on each pupil's graph a number which corresponded to the day the score was obtained: 1 = Tuesday, 2 = Wednesday.

As a result of being able to earn free time, or to escape from spelling, the performances of most children improved. Twice as many 100 percent papers were recorded in the second condition than during the first. Many children for the first time obtained 100 percent scores in the second phase.

To the Teacher   This project, beyond the fact that a system to arrange free time in the classroom was devised, suggests a strategy for assisting teachers to gather data. When teachers are requested to obtain data and plot graphically the academic performances of pupils, spelling is the best place to begin. In the first place, spelling is probably instructed more systematically and tested more regularly than other academic skills. The procedures for instructing spelling are essentially the same from week to week. Furthermore, spelling performance is generally assessed at least once each week. The second reason for using spelling as the springboard for obtaining records of academic performance is that most teachers already record pupil performance in spelling. Many teachers indicate in their record books the weekly percentage scores of the pupils. It is a simple matter to convert these notations into percentage points on a graph.

Although this project dealt with spelling, arrangements similar to those used here could be incorporated in other subjects. The only requirements would be (1) arrange a definite period each day to offer the subject; (2) establish a criterion for satisfactory performance; (3) designate some place for pupils to spend their leisure time; (4) provide reinforcing events.

This strategy, for example, could be used in arithmetic computation. The pupils could be given a set of problems to master each week. A specific period each day could be scheduled to work on those facts. On several days of the week tests could be given. When the students scored perfectly, they could be relieved of math computation for the week. In this project the pupils took free time at their desks. For them this was a satisfactory arrangement. Other pupils might be more reinforced by leisure time if a special room was set aside for games and free play. Several studies have been conducted using special rooms for free time.

Teachers could improve upon this project in terms of individualization. Throughout this project all pupils were assigned the same spelling words. Although all students improved, some had to work harder than others. A teacher could use the same free time contingency, but individualize the spelling words, arithmetic problems, or other academic assignments.

***b-d* reversals**[10]   A problem with many learning-disabled children, at least insofar as their teachers are concerned, is the reversal dilemma. Teachers frequently express concern about children who transpose letters. The classic example used when discussing reversals is the *b-d* transposition.

Reversals appear in both writing and speaking. In the former a pupil could, when asked to write the word *dog,* reverse the *d* and instead write *bog*. At that point the pupil has a spelling problem.

The subject of this experiment was a ten-year-old boy. A teacher in our class had observed that on occasion, when he was asked to write certain words he reversed some letters. Often he reversed the letters *b* and *d.*

An *ABA* design was adopted in this study. During a baseline period the pupil was asked to spell several three-letter words that ended or began with either *b* or *d*. The data during this phase pointed out the frequency and extent of the difficulty. He rarely substituted *d* for *b,* but often substituted *b* for *d*. Further, he substituted *b* for *d* more in the initial than in the final position.

The intervention was simple and effective. Everyday during the intervention phase the teacher showed the pupil the word *dam*. He was then asked to read the word, then name the first letter, then write the word. Next, he was shown the word *bam* and asked to name the first letter. He was again asked to name the first letter of the word *dam,* then instructed to write the letter *d*. After this teaching period, which lasted about 45 seconds, he was asked to spell the same words used throughout the baseline.

The effects of this procedure were noted immediately. After five days his accuracy for all words was 100 percent. Throughout the next phase no instruction was provided. He continued to discriminate correctly between *b* and *d*.

The next concern was to determine the extent to which this newly acquired *b-d* discrimination generalized. Generalization was assessed from two more word lists. The words on the first generalization list were short words which contained a *b* or *d* in final or initial position. Although these were different words than were used on the first list, the pupil spelled them all correctly. The second generalization list was composed of two-syllable words that included a *b* or *d* in final, medial, or initial position. His ability to discriminate again generalized. He spelled all the words accurately.

The teacher became curious about whether this generalization would be noted in a context other than spelling. Although she hoped such a transfer would occur, she knew it was possible for the child to develop a skill in one situation and be unable to extend the skill to other settings. In order to discover whether the discrimination skill had transferred to another situation, the teacher checked through several of his pensmanship papers for a period of time following the *b-d* study. She found very few instances where one letter was substituted for the other.

To the Teacher This project points out the advantage of pinpointing several related behaviors and measuring each over a period of several days. By so doing, the teacher discovered the student's reversal difficulty was not pervasive. He generally substituted *b* for *d*. A precise and extended diagnosis, like the baseline of this study, is called for to determine the extent and frequency of the problem. It is certainly much easier to design a remedial technique for the overuse of *b*'s, than for more global reversal problems. Of those pupils said to have reversal difficulties, it is possible that more of them occasionally transpose certain symbols than invariably transpose all reversible symbols.

A second point is the extent to which generalization was monitored. By measuring the pupil's ability to discriminate with words and in other situations, the teacher knew that learning had transferred; she knew that the remediation was not situation-specific. His dyslexic ailment was apparently cured. It must be emphasized, however, that although generalization occurred, teaching was directed toward the primary behavior of concern.

A third point of possible interest is another example of simple, yet effective, teaching. When the little *dam* procedure was scheduled (which was prompted by the student's behavior), his performance quickly and significantly improved.

Communication Research

Penmanship: Correct Next Day This project was based on a penmanship study conducted by Hopkins and his colleagues (1971). Their subjects were first and second graders whose mode of writing was either manuscript or cursive. In their investigation the total penmanship period was initially 50 minutes, including work and free time. During certain phases of that study, the pupils could go to a playroom when they had finished their writing assignments. In that investigation, the amount of time scheduled for the total penmanship period was systematically reduced and the amount of time available for play was accordingly lessened. The data indicated that as the time for the total penmanship period was shortened, the rate and accuracy of penmanship improved.

The ideas of allocating a specific amount of time for a period, which included work and free time, and allowing pupils free time when they finished their assignments, appealed to us. Further, we were curious about two other aspects of the Hopkins investigation. In the study, although there was not a systematic effort to deal with errors, the pupils' incorrect rates were generally low. It had been our experience in past penmanship studies that unless some attention was directed to errors, rather high incorrect rates could be expected. The second feature that intrigued us was that their students' manuscript and cursive writing rates were so low. Compared with writing-rate data we had obtained from normal first amd second graders, the pupils in their study were not nearly as proficient.

In an attempt to replicate certain features of the Hopkins research and to provide data regarding our queries about that study, we designed a similar penmanship study. In order to investigate whether systematically attending to errors would influence quality of performance, several conditions were scheduled where an error contingency was alternately arranged, then withdrawn. In response to the aspect of proficiency, we obtained writing-rate data from normal children to use as desired rates for our pupils.

Our study began by requiring the pupils to alternate writing styles for a few days. One day they copied a 500-symbol story in manuscript, the next in cursive. The purpose was to determine which mode would be used for initial instruction.

Once we had made this determination, the investigation began. Each day the pupil was given a sheet on which a 500-symbol extract from a reader of each child's reading level was printed. A symbol included a letter, punctuation mark, or space.

An ABA design was used throughout the study. During the first phase the pupil simply brought his completed paper to the teacher. She checked to see if everything was copied. The pupil was then free to go to a leisure-time area.

The total penmanship period lasted 30 minutes. If the pupils finished their assignments in 15 minutes, they were free to play for 15 minutes. Following the 30-minute period, the pupils participated in a social studies activity.

Each day two data plots were entered, correct and incorrect symbols per minute. Errors included case, punctuation, spelling, and penmanship mistakes. Reliability measures were obtained throughout the study in regard to accuracy of checking responses, general procedures, and timing.

Throughout the baseline period the teacher did not attend to errors. During the next condition, however, a quality-control contingency was put into effect. Now the pupils had to correct their errors from the previous day. If a pupil left out some letters or illegibly formed some letters on Monday, he was required, on Tuesday, to complete the regular Tuesday assignment, *then* correct all his Monday mistakes.

This condition was in effect for about 20 days. During the next phase the quality control was lifted. The arrangements were identical to those of the baseline.

For the majority of the students this correct-the-next-day contingency was very effective. Their incorrect rates dropped considerably. For a few pupils, however, this technique did not result in reduced errors. The error rates for two were reduced when they were required to correct their mistakes *twice* rather than once the next day. For a third boy, whose errors were not initially attenuated, the same procedure was used, but he was required to correct his mistakes the *same* day. This alteration resulted in success.

Figure 4-3 illustrates the performance pattern of one of the boys. The correct-the-next-day contingency was effective for him.

During the prebaseline period, it was decided to begin this boy's training with manuscript writing. During the baseline phase his correct and incorrect

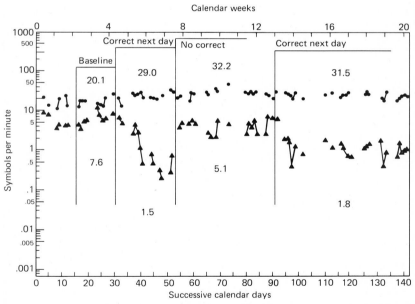

Figure 4-3 Correct and incorrect rates of writing symbols throughout four experimental conditions. For the first six days the pupil alternated between manuscript and cursive writing. Throughout the first condition no quality control was arranged; throughout subsequent phases the correct-the-next-day contingency was arranged, then removed. Correct rates generally improved throughout the study. Incorrect rates were greatly influenced by the contingency; when arranged, the incorrect rates were low, when not arranged, the incorrect rates were high.

rates were fairly close together, indicating very low accuracy. In fact, his errors were increasing from day to day. The data in the next phase were quite different. Immediately, when the error correction rule was imposed, his correct rates increased a bit and his incorrect rates began to plummet. When the error contingency was withdrawn throughout the next phase, the effects were almost as radical and immediate. His incorrect rates suddenly increased. In the next phase, when the error rule was reinstated, his errors once more dropped considerably.

In regard to errors, our project did not totally agree with the Hopkins data. The errors of our pupils were not lessened until a contingency was scheduled. Such an apparent difference in the two studies could have been due to distinctive instructional styles of the teachers. Perhaps Hopkins' teacher had, in the past, attended more to errors than had our teacher, or possibly, the manner in which errors were checked was more stringent in one situation than in the other.

As to writing proficiency, before the study we obtained writing samples from dozens of children in both manuscript and cursive form. We ranked those data and selected as desired rates the seventy-fifth percentile correct-rate score and the twenty-fifth percentile incorrect-rate score. For manuscript, these rates were 22 correct symbols per minute and 0.15 errors per minute. In the figure included here it can be noted that the pupil's correct rates always exceeded the criterion, but incorrect rates were much too high.

In the Hopkins research the rate of the best manuscript writer at any point in the study was far less than the desired rate we had chosen. This discrepancy could be accounted for in part by the fact that they counted only letters, whereas we counted symbols (letters, spaces, and punctuation). A more probable reason for this discrepancy, however, is that the pupils in the Hopkins study copied from a chalkboard, whereas ours copied from a paper at their desks.

To the Teacher   The contingency used here was about the same as that arranged in one of the spelling studies. When work was satisfactorily completed, free time was available. In this study, as in others, errors were categorized so that each pupil's mistakes could be analyzed by type.

Although the same type of intervention was used with all pupils, the exact way the intervention was used depended on the behavior of each child. During the period when the intervention was scheduled, the pupils had to redo all their mistakes. If a pupil had difficulty with a particular letter or letter combination, he had to practice it.

This brings out another feature of individualized teaching that has at least been attended to in this chapter, that is, individualized instruction. Although many people at least pay lip service to individualized teaching, they generally interpret it to mean that individuals are being taught skills at various levels. If instruction is to be truly individualized, it requires that every component of the educational situation be individualized. That would certainly include the program *and* the teaching procedures.

A feature from this study referred to earlier in an arithmetic report was the matter of desired rates. Prior to running our penmanship study we gathered some penmanship data from regular school children. These data served as desired rates. The primary reason for obtaining desired rates from other pupils is for reference purposes. We must have some gauge as to the extent pupils should be taught. In situations where the goal is to normalize children or to send them from a remedial setting to a regular situation when their problems are solved, desired rates should be gathered. If the pupils are expected to survive in a class where the performance levels are currently higher than theirs, they must be instructed to the point where they are equally proficient.

A final point to consider from this study deals with calibration. It will be recalled that in our study we counted symbols written, whereas in the Hopkins study letters written were counted. In many subject-matter areas the teacher can identify the item to be measured along a scale from very broad to very specific. In reading, the teacher could measure the following: books, chapters, pages, paragraphs, lines, words, or phonemes read. Obviously, it is easier to measure books read than phonemes pronounced. The decision, however, as to the amount of precision required should not be based totally on ease. The teacher should generally measure what is being taught. If instruction is focused on specific phonemes, they should be measured rather than the number of books read.

Cursive Writing: Effects of Selected Checking   Second only to reading, penmanship has generated more research, discussion, and controversy than any other academic subject. Perhaps the biggest controversy regarding penmanship instruction focuses on the manuscript-cursive issue. Most schools routinely start all children on manuscript writing, then shift to cursive. Some schools make this shift at the end of the second grade, others as late as the end of the third grade. Convincing research to support the notion that cursive writing is enhanced by manuscript writing, much less that children should print until a certain grade, is to my knowledge, nonexistent.

Another issue relating to the teaching of writing pertains to the sequencing of instruction. Some experts state that instruction should be based on letter families; words that have common characteristics should be introduced and taught together. Others believe certain letters are inherently difficult for pupils to form and specific instruction should be focused on those letters.

This penmanship study stemmed from those two issues. In respect to the manuscript-cursive argument, we simply started all our pupils at the beginning of the year on a cursive program, regardless of their past penmanship experiences. As to the beliefs that instruction should center on certain families or specific letters, we individualized the instruction. Attention was directed to the specific letters each pupil had difficulty with. Another interest we had in conducting this project was to study transfer of training and to determine whether, if teaching is focused on certain letters, other nontaught letters will improve.

A final objective was to establish a cursive writing program that was quick and effective. In the previous year (the preceding project) we were able to change the writing rates, hence the legibility of the pupils, but we believed that program required too much time.

Each day, in this project, the pupils were required to perform several tasks. Two work sheets (lower and upper case) were used to obtain the pupils' responses. On one work sheet they copied, using manuscript letters, from a list of lower-case cursive letters. Next, they spoke the letters, then wrote the alphabet in order, using lower-case cursive letters. On the same work sheet they wrote 16 lower-case cursive words. The other work sheet was similar. The differences were that the two letter-writing tasks on the second sheet were upper case, and the pupil did not write the 16 words.

The reason the pupils were required to write lower and upper-case manuscript letters and to speak the names of the letters was that many writing experts consider these skills prerequisite to cursive writing. Although data regarding these skills were kept throughout the project, interventions never focused on those skills. We were, however, interested in "backward" generalization. By measuring components of manuscript and cursive writing, and by focusing the interventions on cursive writing, we felt we would obtain data regarding transfer effects.

A multiple baseline design was used. During the baseline period no teaching, feedback, or reinforcement was scheduled for any of the writing behaviors. At the end of this phase each pupil's lower-case cursive errors were analyzed. The five letters that were most often illegible in the baseline were selected as target letters. Throughout the intervention period if a pupil incorrectly formed any of those five letters he had to complete a work sheet devoted to each letter. If letters other than the five were incorrectly formed, he was not required to complete the exercise. The pupil was not told which five were selected.

When a letter was perfectly formed for three consecutive days, it was dropped from the program. When one of the five target letters was passed, a new one was selected. This procedure continued until all letters were passed. A second observer periodically checked the scoring of the papers.

The same intervention, once proficiency had been obtained for lower-case cursive letters, was successfully applied to lower-case cursive words, then upper-case cursive letters.

After the baseline period it took pupils an average of 12 days to reach proficiency in lower-case cursive letters. Most students reached criterion on lower-case words and upper-case cursive letters in about the same time.

This study indicates that irrespective of the pupils' penmanship backgrounds, they can be taught to be competent cursive writers. As to the advantages of initially teaching certain difficult words or families, those beliefs are perhaps unfounded. At least in this study when instruction was focused on words that were particularly troublesome for students, the results were positive. As to there being particular letters that are difficult for all children, we found that, to the contrary, each pupil's hard and easy words were unique.

Regarding transfer of training, several instances were noted. As some children were taught to write certain letters, those letters and other nontaught letters improved. In some instances the writing of lower-case words and upper-case cursive letters improved when teaching was keyed on lower-case letters. Finally, in some instances transfer across type of writing was indicated. As some pupils were taught to write cursively, their manuscript writing improved.

As to our final objective, to design a cursive writing program that was quick and effective, evidence supports the latter characteristic. To substantiate the former qualification, only five hours of instruction was generally required for a pupil to complete the program.

To the Teacher   The teaching procedure in this study, like the technique in the preceding study, was individualized. The students practiced only on items that were troublesome for them. In this study they rehearsed letters, whereas in the preceding study they practiced words.

Another feature of the intervention—its intermittency—should be pointed out. During the intervention phase in this study, the pupil had to practice on only five letters which were selected by the teacher. If the pupil missed one of those five letters, he had to write that letter several times. If he erred on other letters, he did not have to practice them. The pupils' penmanship throughout this project was generally good. They did not become sloppy on nonselected letters. Apparently this was due to the fact they did not know which letter, if improperly formed, would result in extra practice.

Intermittent checking could be done in another way. For example, if a teacher, for some reason, does not have time to check all the pupils' papers each day, he or she may check all of them some days or some of them all days. If the teacher's primary aim is to maintain proficiency, such intermittent evaluations could be effective and economical.

Creative Writing   In conceptualizing this research, the word "creative" was used in a most liberal manner. To us, creative writing was any writing by an individual that was unique for him. We were not trying to develop writers who expressed strange, bizarre, or fantastic thought. Rather, our goal, in this research and other similar attempts, was to encourage youngsters to express themselves in a way comprehensible to themselves and to others.

A further long-range objective of our writing efforts has been to conceive of writing as an ideational mediator as well as a communicative device. When people write about something, particularly when they describe what they have done and why, their thinking about that activity is influenced. Often one finds, with the effort of putting thoughts into words, that the logic of the argument is less defensible than it had at first seemed. When a person writes, he or she is forced to use words that precisely convey meaning, to arrange sentences so that their line of thought sequentially unfolds, and to give emphasis to the more important portions of the argument. We have conceived of writing as more than a method of communication.

An initial problem in conducting creative-writing research is to decide which elements of the process should be measured. In a recent study dealing with composition (Brigham, Graubard, and Stans, 1972), the authors measured the number of words, number of different words, and the number of new words. A panel of judges also evaluated the content of the stories on a five-point scale.

In making our selection of components to measure, we wanted to measure enough elements so that both the content and the mechanics of writing would be described. At the same time, we did not want to be overwhelmed with unmanageable data. We selected six elements to be measured daily. Our primary measure was *word frequency*. Although such a measure reveals nothing about the quality of the writing, it does provide a quantitative index. We also measured the frequency with which punctuation and capitalization were used correctly and incorrectly. These were the basic measures of mechanics. In addition, we kept data on the average length of sentences and the number of different words used each session. These latter two measures furnished, to some extent, an index of complexity if not content. The final measure was a creative writing scale developed by Winnifred Taylor (1965).

The pupils wrote for 10 minutes each day. Three different settings were used. On two days the stimulus was "story starters." A portion of a story was read to the pupils and they supplied the ending. Twice a week, story titles were presented. On one day, generally Friday, the youngsters were free to write about a topic of their choice.

In general, it is not advisable in a daily measurement project to change the setting so often. In this case we felt justified in doing so. When we kept the setting more consistent in previous writing studies, our pupils became very bored; their writing was anything but creative. In another effort to sustain interest throughout the project, the boys were allowed to read their stories to their classmates after the period. Most of the time they took advantage of this option.

An AB design was used in this study. Throughout the baseline, no teaching, feedback, or reinforcement was scheduled. During the next phase, two types of feedback were provided. For one group the feedback centered on mechanics; for the other, feedback pertained to content. For each group, six statements were given to the pupils after the teacher had scored their papers. Three of the statements were positive and three were negative. With the mechanics group, the teacher pointed out three places where they correctly used punctuation or capitalization and called to their attention three places that could be improved. With the content group three positive and three negative statements were offered relating to style, syntax, and description.

Following this condition of partial feedback, a "total" feedback phase was instituted. At this time the pupils were given feedback on several details pertaining to either content or mechanics.

Periodic reliability measures were obtained throughout the various phases of this project. These measures were in regard to the scoring of the several writing behaviors, timing, and general procedures.

Following are some general results from this research. Comparisons were made between the baseline condition and the combination of the feedback conditions. Regarding the effect of feedback on mechanics, we found that although both groups improved in their use of punctuation and capitals, the group where feedback was directed to mechanics improved more. As to the effects of feedback on content, both groups showed about the same amount of improvement. The word-per-minute rates of the pupils remained about the same throughout the study. In reference to average sentence length and the use of different words, the frequencies of these elements increased for most pupils irrespective of the focus of the intervention.

When the degrees of feedback were compared—partial versus total—the differences were mixed. For some pupils certain aspects of writing improved more during one condition, and for some pupils other aspects improved more during the other condition.

Of some interest was the fact that mechanics was influenced more by feedback than content. This perhaps has to do with the fact that content is more difficult to define than mechanics, hence is more difficult to evaluate. Finally, in respect to feedback for mechanics, some creative-writing experts have warned about this practice. They have suggested that if mechanics are heavily attended to, creativity will be inhibited. The contrary was the case in this study. Feedback on mechanics positively influenced mechanics *and* content.

To the Teacher   This project illustrates, along with several others, the necessity for obtaining multiple behaviors in order to explain the development of a complex skill. As suggested in this report, enough behaviors should be selected for daily measurement to provide an adequate picture of the developing skill. One consideration in selecting those behaviors has to do with calibration. Some discussion was provided on this topic earlier and suggested that teachers measure behaviors that are being taught. Another consideration, insofar as selecting behaviors to measure, is to be certain that *important* behaviors are being measured, not merely behaviors that are *easy* to measure. The teacher must always keep in mind that measurement of student behaviors is not an end in itself. Measurement merely allows the teacher to determine whether she is teaching what she intended to teach. The skills the pupils develop are of ultimate importance.

Another point brought out in this project is that often, when teachers desire to assist pupils to acquire certain tasks, several individually derived teaching procedures are necessary. In this project, a feedback technique helped the pupils reach competency, but they certainly did not totally master the fine art of writing, not even in mechanical usage. Teachers, even though they may have found a successful teaching technique which helps the pupil make progress, must continually monitor their efforts and file away techniques to be used in the future. A creative teacher must always be on the lookout for individually designed teaching techniques and must amass a huge repertory of potential interventions.

Instructions Were Used to Increase Verbal Behaviors[11]   The pupil in this study was a nine-year-old boy. His speech was very difficult to understand. When a speech therapist attempted to pinpoint his problems, he was unsuccessful. The boy did not consistently misarticulate any sounds and he did not stutter. At times his voice was husky and his speech very rapid, but neither poor quality nor excessive rate appeared to be persistent characteristics. He did use "ghettoese" speech at times and occasionally resorted to current adolescent jargon and even used words and phrases of his own invention. Since we could not pinpoint specific verbal behaviors, yet believed we should improve his speaking, we decided initially to focus on sheer word output.

This study used a pre-posttest and a multiple baseline design. Pre- and posttests were administered before and after several daily measures were obtained. Throughout the period of daily measurement a multiple baseline design was used.

Before the daily measurements began, the boy was asked to describe three pictures from a Peabody Language Development Kit. His descriptions of these pictures began with the phrase, "This is." We, therefore, decided to measure, throughout daily sessions, the ratio of different sentence beginnings as well as the average number of words per response.

Throughout the investigation the daily sessions lasted ten minutes. Picture cards were presented to the pupil one at a time. During the baseline phase the pupil was instructed to tell about each card. He could respond to each card as long as he wished. The data in this condition indicated his average number of words per response was four, and his ratio of different sentence beginnings was low. If a picture of a cup was shown, his response was, "This is a cup."

Based on these data our decision, during the next phase, was to try to alter the ratio of sentence beginnings. Before each session in this phase, the boy was told to use different ways to begin sentences. He immediately complied. Throughout that phase his beginnings were gratifyingly varied. Meanwhile, in this phase his average response length was only slightly influenced. Most of his responses were four to six words.

Therefore, during the third condition, the pupil was still instructed to vary his sentence beginnings, but, in addition, to use more words. He again complied. The data revealed that his average response length doubled, and his ratio of different sentence beginnings remained high.

Following this condition a posttest was scheduled. The pupil was required to describe the same three pictures used in the pretest and three others he had never seen. During the posttest, on both sets of cards, he used over three times as many words as he had during the pretest. Thus, not only did instructions influence his verbal output throughout the daily sessions, this characteristic generalized also to a different situation.

During the final phase of the study, following conditions where the pupil had been successively instructed to vary sentence beginnings and to use more words, no instructions were given. Throughout these sessions the examiner simply showed the pupil a series of cards. The data from this phase were extremely variable. His beginning ratio was high one day, then low the next. His performance in regard to frequency of words was just as inconsistent. Since he had previously been responsive to instructions, it was now as though he was exploring, trying to determine what the examiner wanted him to do.

To the Teacher   In schools and clinics many and varied instructions are used in efforts to teach children. These instructions are intended to serve many functions. They are used to inform pupils *which* response to make. Pupils are requested to walk, run, sing, write. Instructions are employed to tell pupils *how* to respond. They are asked to walk more softly, run faster, sing louder, write more neatly. Furthermore, instructions are used to inform students *when* to respond. They are told to perform now, in five minutes, when the bell rings, and tomorrow.

Sometimes these instructions are effective, sometimes not. Many children, like the pupil in this study, would do what was expected of them if they just knew what it was. When instructions are used, they may not be precisely stated or consistently given. Some children have been instructed to "do better work," to "think before they act," to "improve their performance." Such directives may only confuse children. Their efforts, following such instructions, may be erratic. At other times instructions are clearly stated, but not consistently administered. In a writing session, for example, perhaps one day the teacher requests more words, the next day neater writing, then more imaginative content, then "watch the capitalization," or "be careful of the punctuation." Although some children can cope with such a barrage of instructions, others flounder.

Studies such as this which show that certain behaviors can be influenced by carefully given instructions, should be encouraging to teachers who are trying to influence the behaviors of children. It would appear that if the student is capable of performing the requested skill, the first attempt to stimulate that behavior should be a clearly stated instruction. Furthermore, if that behavior is desired over a period of time, the same instruction(s) should be given.

Obviously, other teaching techniques should be used with the nonmotivated student, the one who *can* but will not perform the requested task. One recommended technique is to couple instructions with reinforcement contingencies; ask for the behavior and pay off when it occurs. This technique was used in an arithmetic project described earlier.

Instructions should also be coupled with or supplanted by other teaching techniques if the desired behavior is not in the pupil's repertory. If, for example, the pupil was requested to say the sound of c or add the digits $2 + 2 = [\ ]$ and had never done so, instructing him to perform these tasks might be futile. Some other form of prompting those behaviors, such as modeling, would of course be recommended.

A final point to be brought out from this study refers to pinpointing. The first task of the teacher setting out to change some behavior is to pinpoint the behavior to be altered. Next, that behavior should be measured and, if necessary, an intervention arranged to alter the behavior. Measurement should continue in order to determine whether the pinpointed behavior is altered.

Sometimes it is not apparent which precise behavior should be changed. Although the teacher knows something is not quite right, he or she may be unable to put a finger on the problem. Sometimes, in cases like this, the teacher will consider the matter a long time and lament the fact he or she cannot isolate the important behavior. No attempt will be made to change the behavior. I believe a more productive strategy is to study the situation and attempt to isolate the behavior of concern. Then, if the problem is not obvious, something should be changed in an attempt to improve the situation. When such a strategy is followed, the general behavior could be improved or the "real" behavior of concern could emerge. Such an approach was taken in this project. Although the teacher evaluated the boy's speaking as poor, the specific speech element that was inadequate and needed correction was not obvious. Rather than prolong the search for the key behavior, the teacher changed two aspects of the boy's speech that could be pinpointed. Once those behaviors were changed, the teacher reevaluated the boy's speech and decided it had, in fact, improved.

Pupil Management Research

Pupil Selects either Math or Reading[12]   This study was designed to determine the effects of selecting either reading or mathematics on performance rates in those two activities. The project was conducted with two boys, one eight years old, the other twelve.

The first pupil was permitted to select whether to work on mathematics or reading for a twenty-minute session each day. The mathematics materials were from Suppes Book 2*A*, and Book 7 of the Sullivan materials was used for reading.

Following this period of pupil selection, two teacher-selected periods were scheduled. During the first such period, the pupil was required to continue for forty minutes in the academic area he had chosen during the pupil-selected period. In the third period, which lasted for sixty minutes, the alternate academic material was scheduled.

The sequence of periods for the second pupil differed. In the first period, one of teacher selection, he was alternately programmed either mathematics or reading for thirty minutes each day. Mathematics was supplied from Suppes Book 3*B* and reading from the Sullivan Books 19 and 20.

In the second period, which also lasted thirty minutes, he was allowed to select either reading or mathematics. Finally, for the thirty minutes of Period 3, the boy was assigned the academic material alternate to that presented in Period 1.

Three calculations were obtained each day, one each for mathematics and reading when the teacher selected the program, and one from the pupil-selected period. The results for the first pupil revealed that on 24 of 26 days, his performance rate was greater when *he* selected the subject than his rate on the same program when it was selected by the teacher. The performance of the second boy was similar, in that during 17 of 25 sessions his correct rate was greater when he selected than on the same material when the teacher selected.

For these two boys it appeared that self-selection was a motivating variable. Being allowed to select, even between two relatively low-strength tasks (mathematics and reading), was for them a reinforcing event.

To the Teacher   We have conducted a number of pupil-management projects during the past few years that have focused on various management components. In some, the pupils have graphed their own data, in others, pupils have specified their own performance objectives and designed their own daily schedules. Projects have been conducted wherein pupils timed their performance and counted and corrected their responses. In a recent project a pupil selected his own instructional technique. In the project that follows, a young man designed his own contingency system.

Invariably, these projects have shown that pupils are motivated when they are given a piece of the action. This motivation is indicated by the fact that during those conditions under which they are partially responsible for their behavior, their performances are generally better than when the teacher manages the entire situation.

Pupil-Specified Contingencies in Academic Areas[13] This experiment was concerned with the comparative effects of teacher-or-pupil–specified contingencies. The pupil in this experiment was a twelve-year-old boy. The investigation consisted of three separate studies—two that manipulated the contingency manager and one that manipulated magnitude of reinforcement. Each study used an ABA design. Throughout these studies the boy received points for academic responses. In reading he was granted two points for each correctly read page. That ratio was 1:2. The ratios in the other academic areas varied. Points were redeemable for minutes of free time.

During Study 1, baseline data relevant to the pupil's academic response rates were obtained for nine days. Each day a response rate figure was calculated for the boy's performance in all his subject-matter areas. Throughout this period no attempt was made to explain to the student the response-per-point ratio in each academic area.

Following this baseline period, the next phase of the study was instituted to instruct the pupil about the relationship between correct answers and contingent points. Each day, in this condition, the teacher verbally explained the contingencies and placed a written copy on the boy's desk. The contract was composed of nine agreements, each of which had a response-per-point ratio. For example, the pupil was granted two points for each page read and one point for 10 correctly answered problems. As he completed each academic assignment, he was shown how many responses had been made and was asked to calculate how many points he had earned.

In the next condition, the copy of the response-per-point requirements was removed from the pupil's desk. He was now asked to specify his own payment for each of the nine areas. These new specifications were copied on a card and attached to his desk. Finally, in the last phase, the teacher-imposed contingencies were again in effect.

During the next quarter, Study 2 began. Procedures for this investigation were exactly like those in Study 1. Teacher contingencies were explained, written out, and attached to the student's desk in Phases 1 and 3, but during Phase 2 the pupil's contingencies were in effect. Figure 4-4 illustrates the data from Study 2.

Following this replication study, Study 3 was conducted. Since during Study

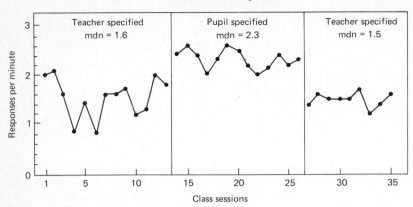

Figure 4-4 Response rates throughout the three conditions of Study 2 (Experiment II). These data indicate the pupil's rate was higher during the condition that he specified the contingencies than when specified by the teacher.

2 the pupil had altered all the teacher-imposed requirements to grant himself more points per response, it was necessary to determine whether being able to specify his own contingencies had effected the academic increase or whether this gain was due to the increased payoff. Study 3, therefore, consisted of three phases: (1) the teacher specified the response-per-point requirements she had placed in effect throughout Studies 1 and 2; (2) the teacher specified the requirements that the *pupil* had instituted during Study 2; and (3) the teacher again specified her original requirements. The only difference between Studies 2 and 3 was that in Study 3 the teacher imposed the contingency requirements throughout, whereas in Study 2 the pupil set his own contingencies during Phase 2.

The data from these experiments indicated that, for this boy, self-specified contingencies were associated with increased academic response rate. This was evidenced in Studies 1 and 2 since during the periods when the pupil specified the contingencies his median performance rate was higher than during the periods when the teacher imposed the contingencies. In addition, the data from Study 3 revealed that the response rate was due to the contingency manager and not to reinforcement magnitude since his rates were about the same across all phases.

To the Teacher   Teachers should consider training their pupils to manage certain of their own affairs. One reason was mentioned in the preceding project. That is, pupils are often motivated when allowed to assume certain responsibilities for their own development. Another reason for teaching pupils to manage certain of their behaviors is that they can assist their teachers. In some classrooms children have been taught to calculate the time they spend on certain programs, to total their correct and incorrect answers, chart their rates, and evaluate their own performances.

Another reason for developing pupil-management skills relates to the academic curriculum. When children are taught to correct, count, chart, and evaluate their own performance, they are learning in functional ways to add, divide, tell time, and compare. The amount of pupil involvement and the extent to which this involvement is incorporated into the math and science curriculum is dictated only by the ingenuity of the teacher.

The primary reason for teaching pupil-management behaviors is that by doing so, pupils could emerge from schools as independent, productive, and creative citizens. To train such students should be one of the primary objectives of education.

EPILOGUE

Curriculum research, particularly when Applied Behavior Analysis procedures are used, is exciting. It is personally reinforcing to identify important behaviors, arrange various techniques and procedures in efforts to develop those behaviors, then be informed daily about the function of those variables.

That Applied Behavior Analysis procedures are suitable for carrying out curriculum research has been demonstrated, not only by the varied projects reported here, but by several researchers throughout the country. The state of the art of Applied Behavior Analysis procedures and curriculum probably corresponds to the degree of sophistication existing ten years ago when behavior modification pioneers were adapting operant techniques to alter talk-outs and out-of-seats in classrooms.

In the basic subject-matter areas many more investigations should be conducted. The behaviors measured in the subject areas reported here were the simplest and most fundamental. In reading, for example, projects were included that dealt with phonics behaviors, oral and silent reading, and some types of comprehension. Future research could identify more complex reading behaviors such as paraphrasing stories, integrating material read from several sources, and criticizing stories.

Our measures in arithmetic were similarly fundamental. They were limited to various types of computation and story problems. A great deal of work remains to be done in the latter area. Research should also focus on other aspects of mathematics such as time telling, measuring, sets, and unions.

In spelling, future researchers need to focus on the matter of sequencing, i.e., which words or letter combinations should be taught before others. Spelling researchers also need to identify which teaching techniques seem to be most useful for certain types of words. Our work in typing is but a beginning. In that research we followed a commercial book. Perhaps by using Applied Behavior Analysis techniques, researchers will be able to identify a better sequence of tasks and more effective teaching procedures.

In penmanship some of the basic issues, including the development of manuscript before cursive writing, remain to be resolved. Applied behavior analysts should focus on such issues. Although the penmanship questions have not been answered, there are other curricular questions of far more importance.

Creative writing offers a wealth of possibilities for the innovative Applied

Behavior Analysis researcher. Curriculum researchers are perhaps the farthest away from identifying the important behaviors of writing and the techniques that will develop those behaviors than in any other area.

Not only does a fair amount of research need to be done by the applied behavior analyst in the basic skills just described, but other, perhaps more complex, subjects must be investigated. There is little, if any, research of the Applied Behavior Analysis variety in such areas as social studies, science, art, music, history, geography.

Whose obligation is it to conduct this research? I believe the primary responsibility rests with research facilities such as ours. Teachers can ill afford to spend time researching the effects of various instructional techniques or identifying behaviors that are measurable. They are in the business of developing behaviors. It is the researcher's responsibility to investigate current curricular practices in schools. The researcher is also responsible for suggesting curricular innovations based on his investigations.

Further, it is the researcher's responsibility to present his findings so teachers can incorporate them in their daily routines. Throughout this chapter I have attempted to present research so certain elements could be used by teachers. The approach was to synthesize several projects and follow each with specific suggestions about which aspects could be assimilated.

Finally, once the curriculum researcher has identified important areas for investigation and clearly presented his findings, it is up to the teacher to blend those findings with basic technology. As I mentioned before, the creative teacher is one capable of extracting various elements from research projects and modifying others so they are functional in her situation.

Teachers will develop in proportion to the extent they can generalize. Some third-grade teachers are willing to learn from only other third-grade situations. To them, research or clinical evidence from other situations is not relevant because of the different setting, type of subject, behavior measured, or remediation technique. These teachers deny themselves many learning opportunities.

The teacher most capable of growth can extrapolate from many situations, some quite different from her own. It is my hope that teachers can generalize from the studies in this chapter, even though most of the research was conducted in a laboratory setting with learning-disabled children.

Many teachers of mildly handicapped, even normal, children should be able to incorporate certain of the suggestions from this chapter regarding the arrangement of materials, designing of materials, diagnosis, error analysis, selection of teaching techniques. Several of the more general notions, for example, those in reference to various reinforcement arrangements, should be applicable to a wide range of individuals.

The reason for the wide extrapolation potential of the research from this chapter is that Applied Behavior Analysis techniques were used. When this approach is used, explicit behaviors are dealt with in a straightforward manner. Generalization in this context, therefore, pertains to identifiable environmental relationships. For instance, a teacher of neurologically impaired children identified a boy whose penmanship skills were inconsistent. One day his writing was beautiful, the next terrible, the next fair, and so on. Following a baseline period the teacher arranged a withdraw-of-positive-reinforcement procedure, similar to the one used in a math project reported here. For each incorrectly formed letter, the boy lost thirty seconds of shop time. Although there were many procedural differences between the penmanship and math project (sex, type of pupil, subject area, reinforcer), the teacher generalized the important environmental relationship from the math project to the penmanship situation. Contingent on errors, reinforcement was withdrawn, and his writing behavior stabilized.

Thus, researchers and teachers are granted two tremendous advantages when Applied Behavior Analysis techniques are used. First, in response to educational researchers, when these techniques are used almost all the features of educational curriculum can be studied. Second, in response to teachers, when the concept of generalization is derived from the Applied Behavior Analysis approach, teachers are provided with infinite opportunities for developing their instructional skills.

DISCUSSION TOPICS
Applied Behavior Analysis Techniques and Curriculum Research

Objective This chapter describes the reciprocal roles of the researcher and the teacher—particularly in terms of the management and operation requisite in a basic curriculum.

Exercises

1 Throughout this chapter, the author recommends that "simple" teaching techniques should be used. Why was this practice recommended and what are some simple techniques?

2 As you remember, from Chapter 1, Ronny Rightson was given certain tests. We also concluded that these scores, although they remain an integral part of his school dossier, were of little value in treating the problem Ms. Spring described. If several popular achievement tests had been administered to Ronny, what would Lovitt have to say about such scores as aids to prescription for Ronny?

3 Discuss the various ways reinforcement contingencies might be used to influence Ronny Rightson's performance.

4 Applied Behavior Analysis in the classroom requires, above and beyond all other factors, *direct and daily* measurement. Discuss what such measurement would mean to Ms. Spring in terms of the following three uses: (*a.*) as a communications tool (to the school, the school system, and the parents—as well as *to Ronny*); (*b.*) as a means of evaluating her instructional competency; (*c.*) as a basis for a precise and ongoing instructional (and management) program for Ronny.

NOTES

1 Lovitt, T. C., & Hurlbut, M. Using behavioral analysis techniques to assess the relationship between phonics instruction and oral reading. *Journal of Special Education, 1974, 8,* 57–72.

2 Eaton, M., & Lovitt, T. C. Achievement tests vs. direct and daily measurement. In G. Semb (Ed.), *Behavior analysis & education–1972.* Lawrence, Kansas: University of Kansas Press, 1972. Pp. 78–87.

3 Lovitt, T. C., Eaton, M. Kirkwood, M. E., & Pelander, J. Effects of various reinforcement contingencies on oral reading rate. In E. A. Ramp and B. L. Hopkins (Eds.), *A new direction for education: Behavior analysis.* Lawrence, Kansas: University of Kansas Press, 1971. Pp. 54–71.

4 Eaton, M. Applied behavior analysis of certain reading skills of seven boys with learning disabilities. Unpublished doctoral dissertation, University of Washington, 1972.

5 Lovitt, T. C., & Curtiss, K. A. Effects of manipulating an antecedent event on mathematics response rate. *Journal of Applied Behavior Analysis, 1968, 1,* 329–333.

6 Smith, D. D., & Lovitt, T. C. The use of modeling techniques to influence the acquisition of computational arithmetic skills in learning disabled children. In E. Ramp and G. Semb (Eds.), *Behavior analysis: Areas of research and application.* Englewood Cliffs, N.J.: Prentice-Hall, 1975. Pp. 283–308.

7 Smith, D. D. The influence of instructions, feedback and reinforcement contingencies on children's abilities to acquire and become proficient at computational arithmetic skills. Unpublished doctoral dissertation, University of Washington, 1973.

8 Smith, D. D., Lovitt, T. C., & Kidder, J. D. Using reinforcement contingencies and teaching aids to teach subtraction skills to learning disabled pupils. In G. Semb (Ed.), *Behavior analysis & education–1972.* Lawrence, Kansas: University of Kansas Press, 1972. Pp. 342–360.

9 Lovitt, T. C., Guppy, T. C., & Blattner, J. E. The use of a free-time contingency with fourth graders to increase spelling accuracy. *Behaviour Research and Therapy, 1969, 7,* 151–156.

10 Smith, D. D., & Lovitt, T. C. The educational diagnosis and remediation of written *b* and *d* reversal problem: A case study. *Journal of Learning Disabilities, 1973, 6,* 356–363.

11 Lovitt, T. C., & Smith, J. O. An analysis of the effects of instructions on an individual's verbal behavior. *Exceptional Children, 1972, 38,* 685–693.

12 Lovitt, T. C. Self-management projects with children with behavioral disabilities. *Journal of Learning Disabilities, 1973, 6,* 138–150.

13 Lovitt, T. C., & Curtiss, K. A. Academic response rate as a function of teacher- and self-imposed contingencies. *Journal of Applied Behavior Analysis, 1969, 2,* 49–53.

Chapter 5

Management Strategies for Teachers and Parents: Responsive Teaching[1]

R. Vance Hall
Juniper Gardens Children's Project, Bureau of Child Research,
University of Kansas
Rodney Copeland
Juniper Gardens Children's Project, Bureau of Child Research,
University of Kansas
Marilyn Clark
Shawnee Mission Unified School District, Shawnee Mission,
Kansas

EDITORS' NOTE

The editors have observed the impact that Vance Hall and his colleagues have had on the classroom practices of hundreds of teachers and administrative and support personnel working in dozens of schools. Their methods are experimentally based, simple, straightforward, and practical. They call their community-based system *Responsive Teaching* (RT).

[1]The preparation of this chapter was supported in part by Research Grant HD 03144 from the National Institute of Child Health and Human Development, Research Grant MH 13296 from the National Institute of Mental Health, and Research Grant OEG-072-0253 from the Bureau of Education for the Handicapped.

Hall credits much of the success of his approach to the training he received and the work he did in the University of Washington Pilot School for the Brain Injured and Retarded (now the Experimental Education Unit of the University of Washington Center for Human Development and Mental Retardation). However, his applications to the practical demands of a community setting began in the classrooms of the Juniper Gardens District in Kansas City, Kansas in 1966.

He first demonstrated to teachers that disruptive events could be reduced and that teachers could use their own contingent responses to accomplish the desired change. These successful classroom demonstrations led to requests from teachers for further instruction in applying behavior analysis techniques. An in-service course was developed for a few teachers. The second offering was greatly expanded, and subsequently hundreds more have taken the course. Three practical workbooks were written for trainees, and a technology for teaching the teachers and other relevant personnel was developed. The term *Responsive Teaching* is used to acknowledge that the content of the courses, the teaching procedures, the trainee projects, and the final training targets were all *responsive* to the special problems and the special children involved.

The adapted nature of the content, the pattern of the teaching, and the effects of the common systems that result from widespread application of Responsive Teaching are all explained in the chapter that follows. However, the effects can only be briefly detailed. The explanations are largely limited to two schools. It should be known, however, that the favorable impact has been extended to a wide radius from the original small beginning in Juniper Gardens. Hall believes that many other communities can initiate similar programs if they utilize competent people who are responsive to the contingent features of teaching.

INTRODUCTION AND BACKGROUND

In 1965 the Juniper Gardens Children's Project was established in the inner-city area of Kansas City, Kansas. This demonstration, training, and research program was designed to develop procedures for remedying the learning and behavior problems of children from depriving environments.

New techniques for dealing with inappropriate behaviors and for increasing academic performances of children in both "regular" and "special" classrooms were soon developed. (See, for example, Hall, Lund, & Jackson, 1968; Hall, Panyan, Rabon, & Broden, 1968; Broden, Hall, Dunlap, & Clark, 1970).

One main research theme of the original Juniper Gardens research concerned inappropriate classroom behavior. Teachers, principals, school psychologists, and counselors of poverty area schools spend a great deal of time dealing with inappropriate and ineffective pupil behavior. Pupils in poverty areas often come to school with a poor foundation for learning academic skills. Because of this, and because many are poorly motivated to achieve, they are likely to fall behind. Many become so educationally retarded that they do not profit by their school experience. They end up in special education classes, drop out, become delinquent, or stay in school without acquiring the skills they need to continue their education or to make them employable.

We were aware of the need to develop procedures to enable teachers to deal more effectively with disruptive and nonachieving pupils. However, when the project staff sought to establish a token reinforcement remedial classroom, we encountered some obstacles. School administrators and the parents of youngsters were reluctant to cooperate. The school district officials had reservations about behavior modification and were concerned about possible exploitation of school staff and children. Parents were wary of the program because it was experimental and there was some distrust because we were a university-related project. Because of these reservations it was necessary to carry out the remedial research after school hours in the basement of a nearby church. Fortunately, the principals of nearby schools were willing to help select candidates for the remedial program and to make achievement records available. This was done without imposing on teachers.

The demonstrated success of the after-school remedial program (Wolf, Giles, & Hall, 1968) in improving academic performance and classroom behavior served as an entré to the schools and allowed us to begin studies in the public school classrooms the following year.

We began working in one third-grade classroom with one teacher who learned to use systematic teacher attention to reduce disruptive behavior.

The scope of our school research subsequently expanded to include classroom groups (e.g., Hall, Panyan, Rabon, & Broden, 1968), the evaluation of systematic reinforcement procedures in the junior and senior high school (Broden, Hall, Dunlap, & Clark, 1970), and the investigation of the roles of principals and school psychologists as modifiers of pupil, teacher, and parent behavior.

While carrying out these investigations, we began working with the people of the Juniper Gardens Community and with members of the school district staffs. As members of the community gained confidence in the project, the reluctance of parents to cooperate and participate disappeared. At the same time, as we carried out applied studies in an increasing number of classrooms and schools, we received more and more opportunities and invitations from teachers, principals, and counselors who wanted to develop and implement procedures for increasing pupil academic performance. Thus, as we developed a technology for motivating poverty area pupils, we also built strong relationships among the project, the schools, and the community.

The teachers and the residents of the community influenced our research emphasis and approach as much as we influenced them. In our early studies, in single classrooms with individual subjects, we, as outside experimenters, sent observers in and suggested procedures teachers could use to change behavior. Then we expanded our research to include entire classroom groups. Principals began to encourage us to enlist beginning teachers who were having problems with whole classes rather than with a few disruptive pupils.

Within a short time, groups of teachers, principals, and counselors were requesting opportunities to learn more about our research methods. These demands led to the development of procedures teachers could use to observe and record behaviors as they taught. Other school staff members were also taught to measure behavior. They became familiar with basic-learning-theory principles and learned how to carry out applied research studies (Hall & Copeland, 1972).

This development has greatly increased our interaction with and impact on the schools both within and outside the Juniper Gardens area. It has also helped move research from the laboratory into the classroom and into the hands of teachers. A large percentage of our school studies have been carried out by teachers, principals, and parents acting as observers and experimenters dealing with problem behaviors with resources available to them in the natural environment (e.g., Hall, Cristler, Cranston, & Tucker, 1970; Hall, Fox, Willard, Goldsmith, Emerson, Owen, Davis, & Porcia, 1971; Hall, Axelrod, Foundopolous, Shellman, Campbell, & Cranston, 1971).

The success of the Juniper Gardens research in classrooms and elsewhere in the community eventually led to requests for instructional classes and to the formulation of additional teaching procedures. As these procedures were planned and implemented we began to refer to them as *Responsive Teaching* (RT).

Two major community developments have been generated from the Responsive Teaching procedures. First, a large number of teachers and other personnel have taken in-service courses for university credit. (See Propagating the RT Model.) Second, the trainees have undertaken major innovations in instructional programs.

These two developments represent related phenomena. As the numbers of trainees from the courses increased within the schools of the community, the impact of the Responsive Teaching design became increasingly apparent. These effects are described in the section on school programs.

FRAMEWORK OF A RESPONSIVE TEACHING COURSE

The Responsive Teaching Model is a training package for efficiently and responsively introducing teachers, counselors, school nurses, psychologists, principals, and other school personnel to an Applied Behavior Analysis approach to educational management. It has proved adaptable also for use in training mental health workers, attendants in institutions, parents, and even children. It is a replicable model which has been successfully implemented not only by its originators but by many others in a variety of settings.

The organization and structure of the RT course is presented here in sufficient detail to enable still others to replicate the course in many instructional forms—short courses, workshops, in-service training for college credit, units, etc. The format as outlined in the following pages is designed as a credit course but has also been adapted and used in the other forms. Although many essential details of instruction are not included, they are referenced so that a complete course manual could be developed from the format and the documentation.

It should be stressed that the RT Model in its present form is the result of the efforts of many persons.[1]

Among the basic elements of the RT course are the following:

1 A format for course sessions which allows the fulfillment of the roles of
   a   Participants
   b   Group leaders
   c   Instructors
2 Course content
   a   Background readings
   b   Practical measurement and recording procedures
   c   Applied behavior-analysis designs
   d   Basic reinforcement principles and procedures
3 Carrying out an applied study
4 Evaluation

Format of Course Sessions

The schedule followed in the Kansas City area has evolved partly from conditions which may not prevail at other locations. The fact that it has been presented in other locations in varying formats, including workshop sessions as outlined above, indicates that sufficient flexibility exists so that it can be adapted to other schedules and formats. The format below is one of a number of possible organization patterns which are effective.

Since the course was first offered through the Extension Services of the University of Kansas, several conditions imposed by Extension Service guidelines helped to shape the class format. These include the following.

1 The course must meet three hours a week for sixteen weeks.
2 There must be a final exam with a grade of 90 to 100% = A; 80 to 89% = B; 70 to 79% = C; 60 to 69% = D; 59% and below equals F.

Another constraint on the course when it was first offered was that most participants were teaching or otherwise employed in the schools. This meant that the course was offered after school hours within the school district.

The course has been presented in several formats, usually as a three-credit class which meets once a week for three hours over the course of a semester (sixteen weeks). An alternative format is a two-credit course presented over a three- to five-day period in intensive workshop sessions. Following the work-

---

[1]Among those who have contributed significantly to its development are Dr. Herbert Rieth, Dr. Rodney Copeland, Dr. Jasper Harris, and Dr. Richard Fox. All are currently or were formerly a part of the school research team of the Juniper Gardens Children's Project. Others who have been involved include Ronald Brown, Donald Lamb, Lowell Alexander, Ace Cossairt, Jeane Crowder, Marilyn Clark, Joe Meyers, Jerry Wyckoff, and the administrators, teachers, and parents in the schools of Kansas City, Kansas, Shawnee Mission, Kansas, Bonner Springs, Kansas, and the Shawnee Heights Unified School Districts.

shop, additional credit is earned when the participants carry out applied studies. Contact with the instructor or a group leader is provided as needed during this time.

In its usual format, the weekly three-hour course is divided into two parts. The first includes the entire class. The second part includes small study discussion groups. During the first hour and a half, lectures (utilizing overhead transparencies), demonstrations, and films are presented to the entire class or workshop group. In some cases these sessions may involve 80 or 90 persons.

After a short break the class is divided into small groups of 10 to 15 participants. These are led by persons who have previously taken the course and who are familiar with the course content. During the first half-hour of each small group session, points covered in the lecture are discussed and a short written quiz is given. The quiz is self-corrected immediately to provide feedback to the participants and the group leader. No individual quiz grades are recorded. During the remaining time the group members present data and discuss measurement problems. Group members as well as the leader offer suggestions regarding solutions to problems.

While the small groups are in session, the instructor is available if questions arise which the group leaders cannot handle.

Role of the Participants

The course should acquaint participants with practical measurement and observation procedures, reinforcement principles, and some of the pertinent behavior modification literature and should prepare them to carry out and write up an applied study. To accomplish this the participants are asked to:

1   Participate in small group discussions following lectures. They also take quizzes each week and report to the group on the progress of their applied studies.
2   Take an examination in week 12 comprised of items similar to those presented in the weekly quizzes. Each must achieve a score of 96% or better or take a final exam during the last session, achieving a score of 90% or better for a grade of A, which counts 40% of the course grade.
3   Hand in seven summaries of articles of outside reading at the end of eight weeks. They must incorporate references to outside readings (at least three) into the write-up of their studies.
4   Hand in a preliminary write-up of an applied project in the tenth class session.
5   Hand in a final project write-up in the last class session (counts 60% of grade).
6   Make a computer abstract of their study. (See Fox, Copeland, Harris, Rieth, & Hall, 1975.)

Students judged most competent and who seem most enthusiastic in carrying out a study and participating in the course become candidates for group leaders in subsequent sessions.

Role of the Group Leaders

From the beginning of the development of the RT course we have recognized the importance of interaction among the participants. It is important, and in keeping with our reinforcement orientation, to provide contact with leaders who answer questions and give feedback.

There were nine participants in the first group to receive instruction. This made it easy for all to follow the progress of each study being carried out in the class and to learn from discussions centering around course presentations, quizzes, and problems encountered in carrying out studies. Each class member obtained whatever assistance was necessary from the instructor. Within one semester, however, the class size increased to 40 members. Sections of 60 to 80 members were soon common.

It became necessary to develop a strategy for handling larger groups efficiently without losing the benefits of continued interaction among participants and close contact with someone knowledgeable in RT procedures. This was accomplished by reorganizing the class to permit interaction in small groups.

The role of the group leader is extremely important. He or she is an extension of the instructor. A good group leader can enhance the course and complement the efforts of the instructor by providing cues (S^D's) to the participants regarding their responses. He must follow those responses with appropriate feedback and reinforcement.

The group leader, who generally receives three hours credit for fulfilling his role, has several responsibilities:

1   Obtain a copy of course lecture notes from the instructor prior to each session and prepare and organize materials.
2   Attend lecture during first half of each course session.
3   Lead discussions, answer questions regarding class lectures, and give in-class written quizzes during small group session during second half of each course session.
4   Monitor data and discussions of studies presented by group members.
5   Carry out at least one reliability check visit for each member in his group.
6   Discuss problems encountered and provide feedback to instructor.
7   Check reports on readings. Help grade exams and projects of group members.
8   Keep records and check lists of progress reports and grades for the group.
9   Give lectures or parts of lectures at the request of the instructor.
10   Check computer abstracts for accuracy.
11   Recommend group members as future group leaders.

In some cases two group leaders may be assigned to each group, especially if groups are large (over 10). Just as the most proficient course participants are selected as group leaders, the most effective group leaders are candidates for continuing in the RT master's or doctoral programs.

Role of the Instructor

After serving as group leaders during two semesters, the group leader may take the major responsibility for teaching a section of the course. To assume the responsibility of the instructor's role, one should have a demonstrated knowledge of Applied Behavior Analysis and its application in school settings and experience as a teacher, psychologist, or other related profession. This is essential if the instructor is to relate to teachers, principals, and other professionals taking the course.

To fulfill his role, the instructor must:

1   Make all necessary arrangements with school district and/or university officials regarding enrollment and place of meeting.
2   Make arrangements for obtaining group leaders.
3   Make arrangements for securing transparency kit, films, texts, and other necessary materials and equipment.
4   Meet with group leaders in preplanning sessions to assign responsibilities and provide group assignments.
5   Provide group leaders with lecture notes and a plan for each session including quizzes, guide sheets for write-ups, and grade sheets.
6   Give or arrange lectures and demonstrations during first half of course sessions.
7   Circulate among groups and meet with individuals to solve problems during second half of each class session.
8   Make reliability checks on grading examinations and feedback on project write-ups and computer abstracts.
9   Arrange to meet with group leaders or participants regarding special problems.
10   Assume responsibility for assigning and recording grades.
11   Select potential future group leaders.
12   Make recommendations for innovative teaching procedures and participate in the development of new course procedures.

As noted above, the instructor must have a background in and an understanding of the theory and principles of behavior. And he must know how to relate these to practical applications to provide appropriate cues (S^D's) to participants as to which responses are appropriate. He must provide feedback and reinforcement for appropriate responses.

His most essential responsibility is to be an expediter who provides an environment which helps group leaders and participants fulfill their roles. The instructor provides positive verbal and written comments throughout the course.

Course Content

The major content covered in the course includes:

1   Background readings of previous research
2   Practical measurement and recording procedures
3   Basic reinforcement principles

Background Reading To provide background on previous research and on acceptable models for reporting their own research, participants are asked to read a number of journal articles.

School and home studies (Hall, 1971*a*) should be included. Other background readings should include the best-known studies in Applied Behavior Analysis (Rieth & Hall, 1974).

Participants were at one time asked to summarize fourteen articles during the course. This requirement was later reduced to seven readings due at midterm. Class members are now encouraged to read articles pertinent to their own particular study and to refer to at least three such articles in the introduction or discussion of their own study report.

In addition to some of the historically significant studies (e.g., Zimmerman & Zimmerman, 1962; Wolf, Risley, & Mees, 1964; Patterson, 1966), studies carried out by previous class members are recommended as background. Acquainting participants with these studies encourages many to pursue their reading further and provides a good background for understanding what has been done in their own areas of interest.

Practical Measurement and Recording Procedures The foundation of research in behavior modification is set on precise observation and measurement of behavior. Beginning in the first session, participants are taught to scientifically define behavior and to begin attempting to record behaviors.

We began teaching behavior management without a text which adequately outlined the basic measurement and recording procedures available to persons working in applied settings. The material was presented through lectures. Lectures were followed by quizzes that gave both the instructor and the participants feedback as to how well the material covered had been learned. We now use a standard text which presents material on measurement and observation (Hall, 1971*a*).

Graphing As soon as participants begin obtaining baseline records of their target behaviors, they record them on conventional graphs or cumulative records. Conventional graphs and cumulative records have a number of advantages:

1 They are more easily understood than complex systems. (For this reason the conventional graph is usually preferred to the cumulative record.)
2 Conventional graphs allow the display of rates as well as percentage levels of behavior.
3 Conventional records more often display behavior in a context familiar to the average person (most persons understand seven episodes of crying per day better than they do 0.28 per hour).
4 Small, but important, changes in rate are more easily displayed on conventional graphs.
5 Graph paper is less expensive.

Data sheets (Figure 5-1) should include entry blanks for the name of the subject, the setting, the author, his position, the definition of the behavior, and the recording procedure used, as well as a scale for recording the level of the behavior along the vertical axis.

The raw data recorded during each observation session is entered just below the point where it will be entered on the graph. Below this are spaces for recording data obtained by a second independent observer during reliability checks.

BASIC REINFORCEMENT PRINCIPLES AND PROCEDURES

Once participants have been introduced to measurement and Applied Behavior Analysis, several sessions deal with reinforcement principles and procedures. Many persons have some previous exposure to reinforcement and most are familiar with some of the basic terms, but few have a firm grasp of what they really mean, and most have not learned to apply these principles systematically in everyday situations. Ensuring that participants know how to select and use reinforcers properly is one of the most critical aspects of this training.

The strategies used in implementing the RT Model are designed not only to teach participants how to use reinforcement principles and procedures as a function of the course content but also by example through the application of the principles in teaching the course.

The application of these principles can be seen along a number of dimensions:

1 Clear-cut S^D's (cues) are provided participants so that it is easy for them to discriminate the responses required to meet course requirements.
   a   At the beginning of the course participants are informed of what will be required for them to successfully fulfill the course requirements.
   b   The content of each session is outlined so that participants know in advance the readings that are necessary and the material to be covered.
   c   In the lecture portion of the class sessions, overhead transparencies are used which outline the important points of the lectures. Thus the participants get visual as well as auditory cues as to the material they are expected to know.
   d   Numerous examples of studies carried out by other persons who have taken the course are made available through (1) graphs presented during lectures via overhead transparencies, (2) required readings of studies reported in the literature and in the text, (3) studies related to the study carried out by class members obtained from those available in the RT computer files.
   e   Guide sheets help shape participants toward carrying out and writing up their studies. Guide sheets are programmed to have participants define a behavior they wish to manage, select and describe an observation and recording procedure, obtain reliability checks, record and graph a baseline record, implement an experimental procedure and carry out a

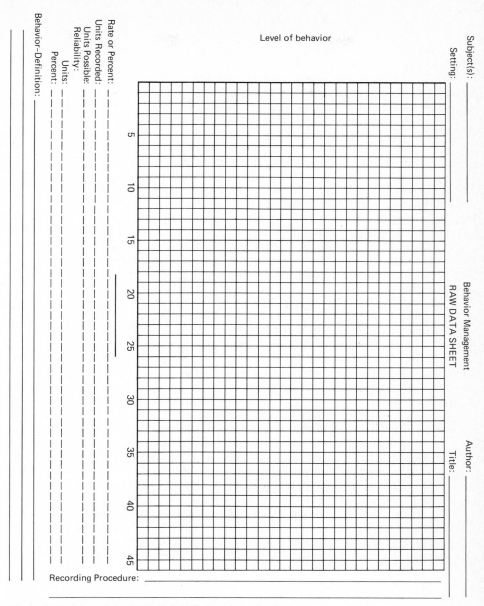

Figure 5-1   *(Copyright 1973, H & H Enterprises, Inc.)*

scientific verification procedure (Applied Behavior Analysis). Model write-ups are also provided as examples to aid participants in reporting their experiments.

2   The opportunity to make frequent responses is incorporated into the teaching model. Participants make frequent responses throughout the course. The texts used have short quizzes over the material covered after each topic is presented as well as exams over the major topics of measurement and research design and social learning theory principles. These give the participants the opportunity to quiz themselves over the material that is read even prior to class lectures. During lectures, opportunities are provided for participants to give examples of applications of principles, to role play situations illustrating the use of various reinforcement procedures, and to suggest solutions to problems. An even greater opportunity to make responses is provided in the small group sessions in which quizzes over the material covered in the lectures are given and participants ask questions, enter into discussion, and report on problems encountered and the progress in carrying out their study. Limiting the groups to no more than 10 or 12 assures ample opportunity for all to participate actively in these sessions.

3   Feedback is provided regarding responses. The answers to quizzes in the text are provided so that the reader may check his answers. The quizzes administered by the group leader following each lecture are self-corrected upon completion, and any misunderstandings are clarified immediately.

It is also the group leader's responsibility to provide feedback to the participants during each session regarding the appropriateness of their efforts to define, observe, and record behavior. They also provide feedback as to the adequacy of the reports on readings, and at least twice they provide feedback as to the adequacy of the write-up of the study carried out. With both the preliminary write-up and the final one, a checklist is filled out as to the adequacy of each section of the write-up from the abstract through the discussion. Group leaders also routinely make their telephone numbers available to participants so that assistance can be provided as needed between class sessions. In addition, they endeavor to make reliability checks whenever feasible in order to provide more meaningful feedback and suggestions than would be possible had they not visited participants in their applied settings.

4   A concerted effort is made to reinforce participants for appropriate responses. During lecture sessions, the presenter attempts to reinforce the asking of questions and participation in discussion through positive comments and by giving direct answers and providing illustrations that are practical and to which participants can relate. If a class member presents a particularly good question or participates in role playing or a demonstration, an attempt is made to comment regarding it after class or a brief note remarking on the contribution is written. Group leaders are also encouraged to make their sessions as reinforcing as possible by providing both verbal and written comments regarding responses made. This is especially important in providing feedback regarding the studies being carried out. It is always a goal for the majority of comments regarding study write-ups to be positive.

Another source of reinforcement is the opportunity for those who meet the criterion of 96% on the first examination to skip the final exam. In some cases almost the entire class has quizzed out of the final.

5   Since the RT Model requires responses from participants, as much reinforcement as possible should be delivered to those making the responses. College or professional credit is desired and needed by most school personnel. That reinforcement should be arranged whenever possible. We have found that the best workshop participants are those who are willing to make a monetary commitment for their participation, even though the only credit for completing the course is a simple diploma or certificate. New techniques for teaching the course are continuously being explored. To expedite this process, an evaluation sheet is filled out by each participant at the end of each course. This feedback is used to modify future presentations. Recommendations by instructors and group leaders are also incorporated.

OTHER BASIC PRINCIPLES AND PROCEDURES

Many other basic principles and procedures are taught in conjunction with Responsive Teaching. These include *generalization, discrimination, chaining, prompting, fading,* and *instructional control.* These procedures are amply described and demonstrated in other chapters of this book.

As participants learn the principles and procedures, they are encouraged to select a technique for modifying the particular target behavior or behaviors they have recorded. They then carry out an Applied Behavior Analysis procedure to demonstrate the functional relationship between the changes brought about and the experimental conditions employed.

CARRYING OUT A STUDY

A major component of the RT course includes studies or experiments by the participants. Participants learn by emitting responses and then receiving differential feedback regarding these responses. In other words, they learn by doing.

Participants learn to incorporate RT procedures into their repertories by using them in practical situations. By following the progress of other projects and seeing them succeed, each person participates vicariously in studies by others.

From the first session of the course, each participant begins employing behavior management procedures. In the regular course this is done over a sixteen-week period. Those in shorter in-service workshops often carry out a study after the workshop ends.

By conducting applied studies, the participants get practice in defining, observing, and recording behaviors; in arranging for and carrying out reliability checks and graphing; in employing reversal, multiple baseline, or changing criterion research strategies; and in writing up and presenting research studies.

Guide sheets distributed to participants help define the target behavior and assist individuals as well as the group leaders and the instructor in monitoring the progress of each study. A preliminary write-up of the study is due at about the ninth session. This is checked over by the group leader and the instructor and returned the following week with feedback about its strength and its deficiencies.

The write-up due on the last class session in its final form includes:

Title:
Author:
Abstract:
Introduction: (cite 3 or more studies)
Subjects and setting:
Behavior measured:
Observation procedures: (reliability)
Experimental procedures and results:
Discussion:

A successful modification of the behaviors chosen is not a requirement for a top grade. Honesty in recording data and checks on reliability of observation are as important as a behavior change.

Participants are encouraged to analyze unsuccessful procedures and to try alternate procedures if their efforts fail. It is as important to discover what does not work (and why) as it is to find out what does work. Thus the interpretation of results in the study discussion section is important in the final grade.

A participant may be unable to complete his study because of circumstances beyond his control (as when a subject suddenly moves to another school). In such cases participants indicate the point at which they could no longer gather data. From that point on they may fabricate the data without penalty. They describe what they would have done in completing the study and what they expected the data to indicate. This is done to reduce the probability that false data will be handed in as legitimate.

The instructor files a copy of each study by the author's name. In addition, each study is abstracted on a computer information form developed by Fox et al. (1975). After the abstracted study is checked for accuracy by the group leader, the study is entered in a master computer file. There are 28 categories of information in the computer file, including among other things, subject, author, setting, behavior measured, observation procedures used, reliability checks, research design, procedures used, results, unusual features, quality of the study, and whether or not fabricated data were used. This makes it possible to retrieve studies relating to particular subject populations, behaviors, and procedures.

RESPONSIVE TEACHING STUDIES

Because carrying out an actual study is so important in learning to use Responsive Teaching, and because the versatility of the model can best be demonstrated by actual examples, the remainder of this chapter will deal mostly with applications of Responsive Teaching in various environments.

There is a major difference between the studies in this chapter and the studies which have been reported in the literature. Generally studies reported in professional journals have been carried out by the skilled researchers who planned them. They have often included complex token systems and extrinsic reinforcers, employed outside observers, or sophisticated equipment for measuring behavior or providing cues to experimenters and subjects.

Responsive Teaching studies carried out in schools, homes, and classrooms, in contrast, are planned and carried out by teachers, parents, principals, counselors, school psychologists, speech therapists, or other staff as they are actively engaged in their regular duties. Because of that fact, it seems logical that other teachers, principals, counselors, parents, etc., will be much more likely to be able to carry out similar procedures than would be the case if the study required outside researchers, observers, or equipment.

RESPONSIVE TEACHING STUDIES CARRIED OUT BY TEACHERS

Since there was no extra manpower or money available for these studies, they were carried out using resources naturally available in classrooms and school settings.

Approximately 60 Responsive Teaching studies have been published in various books and professional journals. In most cases two or more related studies have been published together. Three studies which illustrate the three basic multiple baseline designs are presented in Hall, Cristler, Cranston, and Tucker (1970). Several studies in which teachers modified disputing and talking-out behaviors of students and entire classroom groups were presented in Hall, Fox, Willard, Goldsmith, Emerson, Owen, Davis, and Porcia (1971). A series of studies illustrating the use of systematic punishment procedures in the classroom (Hall, Axlerod, Foundopolous, Shellman, Campbell, & Cranston, 1971) was first published in edited form in *Educational Technology*. Other classroom studies which include a wide range of student populations and experimental procedures can be found in Hall (1971c); Hall, Ayala, Copeland, Cossairt, Freeman, and Harris (1971); Hall and Copeland (1972); and Hall, Cossairt, and Crowder (1973).

A number of RT studies were generated as a result of an international workshop held at the Panamanian Institute of Special Education (Chavez, 1973).

The first study from Hall (1971c) was carried out by Amber Tribble and illustrates how reinforcement in the form of peer approval was used to increase the number of arithmetic problems completed by a third grade boy. It also incorporates a reversal design to show the causal relationship between the reinforcement procedure and the change in behavior.

The second study illustrates the use of a punishment procedure (time out) to decrease tantrum behaviors of an elementary school girl. This study also presents a good example of using a multiple-baseline design to show causality.

Effects of Peer Approval on Completion of Arithmetic Assignments

Subject and Setting   John, a third grader in an elementary public school, was an active and capable participant in group classroom activities; however, he had poor independent work skills. When he was supposed to be working on individual assignments, John engaged in other behavior such as playing with his comb, rolling his pencil up and down his desk, making airplanes, and drawing cars.

Behavior Measured   During arithmetic class, the teacher usually explained and discussed with the students the day's work and had different students work example problems at the board. She subsequently gave pupils an individual work sheet to complete. A daily measure was taken on the percent of the problems John completed on the work sheet in arithmetic.

Procedures and Results

Baseline$_1$ The daily mean of arithmetic problems (Figure 5-2) completed in the 15 baseline sessions was 18%.

Surprise at Home   At the beginning of arithmetic class on the sixteenth day it was explained to John that if he completed 60% of his arithmetic work sheet, he could take a card home and exchange it for a surprise previously arranged with his parents. John responded to the surprise on the first day, but by the fourth day of this condition his percent of work completed was tending to revert back to the baseline level.

Peer Approval and Class Leader$_1$ On the twentieth day of the study the teacher announced a new game. John was designated as engineer, and if he completed his arithmetic work sheet, the whole class with John as leader would line up in train formation and go to the playground where they would get to engage in a special activity. The activities varied, but each day the class would urge John on and clap for him if he got the work sheet done. John's daily percent of assignments completed during this ten-day condition was 100% on all but one of the days, when it was 80%.

Baseline$_2$ For five days the teacher let another child be the engineer and John's mean daily total of the work sheet completed was 21%.

Peer Approval and Class Leader$_2$ John was again allowed to be the class leader of the special activities if he completed his work sheet. He finished his work sheets at a 100% level for the entire five-day period.

Intermittent Reinforcement   In order for the class leader and special activity contingency to affect all members of the class, the teacher began picking the

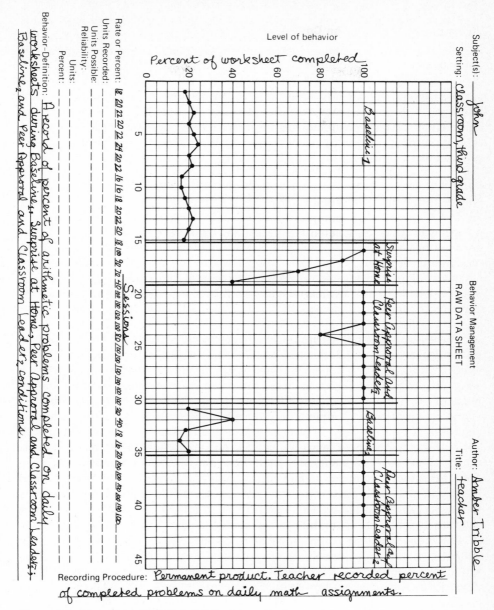

Subject(s): _John_

Setting: _classroom, third grade_

Behavior Management

RAW DATA SHEET

Author: _Amber Tribble_

Title: _teacher_

Level of behavior

Percent of worksheet completed

Baseline 1

Surprise Peer Approval and Classroom Leader 1 at Home

Baseline 2

Peer Approval and Classroom Leader 2

Rate or Percent: 18 20 22 20 22 24 24 22 16 16 18 20 22 20 18 60 70 40 100 100 100 80 100 100 100 100 100 100 100 100 100 100 40 18 16 20 100 100 100 80 100 100 100 100 100 100

Units Recorded: _Sessions_

Units Possible:

Reliability:

Percent:

Units:

Percent:

Behavior-Definition: A record of percent of arithmetic problems completed on daily worksheets during Baseline, Surprise at Home, Peer Approval and Classroom Leader 1, Baseline 2, and Peer Approval and Classroom Leader 2 conditions.

Recording Procedure: _Permanent product. Teacher recorded percent of completed problems on daily math assignments._

Figure 5-2 (Copyright 1973, H & H Enterprises, Inc.)

engineer at the close of the study period. If the chosen person had finished his seatwork, he received the applause of the class and got to be leader. The teacher reported that John as well as others completed more work under this contingency.

Discussion   This study shows that the opportunity to earn an activity for one's peers is a powerful reinforcer for certain individuals. John's rate of completing arithmetic work sheets increased markedly. The study shows how other treatment conditions may succeed where the initially planned treatment program is ineffective.

Control of Severe Tantrum Behavior through the Use of a One-Minute Time-out Procedure on Three Early-Stage Tantrum Symptoms

Subject and Setting   Susie was an eight-year-eleven-month-old girl enrolled in a class for the multiply handicapped. She was labeled "mildly to moderately retarded." She had multiple congenital anomalies including eye and hand deformities, limited vision, hearing, and bilaterally subluxated hips. Teachers and parents were concerned with how to control Susie's numerous and severe tantrums.

Behavior Measured   Three pretantrum events were noted and defined. A screaming event was tabulated each time the subject screamed "no!" or "I won't!" in response to a request from the teacher or the student teacher. Each screaming event was separated from the previous screaming event by a minimum of 90 seconds. Each stamping event was separated from the previous stamping event by a minimum of 90 seconds. A spitting event was recorded each time the subject spit at any person or in any place other than the sink in the bathroom or in the classroom sink. If all three events took place concurrently, an event was tabulated for each behavior. A tantrum was tabulated each time the subject stamped, screamed, hit people or objects with her fists, and had to be physically restrained from injuring herself or others. Each tantrum was separated from the previous tantrum by a minimum of fifteen minutes in order to be tabulated as a separate event. The teacher kept a written tabulation of all events. Reliability was obtained by similar tabulations recorded by the student teacher, who observed one of the three early-stage symptoms on Mondays, Wednesdays, and Fridays, and tantrums on Tuesdays and Thursdays. Reliability checks showed 100% agreement.

Procedures and Results   A multiple baseline design was employed. After concurrent baselines were recorded on screaming, stamping, and spitting events, a one-minute time-out procedure was successively applied first for screaming, then for stamping, finally for spitting events.

Screaming   During a five-day baseline period for screaming events, a mean of 8.4 daily events was recorded. On the sixth day, the one-minute time-out procedure was introduced, and the teacher placed the subject in the hall immediately following each screaming event. After an increase in the behavior on the first day, screaming events steadily declined until zero was reached on the thirteenth day. Figure 5-3 shows that screaming behavior was maintained at this low level throughout the rest of the study.

Stamping   Baseline data were recorded for twelve days with a mean of 7.4 daily stamping events. A similar time-out procedure for stamping events was introduced to run concurrently with the time-out procedure used for screaming events. There was an increase in the number of stamping events recorded on the first day of the experimental procedure, followed by a sharp drop which continued until zero was reached on the nineteenth day.

Spitting   The mean level of spitting events recorded for an eighteen-day baseline was 5.4 events per day. A time-out procedure was implemented on the nineteenth day that was identical to the procedure used for both screaming and stamping events. There was a sharp drop in the level of spitting behavior following the application of the time-out procedure. A zero level was reached two days after the time-out procedure was introduced.

Tantrums   During the first five days of the study when all three early-stage symptoms were still in baseline, a mean of two tantrums per day was recorded. When time-out procedures were in effect for screaming events, a mean of only 1.1 tantrum per day was recorded. Following the introduction of time-out for screaming and stamping, no tantrums were recorded for five consecutive days. On the sixteenth day, which was the student teacher's first full day of teaching, Susie had three tantrums. No more tantrums were recorded during the study.

Discussion   Through pinpointing, defining, and systematically using a time-out procedure on three early-stage tantrum symptoms or behavior components, the author successfully controlled Susie's tantrum behavior in the classroom. The process may be inversely compared to "shaping" a complex appropriate behavior, in that the teacher differentially used time-out procedures on the three tantrum behavior components one at a time until the undesired behavior was eliminated.

RESPONSIVE TEACHING STUDIES CARRIED OUT BY PARENTS

From the beginning, RT courses have generated studies carried out by parents in their homes. Some course participants were full-time graduate students and were not actively teaching, so they chose to observe and record behaviors of their own children. (In some cases participants measure and attempt to change the behavior of a spouse or roommate.)

Some participants who had access to a classroom chose to carry out studies in both settings, especially if they were more concerned about a behavioral

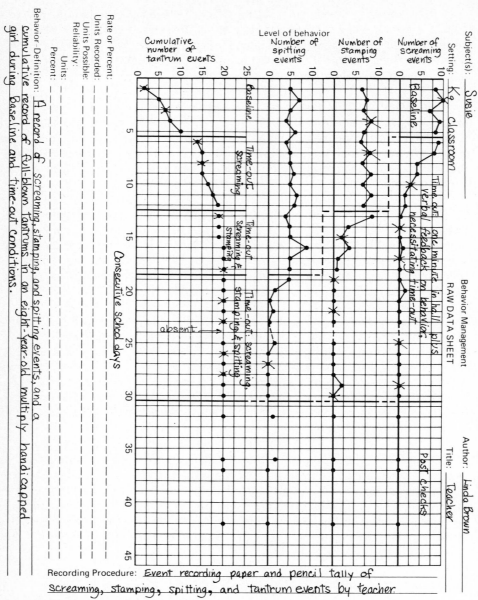

Figure 5-3 *(Copyright 1973, H & H Enterprises, Inc.)*

problem of one of their own children than they were in managing the behaviors of pupils in class. As a result, many RT studies have been carried out by parents enrolled in regular sections of our RT courses. A number have been published (Hall, Cristler et al., 1970; Hall, 1971a; Hall, 1971c; Hall, Axelrod, Tyler, Grief, Jones, & Robertson, 1972).

In addition to continuing sections for parents in the Shawnee Mission suburban area, parent training in the inner-city area of Kansas City, Kansas now includes developing paraprofessional mental health workers from the community to assist parents in carrying out RT procedures.

As with our teacher-implemented studies, our parent studies differ from most because the parents themselves chose the behaviors of concern, the procedures to be used to measure and modify the behaviors, and the research design to be followed to demonstrate causal relationships between the procedures and results. Thus, the parents become researchers, using a scientific approach rather than hit-or-miss tactics.

Much of this outreach work is carried out by a learning specialist in the Office of Special Education of the Shawnee Mission, Kansas, Public Schools. The specialist was assigned to twelve elementary, two junior high schools, and one high school. In her itinerant role she helps teachers and parents deal with special behavior and learning problems. The emphasis of this program is a "mainstream" approach designed to keep pupils in the regular classroom whenever possible. Thus, the work with parents was mainly preventative. Pupils were referred to the specialist either through the schools or by their parents. Whenever possible, the specialist asked the teacher or parent to enroll in an RT course.

The first study was one of a number carried out by parents of children enrolled in regular elementary classes. The parent had requested help from the schools because of difficulties she was having at home with her child.

The second study is one of several carried out by parents who were members of an RT class for parents of adolescents concerned about the behaviors of their teen-agers (Clark & Hall, 1973).

A Token System Increases Completion of Home Tasks without Parental Reminders

Subject and Setting   Debby was a nine-year-old girl who was having no difficulty in her third-grade classroom in a public elementary school. However, her parents requested help through the educational clinic, a service of the school district, because of management problems at home. Debby's parents became participants in an RT parent-education group.

Behavior Measured   Debby had two assigned tasks in the home: to make her own bed and to clear away dishes after the evening meal. Debby was also asked to keep her own belongings picked up and to be in bed by 8:30 P.M. on school nights. Only after constant reminding did Debby ever manage to accomplish these tasks. Therefore, these parents decided that changing the behavior would be their project for the RT parent group. Using a pencil and paper, each task was scored at a certain time each day and the permanent product was counted and recorded for the tasks defined as items left out. Debby's father made reliability checks at least once for each task during each phase of the study. With the exception of one of these reliability checks, their records were in agreement. On that one occasion the mother recorded zero items left out, but Debby's father found three items under her bed.

Baseline₁   As is shown in Figure 5-4, after six days, the baseline record indicated that Debby never made her bed without parental reminder. There was a mean of three of her personal belongings left out. Debby usually removed the dishes from the table, but on five occasions she left some of the dishes, and during the first three days of baseline, she did not remove the dishes without being reminded. Only once during baseline conditions did Debby make it to bed on time.

Points Exchangeable for a Variety of Reinforcing Events   Beginning on the seventh day, Debby was told that she could earn points for making her bed each morning without being reminded. These points could be exchanged on the weekend for a special event such as having a friend spend the night, bowling a line with her father, or a shopping trip with her mother. Debby consistently made her bed from day seven to the completion of the study. On the eleventh day, points could be earned for having no items out of place at the 6:00 P.M. check. In order to engage in a weekend special event, Debby had to have twice as many points. On the nineteenth day, Debby was told she would be issued points for removing all the dishes after the evening meal, and the weekend event would again cost more points. Debby failed to remove all the dishes only once during experimental procedures. On the nineteenth day, Debby was informed that being in bed by 8:30 without being told to retire could earn her points. The special weekend event was now four times as expensive as it once was.

Discussion   This simple multiple baseline procedure incorporating a point system is similar to one previously reported (Hall, 1971a). The point system was an extremely simple operation for these parents to establish. They expressed delight in their new day-to-day living with their daughter. Debby reported she thought it was fun to do her work that way.

A Parent Uses Contingent Driving Privileges To Decrease Negative Verbalizations

Subject and Setting   Charlie, age seventeen, was an eleventh grader in a senior high school. Charlie's school counselor was concerned because Charlie often cut classes and was failing nearly all his subjects. An RT parent education group was started at the high school, and Charlie's mother enrolled. Though the main concern was Charlie's attendance and grades, it was decided to work on home problems first in order to teach the parents more effective manage-

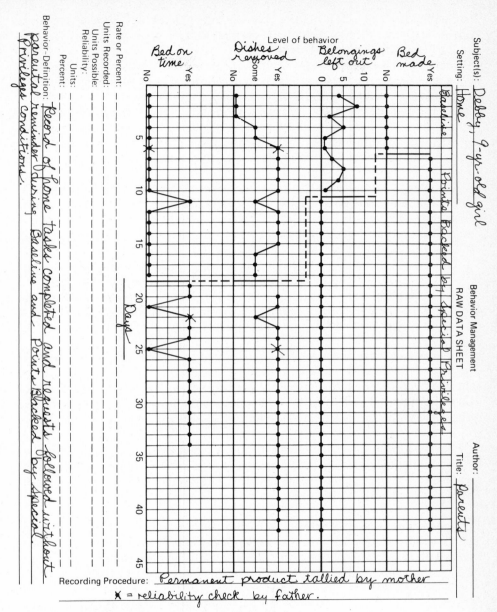

Figure 5-4 *(Copyright 1973, H & H Enterprises, Inc.)*

ment techniques. Charlie's mother was concerned about his negative verbalizations in the home. She picked this as her target behavior.

Behavior Measured   Negative verbalizations were recorded using a simple pencil and paper tally. Charlie's younger brother, age fourteen, made an independent recording during each phase of the study for reliability purposes. Except for two occasions the records were in agreement. During Baseline$_1$, the mother recorded six events and Charlie's brother noted seven. During reinstatement of experimental procedures, the primary observer recorded three events while the secondary observer scored two events.

Baseline$_1$ As shown in Figure 5-5, the operant level of negative verbalizations was at a mean of two. At this time a response from the mother upon each occurrence of a negative verbalization was something to the effect of "you'd better show more respect" or "don't talk to me that way."

Ignore$_1$ Beginning on the thirteenth day, Charlie's mother did not respond to her son with any remark, hoping that an extinction process would decrease the negative verbalizations. However, this did not occur, in fact, the mean rose to three. Charlie's mother stated that she probably did give him a dirty look though she certainly did not say anything.

Ignore and Drive to School$_1$ It was decided to continue to ignore Charlie's negative verbalizations but also to inform him that he could drive the car to school only if he did not engage in the defined behavior. Not until the fifth day did his behavior allow him to drive to school the following day. The mean rate of negative verbalizations fell to less than one during this phase of the study.

Baseline$_2$ During scientific verification when driving to school was no longer contingent on a lack of negative verbalization, Charlie's mean rate increased to three negative verbalizations. During the last two days of Baseline$_2$ he eased back into his old way.

Ignore and Drive to School$_2$ Charlie was informed that he could once again earn driving the car to school contingent upon zero negative verbalizations. With two exceptions he drove every day during this return to experimental procedures phase. The mother continued to ignore negative verbalization.

Increasing School Attendance through Contingent Driving Privilege   Charlie's mother said she was doing the dishes one evening when the "ah-ha" effect hit her. She decided to tell Charlie he could drive to school only if he kept his negative verbalizations down and attended his classes regularly.

Behavior Measured   Charlie's mother checked with a school secretary and received permission to check the permanent daily attendance records. The

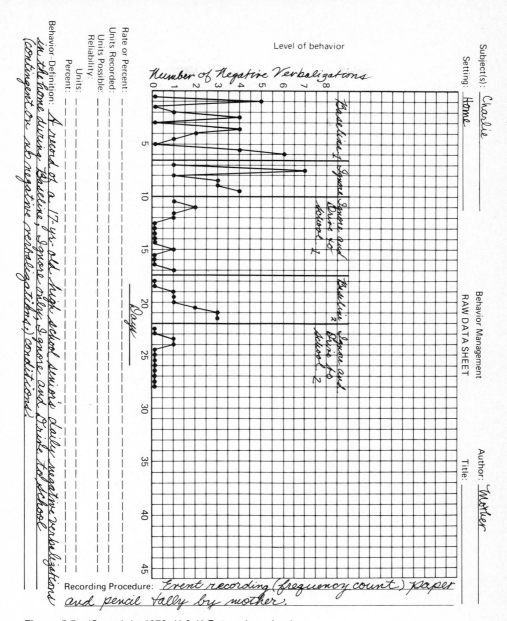

Level of behavior

Subject(s): _Charlie_

Setting: _Home_

Behavior Management
RAW DATA SHEET

Author: _Mother_

Title: _____

Number of Negative Verbalizations

Days

Baseline 1   Ignore and Drive to School 1

Baseline 2   Ignore and Drive to School 2

Rate or Percent: _____
Units Recorded: _____
Units Possible: _____
Reliability: _____
　　Units: _____
　　Percent: _____

Behavior-Definition: _A record of a 17-yr.-old high school senior's daily negative verbalizations in the home during Baseline, Ignore only, Ignore & Drive to school (contingent or no negative verbalizations) conditions._

Recording Procedure: _Event recording (frequency count) paper and pencil tally by mother._

Figure 5-5 *(Copyright 1973, H & H Enterprises, Inc.)*

author checked the same records for the purpose of reliability checks. There was 100% agreement.

Baseline₁   Figure 5-6 indicates a mean of three classes out of four being attended over an eight-day period.

Treatment₁   Charlie was informed that he must not only continue to refrain from negative verbalizations in order to drive to school but that furthermore, he would have to attend all his classes in order to drive the car. If he managed both of these behaviors he could not only drive to school but could also have access to the car after school and in the evenings. An agreement was made between the secretary and his mother that she would be called immediately whenever Charlie's name appeared on a class absentee slip. During Treatment₁ Charlie did not miss one class and had the car regularly. At one of the parent group meetings, Charlie's mother announced that she thought she had a problem. Though the project was going fine, Charlie was expelled from school for three days for smoking. No call came from the secretary saying he was absent. Further checking revealed that Charlie was not absent from class; he had been sneaking into his classes rather than staying out of school for the three required days.

Baseline₂   Both the parent and the school authorities were reluctant to engage in a reversal procedure now that Charlie was attending class on a daily basis. It was decided to shoot for a one-day trial to see if a fast reversal was possible. Charlie was told that he could drive the car free regardless of his attendance to class. On the one day of reversal, Charlie attended one class but skipped the rest of the day.

Treatment₂   Experimental procedures were reinstated, and for the next ten days, Charlie attended class regularly. At this point, recording procedures were stopped, but the secretary continued to call the parent if Charlie was absent. Two postchecks on a weekly basis showed Charlie attending class on a regular basis.

Discussion   A check of Charlie's first and second semester grades revealed a change from failing to passing grades. Teaching a parent to use simple management techniques resulted in dramatic home and school behavior changes in Charlie.

RESPONSIVE TEACHING STUDIES CARRIED OUT BY PRINCIPALS

Principals are no longer thought of as head teachers who have to perform administrative duties in addition to carrying out their teaching responsibilities. One is hard-pressed to find literature demeaning the role of the present-day

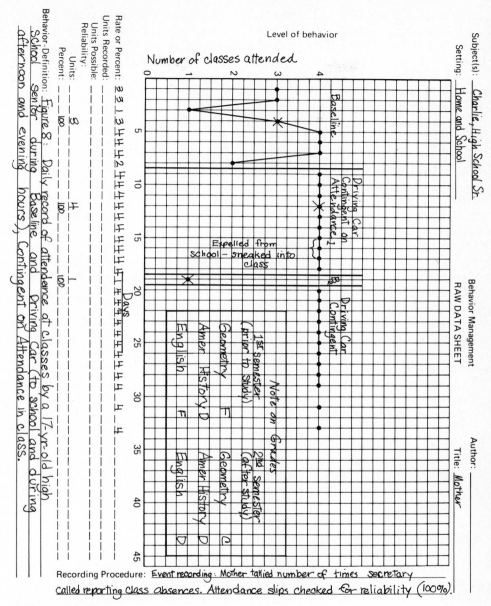

Figure 5-6 *(Copyright 1973, H & H Enterprises, Inc.)*

principal. Essays, books, and articles which stress the importance of the principal are abundant. School principals have contributed greatly to the development of the RT Model. Principals have been successful in using RT research designs while carrying out their professional activities.

In addition to the methodological attributes of the RT approach which finds favor with principals, the operant psychology which forms the basis for developing treatment programs is also welcomed by principals who are disheartened with psychological and educational theories that attribute maladaptive learning and social behavior to internal sources or past events.

School principals have been involved in a number of RT studies (Copeland, Brown, Axelrod, & Hall, 1972; Stanberry & Harris, 1971). It was a school principal that allowed the first RT classroom research to be conducted, which resulted in the Hall, Lund, and Jackson (1968) study. This incident exemplifies the tremendous power and influence principals have in education research. New approaches succeed only with the sanction of a building principal concurrent with teacher, parents, and psychologists. Principals have also been instrumental in organizing a number of RT classes within their respective buildings. Two principals have been the major force in implementing total RT programs within their schools.

The RT approach has much to offer to a principal interested in assessing and upgrading the program in his building. The research designs used in RT (reversal and multiple baseline, changing criterion) are far more relevant to a building principal than the more often used educational research designs that involve sophisticated statistical analysis and rigid groupings that very seldom involve more than pre- and postmeasures of the target behavior. The fact that RT procedures involve daily measures of clearly observable behavior coincides well with the principal's responsibility to monitor the programs in his building on a daily basis.

In the studies carried out by Brown, Copeland, and Hall (1972), the school principal systematically showed his pleasure with elementary school children's appropriate behaviors with various rewards. The behaviors of the children the principal dealt with were arriving at school on time and disruptiveness in the classroom.

A Principal Decreases Absenteeism in a Second-Grade Boy
Through Token Reinforcement

In the first experiment in the Brown et al. (1972) study, a second grader (in a class of 42 pupils) with a record of frequent absenteeism and tardiness served as the subject. A record was kept by the classroom teacher on the number of times the subject arrived at school on time. As can be seen in Figure 5-7, during the 56-day baseline phase, the subject came to school on time 46% of the time. The principal's modification procedure consisted of delivering potential reinforcers contingent on the subject's arrival at school on time. The procedure involved having the subject, Larry, come to the office and sign in with the principal each morning and afternoon. Each time Larry signed in, he earned five tokens which

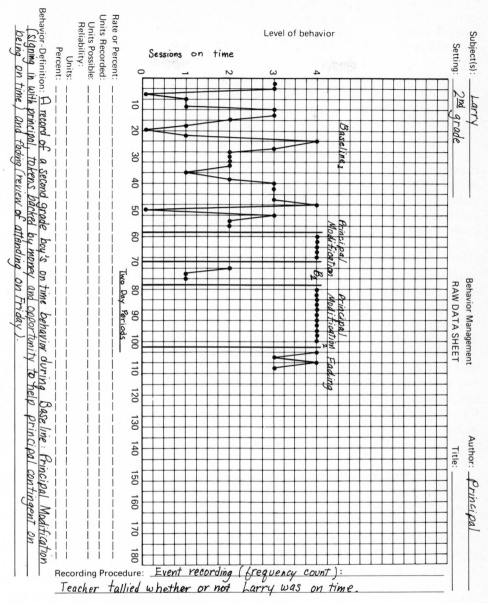

Figure 5-7 *(Copyright 1973, H & H Enterprises, Inc.)*

could be exchanged for a penny each. In addition the principal asked Larry to become his helper. If Larry arrived at school on time, he was allowed to spend approximately ten minutes out of the classroom in the afternoon picking up loose papers in the hallways. The token exchange procedure was abandoned after a few days, and Larry was paid 5 cents for each time he signed in at the office. This procedure had a dramatic effect on Larry's on-time behavior. For the two weeks the treatment condition was in effect, Larry was on-time for 100% of the school sessions. A six-day reversal period resulted in Larry's on-time behavior immediately decreasing to baseline levels. The principal reinstituted the modification procedure, and Larry again arrived at school on time 100% of the time for over four weeks. A fading procedure was implemented in which the subject no longer signed in at the office but rather the principal and Larry went over Larry's attendance record. On Fridays he was paid accordingly at the same five-cents-a-day rate as before. He also continued to help the principal around the building. Larry's on-time behavior decreased only slightly in this fading condition.

Effects of a Principal's Attention on Academic Behavior

In another study, the principal twice weekly entered two third-grade classrooms and recognized improving students and top-performing students regarding their work (Copeland, Brown, & Hall, 1974).

As shown in Figure 5-8, the principal was successful in bringing about increased scores in both rooms although the total time spent in each room was less than five minutes per week. This technique was particularly significant in that it took so little of the principal's time and yet affected so many students.

In other research studies conducted within the RT program investigating the school principal's role, school phobia has been successfully treated (Brown, Copeland, & Hall, 1974) and teacher behavior has been modified (Cossairt, Hall, & Hopkins, 1973). Studies are currently being conducted in which the principal is working with over 300 students regarding their performance with multiplication facts.

Obviously the elementary principal is an integral force in the public schools. Children, teachers, and parents either learn to avoid and escape the principal or to approach the principal. If a principal uses techniques which result in teachers, pupils, and parents avoiding or escaping from his presence, then his office and the school have become stimuli paired with punishment. If, on the other hand, a principal employs positive techniques in his interactions with parents, teachers, and pupils, the school becomes a stimulus paired with positive interactions.

PROPAGATION OF RESPONSIVE TEACHING

Responsive Teaching had its beginning as a class for nine educators working in inner-city schools. Although its originators did not set out to develop a large program, RT has grown and expanded along several dimensions.

Over each of the past few years approximately 200–250 teachers, school psychologists, special-education teachers, principals, speech therapists, school

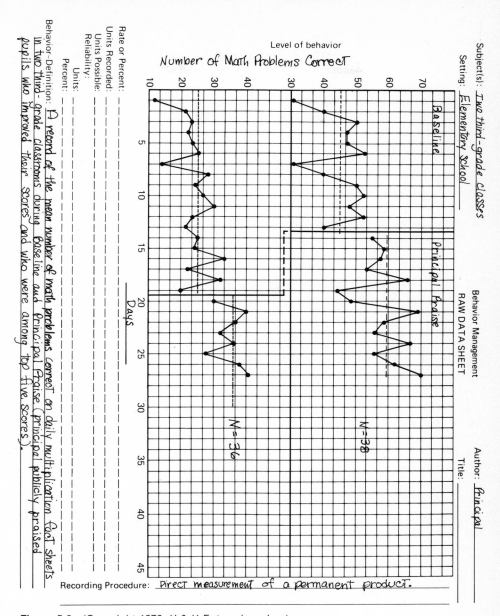

Subject(s): _Two third-grade classes_   Behavior Management   Author: _Principal_

Setting: _Elementary School_   RAW DATA SHEET   Title:

Level of behavior

Number of Math Problems Correct

Behavior-Definition: _A record of the mean number of math problems correct on daily multiplication fact sheets in two third-grade classrooms during Baseline and Principal Praise (principal publicly praised pupils who improved their scores and who were among top five scores)._

Percent: — — —

Units: — — —

Reliability: — — —

Units Possible: — — —

Units Recorded: — — —

Rate or Percent: — — —

Recording Procedure: _Direct measurement of a permanent product._

Figure 5-8 *(Copyright 1973, H & H Enterprises, Inc.)*

nurses, and other school personnel have enrolled in credit classes. Many have acted as group leaders, and a number have gone on to teach sections of the course as a part of their training. Upon graduation a number of graduate students have begun teaching courses in RT at other schools and universities. Still others have attended Responsive Teaching workshops and have brought the RT approach to other school districts and colleges as a result of the training they have received. As a result, in addition to the large number of teachers trained through the University of Kansas, many more are using RT procedures in other parts of the United States.

In addition, Responsive Teaching has been implemented in the Republic of Panama and in Brazil, and basic text materials have been published in both Spanish and Portuguese.

Various persons have modified and adapted elements of the RT approach to fit particular needs and circumstances. Thus, RT has been taught not only as a university graduate-level course but also as a workshop followed by practicum application. It has been presented as an in-service training program sponsored by school districts and taught by district personnel. It is still evolving and undergoing change. Some of those who present it have placed greater emphasis on the research aspects of it and utilize it as a vehicle for training in applied research techniques. Others have placed emphasis on the practical aspects designed to bring about change in teacher practices. A number of instructors have shifted the emphasis from social to academic behaviors. Successful applications have been reported not only by those working with normal and exceptional children in regular classrooms, but also by the teachers of hearing-impaired students, blind students, and by speech clinicians, social workers, nurses, school psychologists, and teachers of the learning-disabled, the emotionally disturbed, and the gifted child.

Special sections of the course have been developed for principals, secondary teachers, and teachers of the handicapped, as well as for secondary school counselors and for attendants working in institutions for the severely and profoundly retarded.

Recently the third author of this chapter adapted the RT approach in working with parents. Although many previous participants have selected home behaviors as targets for the studies they carried out, these sections have focused entirely on working with parents who do not have or are not interested in post-high-school training. Not only have the materials used in training teachers been adapted for parents in these programs but the parents themselves have participated in writing materials to be used for training other parents.

Other adaptations of the RT approach have been made for programs for training paraprofessional mental health workers who work not only directly with pupils who have been referred for behavior and learning problems but also with teachers and parents of these children by enlisting their assistance in maintaining RT procedures once they have been instituted by the paraprofessionals under the direction of the professional mental health staff.

Pilot studies have indicated that elementary-aged children too can be taught to use RT procedures, to observe and measure behavior, and to systematically use contingencies to bring about behavioral change. Currently we are also developing a course for high school psychology students using many of the same materials found to be effective at the college level.

Paraprofessional day-care workers are also receiving training in RT procedures designed to aid preschool children in learning social and preacademic skills necessary for them to be adequately prepared for entrance to school and to function in social situations.

At the University of Vermont, the special education department offers a course in RT to undergraduates in special education to help prepare them for dealing with handicapped pupils in both special and regular classrooms.

The University of Vermont Consulting Teacher program is a highly developed example of a program which incorporates Responsive Teaching procedures. In it special teacher consultants work with teachers, principals, and other school personnel and parents to serve the handicapped learner in the public schools (McKenzie, Egner, Knight, Perelman, Schneider, & Garvin, 1970). A related program has been developed at the University of Kansas. In this program consultants have been given training beyond the basic RT course so they can assist other teachers in using a Responsive Teaching approach with handicapped learners.

Currently we are in the process of extending the RT course to include additional training and experiences. We are often asked to provide further training and experiences so teachers can develop their skills and maintain those they have. Thus we are considering development of follow-up practicum courses in which teachers would have the opportunity to demonstrate proficiency in a number of critical areas such as, in dispensing reinforcers to both individuals and to groups; in delivering praise both privately and from across the room; in maintaining high levels of contact and feedback; in using shaping, extinction, time-out and other systematic procedures; and in demonstrating how to increase academic performance in a given area and to use behavioral objectives appropriately.

In order to illustrate how RT is responsive to the needs of teachers, parents, and others, we have described its effects in Bryant School and Crestview School.

SCHOOL PROGRAMS

Bryant Elementary School is in an all-black inner-city neighborhood of Kansas City, Kansas. Its principal, Ronald Brown, came to the school when it was undergoing transition from an all-white neighborhood school. Two other principals had preceded him six months prior to his appointment. Almost every teacher had asked for a transfer out of the building at the end of the previous school year. Fighting and other disruptions frequently occurred in the school and on the playground. Few parents attended PTA meetings, and most contacts between the principal and teachers, parents, and children revolved around discipline, absences, truancy, and other problems.

Four years ago the second author of this chapter, a former school psychologist who had worked with the principal, contacted him and proposed that they begin working together to carry out some research into ways that a school principal might more effectively deal with discipline, truancy, and attendance problems. The principal had already begun trying some procedures to deal with these problems, and he responded enthusiastically to the opportunity to carry out research and to find better ways. As a result of that initial contact and the success of some of those procedures (Copeland, Brown, Axelrod, & Hall, 1972; Brown, Copeland, & Hall, 1972), the principal invited staff members of the Juniper Gardens Children's Project to introduce him and his teachers to the Responsive Teaching Model. Arrangements were soon made for a section of the Responsive Teaching course in behavior management to be taught in Bryant School.

Four years have passed since that introductory class was offered. Today, as was recently reported in the *Kansas City Magazine,* "the overall atmosphere of the school is one of relaxed, happy people working well together. Students and teachers treat each other with utmost courtesy. . . . The halls are quiet and classrooms have a pleasant hum of activity."

As the principal goes down the hall he is frequently stopped by students who bring exceptional papers for him to autograph. Others are sent to the office by their teachers to receive praise in the form of a pat on the back and a comment such as "That's fantastic," for outstanding work. His office walls are literally covered with pupils' papers of every grade level and subject matter area.

Although five former Bryant teachers who took the original Responsive Teaching course are now DARTS (Diagnostic and Remedial Teaching Specialists) who have been enlisted by the district to go to other buildings to assist teachers in using Responsive Teaching procedures, systematic positive reinforcement prevails throughout the school.

In one fifth-grade class, spelling scores have zoomed. Pupils who have earned it get to take home notes saying:

> Congratulations are in order! Your son/daughter made the TOP SPELLER board for the *3rd* time. Only the students who can spell *all* their words are lucky enough to be a TOP SPELLER.
> I am most pleased aren't you?
>   (signed) Mrs. Almond

In another class each pupil keeps track of how many papers he has had on display on the bulletin board since the year began by listing them with Sam Scarecrow. Each pupil has a chance to display any outstanding paper in any subject. Every child has at least two papers on display at any time, as new ones go up the old come down.

In another classroom pupils bid for classroom jobs with points earned by good behavior and excellent work. Each must earn enough points to attend class parties and to receive other privileges, including free time.

The art teacher has devised a simple system which reduced clean-up time across all classes from ten minutes to five minutes per class as a result of a data-based experiment she carried out as a Responsive Teaching project.

The music teacher reports she no longer has problems with her classes as far as behavior of pupils entering and leaving the music room, caring for materials, posture, and participation in class since she instituted a system in which each class can earn ten minutes of playing favorite records every two weeks contingent on a daily record of appropriate behavior in these four areas.

Pupils in a special reading program can earn certificates and get their pictures taken with someone special by completing a given number of units in a reading program.

Pupils in a special class get stars for good attendance and for making progress in counting. Other charts show their progress in learning color names.

Carey, a youth diagnosed as brain-injured, who had been excluded not only from his neighborhood school but from a special school at a well-known institution in the city because he was unmanageable, was placed in Bryant. At first he ran screaming down the hall and engaged in other bizarre behaviors. His teacher discovered, however, that Carey liked to be a monitor. Using a shaping procedure with that as a reinforcer, screaming was eliminated. Carey is now reading and his teacher is getting a baseline on how frequently he fails to return when sent on an errand. His teacher is confident that behavior can also be modified.

One parent called the principal after receiving a letter from her child's teacher telling how much progress he had made. She stated that the family had planned to move to another neighborhood, but if the teacher cared *that* much about him there was "no way" they would move.

Parents speak glowingly of the principal and proudly tell their neighbors of the calls they have received about the positive things their children have done that have come to his attention. Over 150 parents attended a recent PTA meeting in this area where once only a handful could be expected to participate. Rather than having teachers who request to leave the school Bryant is finding that teachers from other schools request transfers to teach there.

The principal holds informal weekly seminars in his building in which teachers experienced in Responsive Teaching share their data on studies they are carrying out in their classrooms and teachers new to the building learn about measurement, baselines, reinforcement, shaping, extinction, and the other aspects of Responsive Teaching.

In addition to studies designed to help individual children and classrooms, several school-wide studies are in progress. Several directly concern the principal, including one which has successfully reduced after-school playground fights involving pupils from a nearby junior high. Another concerns the school lunchroom. One of the most impressive studies increased the scores of the third-, fourth-, and fifth-grade students multiplication facts to levels far above those in control schools in other parts of the district. Pupils who made weekly increases in their scores got to play Quizmo, an arithmetic game, with the principal.

So pervasive is the influence of Responsive Teaching that even the school custodian and the secretary act as observers and reliability checkers. The secretary is also carrying out a study designed to modify her own junior high school son's school behavior.

One first-grade teacher who became concerned about a high rate of absenteeism in her class was able to decrease absences to a negligible level by getting the principal to recognize those with good attendance records by giving them a three-stage "soul" shake.

Crestview School is in an all-white suburban area of metropolitan Kansas City. Two years ago its principal was concerned because most of his contacts with pupils and parents revolved around discipline problems. Because he took his role as instructional leader seriously, the principal experienced a sense of frustration because he felt he had too little impact on the academic progress and teaching methods at his school. Another area of concern was what he termed a lack of communication between the school and the home. Finally, he was concerned because of the high number of teacher referrals of pupils for special education classes.

At Crestview School the principal asked the learning specialist to bring Responsive Teaching to all teachers and parents in the school. He had observed the effects of her work with individual teachers and parents and, with the urging of the school nurse who had also become aware of Responsive Teaching, decided to bring Responsive Teaching to Crestview.

The first semester sixteen staff members and seven parents took the basic Responsive Teaching course. Most of them carried out individual studies on social behaviors such as talk-outs and other disruptions. The next semester eight teachers continued to carry out studies, but this time most focused on academic behaviors. In addition, one school-wide study involving all the teachers and every student was carried out under the direction of the principal and a graduate student from the Juniper Gardens Children's Project.

In the study pupils earned an all-day picnic at a nearby park by increasing the level of their correct academic responses from 73 to 89%. In addition a local bank proclaimed their success in reaching their goal on its electronic readerboard sign so that the entire community was aware of their success.

The seven parents who took the Responsive Teaching class with the Crestview staff became group leaders for a class for other parents, which they labeled Responsive Parenting. They acted as group leaders and trained 37 parents who enrolled in their first class. During the summer they wrote a manual for Responsive Parenting and another group of parents became group leaders to assist in training the next class of parents. Their aim is to train every parent in the Crestview service area within the next two years, and plans are underway to offer Responsive Parenting training to other district schools.

Parents who have participated are enthusiastic, some are almost evangelistic, in proclaiming that the class has given them not only better ways of managing their children's behavior but a new way of life. They say their new approach is much freer from nagging, scolding, and other ineffective management techniques. Rather than using punishment, they have used reinforcement, shaping, and extinction to make relationships throughout the family more pleasant and productive.

The 47 studies and the many additional ones now in progress that they have carried out provide convincing evidence that they are indeed becoming more effective with their children.

Furthermore, the principal reports that cases involving him in discipline problems have been reduced to such an extent that when asked recently when his last discipline case had occurred, he had to stop and think in order to recall that it had been two weeks since he had had to discipline a pupil. In addition referrals for special education placement have decreased to zero, and the principal is working with teachers and district curriculum directors in establishing minimum academic objectives for the various subject-matter areas.

Many of the over 1,500 other teachers, principals, speech clinicians, school psychologists, nurses, teachers of the deaf, and other professionals and para-professionals who have been introduced to Responsive Teaching report they too have learned to deal more effectively with learning and behavior problems as a result of their contact, though in most cases they have not been implemented as intensively as has been true at Bryant and Crestview.

Because of the success at these schools and in the classrooms and homes of others who have successfully implemented Responsive Teaching procedures, we know that the Responsive Teaching approach is an effective way to introduce educators and others to Applied Behavior Analysis. It is an approach which allows sizable groups to be introduced to this approach and has the advantage of being a replicable model. That is, a substantial number of persons have used the materials and procedures developed for its implementation and have achieved similar results.

DISCUSSION AND SUMMARY

The RT Model is the outgrowth of our attempts to use laboratory approaches and procedures in applied settings, notably schools and homes. Although the RT Model has clearly demonstrated that teachers and parents can use applied research methodologies to increase both social and academic behaviors, the RT Model in its current form is only a first step in the process of helping educators and parents use a more systematic approach in working with children.

Past course participants have included principals, counselors, parents, speech therapists, psychologists, nurses, special education teachers, occupational therapists, and other professionals. Sections for special groups are now being implemented. As studies are carried out in the various specialty areas it is possible to tailor the course more and more specifically for these various groups. Also, school personnel, including administrators, have assisted in teaching courses for special education teachers.

Teachers who work in schools where principals, school psychologists, and supervisors have taught or studied Responsive Teaching are more likely to maintain the positive effects of their own instruction. Nevertheless, further research is needed to determine how to most effectively implement and maintain the elements of the model.

We know that individual pupils and certain classroom groups have derived benefit from the model. We have data to indicate that parents have been able to increase appropriate behaviors of their children. But we still lack generalization data showing how pervasive are the effects of such a training program.

The fact that the RT teaching program has been taught successfully by a number of persons both in Kansas and elsewhere is encouraging. According to these indications, using the materials that have been developed, an RT course or an adaptation of it can be offered in any university training program or in any school district where there are persons with a background in Applied Behavior Analysis to offer the instructions and provide the monitoring necessary to carry out the program.

The RT Model and others which incorporate its features allow us to look not only at the effects of consequences on behavior but also the effects of antecedent events. Each teacher can determine which stimulus materials (including various teaching aids) are most effective. By using Responsive Teaching, and similar programs, all aspects of the teaching process can be strengthened. Our approaches to education need no longer be as nonscientific and ineffectual as they were in the past.

We need to know whether or not parent's and teacher's practices are permanently changed. Do they continue to measure behavior and use Applied Behavior Analysis research designs to assess their effectiveness? Do they at least increase their use of systematic reinforcement procedures?

Furthermore, we need to assess whether or not children exposed to RT procedures over a period of time benefit in tangible ways. Are they less likely to be truant and less likely to drop out of school? Do they make greater academic gains? Can the handicapped child be taught more effectively in the classroom of a RT teacher in areas of social behavior and academic progress?

We are beginning to answer these questions. Through the Juniper Gardens Children's Project we are instituting longitudinal studies designed to follow the progress of children exposed to RT procedures over a period of years. These studies will yield information beyond that provided by the relatively short-term studies presented in this chapter.

The early RT studies dealt with decreasing inappropriate social behaviors such as talk-outs and other disruptions. In the past two years more studies have concerned appropriate academic responses. Our recent research, and that of our colleagues, concerns increasing participation in classroom activities.

It is of paramount importance for us to continue our efforts to acquaint parents and members of the school community with these powerful techniques. If parents and educators work together, it is possible to build a learning environment that will be highly reinforcing for all children. Since ultimately we are all responsible for participating in the decisions of what social and academic skills should be taught, all of us should be informed regarding them.

This is perhaps one of the most positive aspects of this approach. It can be made available to all members of the community. We can all look at the procedures and their effects and base decisions regarding them on tangible evidence rather than on speculation or subjective judgment.

In summary the RT approach fits into existing administrative structures and arrangements. It can be applied and implemented within school districts, individual buildings, or single classrooms without changing schedules and other administrative arrangements.

Another feature is that it does not conflict with the educational goals and moral and ethical standards of teachers and the school social system. It merely allows teachers, principals, psychologists, and others to attain the goals they set for themselves using those procedures which are appropriate to their situations and consonant with their sense of values.

It is adaptable. It allows for reinforcement for all. If a teacher becomes more effective as a result of using the procedures, the children make gains, the principal is faced with fewer problems and sees pupils making increased educational gains, and the school patrons become increasingly approving of the school and its program. Likewise the parents are pleased to see their children respond to the more positive approaches used by the schools and are more inclined to participate in school activities.

Ultimately RT becomes incorporated into the system without disrupting it. It merely allows for better utilization of available resources. It shows the way for teachers, principals, parents, and others in the schools to mobilize the resources available in a way which increases educational outputs.

DISCUSSION TOPICS

Management Strategies for Teachers and Parents: Responsive Teaching

Objective   This chapter is a description of the successful training package for introducing teachers, counselors, principals, and other school personnel to an Applied Behavior Analysis approach to educational management called Responsive Teaching. This community-based system is described along with several successful uses of it.

Exercises

1   A Responsive Teaching class is being taught at North Bend, Nebraska, for teachers and parents. Ronald Rightson's mother has enrolled (see exercises for chapters 1, 3, and 4). Mrs. Rightson decided to help Ms. Spring in her attempt to modify Ronald's classroom behavior. Describe how she might work with Ronald's teacher in this.

2   Mrs. Rightson also decided to carry out a study on Ronny's behavior at home. Using the format in this chapter to describe procedures of Responsive Teaching methods used by parents, write a report that Mrs. Rightson might have written as a result of her study on Ronald.

3 The behaviors of children that principals dealt with in this chapter were absenteeism, disruptive classroom behavior, and academic achievement. What other areas do you think the principal might deal with successfully?

4 Select one of these areas with which you feel the principal might deal to describe the procedures he could use and the expected results.

Chapter 6

The Trainable Retarded: The Technology of Teaching

James R. Lent
Barbara M. McLean
Bureau of Child Research, Parsons State Hospital and Training
Center, University of Kansas

EDITORS' NOTE

This chapter and the next chapter are addressed to teachers and specialists who instruct children with limited social and academic behavior. This chapter focuses upon children whom the schools have long regarded as *trainable*— children usually grouped in special classes. The next chapter concerns children who will require special training in order to qualify for entry into such group training. Taken together the chapters cover a wide range of abilities and disabilities at the low end of the behavioral scale.

Lent and McLean discuss a program for children who are often institutionalized but for whom many schools must now provide training. For them the educational target may be preparation for community living, vocational placement, and social compatibility in community settings. The goals will be only partially attained for many, but nevertheless, the philosophy is one of normalization, and teaching technology must be designed to achieve this objective.

Spradlin and Spradlin, in the next chapter, discuss a group of children for whom the objectives are less clear. For them programs have been limited almost exclusively to institutions and other residential or hospital settings. Schools have not often admitted them, instructional programs have not been devised for them, and schools have not looked closely at issues that unavoidably accompany such training. Objectives for suitable life styles for them have not emerged, at least not as alternatives to institutionalization. The current mood of society is that institutionalization is not a reasonable alternative. Since the schools are now legally obligated to admit severely limited children, new and better ways to teach them must be developed. The Spradlins suggest an approach for undertaking this instructional program.

In the perspective of teaching all special children, Lent and McLean present a useful technology for teaching children who are in the lowest categories of the current educational scale. The Spradlins propose a way to extend the scale downward to include children that have usually been excluded from public education. Both chapters provide a provocative challenge to educators engaged in planning, implementing, and maintaining programs for special children.

This chapter concerns the habilitation of the trainable-level mentally retarded. Although individual characteristics vary enormously within the group, some characteristics overlap those of all other persons.

Man's tendency to classify is basic to his understanding and to his accumulation of knowledge. As useful to learning as this labeling process is, it has disadvantages when applied to individuals. The disadvantage is heightened when the group being considered is the portion of the population known as the mentally retarded: persons whose disabilities are rarely single and about whose condition many unknowns remain. Each person has unique characteristics, and it is unfair to prejudge him because of limitations in one facet of his being. Nevertheless, various professional groups continue to need to use this kind of labeling to plan and execute their services.

CONVENTIONAL DEFINITIONS AND LABELS

There is no agreed-upon definition of mental retardation, nor is there a universal terminology for the degrees or levels of deficiency. However, the American Association for Mental Deficiency has formulated a workable definition which answers some of the criticisms of exclusion or concentration of earlier attempts at definition (Grossman, 1973).

> Mental retardation refers to significantly subaverage general intellectual functioning existing concurrently with deficits in adaptive behavior and manifested during the developmental period.

This definition is useful in determining services that should be provided in schools and community settings or in deciding what type of institutionalization is needed.

Labeling by degree of deficit is still more a matter of preferential usage than logic. The traditional classification system encompasses a broad range from *idiot* upward through *borderline*. These categories were based on the quantitative measurement of intelligence quotients: idiot, 0 to 20–25; imbecile, 20–25 to 40–50; moron, 50 to 70; and borderline, 70 to 80–85 (Kirk & Johnson, 1951).

The National Association for Retarded Citizens has defined four levels of retardation, ranging from profoundly retarded through mildly retarded (NARC, 1972). The profoundly retarded, with IQs below 20, represent 1½ percent of all mentally retarded persons in the United States. The severely retarded are those whose "developmental delay is highly similar during early life to the profoundly retarded children; however, their rate of progress and developmental potential is significantly greater." Approximately 3½ percent of the retarded are severely retarded.

Moderately retarded persons represent 6 percent of the retarded population, having IQs from 36 to 51. With early and community-based training, moderately retarded citizens can live acceptably in community group homes, and "make social and occupational contributions through employment in sheltered workshops or other supervised work settings," according to the NARC definition.

Approximately 89 percent of the nation's mentally retarded are mildly retarded, with IQs of 52 to 67. NARC describes them as "highly similar to their nonretarded peers, differing only in rate and degree of intellectual development."

Contemporary educational terminology concentrates on the two terms, educable (above 50 IQ), and trainable (below 50 IQ with lower limit of 25–30), with some use of the term *borderline* to designate the group who test as slightly below normal. This terminology reflects both the concern of various groups for a less derogatory connotation and the necessity to determine a cutting-off point for the nation's public school systems.

Although an improvement over former classification, the "educable" and "trainable" labels initiated in the 1950s no longer adequately express the fluid nature of the groups. Research and experimentation have indicated that all retarded persons can achieve a far greater step toward normalization—toward becoming more personally fulfilled and productive members of society.

NEWER CATEGORIZATION SYSTEMS

More recently, two other categorical models have emerged: the Adaptive Behavior Checklist'(Nihira, Foster, Shallhaas, Leland, 1970, which is still widely referenced in its original format although revised more concurrently) and the AAMD manual on terminology (Grossman, 1973). Each of these plans provides numbers from one through five to designate levels of deficit in adaptive capacity or degree of retardation. The models are conceptually different and conflicting in their use of numerical indicators. Classification methods and terminologies are not compatible with the public school system of grouping the mentally retarded into educable and trainable classes. Eventually, language must describe function.

The same retarded individual is now evaluated by a range of service groups: home, institution, day-care center, public school, sheltered workshop, and half-way house. These various groups' inability to describe the same client with a common notation system will eventually force a redefinition and relabeling. Such a forced compatibility will expedite diagnosis and therapy processes and will be a first step in making possible an efficient retrieval system for materials, procedures, and data regarding instruction of the retarded. Retrieval of instructional programs and training components must necessarily depend on deficit-specific request input. As Drucker (1969) points out, without one universal notation system as invented by St. Ambrose in the fourteenth century, musicians would today face the same frustrations and problems now facing educators.

Although incompatible notation systems are a fundamental problem that contributes heavily to the dearth of precise, deficit-specific programming, let us also realize that the notion of providing treatment, training, and, indeed, education for the retarded, has a slow and sporadic history.

DEVELOPMENT OF A CONCEPT OF TRAINING

In the past, despite noteworthy attempts to better the lives of the moderately and severely retarded, the prevailing attitude precluded instruction beyond what amounted to custodial care. *Training* which could contribute to the personal growth and satisfaction of the retardate in the community was not a primary goal for most programs. Until recently, too little attention was paid to daily-living behaviors which contribute to acceptance by a normal community.

This has not always been true. Some of the earliest work with the severely retarded was highly systematic and oriented toward returning students to a normal *life-style*. The Montessori sense-training techniques and didactic materials have had an enthusiastic revival in the education of normal and gifted children. Maria Montessori, however, began her efforts with institutionalized children in Italy and achieved such success that, although the children were classified as "mentally deficient" in the terminology of her day, they were able to pass the competitive school examinations for normal children (Montessori, 1912). This might be too optimistic a goal for those we call trainable, but there is evidence that their functioning level can be dramatically improved and their capability to achieve a degree of normalization can be expanded.

Sequin, in nineteenth-century France and later in the United States, sought answers through physiologically oriented training. It is interesting to note that his pioneer institution for the mentally retarded in the United States was intended as a *training* school, not a custodial dwelling (Sequin, 1866, in Rothstein, 1971).

In it [institutional school] idiots and their congeners are expected to remain *during the period assigned by nature for progress in young persons* unless it sooner becomes manifest that they cannot be improved at all or any more, in which case their parents should take them out to make room for new pupils. [Italics, the author's]

However, as more were admitted to institutions, causing overcrowding, those leaving were not successful in adapting to a normal environment. As a result, Sequin's original philosophy of curing or "restoring" to a normal life deteriorated to one of custodial care. And with isolated exceptions, this practice has *remained* until recent times.

CONCEPT OF TRAINING AS A COMMUNITY CONCERN

Prior to the 1950s the educable retarded were allowed in the public school systems of some states. It was in that decade, however, that several forces produced a concerted effort to make this practice more universal. Among the forces changing public attitude toward the handicapped were the World War II disabled veterans, research findings concerning the dynamic nature of intelligence quotients, and the increasing use of an adaptive-behavior philosophy—all of which combined to help modify some earlier attitudes about the educability of the retarded. Perhaps even more important were the efforts of parent groups who banded together to seek support and recognition for mentally retarded offspring. Beginning with experimental programs and schools which were privately financed, this movement affected and continues to affect local school systems, state legislatures, and federal government agencies.

Local organizations were ingenious in their efforts to secure space wherever possible—in churches, in community buildings, and in abandoned school buildings. Even more impressive was their ability to get financial assistance from local service groups to help finance day-care centers. These early efforts were not philosophically coherent, but they were important for solving immediate problems. As they grew in number and in variety, there was increased effectiveness.

During the 1950s what had been primarily a local concern became a working network of state and national organizations whose focus was the provision of direct services for retarded children. In the 1960s the emphasis shifted to overall planning and participation in governmental agencies and commissions. An international league was formed, the impact of which is evidenced in the Declaration of the Rights of Mentally Retarded Persons by the General Assembly of the United Nations on December 20, 1971 (Dybwad, 1973).

TRAINING AS A CONCERN OF PUBLIC EDUCATION

The growth in numbers of special education classes within the public school systems of the country has been steady. Nevertheless, special education has been beset with serious problems, including a lack of technologically trained teachers; a shortage of university-level personnel qualified to train them; the financial burden of such programming; an inadequate number of appropriate facilities; and scarcity of specific curriculum guides and validated, replicable program materials. Too often special education classes offer a watered-down academic curriculum or are a "dumping ground" for heterogeneous problem children who are taught by an unqualified teacher in unsuitable, leftover, or improvised space.

Action in the 1960s regarding civil rights for minority groups encompassed the rights of another substantial minority group, the mentally retarded. Added to the inadequacies of the classification system already noted are the discriminatory results of ability testing among the culturally disadvantaged. What has been labeled retardation in many cases is really educational and cultural deprivation. In the past decade there has been considerable research in early childhood development. The findings emphasize the need for reliable identification of retardation well before school age—the point at which it has most often been discovered in the past.

These are among the problems and developments which are causing a current self-evaluation in the field of mental retardation. The current trend in special education programs within the school systems is toward returning the educable child to the regular classroom and making available to him the added aids of resource rooms where qualified specialists with appropriate equipment and materials can offer individualized services.

Such *mainstreaming* (as this process is called) requires painstaking analysis of needs and provisions for nontraditional public school facilities and assessment procedures. An emerging diagnostic study labeled "Programmed Re-entry Into Mainstream Education" (PRIME) will lead to guidelines for successful mainstreaming and is currently an intramural project of the Bureau of Education for the Handicapped (USOE).

As complex as the planning for the educable is, the planning for the trainable is even more complicated. Estimates reveal that, of the 6 million mentally retarded persons in the United States, the trainable (including moderate and severe levels) number approximately 570,000. Of these, 295,000 are under 20 years old (HEW, 1972). About 40 percent of the school-age children of this number are institutionalized, and about 60 percent remain in the community (Cruickshank & Johnson, 1967, in Waite, 1972). The current direction of planning in the country's institutions is toward a return to the community. This is a necessary and healthy development, but most communities are not ready to provide services to increasing numbers of the trainable retarded.

COMMUNITY TRANSITION AS A TRAINING GOAL

The community can serve as a "classroom" for those retarded who are not institutionalized by providing a learning environment filled with examples of acceptable behavior. Such models can help each person achieve a degree of normality. As the individual learns to adjust to the normal community, adopting the behavior patterns he learns there, he becomes more acceptable to that community.

Whether institutionalized or not, the trainable can best learn to adapt to community life through daily-living experiences in that community. Such experiences help him appear more normal and prepare him for at least semi-independent living in the community.

Truly successful adjustment from the institution to the community has not occurred on a large scale for three reasons:

1 The target behaviors necessary for success have not been delineated or specified in a manner to make them teachable.
2 There has been no realistic plan of implementation with specific program materials.
3 Few institutional administrative structures ideologically or functionally support such behavior specification and training materials.

It should nevertheless be remembered that there are concerted efforts by many groups to return to a "restoring" philosophy for retardates either in or out of institutions. Special classes are being mandated and community facilities are being provided. Do these new developments represent a faith in new-found knowledge or merely hope? A bit of both, really. The mere commitment to a philosophy of normalization will guarantee a measure of success to any program. In addition, there is quite a bit of new technology available to assist in selecting target behaviors and implementing them. This technology provides the central theme of this chapter.

INDIVIDUALIZING TRAINING

There has been a gradual trend toward integration of the educable-level mentally retarded into the regular grades. Such a development is possible because the difference between the intellectually normal and the educable is small enough to be indistinguishable or tolerable. In classes where subject matter is more concrete than abstract, the two groups may meet on relatively equal ground. In reading, math, English, and other academically oriented subjects, the educable can be provided special instruction in a resource room where students compete against their own standards of achievement.

This trend recognizes that the difference between intellectual groups is one of degree and that frequently the groups can be mixed to mutual advantage. To date, there has been no move to integrate the trainable into the regular grades or into classes for the educable. This too is recognition of a difference between the groups, a difference sufficiently great that bridging the gap is difficult. The trainable are more difficult to teach. The difficulty may have been exaggerated, but it is real. Compared to the educable, the trainable will learn less rapidly and will generalize less. This implies a need for more individualization of instruction, better classroom organization, better use of times available for training, and more naturalistic training environments.

Teacher-Pupil Ratio

The need for a more individualized instruction has been acknowledged but not provided. Most state departments of education and local school districts recommend a teacher-pupil ratio for the trainable of one to ten or one to twelve. That ratio may be as advantageous as can be expected, but it is not realistic. A provision for a teacher-aide in the special class is the most hopeful development of recent times. It makes the professional teacher twice as effective by allowing her to provide instruction to small groups and individuals while the aide is occupied with the remainder of the group. A teacher-pupil ratio of one to five is not idealistic in relation to the demands of the job. It is very realistic if we are committed to real behavior change in the learner. It should be made clear, however, that a proper number of adults in the classroom is not the only condition for better learning. Many day-care centers and institutions can provide a favorable teacher-pupil ratio without being able to provide functional measurable changes in pupil behavior. This is due to poor organization, lack of systematic program materials, poor choice of instructional objectives, or all of the above.

In a properly engineered classroom—or as Skinner (1968) would put it, if the total learning environment is properly arranged—the problem of individualizing training is markedly lessened. Hewett (1972) details a discussion of such engineering in the classroom. It *is* possible for the teacher to devote attention to a single student or to small groups while other students are productively employed elsewhere in any "classroom."

Systematic Teaching

It would be impossible to stress too greatly the role systematic teaching, appropriately programmed materials, and suitable resource materials—not to mention resource personnel and training aides—can play in facilitating the learning process *whatever the teacher-student ratio*. In fact, if the prognosis for the number of teachers immediately available from training institutions is considered, along with the prognosis for the numbers of students to be immediately serviced by public institutions, it is clear that our concentration must be on systematic training procedures and appropriate materials development. Peter Drucker (1969) has said that any technology consists of only two factors: appropriate tools and the organization of work. Further to the point, he adds:

> There is a great need for a rapid increase in the productivity of learning. There is, above all, great need for methods that will make the teacher effective and multiply his or her efforts and competence. Teaching is, in fact, the only traditional craft in which we have not yet fashioned the tools that make an ordinary person capable of superior performance [Drucker, 1969].

CREATING A TRAINING ENVIRONMENT

Public schools have been relatively selective in their choice of students in the past. They have been able to insist that children be toilet trained, have useful receptive language, functional expressive language, be capable of simple self-care skills, and not be "too hard to manage." Some administrators and teachers expect a whole new set of problems if they are forced to accept children with lesser abilities and fewer skills. Those fears are exaggerated. Unnatural restrictions such as insisting that training be conducted in a school-like environment create more real problems.

Another crippling restriction is the insistence that training be conducted during school-like hours. Training can and should be conducted during the evening hours when a variety of daily-living and leisure-time behaviors occur naturally. In institutions training should take place in the cottage or residence hall until bedtime. Community halfway houses should provide training during the evening hours rather than simply offering residence during this valuable time. Public schools should provide active and systematic training in recreation and leisure-time skills during evening hours. They should also train parents to provide follow-up support training in the home and in the community.

Need for a Realistic Training Setting

One of the most conspicuous reasons for lack of success in preparing the trainable mentally retarded for life in the community is that most training environments are not natural. They are limited in both scope and realism of experiences offered. Although recent research findings suggest the mentally retarded are indeed capable of generalizing some kinds of learning from one situation to another, in a real-world, nonlaboratory setting, the trainable generalize less than do persons with higher mental ability. Although persons who work with the retarded are aware of this, they seldom make provisions for it. The best quality education provided in an institution does not provide sufficient skill for adjustment to life in any other special environment.

Not all training can take place in a natural setting because we cannot arrange conditions in the real world to provide repeated lessons at convenient times. On the other hand, certain adjustments can be made. First, nearly all training environments can be designed to more nearly simulate required community experiences. Second, more training can take place in the real environment. The problem is due in part to the fact that too few programs are committed to community transition. Perhaps not enough people really believe the trainable are capable of a meaningful life adjustment. Another factor contributing to the faulty training environments is that most facilities were constructed without considering a community-transition philosophy.

Modifying the Institutional Setting

Classrooms in schools and cottages in institutions can usually be modified to accommodate more realistic training. Mimosa Cottage at Parsons State Hospital and Training Center was originally designed for custodial care and was totally unsuited to training (Lent, 1968 and 1970). The diagram of the middle floor of the building (see Figure 6-1) illustrates this. To create a training environment, several simple changes were made in the floor plan (see Figure 6-2). These changes made it possible to provide training in housekeeping, cooking, sewing, ironing, clothes washing and drying, and clothing storage. These accommodations to reality were still not sufficient. For instance, to train girls in housekeeping, the house-like areas in the cottage provided only the first step. When a student house-keeper had been trained to criterion on the cottage, she was placed in a community home under continuous supervision for additional training. Next, she was placed in a series of different community homes with increasingly less supervision. A worker was not expected to generalize from one home setting to another and from the supervisory conditions of one housewife to another. Rather, the variety was systematically provided in order to enhance ultimate generalization. One thing is clear. Abrupt transitions from school or institution to the real world are seldom successful. Without systematic planning and en-vironmental restructuring, training in the institution prepares children to live in the institution—nowhere else.

Other Methods for Providing Realistic Training

In all cases, more experience can and should be provided in real-life settings. The educators' old standby, the field trip, is not sufficient. Field trips are too infrequent and too passive. There is seldom a chance for children to participate. They merely observe. What *is* required is a planned series of *assignments* in the community. Town orientation—learning to get about the community by one-self—is a long-term, gradual process. It involves having students go places and do things, run errands, make simple purchases, deliver messages.

Distributive education is another possible solution for providing realistic

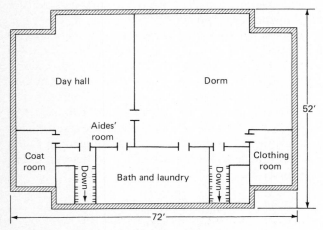

Figure 6-1   Mimosa Cottage Floor Plan A.

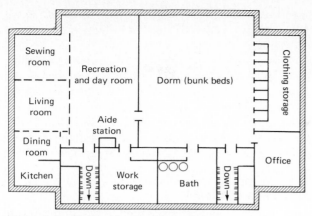

Figure 6-2 Mimosa Cottage Floor Plan B.

training. If the trainable are actually given training by the business community of their residence in the same systematic ways as normal distributive education students and many educable retarded, if they are assigned roles for which the rewards and the performance criteria are clearly stipulated, if they are allowed to interact with and work beside those who will become their daily-living skill models, we shall begin to realize the goal of normalization for the retarded. Such a program might well be underwritten by industry and by government on any or all levels from municipal to federal; this, in fact, is being successfully attempted in some European countries.

EDUCATION FOR ALL

Recent interpretations of law resulting from several court decisions will have a decisive impact on planning for and providing services for the mentally retarded. We need to look briefly at the development of educational responsibility in the United States to understand the recent change of direction. The authority for education has rested always with the states. There is no reference to education as such in the federal constitution.

Traditional State Legislation

States have various guarantees of free public education. This is reflected in legislation containing exclusion clauses. These have been of two kinds: (1) Statutes which guarantee a free public education on the basis of qualifications— such as independence of locomotion, absence of severe motor and/or emotional handicaps, absence of serious communication disabilities—all of which have had the effect of excluding some of the physically and mentally handicapped; (2) Statutes concerning compulsory school attendance which *excuse* the physically and/or mentally handicapped from the regulations applied to the normal student. By 1955, 25 states had enacted legislation either permitting or requiring classes for the severely retarded, the lower reaches of the group now referred to as trainable. The states which had achieved enabling legislation were still limiting services because of exclusion clauses.

Most states have delegated operative responsibility to the local governing units: the school districts. However, the past decade has seen a growing participation by the states in local school matters. This is due in part to the need to provide certain services which cross local district boundaries; the provision of education for the handicapped is a case in point (Weintraub, Abeson, Braddock, 1972). The body of pertinent legislation can be summed up as pertaining to three overriding issues: (1) the right to education, (2) the right to treatment, and (3) the guarantee of due process.

Changes in State Responsibilities to All Children

The decade of the 1960s was a period when minorities in the United States began to claim their rights. The particular case which has become a bellwether on the "education for all" issue started as a public concern for the residents of Pennhurst State School and Hospital, a Pennsylvania institution for the retarded. Investigations, newspaper reports, visits by public officials, and protests by parents disclosed that this institution housed 30 or more residents in a room and afforded them literally no habilitative services.

When the Pennsylvania Association for Retarded Citizens, an affiliate of the National Association for Retarded Citizens (NARC), retained counsel and brought litigation, the milestone ruling ordered the state of Pennsylvania and its public agencies to provide educational services for every child (Lippman & Goldberg, 1973). The corollary is that all retarded children, regardless of what traditional label might be attached to them, must have training or education which will benefit them.

Other cases, e.g., Mills versus Education (in the District of Columbia) and Wyatt versus Stickney (in Alabama), had, through their interpretations, already begun to shift the burden for education from community and state services and institutions to the public schools.

The right-to-education rulings are matched only by the parent movement, after World War II, in its effects on change in the training of the retarded. These two shaping events are forcing a new technology for the public education of the retarded.

Extensions of the Pennsylvania Decision

Since the Pennsylvania final court order in May 1972, there have been numerous extensions of the right-to-education principle (Lippman & Goldberg, 1973). Interpreted broadly, the Pennsylvania decision opened the way for a doctrine of universal education. It calls for equal access to education for all children, regardless of their situation.

A position paper adopted by the Council for Exceptional Children at its Miami Convention in April 1971 explains that universal education has been "translated as a commitment to provide educational opportunities for every child, whatever his socio-economic status; cultural or racial origins; physical, intellectual, or emotional equipment; potential contribution to society; and whatever his educational needs may be" (Lippman & Goldberg, 1973).

Inherent to the universal education doctrine is the obligation of each state to locate children who are not being trained, test them, and place them in classes with trained teachers, where they will have equal opportunities for education.

DEVELOPING CURRICULUM GOALS

Special educational provisions for the mentally retarded have been a feature of the American education system for many years. It would be reasonable to assume that the issue of curriculum content had been settled by trial and error— or directed by research findings. In one sense such content has been determined: public school curriculum guides are relatively standardized.

Curriculum guidelines issued by most state departments of public instruction are nonspecific and nonbehavioral. (A limited number of states are now developing behavioral, deficit-specific guides.) In general the state plans list certain life functions necessary for adjustment to society: citizenship, communication, home and family life, leisure-time pursuits, management of materials and money, occupational adequacy, physical and mental health, safety, social adjustment, and travel. The skill areas necessary to implement the life functions are arithmetic, fine arts, language arts, physical education, practical arts, science, and social relationships. These are the same educational goals educators have agreed upon for children in the regular grades. It is understood, of course, that the mentally retarded will not attain all the goals listed in the curriculum guides, at least not at the same level as their normal counterparts.

Adapting Curriculum Goals to the Retarded

The special education curriculum is, then, not as "special" as it is watered down. This is not to imply that the goals for the retarded should be different, or even "special." Indeed they *should* be the same, but through the process of watering down the curriculum, the student is given an imitation education. For example, the academic community had decided that the trainable retarded cannot learn academic materials (Johnson & Capobianco, 1958; Johnson, 1958; Doll, 1931; Louttit, 1957; Kirk & Johnson, 1951). Warren (1963) presents evidence to support the generally accepted notion that children with IQs below 55 seldom learn reading and arithmetic sufficiently well to use them in solving life problems.

Although studies do not specify that the trainable *could not* learn academic content, it has been *accepted* that they *cannot*. Consequently, there has been a trend to stress the development of social adaptability in special classes in public schools and in institutions. The exclusion of academic content in favor of special skills would perhaps be justifiable if it resulted in usefully improved social behavior. However, even this evidence seems lacking. Johnson and Capobianco (1958), in a survey of classes for the trainable in New York State, found only slight increments of improvement in habit development and social skills over a two-year period.

Cain and Levine (1961) investigated gains in social competency in institutionalized and community-based children. Each group was further divided into those who attended school and those who did not. The institutional-based children, both in school and out of school, showed significant decreases in social competency over a two-year period. The community group showed significant increases in social competency, but there was no difference between the group attending school and the group remaining at home. The implications are that institutions, under the best of conditions, are not effective in developing social skills, and that the community is a better environment for such development. The school program, in any event, could not be given credit for improvements.

Precise Goals—The Responsibility of School and Institutional Personnel

A less-recognized reason for the lack of success reported in most studies probing education of the trainable retarded is that educational goals are not stated with sufficient precision to be implemented. Failure to determine precise goals is not the fault of those who write curriculum guides. Their purpose is to guide. It is the responsibility of school and institutional personnel at the local level to translate broadly stated educational goals into more precise and usable forms. When goals have been made more explicit, two things are possible. First, it is possible to begin to design and write training programs. Second, the process of making *behavioral* definitions from generally stated goals allows the educator to make a critical discrimination; namely, which of the goals—all of which are valid—are the *most* teachable.

Failure to delineate teachable goals has hindered progress in teaching the retarded. When one is considering the trainable retarded group, the most teachable things are those which consist of components which are identifiable and observable as discrete units. In other words, skills can be more easily taught than concepts. But even here we must be cautious. Some skills do not lend themselves to detailed analysis. It is easy to agree that there are a number of "citizenship" skills required for community adjustment. However, citizenship has always been difficult to teach because it is difficult to define, divide into components, and sequence into a program of instruction. This is not to imply that we should not teach "citizenship." Rather, the most teachable parts of the citizenship role must be given first priority.

The process of writing instructional objectives has received considerable attention in recent years (Mager, 1962; Kapfer, 1972; Wheeler & Fox, 1972). Most materials are designed for persons with normal intellect. Wheeler and Fox (1972), however, described a method which lends itself very readily to materials which are complex and abstract or simple and concrete. There are three terms used to describe educational outcomes: educational goals, educational objectives, and instructional objectives. In this classification scheme, an *educational goal* reflects the ideal purposes of education. It is an abstract statement of future educational outcomes, e.g. "to produce citizens who have an appreciation of their American heritage." The next category, in terms of degree of specificity, is an *educational objective*. "Upon completion of the reading program, students will enjoy recreational reading" is an example of an educational objective. Such a concept is not directly observable; therefore, its use is potentially hazardous. It could be assumed that exposure to the reading program will produce the desired outcome. Although the outcome could be more accurately inferred from other observations, it would still be only an inference. Despite the built-in dangers, educational objectives can be helpful. A careful analysis of educational objectives will allow the educator to determine which objectives *are* observable and therefore teachable. This process necessitates an attempt by the educator to make components of instruction more specific in terms of one or several *instructional objectives*—the final and most functional category. There are three main features of an instructional objective:

    1   It contains a description of the behavior in observable terms.
    2   It contains a description of the conditions under which the behavior may be observed.
    3   It contains a description of the criterion by which the behavior may be judged (Mager, 1962).

    The Wheeler and Fox (1972) system is illustrated in Figure 6-3 in an application to daily-living skills derived from valid but general educational goals.

Educational Goals
    To educate individuals to achieve personal competency
    To educate individuals to achieve social self-realization

Educational Objectives
    Each student will know how to eat family style
    Each student will know how to use the telephone

Instructional Objective
    The student places the tablecloth and salt and pepper shakers in designated areas on table
    Before the telephone has rung five times the student picks up his telephone and holds it to his mouth and ear correctly

Writing Instructional Objective

Conditions	Behavior	Criteria
In simulated dining room in class	The student places the tablecloth and salt and pepper shakers in designated areas on table	100% correct on 3 consecutive trials

Conditions	Behavior	Criteria
In room with one-way observation and trainer telephone	Before the telephone has rung five times the student picks up his phone and holds it to his mouth and ear correctly	100% correct on 3 consecutive trials

Figure 6-3 *(From Wheeler and Fox, 1972.)*

Selection of Target Behaviors Based on Community Norms

Educational goals or curriculum-guide objectives are good for, and needed by, all children, and specifying instructional objectives provides latitude for individualization. Target objectives should vary somewhat according to age and ability level of the student population and according to the community setting for which they are being prepared. This latter criterion is all too often ignored by educators, institutional personnel, and parents. All instructional objectives should have community-transition value. There is no one set of behaviors appropriate to the home, one to the institution, one to the school, and one to the town—or at least there should not be.

The most adaptive and useful behaviors in any setting are those which are normal in a community setting. The standards for speech and language, dress, manners, and work should be the same in every living and training environment. It is difficult enough to train a retarded child to any one criterion, let alone several. Unfortunately, educators and even parents persist in allowing one standard of behavior for the retarded and another for normal persons. They permit one standard of behavior for the institution, yet idealize another for the community. Often the rationale for these dichotomous standards is that *he doesn't have a chance of making it in the real world*. Following the law of self-fulfilling prophecies, that fact is virtually assured.

To become as normal as possible is the only way the retarded person can expect to make a satisfactory adjustment in the community. The fact that normal society has constantly changing standards of acceptability is beside the point. It does not matter that many persons are apparently successful in spite of idiosyncratic behavior and appearance. For one thing, many "different" people are not successful. More importantly, of those who are getting by, most are not retarded. In fact, they are usually so skillful or talented occupationally that their deviations are tolerated. They may even be regarded as quaint or interesting. Retarded persons, on the other hand, do not have compensatory characteristics which compel their acceptance. They are peculiarly dependent upon not appearing to be different from the norm of their immediate community environment.

CURRICULUM FOR THE TRAINABLE

Lack of precision in stating goals for the retarded is a major fault in our educational system. Another fault is a lack of accuracy in selecting target behaviors. How do we know the selected instructional objective is on target? It might appear that if we have selected the community norm as our criterion model, the task would be easy. Not so. In fact, the wise selection of instructional objectives is made difficult for two reasons. First, the goals are usually selected by persons who have little association with the community environment for which their students are being prepared. Second, the persons who make curriculum decisions often tend to reject "common" behavioral objectives in favor of "important" ones.

In regard to the first point: The first author decided during the Mimosa

Cottage experiment that social dancing was a useful skill for community transition of the adolescent trainable-level girls of Mimosa Cottage (Lent, 1970). A dance program was designed and taught. It was not until a movie of a class session—a dance—was shown that the problem became plainly and embarrassingly apparent to the staff. The teen-age boys and girls in the film were too well-dressed for a Friday night dance. The girls wore their best long dresses; the boys wore suits, white shirts, and ties. They were painfully well behaved. The boys were courteous, the girls demure. The music, though lively to the author's ears, was probably dead to the ears of a teen-ager. In short, the real-life dance program had been developed by a hopelessly out-of-touch middle-aged man. A visit to a teen-age dance at the Town Hall was revealing, though traumatic. Most adults tend to impose their standards of normal in the selection of instructional objectives. There is only one way to be sure target selections are accurate and relevant—go see it as it is, where it happens.

Determining "Important" Target Behaviors

The other problem in selecting instructional goals concerns our concept of what constitutes an "important" behavior. It is easy to say, "whatever contributes to community adjustment," but difficult to believe that for certain individuals "toothbrushing" should take priority over knowledge of income tax laws. Daily-living skills that contribute to normality may be the most important skills needed by the trainable retarded because they make them less distinguishable from other citizens of the community. They give a retarded person a chance to get his foot in the door and keep it there.

Certain common behaviors are taken for granted in most parts of our society: bathing, shampooing, toothbrushing, and other such personal skills. It is only when these functions are not performed that we pay attention. Body odor, dirty hair, and bad breath are a detriment to the offender.

Daily-Living Skills as "Important" Behaviors

Not only are these simple skills not considered as important as some other behaviors, but there is confusion as to who should teach them. Few public school or day-care centers give daily-living skills priority as curriculum objectives. Some personnel frequently consider such teaching appropriate for the home, rather than the school. It is difficult to teach the trainable retarded to perform independently in the daily-living skills. The schools are better equipped than parents to provide such training, and they should accept a major share of the responsibility. Parents find it too difficult and frustrating to teach such behaviors well enough for the child to perform independently. They help the child bathe and select clothing and, in turn, the teacher may be lulled by the child's relatively acceptable appearance at school. If so, the teacher has missed the point: The student has not learned until he can perform the behavior independently.

Mimosa Cottage Experiment—A Means Toward Adjustment During the five-year course of the Mimosa Cottage experiment the residents of the experimental cottage made better adjustments to community life than was typical for institutionalized, trainable-level subjects. Of the original 71 residents, one of the girls is married and has made a marginal adjustment to the community (Lent, Dixon, Schiefelbusch, McLean, 1972), 40 returned to the community and have remained (Lent et al., 1971). Most of the girls are semi-independent. They are able to work full- or parttime, but require supervision for the management of their affairs. The most common type of placement is in the service occupations, such as aides in nursing homes. The girls live in the nursing homes and in return for their work, receive board and room, supervision and support, and a small salary. Some are living in their own homes with their parents, with foster parents, or in halfway houses. Seven of the girls were unable to adjust to competitive employment of any kind but have been continuously employed in sheltered workshops for more than four years.

Identifying Target Behaviors   The instructional objectives of the program were drawn largely from observations of life settings in the community. The questions which guided the observations were: "What specific, observable features of behavior do people in the community object to in the retarded?" and "What is the desired, appropriate, alternative behavior?" Townspeople, storekeepers, and casual observers were often able to identify residents of the institution by simple observation. The first clue was that they walked differently. Secondly, they looked different, and, thirdly, "You could tell when you talked to them."

Employers gave few behavioral definitions when pressed for reasons for their dissatisfaction with retarded employees, but they were quite articulate about some obvious features of behavior. Observations confirmed that, assuming the work placement was within the individual's capabilities for performance, mental retardation was not the most handicapping behavior feature. Employers complained, for instance, that workers were dirty and smelled bad, had bad breath, were careless about shaving, had hairy legs (girls), and paid too much attention to members of the opposite sex. In a study of the work behavior of the retarded (Lent, 1965), a careful observational procedure in a sheltered workshop setting revealed several observable, measurable behaviors which contributed to an employer's negative feelings toward a worker.

The categories of negative work behaviors and the behavioral definitions are summarized in Figure 6-4. Positive behaviors included those items listed in Figure 6-5.

This category of positively reinforced behavior was selected because it was incompatible with the negative behaviors and also because it made the worker *look* like he or she was working. The workshop supervisors, like other employers, were originally unable to state precisely why they were dissatisfied with some workers. They used such terms as "bad attitude," "not responsible," "fools around too much," and "doesn't work hard enough." The author was convinced that such opinions were formed, perhaps without conscious aware-

1 Talking and/or laughing while working
  a) Talk is nonwork oriented
  b) Excessively loud talk or vocalizations under any conditions
  c) Humming, singing, whistling, or talking to self
2 Nonverbal play
  a) Performance of work in ludicrous manner by use of grossly exaggerated motions or facial grimaces
  b) Playful bodily contact—characterized by light touch and usually accompanied by talking and/or laughing
  c) Throwing objects
3 Nonproductive work
  a) Working at what appears to be a markedly slower rate than is normal or acceptable, i.e., head in hand, slumping in chair, even though may be working at normal rate
  b) Sitting motionless
  c) Nonwork-oriented movements which cannot be characterized as ludicrous or exaggerated
4 Defiance of authority
  a) Verbal or nonverbal behavior intended to derogate the authority figure— includes passive resistance such as failure to respond immediately to commands or requests by authority
5 Unmannerly behavior
  a) Gross violation of code of courteous behavior—characterized usually by tone of voice which implies aggression or lack of respect, i.e., use of "Gimmee"
  b) Motions or gestures which place subject at social disadvantage in working setting, i.e., girl sitting with legs crossed and skirt open
  c) Whispering
6 Sexual contact
  a) Verbal—sexually suggestive words
  b) Nonverbal—arm around shoulder or waist of partner, hands contacting breast, buttock, stomach, or thigh of partner
  c) Allowing partner continued use of (a) or (b) above
7 Grossly immature behavior
  a) Words or gestures which are grossly immature, i.e., appropriate to person one-half the subject's life age

Figure 6-4 *(© 1973 by The University of Kansas [Project MORE].)*

The single category of behavior which was positively reinforced was: work-oriented behavior
  a) Nearly continuous eye contact with work
  b) Handling materials necessary for work
  c) Working at normal or near-normal rate
  d) Not engaged in any listed, categorized, negative behavior

Figure 6-5 *(© 1973 by The University of Kansas [Project MORE].)*

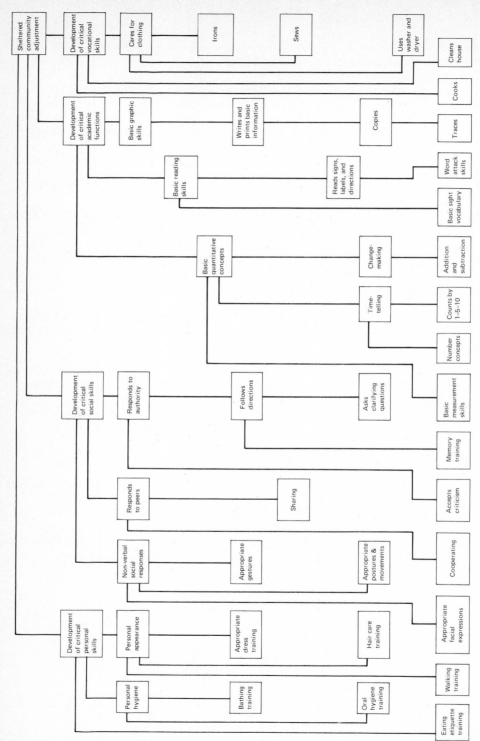

Figure 6-6 Mimosa Program Lattice. *(© 1973 by The University of Kansas [Project MORE].)*

Adaptive Behavior Checklist

Independent Functioning	Eating skills	_____
	Toilet use	_____
	Cleanliness	_____
	Appearance	_____
	Care of clothing	_____
	Dressing and undressing	_____
	Locomotion	_____
	General independent functioning	_____
Physical Economic Development Activity	Sensory development	_____
	Motor development	_____
	Money handling and budgeting	_____
	Shopping skills	_____
Language Development	Speaking and writing	_____
	Comprehension	_____
	General language development	_____
	Number and Time concept	_____
Occupation Domestic	Cleaning	_____
	Kitchen duties	_____
	General occupation Domestic	_____
	Occupation, General	_____
Self-Direction	Sluggishness in movement	_____
	Initiative	_____
	Persistence	_____
	Planning and organization	_____
	Self-direction (general)	_____
	Responsibility	_____
	Socialization	_____

Figure 6-7 Adaptive behavior checklist.

ness, on the basis of observing the workers engage in the negative behaviors previously listed.

Results   A simple behavior modification routine was inititated which effectively reversed the pattern of behavior in three experimental subjects from almost totally negative to almost totally postive. At the end of the three-month experimental period, the workshop supervisors reported that they thought the experimental subjects were the best workers in the workshop. The experiment gave some credence to the notion that *important* behaviors such as *poor attitude* are often made up of *common behaviors* which are observable and, therefore, modifiable.

The conclusions drawn from this study, plus the live observations in the community, allowed the Mimosa Cottage staff to develop a systematic plan for training. The lattice in Figure 6-6 (Lent, 1970) does not represent a complete listing of critical behaviors needed by all trainable retarded. It merely shows the priority targets selected for the Mimosa Cottage population.

Support Sources for Daily-Living Skill Targets

During the work behavior study, a parallel project (Nihira et al., 1970) was developing an instrument to assess the adaptive-behavior level of retarded children. This instrument was designed to replace the traditional measured intelligence level used by most schools and institutions. In the development of the instrument (the Adaptive Behavior Checklist) the authors identified several life skills deemed essential for successful adjustment to life in the institution,

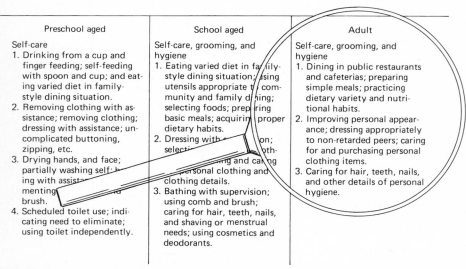

Figure 6-8   Suggested areas of program emphasis for moderately retarded residents: National Association for Retarded Citizens (NARC).

home, and community. It is in agreement with Mimosa Cottage curriculum but it is more comprehensive, since it covers all ages and levels of mental retardation. Samples from the checklist are provided in Figure 6-7.

Most recently, the National Association for Retarded Citizens (NARC) has published its guidelines to appropriate target behaviors for retarded children. Selections from the NARC guidelines are illustrated in Figure 6-8.

Currently, Project MORE, an outgrowth of the Mimosa Cottage experience at Parsons State Hospital and Training Center, is developing systematic training programs based on the concurrent recommendations of the three sources cited above. The programs currently under development appear in Figure 6-9, and several sample program lessons appear as Figure 6-10.

The best way to select program goals is to consult the sources cited in this section and adapt them to the characteristics of different populations.

I Personal appearance	**III Mealtime skills**
Hair combing	Self-feeding
Hair brushing	Eating etiquette
Hair setting and rolling	Selecting simple meals—cafeteria
Face shaving	Ordering simple meals—restaurant
Leg and underarm shaving	**IV Communications**
Toenail trimming	Response development
Shoe polishing	Articulation—stimulus shift
Handwashing	Use of telephone
Toothbrushing	Selecting simple meals—cafeteria
Nose blowing and wiping	Ordering simple meals—restaurant
Care of complexion	Communication of emergencies
Care of fingernails	**V Direction following**
Use of make-up	**VI Domestic skills**
Use of deodorant	Washing clothes by machine
II Personal hygiene	Drying clothes by machine
Handwashing	Washing dishes
Toenail trimming	Ironing
Hairwashing	
Nose blowing and wiping	
Showering and bathing	
Toothbrushing	
Care of complexion	
Care of simple injuries	
Care of fingernails	
Use of deodorant	
Use of sanitary napkin	
Communication of emergencies	
Taking simple medication	

Figure 6-9   Project MORE programs (under development or consideration). *(© 1973 by The University of Kansas [Project MORE].)*

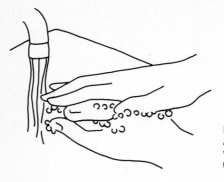

Figure 6-10 (a) Work the soap into a lather.
A step from the Project MORE hand-
washing program. (© 1974 by The University of Kansas [Project MORE].)

Creating Instructional Materials

Project MORE is one of five or six projects in the country to develop the
technology to write, validate, and mediate curricular materials for the retarded—
and one of only two or three such projects actually producing materials for
teachers of the trainable. While there are others, both privately and publicly
funded, tooling up to meet the burgeoning, newly mandated educational
demands, teachers of the trainable are still faced with a dearth of teaching tools.

For teachers of the trainable, the materials shortage amounts to an absence.
Since there are so few materials developed specifically for the trainable child,
teachers are forced to adapt materials intended for educable or normal children
or to design and write their own materials. If they have the time and motivation
to do this, they will experience more success in teaching. Considering the time
and difficulty required to write training programs, it is unrealistic to expect many
teachers to engage in such behavior. There are other solutions, however.

If teachers are provided with time and stipends during the summer months
when there is time to design and develop materials as a group, the idea suddenly
becomes feasible. Not only is this format effective for producing materials, it is
strongly recommended for other important reasons. It is an opportunity for

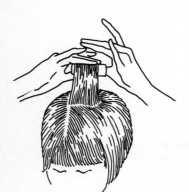

Figure 6-10 (b) Rolling hair. A step from
the Project MORE hair-rolling program.
(© 1973 by the University of Kansas
[Project MORE].)

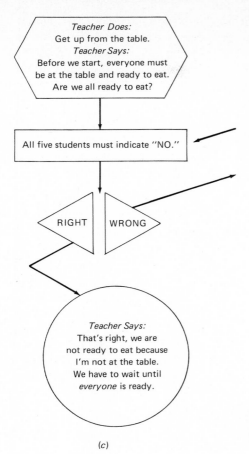

Figure 6-10 *(c) Waiting for others.* A step from the Project MORE eating program. *(© 1973 by The University of Kansas [Project MORE].)*

(c)

teachers and administrators to decide together upon their educational and instructional objectives. In many educational settings this has never been done as a joint effort. Educators have made decisions at the general educational goal level, but not at the level of specificity required for skill teaching. When the staff within a single school, or institution, has not agreed on exactly what should be taught, there is little chance for coordination and support between and among classes. As children progress from class to class each year there should be a logical continuity in their educational experience.

Another reason for a consensus opinion regarding curriculum is to ensure parental support. Teachers lament the lack of support and understanding on the part of parents. What teachers do not realize is that most parents have heard it all before—differently. From the parents' point of view the reasons and rationales for cooperation seem to change from teacher to teacher and from year to year. The schools often lack credibility with parents for this very reason.

The writing of functional, usable program materials has become more feasible with recent advances in educational technology. Ultimately, the solution to the materials shortage will be met by professional program developers such as Project MORE. Such program development is being encouraged by the U.S. Office of Education, Bureau of Education for the Handicapped. In the meantime, the crisis brought on by mandatory education rulings will have to be met by developing teacher-made materials.

Implementation of the Training Program

Once target behaviors have been selected, a lengthy and painstaking implementation process must begin. Without such a process (see Figure 6-11 for the graphic representation of the implementation procedures adopted by Project

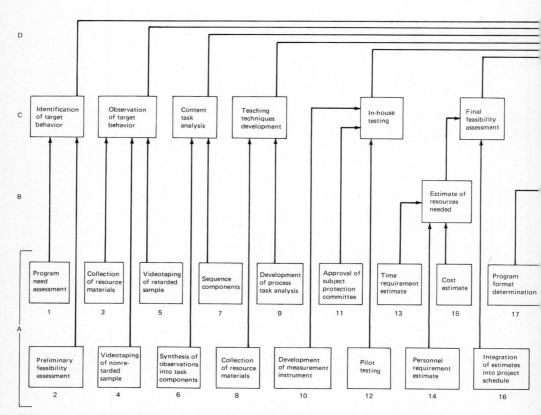

Figure 6-11 Project MORE: Implementation Lattice, February 1974. (© *1973 by The University of Kansas* [*Project MORE*].)

MORE), the chance that an actual program will evolve is slight—the probability of producing a programmed product which will be useful to others is very low. The technology of program development and production depends on a systematic procedure such as the Project MORE implementation process.

The steps outlined for program development are detailed according to the technology developed under the aegis of Project MORE. Teachers developing their own programs will be restricted, in most cases, at each juncture in the systematic procedures, but the steps outlined can be used by teachers and other program developers as models for their own, however restricted, program writing and utilization. The Project's mediation and validation procedures, for instance, cannot be emulated by most teachers—but teachers may profit from a

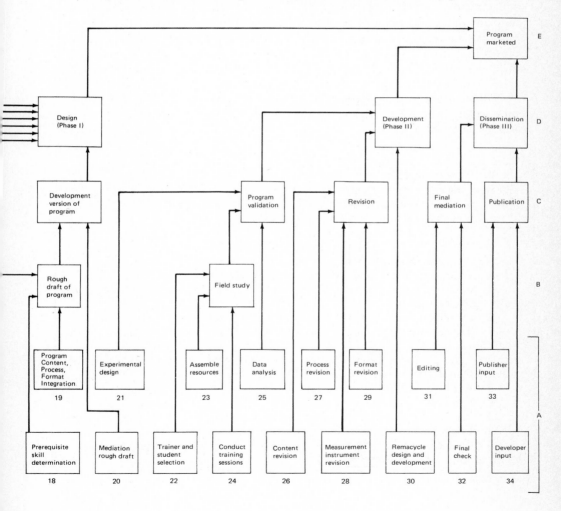

knowledge of the processes and may simulate them according to their own needs.

Figure 6-12 illustrates 13 steps designed by Project MORE for developing a training program. The steps in Figure 6-12 are used in Project MORE workshops to help train teachers to use the Project's educational programs.

Analyzing Target Behavior Steps

Programmers must analyze carefully the single but sequential steps which make up the target behavior they have selected to program. The first step is "the search of the literature." Using professional journals, indexes, catalogs, references, and commercial-product listings, they must gather and scrutinize all similar materials and program designs. Project MORE developers discovered that many of these materials already available require, at the least, adaptation for use with the trainable retarded, and, indeed, many offer programmers little more than format ideas. Nevertheless, this initial step cannot be bypassed: a certain defeat will come to the programmer if the project's investment in technology succeeds only in "reinventing the wheel."

The next procedural step involves careful observation of the target population—in this instance, the trainable retarded—as they actually attempt to perform the targeted behavior. It is necessary for trained observers to record, item

---

1 Define target behavior.
2 Conduct task analysis:
    a Use existing task analysis.
    b Observe nonretarded population.
    c Observe target population.
    d Supplement by introspection.
3 Analyze task analysis.
4 Determine the sequence of steps in the behavior.
5 Place sequential listing of steps into frames usable in a classroom; design teaching format.
6 Develop measurement system—observer's checklist.
7 Teach target behavior to one student currently lacking all or part of the target behavior.
8 Arrange for another trainer unfamiliar with program to teach one student currently lacking all or part of the target behavior.
9 Analyze results of testing and revise the program if necessary.
10 Duplicate final program.
11 Provide in-service training for others interested in using the program.
12 Each trainer teaches the program to three students.
13 Trainers confer and analyze results of training for further revisions in the program.

Figure 6-12 Developing your own training program. (© 1973 by The University of Kansas [Project MORE].)

by item, the behaviors as the students perform them—whether they perform successfully or not—i.e., whether or not their behaviors actually culminate in the targeted behavior or an approximation of it. The student performers should vary in skillfulness to provide an adequate sampling of potential problem areas. The Project MORE staff, for instance, task-analyzed a group of trainable retarded attempting to blow their noses. As the Project began to write a program for training this behavior, they video-taped a group whose skills reportedly ranged from fully competent to fairly competent to not competent.

Observation of the control group, which consists of students whose abilities vary widely, is necessary to determine exactly what steps are occurring during each behavior attempt. Through the control group the researchers can learn which steps in the behavior pattern are easiest and which are most difficult for the students to accomplish so that the training program can be planned accordingly.

Not the least important consideration in the task-analysis process is observation of a normal population. These persons may be staff personnel whose responsibilities span program design, evaluation procedures, testing and training, and mediation.

Determining a Teaching Strategy

Once the task analysis and sequencing of steps is completed for first-draft and testing purposes, the programmer must decide on a teaching strategy. (See Figure 6-13 for an illustration of a modified PERT chart strategy. Refer also to Figure 6-10 for an illustration of several sample Project MORE program lessons.) This format for teaching or training must include the exact sequence of steps, the criterion for the student's progress from step to step, alternatives for retraining each step, and exact directions to the trainer. Sometimes even the explicit words and phrases the trainer uses to direct the student's behavior must be included. Such strategies include first a verbal direction to the student, then an alternative verbal-plus-demonstration direction, and finally a verbal-plus-physical-prompt direction.

Provisions for fading or withdrawing the teacher's cues must be written into the program. This strategy must be tested carefully according to a predetermined evaluation procedure. Arrangements must be made to train enough students systematically, with strict adherence to the programmed content, and with more than one trained observer recording performance data at each training session. One, two, or more observers, in comparing their recorded observations, can aid the programmer in determining procedural reliability. However well the targeting of the behavior, the task analysis, the program sequencing, and the teaching procedure have been accomplished, the evaluation will yield a revised program. Some steps will need expansion and more detail, and some units or frames will require less specificity. During development of the Hair Rolling program (Lent et al., 1972), one entire unit was found, in test, to be unnecessary—largely because the students learned the unit while it was simply demonstrated in the

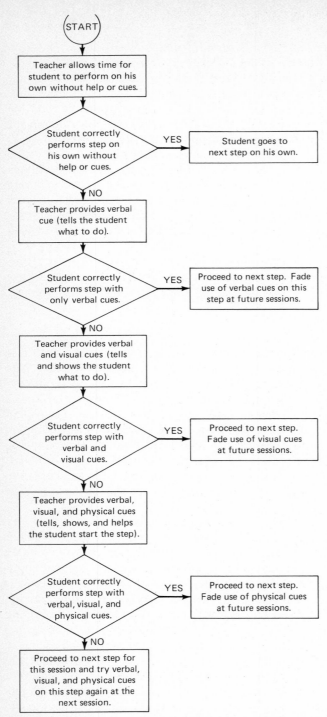

START

Teacher allows time for student to perform on his own without help or cues.

Student correctly performs step on his own without help or cues. — **YES** → Student goes to next step on his own.

NO

Teacher provides verbal cue (tells the student what to do).

Student correctly performs step with only verbal cues. — **YES** → Proceed to next step. Fade use of verbal cues on this step at future sessions.

NO

Teacher provides verbal and visual cues (tells and shows the student what to do).

Student correctly performs step with verbal and visual cues. — **YES** → Proceed to next step. Fade use of visual cues at future sessions.

NO

Teacher provides verbal, visual, and physical cues (tells, shows, and helps the student start the step).

Student correctly performs step with verbal, visual, and physical cues. — **YES** → Proceed to next step. Fade use of physical cues at future sessions.

NO

Proceed to next step for this session and try verbal, visual, and physical cues on this step again at the next session.

Figure 6-13 *(© 1973 by The University of Kansas [Project MORE].)*

backward-chaining teaching strategy. Major revisions in strategy or format of any program should be *expected* to require a second round of testing.

Mediation to Facilitate Learning

Mediation, which will have been in process throughout program development, from the task-analysis stage, will enter its final stages only after testing and evaluation has been successfully concluded. Mediation should not be construed as simply the rendering of the program into readable or watchable or listenable form; it entails the *structuring* of a program in a design which facilitates or controls the actual learning/training process. Media specialists need to work in concert with research personnel throughout program development if the program design and feasibility are to prove efficient for and compatible with the consumer for whom the program is developed. It has been found, for instance, that many forms of audiovisual mediation requiring esoteric hardware systems are not feasible or efficient for use with the trainable retarded. This is because most settings where the trainable are taught do not have and cannot afford the necessary equipment. Program formats must often be confined to printed materials—although every attempt should be made to ensure that programming is viable and adaptable to other forms of mediation, should the program be widely disseminated in the future.

Bridging the Research-Consumer Gap

The implementation procedure as described is obviously costly in terms of personnel and time. This does not mean the development, production, and the dissemination of such materials for the trainable retarded is more costly than commercial development and production of "thin-market" instructional materials. Indeed, in terms of cost-benefit, which takes into account not only actual consumer cost but also such factors as efficiency and effectiveness of programming, materials produced under such optimal conditions are truly more economical. The extensive and time-consuming validation process these materials undergo assures program replicability, and efficiency and effectiveness quotients.

The publishing industry regards "thin-market" materials as high-risk investments. This is true although only a few full-process publishers (as distinct from those providing mail-order services for products consigned to them by others who have actually handled the production phases) have surveyed markets and reassessed market potential among special groups, such as the trainable retarded. In light of new dimensions and demands—not to mention federal and state mandates—in regard to training for such special groups, this market *does* need studying. It promises to quickly become large and voracious.

The normally conservative offices of the federal government have, in this instance, provided leadership in bridging the research-consumer gap. The U.S. Office of Education has provided procedural facilitation for the developers who wish to promote the products of special-education research to enable these products to reach their intended consumer speedily. It has rescinded an old policy which required that the government receive all royalties from such products and has set forth guidelines which allow program developers to petition for developmental copyrights (See Figure 6-14). Such a provision allows for the gathering of market data and determination of consumer feasibility factors.

Surely the day is not far away when publishers will understand the complete technology which must be implemented to produce *reliable* instructional products. With this understanding, publishers will see fit to invest in the dissemination of high cost-benefit, but low consumer-cost, materials. Indeed, if they do not, alternative methods will develop, and these products will emerge, through new dissemination systems, in order to meet the burgeoning public demand. The technology of development will undoubtedly spawn its own technology of dissemination if traditional procedures do not adapt to the demand. The ever-increasing need for efficiency in retrieval of instructional methods and materials depends literally on solutions to such dissemination problems.

The hardware exists for efficient retrieval systems and networks; what does *not* exist are organized, concerted efforts and sufficient, stable funds along with a uniformly specific notation system—which this chapter has already mentioned. All we have to enable any information retrieval are tradition-bound libraries, systems of educational materials' storehouses (regional storehouses and satellite storehouses), and conventions of educators meeting in special curricular subdivisions to exchange program ideas—all heavily underwritten by federal and organizational enterprise but often ineffective and cumbersome.

CONCLUSIONS

The authors have suggested that there are three ingredients prerequisite to changing the lives of the retarded. These are:

1   More careful and realistic selection of target behaviors
2   The technology for implementing systematic training
3   An administration which grants systematic support for targeting and the implementing procedures

The first two ingredients have been covered. Although there is not yet a technology in regard to the third ingredient, it is instructive to note recent attempts to address the problem. One such attempt is occurring at Parsons State Hospital and Training Center, an institution in most important ways representative of others in the United States. Parsons State Hospital has recently undergone an analysis of hospital policies and procedures and has designed a new administrative organization in which accountability for the training of residents is a key feature.

Accountability is indeed the key word in programs which need to be devised for teaching the trainable retarded. Without this factor—and all that it portends and stimulates—there is little chance for normalization of the trainable. There will be no chance for them to be returned as functional though semi-independent members of this or any other society.

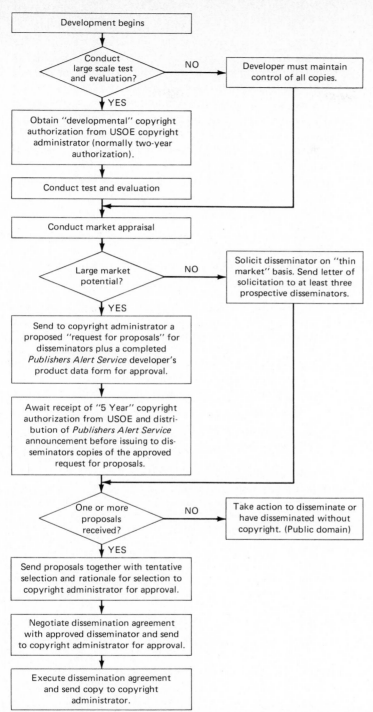

Figure 6-14 *(Revised according to the direction of Morton W. Bachrach, Copyright Administrator, National Institute of Education, USOE.)*

In this country there is a trend toward realizing the goal of normalization for the retarded. However, the movement has used its energy to outline the needs such programming will entail. Little has been done, as far as public or private institutions are concerned, toward even the beginning work on actual programming. The previously discussed technology for teaching daily-living skills to the retarded can lend itself appropriately to such implementation. The authors hope this brief discussion will aid others responsible for such programming.

The precedents underlying and giving impetus to programming for change in the training of the retarded are summarized in the following institutional reorganization plan, with normalization of its residents its goal (Brown and Devine, 1973):

I   Administrative reform
   A   The personnel management system shall meet the habilitation needs of residents with regard to the allocation of staff.
   B   The personnel management system shall provide procedures for staff accountability in the training of residents.
II   Training reform
   A   Written measurable training objectives shall be available for each student.
   B   A written measurable training curriculum shall be available for each department.
   C   Training services shall provide specific entrance and exit criteria for resident transition into living units and training programs.
   D   The quantity of available training programs shall be sufficient to meet training goals and legal mandates.
III   Policy reform
   A   All practices, policies, and procedures shall satisfy normalization principles as specified by the Joint Commission on Accreditation of Hospitals in the Standards for Residential Facilities for the Mentally Retarded.
   B   A statement of policies, practices, and procedures shall be available to all staff.

Such administrative support is essential to overcoming the tremendous and immediate problems of what, where, and how to teach the trainable retarded. We have a technology, and we must now attend to the task.

DISSCUSSION TOPICS

The Trainable Retarded: The Technology of Teaching

Objective   This chapter discusses the habilitation of a specific group of retarded persons; those classified as the "trainable mentally retarded." In this discussion, the authors suggest strategies for this habilitation by examining:

1   The labeling of the mentally retarded
2   Realistic selection of target behaviors

3 Implementation of systematic training
4 Administration to support such procedures

Exercises These exercises are best suited for a two-student team to be completed as a project for this chapter. The simulations suggested require one student to assume the role of a retarded individual and the other student the role of the trainer. (If training sessions or classrooms of retarded are open for observation, it is suggested that students observe them as a basis for simulation. Films of retarded persons performing skills might be beneficial to students prior to simulation.)

1 Select a *teachable* educational goal for a preadolescent trainable mentally retarded (TMR) student and justify it as a needed social competency.
2 Using the illustration from Wheeler and Fox, determine the instructional objectives for this educational goal.
3 Select one of the instructional objectives and conduct a task analysis of the objective. If material is already available, justify its use as written or the adaption for its use with the target population it would require. If no material is available on the objective, conduct a task analysis through simulation. After task analysis is completed, sequence the steps in a logical, teachable order for training with the retarded.
4 Test the sequential listing through simulation by applying the strategy employed by Project MORE. After testing, suggest revisions and adaptations of the sequencing or teaching strategy determined by the simulated testing session.
5 As a TMR trainer, write a rationale for including the program you just developed into the overall training program for the mentally retarded in a public school.

Developing Necessary Skills for Entry into Classroom Teaching Arrangements[1]

Joseph E. Spradlin
Bureau of Child Research, University of Kansas
Rita R. Spradlin
University of Kansas

INTRODUCTION

A major problem facing our educational system is how to best provide for children who have such severe behavior deficits or excesses that they cannot be integrated into public school classrooms.

Many of these children have been classified as profoundly or severely retarded. Others are called autistic, aphasic, or brain-injured. Most cannot be tested with standardized intelligence or achievement tests, and they are excluded from the public schools. Programs for these children have in the past been restricted primarily to institutions or to parent-sponsored day-care programs.

Information concerning teaching such children may be found in the *American Journal of Mental Deficiency,* and the *Journal of Applied Behavior Analysis.* There is almost no literature in educational journals such as *Exceptional Children, Journal of Special Education,* and *Teaching Exceptional Children.* Although *Methods in Special Education* edited by Haring and Schiefelbusch

(1967) gave extensive attention to educating most groups of handicapped children, it contained no chapters on the education of these severely handicapped children. Perhaps the clearest acknowledgement that such children are entitled to education is to be found in Hollis and Gorton (1967).

The lack of information in educational journals and books on teaching these children is not surprising. As late as 15 years ago there was considerable disagreement about whether or not trainable retarded children were even entitled to a free public education (Goldberg & Cruickshank, 1958).

Even with much parental pressure, public school programs for the severely handicapped have often been viewed as a favor by the school system to the child and parent rather than a public responsibility. Nevertheless, recent court decisions in Pennsylvania and the District of Columbia have established that all children have a right to a free public education (Abeson, 1973). These court decisions, coupled with new community models for managing handicapped children, will result in more of these children remaining in the home communities and attending public school (ENCOR Annual Report, 1973). Since these children do not fit into traditional educational groups, individualized methods must be developed to prepare them for group instruction.

During the past few years the term *accountability* has become fashionable in discussions of public education. This term implies that there is a contract between two parties and that one of the parties, the teacher, is accountable for delivering the services defined in the contract. The responsibility of the second party, the taxpayer, is relatively explicit. It consists of providing tax money to be appropriated for the operation of the school system. Exactly what educational services should be provided is far less explicit. It is presently extremely difficult to determine whether or not teachers are providing the services required by the contract.

Principles of mutual agreement for developing reasonable contracts are lacking. This is true, not only in the field of special education, but also in general education. Part of this problem stems from difficulty in developing educational goals. Indeed, one writer has questioned whether general public goals can be reached in a pluralistic society (Bowers, 1971). If there were such goals and also techniques for measuring whether these goals had been achieved, reaching a fair and equitable contract between society and public education might be possible. Until such goals are developed and agreements have been reached concerning how many of these goals should be developed at a particular cost, then accountability will remain an undefined word found in polemic attacks on teachers.

The education of persons with severe behavioral handicaps presents tremendous problems regarding what is a reasonable achievement. There are few, if any, norms for the development of skills. In comparing what handicapped children learn in school with what normal children learn, the accomplishments of the handicapped are meager. For this reason, it is extremely important that appropriate behavioral targets be set and that appropriate measures be developed to determine whether or not these targets have been reached.

DEVELOPMENT OF BEHAVIORAL TARGETS AND PROCEDURES FOR EVALUATING THEM

Considerable material to aid teachers in developing behavioral targets for teaching is now available. This material suggests that targets should be stated in terms of observable actions or behaviors (Mager, 1962; Panyan, 1972; Wheeler & Fox, 1972). The teacher may obtain aid in selecting areas for developing behavior targets by referring to the AAMD Adaptive Behavior Scale (Nihira, Foster, Shellhaas, & Leland, 1970), the Cain-Levine Social Competency Scale (Cain, Levine, & Elzey, 1963), and the Vineland Social Maturity Scale (Doll, 1947). Teachers will also find helpful models for establishing goals and developing specific programs for accomplishing those goals in the preceding chapter.

The development of behavior targets or curriculum for children is usually left to professional educators. Parents normally have minimal participation in this endeavor. In the area of education of the severely handicapped, the parents should be more active participants, both in selecting targets and in aiding in the evaluation of teaching programs.

To begin this process, the teacher should observe the child in the school situation and then compare notes with the parents concerning skills which the child does and does not exhibit. This meeting should be the first step in developing targets for evaluating the child and for developing the teaching program. During these planning sessions the parents and the teacher should reach agreements about how they describe the child's skills. Discrepancies between home behavior and school behavior should become apparent. Behavior is often lost when a child encounters a new environment, and it may take some time to reestablish the behavior in the new environment, that is, when the child goes from home to the school.

Once the parents and teacher have agreed on the behaviors which the child does or does not exhibit, they should plan targets (goals) to be worked on during the year. Targets should reflect the demands of the home as well as prepare the child for school experiences. When parents and teachers agree on the behavioral targets to be taught, the first step toward evaluating the child and developing the teaching program will have been made. Schools must develop new strategies, and joint parent-teacher planning, evaluation, and teaching must be included in them.

We already have discussed the gross initial evaluation of the child's behavior made by the teacher and parent. This evaluation aids in deciding what will be taught. Evaluation must also take place within each teaching session. Each time the teacher requires a performance, she must evaluate whether or not that performance was accomplished. This type of evaluation indicates whether or not reinforcement is to be delivered or whether the child should try again. In some situations the teacher will record these evaluations. However, most recording must be restricted to limited performance samples. Otherwise, the teacher's records will become voluminous, and more time is required to record than to teach.

Data must be recorded to evaluate trends which take place over sessions. If

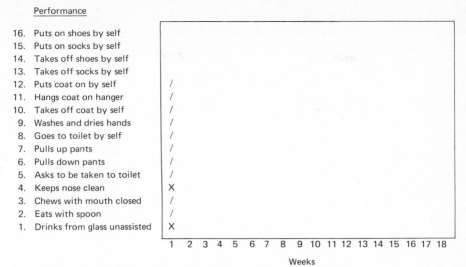

Performance

16.	Puts on shoes by self	
15.	Puts on socks by self	
14.	Takes off shoes by self	
13.	Takes off socks by self	
12.	Puts coat on by self	/
11.	Hangs coat on hanger	/
10.	Takes off coat by self	/
9.	Washes and dries hands	/
8.	Goes to toilet by self	/
7.	Pulls up pants	/
6.	Pulls down pants	/
5.	Asks to be taken to toilet	/
4.	Keeps nose clean	X
3.	Chews with mouth closed	/
2.	Eats with spoon	/
1.	Drinks from glass unassisted	X

1 2 3 4 5 6 7 8 9 10 11 12 13 14 15 16 17 18

Weeks

Figure 7-1   A hypothetical list of behavioral targets and the symbol for meeting criterion (X) or not meeting criterion (/) on those targets.

no improvement in the performance is shown, then the trend suggests a change in the teaching procedure; but if improvement is shown, the same procedure should be continued.

A third level of evaluation involves the child's overall progress during the school term. To evaluate progress in a rehabilitation or education program, the teacher must be able to evaluate the child's acquisition of various skills. Education traditionally trains various performances simultaneously. Moreover, the effects of education are cumulative. A good teacher is not satisfied with teaching only one skill, but continues to teach or add skill after skill. The teacher must have a method of getting a quick evaluation of the type and number of performances acquired over time. Figure 7-1 is a sample chart to aid in the evaluation of the progress a child makes over time in training programs which are in effect.

On the ordinate is a list of performances 1 through 16. Note that each item is something that the child does. The performances must be delineated more precisely than is done with the three- or four-word phrases shown on the sample chart.

Time units were recorded on the abscissa. Dividing the abscissa into weekly periods is adequate if the progress is to be evaluated over the school year. If progress is to be evaluated over several years of teaching, correspondingly larger time units are used.

The charting method requires a specific criterion for each performance listed. Each time the performance is evaluated, a mark is made on the chart to clearly indicate whether or not the child reached criterion. A simple "/" mark is used if the performance does not meet criterion. An "X" mark is used when the performance meets criterion. The hypothetical child in Figure 7-1 was evaluated during the first week on performances 1 through 12. He met criterion on performances 1 and 4, but failed to meet criterion on all other performances. The blank spaces beside items 13 to 16 simply mean that these performances were not evaluated during the first week.

Figure 7-2 introduces three more symbols:

(T) indicates teaching or training is being conducted.

(-) indicates performance was not evaluated during week 2; however, criterion was not met during the first week.

(■) indicates the performance was not evaluated during week 2; however, performance was at or above criterion when last evaluated.

Figure 7-1 shows that neither drinking with a glass nor keeping nose clean were subjected to formal evaluation, but both were present when last evaluated. It also shows that during week 2 training was initiated in eating with a spoon, pulling pants down, and taking coat off. Putting coat on and pulling pants up were evaluated, but neither was at criterion level. Performances 3, 5, 8, 9, and 11 were neither taught nor evaluated, even though they were not at criterion when last evaluated.

Figure 7-3 shows that during week 3 training was introduced for item 12, "putting coat on by self," and that criterion was reached on item 6, "pulls pants down." All other items remained as they were during week 2. During the fourth week, two new items were evaluated. Criterion was reached for item 13, but not for item 14. Moreover, four other performances were evaluated, and all reached criterion. Two performances, 1 and 4, had been evaluated previously and were at

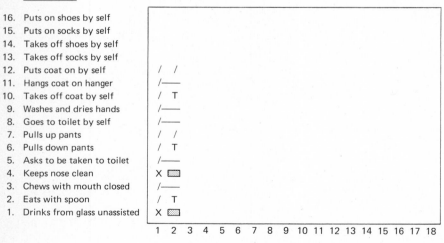

Performance

16. Puts on shoes by self
15. Puts on socks by self
14. Takes off shoes by self
13. Takes off socks by self
12. Puts coat on by self   /   /
11. Hangs coat on hanger   /——
10. Takes off coat by self   /   T
 9. Washes and dries hands   /——
 8. Goes to toilet by self   /——
 7. Pulls up pants   /   /
 6. Pulls down pants   /   T
 5. Asks to be taken to toilet   /——
 4. Keeps nose clean   X ▨
 3. Chews with mouth closed   /——
 2. Eats with spoon   /   T
 1. Drinks from glass unassisted X ▨

1 2 3 4 5 6 7 8 9 10 11 12 13 14 15 16 17 18

Weeks

Figure 7-2 The same hypothetical list or chart as Figure 7-1, but it has been extended to the second week of observation and introduces three new symbols, T for Train—for not evaluated but absent when last evaluated and ▬ for not evaluated but present when last evaluated.

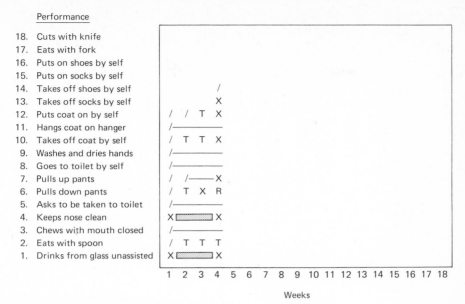

Performance

18. Cuts with knife
17. Eats with fork
16. Puts on shoes by self
15. Puts on socks by self
14. Takes off shoes by self
13. Takes off socks by self
12. Puts coat on by self
11. Hangs coat on hanger
10. Takes off coat by self
9. Washes and dries hands
8. Goes to toilet by self
7. Pulls up pants
6. Pulls down pants
5. Asks to be taken to toilet
4. Keeps nose clean
3. Chews with mouth closed
2. Eats with spoon
1. Drinks from glass unassisted

1 2 3 4 5 6 7 8 9 10 11 12 13 14 15 16 17 18

Weeks

Figure 7-3 An extension of Figure 7-2.

criterion. Two performances, 7 and 10, had not been at criterion during the week they were first evaluated. Criterion was reached on performance 10 after formal training, but without formal training on performance 7. Finally, a new symbol, "R" indicates that review trials were given during this week.

Figure 7-4 shows the overall view of the training program and acquisition of skills for a hypothetical child. This chart shows that during the 18-week period the child acquired 14 performances. Of these 14 performances, 12 were acquired with training, and 2 of the 14 performances without training. Two tasks on which training was given failed to reach criterion. Only one behavior which had been acquired was demonstrated to be lost during the 18 weeks. The chart also shows that the child never learned to ask to be taken to the toilet even though training was given on this aspect of toilet-training throughout the 12 weeks.

In addition to graphically presenting a general view of the child's accomplishments during the 18 weeks, the chart contains considerable information about the overall training program. For example, no more than four performances were being trained at one time. Toward the end of the program, learned behavior was not being evaluated to make sure that it was at criterion level.

Figure 7-4 can represent either individual or group data. It is simple, yet it clarifies almost any individual or group training program involving cumulative skills. Note also that the method of graphing is extremely flexible. Points along the time line can be added ad infinitum. New performances can also be added. These characteristics are quite important when graphically representing the education process. Education occurs over time, altering or adding to what is being taught. Graphic methods must be capable of showing this.

Performance

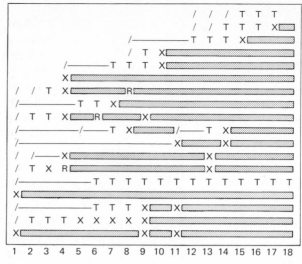

18. Cuts with knife	
17. Eats with fork	
16. Puts on shoes by self	
15. Puts on socks by self	
14. Takes off shoes by self	
13. Takes off socks by self	
12. Puts coat on by self	
11. Hangs coat on hanger	
10. Takes off coat by self	
9. Washes and dries hands	
8. Goes to toilet by self	
7. Pulls up pants	
6. Pulls down pants	
5. Asks to be taken to toilet	
4. Keeps nose clean	
3. Chews with mouth closed	
2. Eats with spoon	
1. Drinks from glass unassisted	

1 2 3 4 5 6 7 8 9 10 11 12 13 14 15 16 17 18

Weeks

Figure 7-4 The hypothetical progress chart for one-half of a school year.

One other note on the charting method. Behaviors or performances must be stated positively. Those behaviors or performances deemed positive should be more frequent at the right of the graph than at the left.

Although the graphing system in Figure 7-4 is simple, it provides a variety of data for teachers, parents, and public school administrators. First, it lends itself to *portraying the list of performances* to be established. Thus, anyone walking into the teacher's area would have an immediate general indication of the performances the teacher was trying to establish for each child. Such a public list established by agreement of teacher and parent helps reduce criticisms concerning relevance of curriculum. Moreover, just as the time is open-ended, so is the list of performances. That is, if during the year the parent and teacher see the need for new performances, they may easily add them to the list.

Although the procedure for displaying the program lends itself to the development of hierarchical skills, it is not limited to such skills. Skills may be sequential, such as saying words and then saying word combinations, or the skills may be unrelated, such as saying words and walking down stairs in alternating steps.

The procedure also should aid in evaluating program planning. For example, if a teacher has a chart which shows that she has been teaching for two or three months and the child has acquired no new performances, the teacher's performance goals are probably unrealistic. She needs help in either selecting more appropriate performance goals or in breaking the performance goals into smaller units.

A second possible explanation for no change in performance is poor teaching technique. Failure to show progress on the chart may indicate that the program is not adequate.

This type of performance chart also helps in discriminating between teaching aimed at changing specific performances and mere exposure teaching. Exposure teaching is merely presenting stimuli in a teaching session, even though those presentations make no changes in the child's performance. The chart also indicates the frequency with which the teacher tests to determine whether specific performances are acquired or being lost. In short, the charting procedure combines evaluation, teaching, and performance acquisition, all of which may eventually aid in devloping reasonable agreements concerning how much children should learn during a given time.

CONCEPTUAL APPROACH USED IN DEVELOPING METHODS

Thus far we have discussed some possible procedures for establishing performance targets for teaching children with severe behavioral problems and some ways of evaluating and graphically displaying the overall educational progress of a child. Nothing has been said about principles of behavior or methods for teaching the performances selected as targets.

The principles of the functional analyses of behavior have been used by special education with increasing frequency during the past 10 years (Lindsley, 1964; Haring & Lovitt, 1967; Hall, 1971a, 1971b, 1971c; Schiefelbusch, 1967; Hewett, Taylor, & Arturo, 1970; Gardner, 1971). Numerous investigators have shown that the behavior of severely handicapped children can be changed through the systematic application of principles of operant conditioning (Wolf, Risley, and Mees, 1964; Baer, Peterson, and Sherman, 1967; Spradlin, Girardeau, and Corte, 1966; Spradlin, 1964; Lovaas, Koegel, Simmons, and Long, 1973; Hall, 1971c; Hollis, 1967a, b).

The primary principle used to bring about these changes is the reinforcement principle. The power of the applied principle has been so well demonstrated that most workers, regardless of theoretical persuasion, recognize that any training or management program must attend carefully to the consequences of behavior. The consequences of behavior and their effects are shown in Table 7-1 below.

Table 7-1 The Effect of Presentation or Withdrawal of Positive Reinforcers or Aversive Stimuli

	Withdraw	Present
Positive reinforcer	Decrease in behavior	Increase in behavior
Aversive stimulus	Increase in behavior	Decrease in behavior

Developing effective reinforcement systems for use with severely limited children is often difficult. One chief problem is finding a durable and effective reinforcer. The importance of finding a durable effective reinforcer for these children cannot be overstated since *without an effective reinforcer any teaching program is doomed to failure*. Many severely limited children may be reinforced with rather conventional reinforcers such as social praise, pats on the back, caresses, or hugs and kisses; however, for some children, these typical reinforcers are not effective. When they are not effective, other events have sometimes proved useful. These include vibratory stimuli, music, moving pictures, colored slides, and mechanical toys. Sometimes foods such as candy, popcorn, cereals, ice cream, and yogurt serve as a reinforcer even when the child has been freely fed at mealtime. Liquids such as milk, Tang, juice, and soda pop have been used for other children. However, there are children for whom none of these events are effective. Striefel (personal communication) worked for over two years with a severely retarded child in an attempt to find a reinforcer which he could use in a program to teach a severely retarded child to imitate and to follow simple commands. The list of events he used in an attempt to find a reinforcer is shown in Table 7-2. None of these events proved to be a reinforcer for the child. Striefel was aware of research (Hollis, 1967*a*, *b;* Spradlin, 1964; Wolf, Risley, and Mees, 1964; Baer, Peterson, and Sherman, 1967; Lovaas, Koegel, Simmons, and Long, 1973) demonstrating that when such a child receives all or most of his meals in a training, he can develop self-feeding, imitation, direction-following, and other motor skills. However, since institutional policy currently does not allow the child's meals to be used as a reinforcer to teach skills, Striefel discontinued attempts to teach this child. This institutional policy seems to be in line with the views held by persons in the general society. Persons who establish such policies must change these views concerning the use of such basic reinforcers as food and water as reinforcers in teaching programs, or we must simply give up teaching some severely handicapped children. Children for whom food or water are the only feasible reinforcers are very few in number, constituting a small percent of those with severe behavioral limitations. Nevertheless, they do exist. When we encounter them we are faced with a severe ethical and perhaps legal dilemma. Shall we simply give up in our attempts to teach? Or shall we provide the child's basic reinforcers contingent on making responses in the teaching setting?

This should not be construed as a plea for widespread use of meals as reinforcers for children—that is unnecessary for the overwhelming majority of handicapped children. But if meals *are* used in teaching, they must be used by a trainer who is extremely skilled in recognizing what behaviors are possible for the child. Using meals as reinforcers and demanding more than the child is capable of accomplishing is cruel as well as ineffective.

Timing the delivery of a consequence is frequently overlooked. *Reinforcement must be immediate*. Certain self-teaching devices probably owe their success in part to the fact that they provide immediate consequences for a correct response. Learning to use adequate timing of consequences is one of the most difficult aspects of behavior management. It is not at all unusual to see a

Table 7-2   Items Used by Sebastian Striefel in a Two-year Attempt to Find an Effective Reinforcer for a Severely Retarded Child

A *Social*
  1 Praise
  2 Pat on knee
  3 Hug
  4 Hand-squeeze
  5 Tickling ribs
  6 Stroking face
  7 Verbal comments such as, "good girl," "that's the way," "great"
  8 Another child who gets reinforced for correct responses

B *Liquids*
  1 Tang (orange and grape)
  2 Lemonade
  3 Koolaid (variety of flavors)
  4 Soda (variety of flavors)
  5 Water

C *Edibles*
  1 Ice cream (variety of flavors)
  2 Candy
  3 Marshmallows
  4 M & M's
  5 Mints
  6 Cheetos
  7 Pretzels
  8 Candy corn
  9 Peanuts
  10 Butterscotch candy
  11 Corn chips
  12 Potato chips (plain and barbecue)
  13 Dry cereals (variety)
  14 Sweet and sour candy
  15 Pudding (chocolate and butterscotch)
  16 Chocolate-covered peanuts
  17 Lollipops
  18 Dried fruits (variety)
  19 Cookies (variety)

D *Toys*
  1 Magazines
  2 Picture books
  3 The Farmer Says (talking toy)
  4 Music box
  5 Noisemaker
  6 Horns
  7 Teddy bear
  8 Barking-walking dog
  9 Balls
  10 Toy adding machine
  11 Santa Claus
  12 Dolls
  13 Helicopter
  14 Wind-up monkey
  15 Chatter telephone
  16 Cars
  17 Trucks
  18 Scissors and paper
  19 Play dough

E *Tokens (Backups included)*
  1 Wide variety of nickel candy
  2 Wide variety of penny candy
  3 Wide variety of carnival-type toys

F *Other*
  1 Mirror
  2 Tape-recorded music (wide variety)
  3 Video tapes (children's programs, commercials, feedback of self)

person trying to teach a child to attend (look at a picture, or an object and/or the trainer), but consistently delivering a positive consequence long after the child's attending response occurred. Such training directly increases the rate of looking at the ceiling or out the window. If it does increase the rate of attending to the training situation, it is only because such attending is a component of a chain, the end point of which leads to an immediate consequence.

Behavior modification includes procedures for bringing behavior under stimulus control. Since much of education involves teaching the child to make the correct response to a specific stimulus, methods for establishing stimulus control are important. The primary condition for establishing stimulus control is differential reinforcement. Reinforcement is presented for a response after one specific stimulus has occurred and not after other stimuli have occurred. For example, a child may receive approval if he closes the door in response to the command, "close the door, please." He is not likely to receive approval if he closes the door in response to the command, "open the window." There are three rather common ways of establishing such stimulus control. The first is trial-and-error discrimination learning. The procedure consists basically of simply presenting the stimulus and, if the desired response occurs, giving reinforcement. The child is not reinforced if the desired response occurs other than when the stimulus has been presented. In some situations this procedure is adequate, but for the most part, it is inefficient (Sidman & Stoddard, 1967; Dixon, 1972). For this reason, trial-and-error methods for establishing stimulus control will not be discussed in this chapter.

Terrace (1963) describes a procedure for establishing stimulus control beginning with a stimulus which already controls the subject's performance and using that stimulus to establish control by other stimuli.

This procedure, properly administered, can result in extremely efficient and rapid learning of new stimulus control. Sidman and Stoddard (1967) developed a procedure for teaching severely retarded persons to discriminate between a circle and an ellipse. The procedure starts by presenting the child with a set of eight keys. Only one key is lighted. This lighted key has a circle form on it. The subject is more likely to press the lighted key than the dark keys. He responds to the lighted key and is reinforced. Over successive trials the light is gradually introduced on the other seven keys until all keys are at the same intensity. Light increase is programmed so that the subject continues to respond to the key with the circle. Once all keys are at full illumination, ellipses are gradually faded in on the seven distractor keys until they are at the same intensity as the circle. The subject continues to select the circle throughout.

A similar program was developed by Dixon to teach the concept *in front of*. Dixon's target behavior involved having the child select an object in front of a referent animal when given the command, "find the ball in front." Like Sidman and Stoddard, Dixon started with discriminations the child could already make and then gradually programmed to the terminal performance. Using this technique, Dixon was able to train a severely retarded child the concept *in front of* in two 15-minute sessions.

On the surface, programs such as Dixon's seem promising. However, we must remember that there are few guidelines. Developing such programs may take years, and there may be some inherent limitations in using one type of stimulus control to establish another, e.g., attempting to use visual stimulus control to establish auditory stimulus control. Suppose that a child understands some gestures but understands no speech. Then suppose that the trainer pairs the verbal commands with the gestures, then gradually fades the gestures until the subject is solely under the control of the verbal command. The teacher may find that the child performs adequately until the last trace of gesture is faded, whereupon he no longer responds. In other words the teacher has developed the child's ability to understand minimal gestures but the child has not learned to understand spoken commands.

Still a third procedure for establishing a new discrimination was reported by Risley and Wolf (1967) and has been refined in a laboratory situation by Touchette (1971). Touchette trained a subject to press a red key in contrast to a white key. The second discrimination which Touchette taught was the letter E with the legs pointed down versus the letter E with the legs pointed up. The letter E with the legs pointed up was the positive stimulus and the letter E with the legs pointed down was the negative stimulus. Touchette presented the positive stimulus on the red key and the negative stimulus on the white key. The child made the correct response on the first trial. Then on successive trials the onset of the red light behind the positive key was delayed an additional 0.5 seconds on each trial. All three of Touchette's subjects learned the discrimination virtually without errors. This technique was used to teach command-following to subjects who had already learned to imitate motor acts (Striefel, Bryan, & Aikens, 1973). Striefel presents a command such as "raise your hand" with the model raising his hand. With each succeeding trial, the delay is increased between the time the command is given and the time the model demonstrates the behavior. Preliminary results indicate that the delay procedure is effective. It is too new to predict its impact on education, but it seems to avoid two of the problems encountered in fading programs. First, it does not take great skill or time to develop the delay program. Secondly, it does not force finer and finer discrimination of an irrelevant stimuli.

To summarize, the contributions of a functional analysis of behavior to education have been significant during the last few years. These contributions have been emphases on (1) procedures for measuring behavior, (2) procedures for charting behavior, (3) consequences and the demonstration of the effect of controlling consequences on behavior change, and (4) the development of techniques for establishing stimulus control.

For persons who are unfamiliar with operant principles and techniques, or who have only a superficial knowledge of such techniques, we would suggest a careful study of Ferster and Perrott (1968), Lindsley (1964), and Chapter 10 by Hopkins and Conard in this volume.

Although behavior modifiers tend to emphasize the importance of teaching specific behaviors, many cognitive theorists emphasize the organization of behavior (Miller, Galanter, & Pribram, 1960; Brown, 1970; Bruner, Goodnow & Austin, 1956). These writers place importance not in specific behaviors, but in the rules or organizational structures which underlie such behavior. Cognitive theorists point out that some behaviors occur without being directly trained. Such behavior is important, especially in language. For example, most five-year-old children will never have been commanded to bring the "green cup with the yellow handle" to an experimenter or tester. Indeed, it would not be surprising if most had never encountered the phrase "green cup with the yellow handle," but it is doubtful that many would fail to grasp the meaning. They would be able to execute that command if they had to select such a cup from a variety of other cups including a green cup with a yellow handle. Certainly language and mathematics have rule-like characteristics which allow us to understand and produce sentences we have never before heard and to solve arithmetic problems we have never before seen.

Perhaps no behavior is quite as specific as we sometimes assume. Learning more than what is directly taught may be the rule rather than the exception. Most good teachers do more than simply increase and decrease the rate of specific responses applicable only in the classroom. Good teaching gives the child a means of effectively mastering situations which extend beyond the classroom. This is true whether the child is taught to dry his hands after washing or to apply the rule that the sum of the squares of two sides of a right triangle is equal to the square of the hypotenuse. Both skills must extend beyond the limitations of the classroom.

How then can we resolve the apparent contradiction between behavior modifiers and cognitive theorists? The answer may be simple. In teaching, we must develop a series of specific behaviors, using the best reinforcement and stimulus control techniques in a functional analysis of behavior. In selecting our goal for teaching, we insist that the child be able to respond appropriately to situations requiring novel combinations of performance. The child's behavior must operate in a rule-like fashion. Suppose we want to teach a child to follow simple commands involving a single noun phrase and a single verb phrase. There are two ways to approach the problem. The child might be trained to execute a series of commands, each of which has no relation to any other command. This type of training is shown in Table 7-3.

These commands are easily discriminated from each other; however, there is no reason to assume that the child, after learning these commands, will be able to follow a command (such as "drop spoon") which has not been directly trained (Striefel & Weatherby, 1973; Striefel, Bryan, & Aikens, 1973).

Table 7-3   Learning Commands Involving Six Noun Phrases and Six Verb Phrases[1]

Verb phrases	Nouns					
	Spoon	Block	Cup	Paper	Bread	Ball
Pick up	T					
Drop		T				
Give me			T			
Hit				T		
Push					T	
Throw						T

[1]This table represents a type of training in which the child is taught to follow commands involving six noun phrases and six verb phrases. For example, "pick up spoon" or "drop block." No command has any components in common with any other command.

Table 7-4   A Suggested Procedure for Selecting Verbs and Nouns for Teaching Which May Be Effective in Developing Generative Understanding of Verb-Noun Commands

Verb phrases	Nouns					
	Spoon	Block	Cup	Paper	Bread	Ball
Pick up	T	T	T	T	T	T
Drop	T					
Give me	T					
Hit	T					
Push	T					
Throw	T					

A second way of training command-following would be to teach each noun phrase and each verb phrase in combination with more than one other component. This type of training is illustrated in Table 7-4.

Thus, "pick up" is trained in combination not only with "spoon" but also with "block," "cup," "paper," etc. "Spoon" is trained in combination with several verb phrases. This training is more time-consuming than the type shown in Table 7-3; however, it will result in the child's being able to respond to untrained combinations of components. For example, it is possible that the child would respond appropriately to the command, "throw cup," even though he had received no direct training on this combination. The rule-like behavior is the aim of teaching. Specific tests must be made to determine if children are learning generative behavior (See Chapters 8 and 9).

EDUCATIONAL PROCEDURES FOR SEVERELY HANDICAPPED CHILDREN

The previous sections described methods for designing a curriculum and evaluating overall progress for severely handicapped children. They also included a discussion of the principles of behavior used in developing educational procedures. The following pages provide examples of techniques to eliminate interfering behavior and to teach self-help skills, social skills, and motor skills. Although language development is extremely important for severely handicapped children, it will not be discussed here because it is covered in Chapter 8 by Schiefelbusch, Bricker, and Ruder and Chapter 9 by Bricker, Ruder, and Smith. Many of these techniques are drawn from studies of children in institutions or studies of children within the home. Studies of severely handicapped children have not been conducted in schools because these children have been excluded from the public school until recently. Exclusion of these children in the future is less likely, but many will require extensive individual tutoring or training before they can profit from classroom instruction. Two informative books are available for persons interested in teaching children with severe behavioral limitations. They are *Teaching the Mentally Retarded* (Bensberg, 1965) and *Itard, Seguin and Kephart: Sensory Education—A Learning Interpretation* (Ball, 1971).

All examples of behavior modification or teaching described in the following pages are intended to effect changes which will make a child more acceptable for classroom learning. Behavior must be eliminated when it interferes with learning, disrupts the learning of other children, or is dangerous to the child or his peers. A child who rocks most of the time, has frequent violent temper tantrums, bangs his head, or kicks other children is not ready for group learning. Most teachers also prefer that each child in the classroom be toilet-trained and capable of feeding and dressing himself. Finally, the teacher must have some way of communicating with the child. Two common methods of communication are demonstration and verbal instruction.

The reader should not look at the examples below as the total set of performances required for classroom adjustment. They are only examples of important educational targets and procedures. Good teaching involves providing the student with concepts and principles which may be used far beyond the immediate situation.

Elimination of Interfering Behavior

Many children with severe behavioral limitations exhibit such stereotyped behavior as rocking, head-swaying, and manipulating their fingers in front of their eyes. These behaviors interfere with other appropriate performances (Lovaas, Litrownik, & Mann, 1971). Children also may engage in self-destructive behavior such as scratching themselves, biting themselves, or banging their heads. Some may bite, choke, or scratch other persons. The public education system may handle children who bite their nails or suck their thumbs, but it has not developed programs for dealing with severe excesses of stereotyped behaviors. Totally acceptable procedures for eliminating such behaviors have not been developed, either inside or outside the public school system. The most effective procedures for reducing the frequency of such behaviors involve aversive control. Dealing with stereotyped behavior will present one more dilemma as these children are admitted to public schools. Will the teacher, the administration, and the public be willing to use aversive procedures if they are shown to be the most effective (or perhaps the only effective) procedures for eliminating stereotyped behaviors? This is not a simple situation. Some parents, as well as others, may believe that eliminating stereotyped behaviors does not justify the use of aversive control.

Several persons have suggested procedures for reducing stereotyped behavior: Spradlin and Girardeau (1966); Hollis (1967c); Lovaas and Simmons (1969); Foxx and Azrin (1973). Perhaps the most promising method is that suggested by Foxx and Azrin. They report on an overcorrection procedure with four severely retarded children in a day-care program. Each of the four children had a different stereotyped behavior. One mouthed objects, a second placed her hands in her mouth, a third rolled her head back and forth, and a fourth engaged in stereotyped handclapping. The overcorrection procedure for mouthing objects and parts of the body consisted of brushing the child's teeth and gums with an antiseptic mouthwash and washing the child's outer lips for two minutes with a washcloth using the antiseptic solution. After each application, the washcloth and toothbrush were washed out and soaked in fresh antiseptic. Foxx and Azrin also report using the procedure successfully with a patient who bit other patients. The overcorrection procedure for head-rolling consisted of functional movement training for five minutes each time the child rolled her head. Initially the teacher used her hands to restrain the child's head. The teacher then told the subject to move her head in one of three positions. For example, "turn head up." If the child did not move her head in the desired direction immediately, the teacher manually guided her head. After a time the child would move her head in response to verbal direction. Then the child was required to hold her head still for 15 seconds and a new command was given.

A similar procedure was used to eliminate handclapping. When the stereotyped behavior had not occurred for several days, Foxx and Azrin introduced a verbal warning. The first time the child exhibited stereotyped behavior on a given day, he was warned. If he continued or if he engaged in stereotyped behavior again, he was given five minutes of overcorrection training. Marquesen (1972) used a procedure somewhat similar to the overcorrection procedure to reduce the percentage of time that a four-year-old severely brain-damaged child mouthed objects. The procedure consisted of holding the child's hands in front of him and his chin up facing the teacher each time he placed an object in his mouth. The child was restrained for only ten seconds unless he struggled or tantrumed, then he was held until he relaxed and was quiet for ten seconds. While the procedure involved relatively little aversive control after it had been applied for a few days, it was initially quite aversive for both the child and the teacher. At times the child would tantrum for periods up to 45 minutes. Foxx and Azrin also report tantrum behavior. The Foxx and Azrin procedure is functionally quite similar to the restraint procedure used by Marquesen; however, they add training on an incompatible response. Whether their procedure is superior to simple restraint remains to be seen.

Persons with severe behavioral problems have few ways of controlling their environments, and many handicapped children, have compensated by developing extremely intense tantrum behavior. When a child exhibits this behavior in its extreme form, it is difficult to keep from reinforcing it. Such behavior elicits pity from those around the child, and there is always the chance that the child may injure himself. A responsible teacher is tempted to do anything to terminate the tantrum. Such teacher compliance, of course, strengthens the tantrum behavior and robs the child of an opportunity to learn to control his environment in more appropriate ways. Nevertheless, only a strong teacher can resist the temptation to give in. Some notable persons who have resisted this temptation are Itard, Seguin, and Ann Sullivan (reported in Ball, 1971). Their rewards have been more compliant children who learned to control their social environment by socially acceptable means.

The behavior we have been discussing is not subtle. If it occurs once a day that may be too often. Thus, setting criterion for when the behavior has reached a satisfactory low level is not difficult. Initially it may be important to keep careful daily records so that changes in rate can be recognized and treatment continued or changed accordingly.

Teaching Self-Help Skills

Most teachers of normal children consider self-help skills something the child should have learned prior to entering school. Indeed, some schools have used self-help skills such as toileting as a criterion for entering school. (Rothstein, 1953; Kirk, 1962). However, when one works with children who have severe behavioral limitations, it is not unusual for the children to be untrained in self-help skills as toileting, washing, dressing, grooming, and feeding themselves in a neat and acceptable manner. The development of such skills (especially cleanliness skills) is extremely important. The lack of these skills will often preclude social educational exchanges. A child who has a runny nose, wet or soiled pants, or dirty hands is likely to be avoided by others. This is true both in formal teaching from the teacher and in the informal teaching by peers and nonteacher adults in the child's environment. The teacher of the child with severe behavioral limitations thus has an obligation to teach the child skills which will make him acceptable to other persons in his environment. As yet there is no highly developed technology for teaching self-help skills; however, one is developing. For aid in breaking self-help skills into manageable steps, consult *Managing Behavior, Part 4,* by Panyan (1972). Panyan's steps for developing self-help are not graded finely enough to ensure that all children will acquire the performance, but they will aid in breaking down self-help tasks.

Toilet Training   There have been numerous reports of toilet training attempts with children with severe behavioral limitations (Dayon, 1964; Baumeister & Klosowski, 1965, Giles & Wolf, 1966; Hunziak, Maurer, & Watson, 1965; Mahoney, Van Wagener, & Meyerson, 1971; Azrin, Bugle, & O'Brien, 1971). Nearly all procedures for toilet training involved increasing the probability of urination or defecation by inducing the subject to drink large quantities of water or by giving a laxative or suppository. Most procedures use positive reinforcement for elimination of the stool. A major problem in toilet training is detecting either appropriate or inappropriate elimination so that it can be quickly consequated. Both Azrin and Mahoney have developed devices to make immediate detection possible. The devices developed by Azrin et al. are both economical to construct and are commercially available. The first device consists of two metal snaps which can be attached to ordinary cotton pants. These snaps are placed about one and one-half inches apart and are connected by two small flexible wires to a small circuit box and worn on a belt underneath the child's shirt or blouse. When moisture shorts across the two snaps, a high frequency tone is produced. The tone can be heard both by the child and the caretaker. A similar device with a different noise is attached to a standard plastic "potty" chair. Moisture conducts electricity between the two snaps, producing a noise until the wires have been unsnapped. According to Azrin et al., these devices can be assembled from components for about $10 each, or they can be purchased for about $40 each from Lehigh Valley Electronics, Inc., Box 125, Fogelsville, Pennsylvania 18051.

The basic procedure used by Azrin et al. (1971) to toilet train four profoundly retarded girls consisted of using the two devices just described. Initially, the child was required to drink one glass of water every half hour to increase urination. Each half hour the child was given manual assistance in removing her clothes and sitting on the potty. The child remained on the potty 5 to 20 minutes unless urination occurred. If urination occurred the teacher hugged and praised the child, gave her a bit of candy, and allowed the child to leave the potty. The teacher could easily detect urination because of the moisture-produced buzzer sound. If the child urinated in her clothes, the high-frequency tone occurred. The teacher gave the child a single spank on the buttocks followed by 10 minutes without social interaction. This procedure was successful in toilet training four severely retarded children between 3 and 6 years of age.

The procedure described by Mahoney et al. (1971) is more complex, but is also effective. This procedure also employs a signaling device attached to the child's pants. However, prior to teaching the child to eliminate, the child is taught the chain of behaviors associated with elimination. These include walking to the stool, lowering the pants, sitting on or facing the stool, urinating, and pulling the pants back up. Training is broken into phases. The child is first taught simply to walk to the commode in response to the auditory signal which is initially actuated by the experimenter. This is done by placing toys near the commode and then presenting the tone for five seconds while saying "let's go potty" and leading the child to the commode. The child is praised and given consumable reinforcers once he reaches the commode. Gradually the teacher fades out the verbal and physical prompts and moves the toys to a place in the room which is farther and farther from the commode. Phase 2 trains the child to go to the commode and pull his or her pants down. This is done by presenting the buzzer, and when the child goes to the commode, the teacher says "pull your pants down," while aiding the child. Reinforcement is delivered when the pants are pulled below the child's knees. Once again, the verbal prompt and the physical help are faded until the child completes the act on his own. Phase 3 teaches the child to go to the commode, pull his or her pants down, take a sex-appropriate position at or on the commode, and remain in that position for 30 seconds.

Initially, the teacher prompts the child by physically placing and holding the child in position for 10 seconds. Reinforcement is then delivered. Gradually the time interval is increased until the child remains in position without help for 30 seconds. At this point Phase 4 is introduced. The child is equipped once again with the buzzer. The auditory signal is introduced either by the teacher or by urination by the child. During Phase 4 the child is given large quantities of fruit punch to increase the chance of urination. If the child appears about to void, the teacher presents the buzzer and the child goes through the sequence. If by chance, the child voids in the commode, reinforcement is delivered. If the child voids in his pants, he is still required to go through the sequence. If he then voids in the commode, he is reinforced. Once the child is voiding in the commode, Phase 5 is introduced. During Phase 5 the child is trained to pull up his or her pants after voiding. Phase 6 involves removing the auditory signal. This is done by waiting until the child shows some signs of being ready to void. These might be fidgeting, grabbing the genitals, or tugging at the pants. At this point the teacher introduces the buzzer and the child goes through the chain. After several such presentations, the buzzer is eliminated and the child performs the chain without assistance. The final phase is to instruct parents in training all phases not requiring the signal so that carry-over to the home environment is accomplished. The procedure results in the virtual elimination of "accidents" by the three normal children who were less than two years old and by the five moderately and severely retarded children.

The two cases above are examples of toilet-training procedures. Not every child who is not toilet trained will need the elaborate training given by Mahoney et al. In fact, with normal preschool children under three years of age we have found that the mere use of the sensing device and the buzzer was satisfactory to eliminate voiding in clothing in less than one week. The apparatus described by Azrin et al. emits a continuous buzzing from the time the child voids until the clips are removed from the pants. The buzzer is aversive for both child and attendant. The natural aversive contingencies produced by urinating on the apparatus may be enough to ensure that the child uses the commode if he already has developed the prerequisite skills described by Mahoney et al. However, the Mahoney et al. article demonstrates many aspects of good teaching. First, the teachers break their task into small enough steps so that even the most limited child can be trained to perform the steps. Second, the procedure provides immediate reinforcement. Third, the procedure helps the child to begin to perform and then gradually fades the physical and verbal prompts until the child performs independently. Fourth, they work with the parents to ensure that the newly learned skills are transferred into the child's nonschool or home environment.

Cleanliness Training   Another skill often considered external to the education process is cleanliness. Like the child who is not toilet trained, the child who fails to wash and bathe will be unpleasant to be near. In teaching a skill such as washing and drying the face and hands, first determine exactly what skill you wish to teach. This may be done by running through the sequence yourself and seeing exactly what movements are involved or by watching another child who has these skills and seeing exactly what he does.

The beginning training for the child you are working with may consist of taking the child's hands and physically putting him through each aspect of the washing sequence. After completion, the child is praised and reinforced with a previously determined reinforcer. The next time the child is put through the washing exercise he may be prompted to do the last part of the sequence himself (that is, put the towel back on the rack). After putting the towel on the rack is firmly established, he should be required to perform the other acts in the chain. Each new act immediately follows the performance which the child has last mastered. Exactly how large each behavioral step is depends on the already existing behavior of the child. Some children will require small steps with gradual removal of support. Others may require little training. Training should be carried out when the child is ordinarily required to wash, such as after outside play, after toileting, or before meals and snacks. Such training helps bring the washing under the control of situations which ordinarily control washing in other persons. After the child has learned the skill, it can often be maintained by simple cleanliness checks before lunch, snacks, or return to normal play activities. A child who does not meet the standard simply is refused entry into the lunch area, play area, or snack area.

Two other aspects of personal care which are important to a child's acceptability for teaching or any other social exchange are proper use of a handkerchief and elimination of drooling. Running noses and wet chins, throats, and blouses or shirts are common in children with severe behavioral limitations. The adult who overlooks these in training is doing the child a major disservice. Once again, a child should not be allowed to engage in reinforcing activities such as dining, snacktime, or play if he is drooling or has failed to use a handkerchief properly. Moreover, in some cases it will be necessary to teach the child step-by-step how to wipe his nose, his chin, and other parts of his body. Once the child is able to engage in these skills, the skills must be executed whenever the nose is running or the mouth is full of saliva and not just when the teacher or parent tells the child to clean his nose or chin. This may be done by periodically reinforcing the child for having clean nostrils or a dry chin. When this skill is well established, it may be possible to maintain the skill with a single reinforcer given at the end of the day. The ease or difficulty with which drooling may be handled depends upon motor involvement or handicap. Teaching a severely cerebral-palsied child to keep a dry chin may be a nearly impossible task. However, Garber (1971) has described a procedure for eliminating drooling in a cerebral-palsied adolescent.

Care of teeth, hair, and fingernails also improves the child's chances of being accepted by other persons. Similar attention should be given to developing these skills. Programs of this kind are described in the preceding chapter. Proper cleanliness and self-care skills cannot be overemphasized because they are prerequisites for many other social interactions.

Dressing Skills   Breland (1965) has described procedures for teaching severely retarded children to dress themselves. The procedures are similar to those described above for teaching a child to wash and dry his hands and face. First, the task is broken into small steps. The trainer goes through the complete task, allowing the child to finish the final step on his own, after which the child is reinforced. As performance on the final step becomes established, the teacher requires the child to complete a little more of the dressing task. Gradually all help is faded.

Despite the importance of dressing and undressing, there has been little good work detailing exactly how one teaches dressing skills. Even though Breland's chapter suggests procedures for teaching dressing and undressing, the procedures are not sufficiently detailed to ensure success. Teaching a child self-dressing skills appears simple until attempted—then it immediately becomes complex. The first author of this chapter recently observed members of the occupational therapy staff of the University Affiliated Facility at the University of Kansas teach a profoundly retarded child to remove a polo shirt. The procedure used was similar to one described by Breland (1965). A special polo shirt about two sizes too large for the child was used. The initial phase involved taking the child's right hand, gripping it around the upper part of the left sleeve of the polo shirt. Then the shirt was gripped by the left hand and pulled over the head. The final step involved pulling the shirt off the right arm.

All this training procedure seemed appropriate; however, several problems were encountered. The first problem was reinforcing the child precisely when he was engaged in the right movement. This was accomplished by the use of a whistle as a bridging stimulus. This whistle was blown immediately after the child had completed a desired act and was followed by reinforcement (a bit of candy, cereal, or playing with beads).

A second problem resulted from slight differences in procedures between trainers. Early in training the sequence of steps had been established, but one trainer was starting with the right hand of the child while the other was starting with the left. Thus, the responses that one trainer was requiring of the right hand of the child, the other trainer was requiring of the left. When the trainers worked out these details, training went rather smoothly and the child learned to remove his polo shirt after approximately eight hours of training. This illustration points out some of the problems in developing programs for teaching the common dressing skills which most children learn without formal training.

Self-Feeding   Probably no child ever grew to maturity without at some time eating in a manner unacceptable to the adults around him. Eating habits or table manners are not usually critical for success. However, when a child exhibits extremely limited or unacceptable eating habits, he may not be accepted in some settings. Since normalization is a primary goal for the person with severe behavioral limitations, developing acceptable mealtime behavior is an appropriate educational goal. Once again, when most children enter school, the are usually able to feed themselves in an acceptable fashion, or they learn these skills rapidly. Schools have thus had no need to develop elaborate procedures for teaching children acceptable eating habits.

A number of studies have concerned self-feeding and appropriate mealtime behavior (Whitney & Barnard, 1966; Spradlin, 1964; Henricksen & Doughty,

1967; O'Brien, Bugle, & Azrin, 1972; O'Brien & Azrin, 1972; and Barton, Guess, Garcia, & Baer, 1970).

Spradlin (1964) reported a procedure for teaching a severely retarded child to feed herself with a spoon. The ten-year-old child had been fed by other persons all her life. When her hands were free at the table, she would pat her food or push the tray to the floor. For this reason the child normally had her hands tied to her sides when she was fed.

The procedure for teaching self-feeding first involved untying the child's arms and hands. The teacher then stood behind the child and molded the child's right hand around the handle of the spoon and held it in this position with his right hand while holding the child's left hand down with his left hand. The next step in training involved taking the child's right hand and the spoon, filling the spoon, and moving it passively toward her lips. When the spoon was within an inch of the child's mouth, the teacher stopped the movement and waited until the child opened her mouth. The food was then placed in the child's mouth. Gradually the teacher offered less and less help. The teacher brought the filled spoon to perhaps two inches from the child and then required the child to move the spoon the remaining two inches. The distance the child had to move the spoon was gradually increased until the child was moving the spoon from the tray to her mouth.

There were periodic problems. First, the child did not respond well to the procedure for several meals, and crying occurred frequently. This meant that the child received little food during the early part of the training. Throughout ten years of her life she had been taught that all good things come to those who wait and cry. Now she was suddenly being required to respond if she wanted to eat. The change did not come easily.

A second problem was throwing the spoon on the floor. Early in training the teacher simply replaced the object which had been thrown on the floor and held the child's hands down by her side for about 30 seconds each time she threw something on the floor. Throwing objects on the floor gradually stopped.

When the child could move the spoon from the tray to her mouth without help, the next problem was to get her to fill her spoon. This was accomplished by manual guidance and the use of very soft food which could be easily spooned. The final step in the chain involved having the child bring the empty spoon from her lips to the food in the tray. When the child could feed herself while the teacher supervised, the teacher shifted the responsibility for supervision to a child helper. Within a few days this supervision was faded out and the child ate with a spoon without help.

Spradlin's procedure was designed to teach self-feeding to a child who had never fed herself with a spoon. Barton, Guess, Garcia, and Baer (1970) and O'Brien and Azrin (1972) have developed procedures for training appropriate mealtime behaviors with retarded persons who are not as limited in their self-feeding skills as the child reported by Spradlin. O'Brien and Azrin's procedures will be summarized at this point since they present an overall program for teaching retarded persons in a group to eat in a manner appropriate to the community.

O'Brien and Azrin first defined a group of eating performances which were correct and a group of eating performances which were incorrect or inappropriate. Some of their correct responses were eating soup with a spoon, eating beets, meat, etc. with a fork, drinking from a glass without spilling, and eating bread or cookies with hands. Some incorrect responses were eating potatoes with hands, spilling drinks, eating pudding with a fork, or eating butter with a spoon. Inappropriate behaviors described were drooling, licking fingers, plates, or table top, throwing utensils, etc. Their first phase of training consisted of teaching the child to eat properly. They gave verbal praise for correct eating and said "no" and interrupted incorrect responses. Teaching consisted of three types of assistance: (1) instructions only, (2) instructions and imitation, and (3) instructions and manual guidance. The first type of teaching used was instructions only. If the subject failed to respond appropriately to instructions alone, he was given instructions and the task was demonstrated. If instructions and modeling were insufficient, instruction plus manual guidance were given. Once the subject had learned to eat correctly, a maintenance program was established which consisted of verbal praise for correct responses and reprimands, warnings, and removal of food for 30 seconds if the subject ate incorrectly. Their procedure reduced eating errors to near zero. The O'Brien and Azrin article should be given careful study by those persons working on feeding problems with severely handicapped children.

Teaching Social Skills   Imitation is not considered a great skill for children who imitate. However, we need only look at a child who does not imitate to see its importance. Imitation is a useful skill in acquiring at least a crude approximation of new behaviors. Imitation and the ability to follow simple commands are two important skills for the child if he is to adapt and learn from group instruction.

Young children exhibit an extensive imitation repertory and learn a variety of new skills such as sex-appropriate stances in the restroom and how to play with toys and use tools. Much social behavior such as greeting, criticizing, and complimenting other persons is learned through imitation. This is also true of speech. Almost any normal person may find himself resorting to imitation if he is faced with a complex novel situation. Indeed, it takes a rather rare individual not to imitate others when he is engaged in a novel situation in which there are other human models. In the public education classroom for young children, imitation is often used as a procedure for developing such skills as drawing and playing games.

Baer, Peterson, and Sherman (1967) described a procedure for establishing imitative behavior among severely retarded children. The procedure has been used many times to establish imitative behavior among retarded and autistic children. Under the procedure, a child was taken into the experimental room and seated in a chair opposite the teacher. Training sessions were frequently held at mealtime. The child's regular meal was used for reinforcement. The teacher would give the command "do this," then engage in some act such as arm raising. The experimenter took the child's arm, put him through the act, then immediately reinforced the child.

As training proceeded, the experimenter gradually reduced his help in putting the subject through the response. Once the child reliably executed the first imitative response, the teacher started training on a second response. Training was carried out exactly as it was for the first imitative behavior. Once this behavior was learned, it was intermixed with the other behavior. Once the subject reliably discriminated between the two behaviors to be imitated, a third behavior was introduced. This behavior was also trained independently until it reached criterion. It was then intermixed with other behaviors. Training was continued until the subject could engage in each of the three behaviors when the appropriate model was presented. This training was continued with new imitative behaviors until the subject could imitate a new behavior the first time it was presented. With some children this will not come easy. Baer, Peterson, and Sherman report that one of their children did not acquire this generalized imitation ability until she had been trained to imitate 130 different behaviors. However, once generalized imitation was established, new behaviors were imitated even though they were not reinforced. Only selective responses need to be reinforced in order to maintain the whole class of imitative responses. Once an imitative repertory is established in the presence of one teacher, it is easily transferred to other teachers if these teachers use similar reinforcement contingencies. Indeed, it is possible for imitative responses to be transferred to another child provided that the severely handicapped child is reinforced for imitating the behaviors of other children. Such imitation is of inestimable value in managing a child in a group situation. Ideally, the child imitates the behavior of other children when they are seated at a small table drawing or writing with pencils, when they are getting their coats on or off as they prepare to go outside, or when they come in from play. Although other stimuli also control such behavior, a good imitative repertory helps the child adjust to group teaching situations.

As was the case for earlier performances, imitation lends itself to evaluation. Criteria which allow for the type of graphing described earlier can be established rather easily. Moreover, a criterion for imitation must include responding to a novel model without direct training on the behavior to be imitated. In imitation, the child learns responses which are never directly trained. In short, he learns a rule.

Instruction-following is an important behavior for any child or adult. Although commands occasionally involve only an auditory or speech stimulus, the spoken command is usually accompanied by a gesture and a particular situational context. For example, "sit down, please" is usually made while looking at the person and a chair. A gesture frequently accompanies this command. A child who follows a number of such commands is much easier to manage in the public school than one who does not. In the future it will be necessary for the public school to educate children who do not follow commands, instructions, or directions. Rather than the ability to follow directions being a prerequisite for entering school, direction-following for some children will become the goal of teaching.

Recent research suggests several procedures for establishing instruction-following (Whitman, Zaharas, & Chardos, 1971; Striefel & Weatherby, 1973; Striefel, Bryan, & Aikens, 1973). Whitman et al. taught two severely retarded children to follow a series of commands such as "sit down" and "put the pencil in the box." The command was given, followed by physically putting the child through the action. Each time the child completed the command, he was reinforced with Fruit Loops or bits of chocolate. The child received less and less help in following the command until finally no help was given. Reinforcement continued.

This procedure established ten behaviors in the laboratory situation. When the children were tested with commands which had never been trained, their performance also improved. This suggests that the children had learned to follow commands in another situation and that the behavior was simply re-established or transferred into the lab situation. This does not reduce the importance of demonstrating that direction-following can be made to occur in a specific situation to a certain person through physical prompting, fading, and reinforcement techniques such as those used by Whitman et al.

Striefel and Weatherby (1973) succeeded in teaching severely retarded children to follow commands using procedures similar to those described by Whitman et al. (1971). However, they obtained no transfer to untrained commands. They found also that the subject was not always responding to the total command. Sometimes only one or two words from the command were sufficient to result in the commanded action.

The teacher should recognize that a retarded child may respond to a command differently than a normal child. For this reason, after training the child to follow one command, the teacher may wish to give a different command with the same intonation pattern. This type of experiment should tell the teacher whether the child is responding to the words or to the intonation pattern. Once command-following is firmly established with one teacher, another teacher or perhaps the parent should present the same command to determine if generalization has occurred. If not, the child should be trained to follow the command when it is given by a different person. This training should continue until the child will follow the command given by any adult. Once again, the effect of good teaching must extend beyond the initial teaching situation.

This technique for establishing command-following involved the fading of the physical prompt. More recently, Striefel, Bryan, and Aikens (1973) have experimented with a procedure which more nearly approximates the delay procedure for shifting stimulus control developed by Touchette (1971). The children in Striefel's study had been taught to imitate prior to being given instruction in command following. With the delay in procedure, the teacher gives the command, then waits two to five seconds before providing a model for imitation.

The child is taught to follow one command, then to follow a second command independently, and finally, to follow the commands when they are intermixed. This forces the child to discriminate between them. As new commands are taught the same procedure is followed.

A few commands which have special importance to the management of the child are "come here," "sit down," "stand up," "give it to me," and "stop!" However, an infinite number of commands may be given. Normal adults and children understand or respond appropriately to commands involving combinations of words they have never heard before. In this sense, command following may be generative. The question is, how can one teach direction-following so that the child learns to follow commands involving novel combinations? One strategy is to teach commands which have immediate utility for the child in his natural environment. Such skills are likely to be maintained in that environment. However, this strategy may teach a child a set of specific command-following responses. For example, the common commands "stop," "give it to me," "stand up," "sit down," and "come here" contain no components in common. In some instances, this is ideal. The commands have minimal probability of being confused. Stated differently, they have a maximum chance of being discriminated from each other. However, since they have no components in common, there is little chance that the child will learn to respond appropriately to commands involving novel combinations of components. Striefel is currently teaching severely retarded children to respond to commands in which several different verbs are combined with a single noun and several different nouns are combined with a single verb (Striefel, personal communication).

This strategy of teaching is time-consuming and demanding. The child may take several days to learn to execute two commands involving different verbs. However, after the child has learned to combine several verbs with two or three nouns, he may be able to follow a command involving a unique combination of learned verbs and nouns without direct training on the combination. The child has been trained with specific commands, but, because of a particular strategy or organization during the training, he has learned something that may extend to untrained novel combinations. This is good teaching.

The behavior which has been trained is observable, recordable, and countable, and at each step Striefel has a specific criterion for determining whether the subject has or has not succeeded on that task step.

Thus far, Striefel has not determined the degree that such command-following extends to new teachers or adults. The direction-following experiment has been confined primarily to the laboratory setting. It is likely that practical training in command-following could be introduced into the natural environment and extended throughout the entire teaching day by periodically presenting commands. Each command would be presented once without a physical prompt. If the child followed the directions, he would be reinforced immediately. If not, the teacher would put him through the action directed by the command and then reinforce him. All commands would allow the teacher to put the child through the actions. No command would go unexecuted, since this would allow the child to ignore commands. The delay between the command and the physical prompt would be brief, probably two to five seconds. Data collected would be the percent of commands executed prior to a physical prompt during a sample period. That sample might be made one afternoon per week. Following commands which involve novel components is the aim of such teaching. Criterion for success is based on such responses rather than on responses to directly trained commands.

Teaching Perceptual or Motor Skills

Many children with severe behavioral limitations will have trouble crawling, walking, or running. Few of these children will exhibit the gross perceptual motor skills needed to enjoy games. Most will not be able to catch or throw a ball with accuracy. Many will also have problems with finer perceptual motor tasks such as putting pegs in holes, working puzzles, and putting taps on bolts. There are few systematic procedures for training perceptual motor skills in severely handicapped children. Nonetheless, some of the same principles used in developing other skills may be applied. Certain components of instruction-following programs and self-dressing programs can be used to develop motor skills.

Hollis (1962, 1967a, 1967b) worked on a procedure for developing eye-hand coordination. The task involved taking a chip with a hole in it off a bent rod. At first, the severely retarded children were unable to remove the chip from a stationary straight rod unless the chip was at the very end of the rod. Even then, they would sometimes push it on farther. Hollis's technique required the child to hand him the chip, after which the child received a bit of candy, cereal, or other food. The next step involved teaching the child to retrieve the chip from the very end of the rod. The chip was gradually moved farther and farther from the end of the rod. When the child could readily retrieve the chip from a straight rod, the rod was bent to a 45-degree angle. When this task was successfully completed, the rod was bent to a 90-degree angle. Additional bends in the rod were added until the child was successfully removing the chips from a rod with three 90-degree bends.

The procedure did not work with every child. One child exhibited stereotyped hand wringing and made only a few manipulative responses to her environment. She made no response to the chip. With this child, meals were used as reinforcers. She had to respond to her environment to receive bites of food. Under these conditions she soon learned to pick up the chip and hand it to the teacher. Training on the bent-rod problem then proceeded much as it had for the other children.

Most children learned to perform on the bent rod task when they were given free access to regular meals. That is, they worked when candy or other edibles were used even though they were relatively satiated. Some of these children performed these tasks solely for social reinforcers. When children will work for social reinforcers, those reinforcers should be used. However, social events are not always effective with severely limited children.

Research clearly indicates that severely handicapped children will work at a task when their meals are used as reinforcers (Baer, Peterson, & Sherman, 1967; Hollis, 1967a, 1967b; Spradlin, 1964, Hamblin, 1971). Once again, this presents a problem for the school and society. Are we ready to use meals to reinforce behavior? Certain circumstances make this advisable. However, this powerful reinforcer should be combined with a finely graded program which results in the child receiving a high density of reinforcement. A child who has seldom been required to respond in order to receive reinforcement may exhibit emotional behavior even though the response requirements are minimal. The child may seem to have made a general decision not to comply for reinforcers. Once this breaks down, the child makes rapid progress (Hollis, 1967a; Spradlin, 1964).

The girl for whom Hollis used meals as reinforcers had extremely limited use of her hands, especially her left hand. She had at various times been considered autistic or subject to some progressive neurological disease which resulted in the loss of the hand movement she had previously exhibited. Nevertheless, when Hollis placed contingencies on the use of her left hand, she slowly and gradually increased the skill with which she used this hand. In order to get her to use her left hand, Hollis restrained the child's right arm by strapping it to the arm of a school chair. Under these conditions the child began to reach for the chip with the unrestrained hand. Her skill with her left hand remained less adequate than with her right hand; nevertheless, it did improve. Although the use of her hands improved in the laboratory, there was little indication that this improvement continued outside the laboratory. This indicates that different contingencies were in effect outside the laboratory.

The work by Hollis was designed to improve the use of the hands by a child who almost never used them. It demonstrated that even with an extremely retarded child, perceptual motor skills can be taught by breaking the performance into small steps and by using powerful reinforcers.

A few severely retarded children have extreme problems in locomotion. They may not be able to walk because of severe physical disabilities, or simply because of lack of training.

Meyerson, Kerr, and Michael (1967) have reported a procedure for teaching a severely retarded child to walk. The child was nine years old, institutionalized, and had never walked. She was carried or pushed in a wheelchair. If it was necessary to move by herself, she scooted on her buttocks by pushing with her hands and feet. She would not support her weight on her feet and legs. However, she could be pulled up if the teacher supported most of the child's weight. During a preteaching observation period, the teacher found that the child was highly reinforceable with a variety of foods such as popcorn, raisins, crackers, nuts, and ice cream.

During Phase 1, which was only one session, the child was lifted into a standing position and then given a bit of food as a reinforcer. Gradually the child was required to bear more and more of her weight until she was standing for five to 10 seconds unsupported. Phase 2 consisted of placing two chairs with their backs toward each other and approximately 30 inches apart. An adult held the back of each chair while the child was trained to pull herself up to the back of one chair, turn to grasp the other chair with one hand and finally with both hands. Reinforcement was contingent upon the child's turning and grasping the chair which she was not holding. At first, the distance between the two chairs required only an unsupported step, but as the distance was gradually increased, the child took several unaided steps. Phase 3 consisted of one experimenter holding the child and walking toward the second experimenter who was offering a piece of candy. As quickly as the child took steps, the first person released the child's hand and the child continued to walk toward the second person who was walking backward away from the child. After the child had learned to start walking while holding an adult's hand the teacher simply required the child to walk across the room unsupported. Within nine teaching hours, the child had learned to walk alone. The procedure once again involved choosing an observable behavior, breaking it down into definable steps, reinforcing the child for successively longer chains of behavior, and carefully evaluating the changes which took place. The child described in the study by Meyerson et al. had no apparent physical difficulties other than weak leg muscles.

Horner (1971) taught a five-year-old child with hydrocephalus and spina bifida to move around with crutches. The child had extensive paralysis of the lower extremities. Prior to training, the child could sit alone, pull to his knees while holding on to a crib rail, and get into a creeping position. He could scoot across the floor by pulling himself with his arms. Like Meyerson et al., Horner determined a reinforcer prior to training. He found that the child would crawl a distance of 50 feet to obtain a tablespoon of root beer. However, after about 25 tablespoons during a session the child would no longer crawl for the root beer, and so the sessions were limited to 25 trials. The first phase of training consisted of teaching the child to walk using parallel bars. During this phase, two stools were placed between the parallel bars so that the teacher and the child sat about two feet apart facing each other. Initially, the child was required only to grip the left bar with his left hand and the right bar with his right hand, and was reinforced with root beer. He then pulled himself into a standing position on the parallel bars and had to maintain this standing position long enough to consume the root beer. As training progressed, the child took three steps, five steps, and finally ten steps before he was reinforced. The child had to be successful on 23 or more trials for each three consecutive sessions before beginning a new phase. In this next phase, divided into ten stages, the child was taught to use crutches. Crutches were taped to the child's hands. The experimenter demonstrated their use by placing the crutches on two dots 18 inches in front of the child and 18 inches apart. The child was reinforced if he put his crutches on those dots. The next stage involved having the child swing his body into an erect position with assistance from the teacher. The teacher used underarm pressure and provided total support. At the next stage, the teacher gave assistance only at the beginning of the movement. The child was then required to hold his crutches without their being taped on and to swing himself forward without aid. Next, the subject had to place the crutches forward while the teacher held his hand on the child's back to balance him. This gradual increase in the complexity of the task continued through the last step, when the child was able to make 12 cycles with crutches using forearm clamps rather than underarm support. Training took 120 sessions. After this training was completed, the child was taught to use his new skill in walking around the hospital grounds. This allowed the child to engage in meals, play, school, speech, and bus rides only if he walked to these activities with his crutches. This teaching, of course, required helpers. If the child had been at home rather than in an institution, the training could have been accomplished with the aid of parents and siblings.

The examples above involved children with severe limitations. Even with these children, breaking the task into small components and building the behavior gradually with support and reinforcement resulted in improvement.

To the writers' knowledge, no systematic work has been reported on teaching children with severe behavioral limitations such physical fitness and motor performance activities as pull-ups, sit-ups, standing jumps, running, and throwing. Rarick, Widdop, and Broadhead (1970) have reported that even educable mentally retarded children are deficient compared to normals in these skills. We can be sure that children of the type we have been discussing are even more limited in these areas. The same procedures which were demonstrated so successfully by Hollis, Horner, Meyerson, Kerr, and Michael could be readily adapted for such training.

The authors of this chapter have made no attempt to review articles on the vocational training of severely retarded persons. However one effort in this area deserves special mention. Gold (1969) has reported procedures for teaching severely and profoundly retarded persons to assemble coaster brakes for bicycles. The theory and procedures used by Gold are too extensive to be reported here; however, the reader who is interested in vocational training of severely retarded persons should study Gold's work carefully.

INCREASING TEACHER EFFECTIVENESS

Admitting children with severe behavioral limitations into the public school system is going to be costly, but over a long period, it will be less costly to the public than are institutionalizations (Wolfensberger, 1971). Since teaching these children requires a high teacher-pupil ratio, plus special equipment, the expense of public education must obviously increase. The question is, "How can these children be taught effectively and efficiently?" We do not know all the answers. Regardless of the programs developed, it will require teachers who are highly trained and effective.

Most of this chapter has been devoted to the use of rather traditional behavior modification skills. These skills are extremely important, and we would predict failure for those persons who do not develop procedures which include breaking performances into small steps, recording behavioral changes, and promptly reinforcing appropriate responses. Nevertheless, these are probably the easiest skills to teach an inexperienced teacher. Other skills such as determining what to teach a child and how to teach parents and peers so that training extends beyond the teacher will be extremely difficult. Numerous suggestions have been made concerning ways teachers can be more effective in educating persons with severe limitations. Four of these will be discussed here: the use of educational television and other media, teaching aides, age peers as teachers, and the use of parents as teachers.

Use of Educational Television

Programs such as "Sesame Street" control children's attention much of the time. This is true not only for normal children but also for children with severe behavioral limitations (Striefel, 1972). There is less evidence concerning what, if anything, children with severe behavior limitations learn from such programs. Striefel and Eberl (1973) have conducted preliminary research which indicates that once severely retarded children have been trained in generalized imitation, imitation can be transferred rather readily to the model presented by television. The ability to present a model by television does reduce some of the burden placed on the teachers. A teacher is still required to determine whether or not the child's imitation meets criterion, to put the child through the procedure if he does not imitate, and to record and reinforce responses. The use of television allows the teacher to work with two or three children simultaneously, provided the children exhibit a high degree of imitation. If the child already imitates several actions reliably, television may be used to teach command-following using a delay procedure. The speaker on the television might say to the child, "raise your hand," and wait for two or three seconds, then repeat the command with a demonstration. The teacher's task would be to reinforce the child's appropriate response when it occurred or prompt it if it did not occur.

It also is quite likely that a television program might be used to program a parent or teacher to conduct a class. Let us suppose that a teacher wanted to teach a child to put on his coat. A television tape might be played that would explain and demonstrate each step of the program. For example, while giving the instruction, "take the child's left hand and place it so it grasps the right side of the collar," the television person would demonstrate this action with a child. The model would also demonstrate the prompt delivery of reinforcement. Instruction and demonstration on the television may be paced so that the teacher plays an active role in instruction. Perhaps the greatest value of a television system is being able to replay the teaching session. Many times when a teacher reviews a teaching session on television she notices inadequacies in her teaching procedure which, when eliminated, result in better progress by the child.

The video system is a valuable tool. When used appropriately, it results in better teaching, but it will not result in cutting expenses unless we evaluate the cost of teaching in terms of performances taught.

Use of Teacher Aides

Another type of support for the teacher of children with severe behavioral limitations is the teacher aide. Once trained, an aide can carry out many of the programs previously discussed. In fact, there are no data which indicate that either educational level or psychological training is related to successfully teaching these children. The use of teacher aides provides the teacher time to plan, locate, and develop materials. Regular class teachers have curriculum and materials to guide teaching, but the teacher of children with severe limitations faces problems for which no specific program has been developed. Even when procedures have been developed, they may require adaptation and modification before they are effective with a specific child. The use of teaching aides is not a complete solution, since they require salary and increase the costs of the public school system, but aides are not as expensive as professionally trained teachers.

Use of Age Peers as Teachers

Another type of support for the teacher is the child's peers (Whalen & Henker, 1969, 1971; Hamblin et al., 1971; Surratt, Ulrich, & Hawkins, 1970). Children enjoy playing teacher. Moreover, some researchers report that both normal and retarded children are able to teach specific skills after they learn how to present stimuli and reinforce behavior. There are, of course, limitations on the use of children as teachers. Children are in the public schools for their own education. In addition, some aspects of an educational program could not and should not be left to children. For example, young children should not be allowed to use procedures such as Foxx and Axrin used in eliminating stereotyped behavior.

There may also be objections from both the parents of the children being taught and the parents of the children doing the teaching. Even so, the advantages of children doing some of the teaching could be twofold. First, they may learn that handicapped children are not "monsters" to be feared or organisms incapable of learning. Second, they learn some things about teaching: (1) any person can be taught provided the task being taught is appropriate for the person's current skill level, (2) the type of materials are important, and (3) contingencies of reinforcement are important.

Use of Parents as Teachers

Parents may also be used as aides in some educational programs for severely handicapped children (Wahler, Wenkel, Peterson, & Morrison, 1965). Parents who help teach children within the school situation can be taught the procedures for managing the child's behavior in the home. The chances for generalization into the home are increased for the parent and child who work together in the classroom. It can be done with a minimum of cost to the school system. Moreover, Lovaas et al. (1973) obtained the best overall results with autistic children when parents were used to mediate the program. There are, however, some limitations. Many parents are unable to be at school because they work or have other children. Attempts to compel parents to aid in the teaching of the child could be viewed as discriminatory, since parents of normal children are not required to do the same.

Many educators believe that adequate teaching can take place only if the home situation supports that teaching. No doubt such home/school relationships aid in teaching; however, the entire literature on discrimination indicates that children learn to behave quite differently under different stimulus conditions. The teacher who teaches a child self-help skills such as feeding, toileting, and dressing himself at school may be disheartened to find those skills not required or reinforced at home. The training is not fruitless, however, because these skills better enable the child to fit into the school system, as well as other situations outside the home.

ISSUES INVOLVED IN EDUCATING THE SEVERELY HANDICAPPED

The Use of Powerful Consequences in Teaching

The leaders of our society must face the problems associated with using teaching procedures which are not typically found in our education system. Most children are easily controlled by social consequences such as compliments, approval, reprimands, and disapproval. Some severely handicapped persons are not so easily controlled. They are reinforced only by such basic things as food and water. Teaching these children may require presenting food and water contingent on the behavior being taught. If these powerful reinforcers are used, however, they must be used in combination with a program which allows the child to succeed. Otherwise the contingent use of food and water is both cruel and ineffective. Moreover, our society generally holds that food, water, and shelter should be provided regardless of the child's behavior.

   Some children have behavior which interferes with learning. The most effective techniques for eliminating interfering behaviors have been severe physical punishment, use of time-out or seclusion, restraint, and overcorrection procedures. All these procedures can result in emotional behavior. We are faced with a choice of whether we will use strong consequences or fail in our attempts to teach many children. This is an issue the public and educators must face.

Cost of Individualized Instruction

Discussion among educational groups about individualized instruction is not new. Ritter and Wilmarth (1925) pointed out the necessity for individualized instruction in rural schools fifty years ago. Yet, in reality, education is not individualized. In the typical classroom each child receives a program similar to the program of every other child. These group-teaching methods are not likely to be successful with children with severe behavioral limitations. Individualized programs are necessary if these children are to be taught the crucial performances required for even minimal adjustment in social groups. These individualized programs will be expensive. It is likely that one teacher can teach no more than three or four such children even with the aid of capable nonprofessional assistants. This means that the cost per child is likely to be between $5,000 and $7,500 per year. Critics will say, "Seventy-five hundred dollars to teach a child to feed and toilet himself, you could send him to Harvard for that!" True, but Harvard does not provide an adequate education for such a child. The question is whether society is willing to pay the price of education for severely limited children.

Parent Participation in Curriculum Planning

Educational planning and curriculum development have traditionally been the domain of the professional educator, yet professional educators may not be adequately prepared to make decisions concerning programs for severely handicapped persons. We have already suggested that in order to develop an adequate program for a child, the educator must draw on a variety of resources. Parents should be brought into the curriculum development and training programs. These changes in the educational decision-making procedures will not be easy. Many school administrators will find the input of parents and other members of the community to be a bother and a threat. A functional system also requires that teachers be more sensitive to the demands of children and parents than to the traditions of the educational system. Can the public school system make the changes needed to develop functional programs for severely limited children?

The Severely Handicapped Person in Society

The issue of curriculum development cannot be isolated from our decisions concerning the role of severely handicapped persons in our society. Many of these persons have in the past been placed in institutions. If this were the goal for handicapped persons, we would do well to examine institutions and design educational procedures to teach children to live in such environments. However, current trends suggest that fewer and fewer handicapped persons will be cared for in institutions (Wolfensberger, 1971). This trend away from institutions is reasonable. Institutions are not only expensive, they are often inhumane. Unfortunately, adequate alternatives to institutionalization have not been spelled out. Even the most idealistic among us would not suggest that most retarded persons can live independent lives in a complex society involving door-to-door salesmen, income tax returns, and credit cards without a great deal of support and training.

Court decisions which require that severely handicapped children have the same educational rights as other children raise some interesting issues. Do the older severely retarded have the same rights as nonretarded? For example, do they have the right to sexual relations? Do they have the right to procreate and raise children if they are physically and behaviorally able? How shall we define "behaviorally able"? These are some of the questions which must be faced in the next few years. The answers will have implications for curriculum planning as we decide what role society will allow for the severely handicapped adult.

SUMMARY AND COMMENTS

Public opinion against the institutionalization of retarded and other handicapped children has been increasing over the past two decades. Recent court decisions hold that all children are entitled to a free public education. These pressures will lead to more and more handicapped children being admitted to public school programs even though most public school facilities and personnel are not equipped to teach them. Until very recently these children were excluded from public school programs. The reasons for exclusion were behavioral deficits such as failure to attend, failure to follow instructions, and failure to care for toileting needs. Now these deficits will be targets for remediation rather than criteria for exclusion. The inclusion of severely handicapped children will necessitate changes in ways that curricula are developed, changes in evaluation procedures, and inclusion of teaching procedures not currently used in the public school. Since there is no standard curriculum for severely retarded children, one will be needed. Parents must play an active part with the teacher in developing educational goals. Moreover, parents will have to play a part in initial and periodic evaluation of the child. The aim of education is not simply performance at school but also performance in nonschool situations.

Self-help skills, social skills, perceptual motor skills, and verbal skills are important target areas for severely handicapped children. The behavior modification literature now includes a number of studies of teaching in each of these areas. The results are consistent. Severely handicapped children can be taught if powerful reinforcers are used and finely graded teaching programs are developed. When properly taught, these skills can be generalized into new situations.

The inclusion of severely retarded children in the public school raises serious questions and issues both for public education officials and for the public in general. Effective teaching procedures for some handicapped children may require the use of consequences not usually used in the public school. Can the public and the school accept the use of both positive and negative consequences which are ordinarily not required or desirable with normal children? Is the public willing to pay for individualized programs for educating their least fortunate and least productive members? Will the public education system be able to make the changes in curriculum development, measurement procedures, and teaching techniques necessary for educating severely handicapped persons? Will society have the tolerance and intelligence to establish dignified roles in the community for severely handicapped persons? If not, any attempts we make to improve the education of the severely handicapped will be empty exercises.

DISCUSSION TOPICS
Developing Necessary Classroom Entry Skills

Objectives This chapter concerns the problems faced by our educational system in integrating children with severe behavior deficits into public school classrooms. In discussing the need for establishing a standard curriculum to accomplish this, the authors offer suggestions in:

1 Selecting performance targets and evaluating the progress of a child.
2 Methods of developing programs to teach the performance targets.

3 How to teach specific target areas intended to make a child more acceptable for classroom learning.

4 Specific ways teachers can be more effective in the education of students with severe limitations.

5 Considerations that must be made in dealing with issues and questions raised in educating the severely retarded in the public schools.

Exercise   This exercise is designed to give the student individual exploration of the problems dealt with in this chapter concerning the major problems of integrating the severely retarded student into the public school system. The student should be given the option of using any format but closely attuning the procedure to the suggestions outlined by the authors.

As a "special education" teacher going into a school district that is integrating the severely retarded into their schools for the first time, describe the procedures required for integration and give the sequence of adoption using specific suggestions made in this chapter.

NOTE

The preparation of this chapter was partially supported by NICHHD Grants HD 00870 and HD 02528. The authors thank John Hollis and Sebastian Striefel for their many contributions to the preparation of the manuscript.

Training Strategies for Language-Deficient Children: An Overview

Richard L. Schiefelbusch
Bureau of Child Research, University of Kansas
Kenneth F. Ruder
Bureau of Child Research, University of Kansas
William A. Bricker
Mailman Center for Child Development, University of Miami

INTRODUCTION

This chapter and the one following concern the teaching of "early" language, but instructions and illustrations for teaching language to children at more advanced levels are also presented. The teacher-clinician may extrapolate from the information provided to enhance language acquisition by any child. A comprehensive generalized program suitable to all children is unavailable, but the information presented here will help any enterprising teacher-clinician who wishes to teach language to special children.

Chapter 8 includes the rationale for language training, a discussion of language structure and function, and a general analysis of language training programs.

Chapter 9 expands upon the analysis of language as a curricular system and provides a careful description of an actual language program. Both chapters describe systematic approaches to teaching with a complex program.

Information is also included for specialists who wish to go beyond current guidelines and to research additional features of language acquisition and intervention. New developments in language must continue to be an important part of the teaching program for special children, and the teacher-clinician will be the most important professional in instrumenting new developments.

Increasing numbers of special teachers and clinicians are teaching language. This trend reflects expanded knowledge of the structures and functions of language, a growing interest in how language is acquired, and a confidence that language behaviors can be taught. Language must be a critical part of any educational plan for special children. Each child's success in his educational environment—both the social and the academic domains—depends largely on how he uses language. The child's ability to express language (speech) and to utilize language interpersonally (communication) is enhanced informally by activities built into teaching programs.

Language acquisition is a special problem for many children. Special language programs must be designed to combine features of psycholinguistics, cognitive structure, and behavior modification. A technology for teaching language must be created to assume a place in education similar to techniques for teaching reading or arithmetic, despite the fact that there are important and perhaps unique differences between language teaching and other teaching programs.

To begin with, the child may have no language through which a teacher can provide basic instructions to explain the "assignments." Instead, the lessons may require a special "clinical" presentation.

Secondly, many of the activities performed in classroom groups require the communication of messages. A language-deficient child can hardly become a part of this classroom process until he can transmit and receive information. Therefore, language training is antecedent to other teaching activities.

Finally, language is a basic part of cognitive behavior. Language is evaluated by the schools in assigning the child to an on-going program. Plans for an individualized curriculum and for individualized instruction must include language training. Until the child's language is evaluated and, indeed, until the range of progress in language training is estimated, the status of the child as a learner cannot be determined.

LEVELS OF LANGUAGE DEFICIT

Several levels of language deficit are found in special children. The most severe is the child who is nonverbal. He may make a few gestures and produce primitive vocal signals, but *he does not use a conventional language system*.

More frequent forms of language deficit involve incomprehensible speech. Even though the child may have (or may seem to have) considerable comprehension of language, his limited ability to express language limits his communication with adults and peers. More common forms of severe language deficit involve poor conceptual development. The child may have echolalic speech but not comprehend or use language appropriate to the context in which he speaks. This is delayed language in a semantic sense.

Most of the children discussed in Chapters 6 and 7 have some language deficit. For them language training should be introduced early—the earlier the better. This urgency underlies the early-intervention program described in Chapter 9. If language development can be accelerated through early-intervention procedures, the child's subsequent education program will be enhanced.

Another level of inadequate language functioning is indicated by poor communication. A child may have considerable understanding of language and a relative ability to express language under optimal circumstances, but overall he may be an ineffective communicator. He may not listen to the teacher or comprehend instructions in a normal, noisy, cluttered group setting. Perhaps he never asks questions, gives instructions, volunteers information, or talks with his peers. In other words his language functions are not adapted to normal social and learning task requirements. He has a *communication problem* even though his language does not seem to be seriously delayed.

Communication problems are often found among children with social disorders and experience defects and deficits. Consequently, communication problems may be found among any assembly of "handicapped" or "normal" children. The most difficult communication problems to eliminate are those which accompany a language lag or a speech defect. To help overcome these problems, most classrooms include "show and tell" activities and other functional communication experiences.

Another reason for language intervention activities is that certain *speech behaviors* are objectionable to listeners. These behaviors are often subtle and call for fine program tuning to produce behavioral change. Areas of concern include articulation defects, voice disorders, and stuttering. Although the defects may represent only a small feature or segment of the total language of the speaker, they may nevertheless interfere with communication. There are apparently more speech problems than language and communication problems. Thus there are more minor than major problems. However, minor problems often lead to major consequences for the speaker. The appropriate context for evaluating speech problems (as well as language and communication problems) is the child's total environment. Important "evaluators" include the family, peers, teachers, other adults, and the child himself. As W. Johnson (1967) has said, "A problem has members."

This brief overview of language problems suggests that we must allow for differences in the level of language already acquired. Some children have language with near normal syntax and phonology while others are virtually lacking in all linguistic structures. Some have functional receptive language but are limited in expressive features. Since language instruction programs often include a wide range of deficits among their clients, a technology for language intervention should be developed to take into account these wide divergencies and still include procedures appropriate for individual instruction.

In defining *language* one must also define *speech* and *communication*. The same issue holds in describing speech or communication. It is sometimes more meaningful to talk about language users, speakers, or communicators (all the same people).

LANGUAGE DISCRIMINATIONS

Premack (1970) suggests that the language user must make four essential discriminations. First he must determine that a symbol stands for a referent (usually an object, action, or agent). Second, he must discriminate between two or more symbols. Third, he must discriminate between different referent symbols. Fourth, he must differentiate between different sequential arrangements of the symbols.

Let us examine what each entails for a child learning a language.

The first discrimination requires the child to learn that language symbols (words) exist and that they can be and are used to represent events and objects in the environment. This discrimination is the recognition that the symbol stands for, or represents, an object. The most commonly used symbol is the spoken word. Gestures and written words likewise suffice as symbolic exemplars of behavior.

A second basic requirement of any competent language user is that he be able to discriminate among environmental events. The range of these particular discriminations as well as the particular environmental events which must be discriminated are mapped by the language systems.

Many environmental events are viewed similarly by all cultures. These events are classified as language universals. All cultures of the world, for example, discriminate between objects and actions and between initiators of actions (agents) and recipients of the action (objects). The important notion here is that to be a competent language-user an individual must make the basic environmental discriminations and conceptual categorizations mapped by his culture's language system.

The third requirement of a language-user is discrimination among symbols. For example, the competent user of English must be capable of discriminating between such language symbols as "pin," "ten," and "men." These are fine discriminations. The same criterion holds, however, for more gross discriminations such as between "cow" and "scissors."

Finally, a language user must discriminate among sequential arrangements of the symbols. In English, for example, it makes a great deal of difference if one says "John hit Mary," rather than "Mary hit John." The sequential arrangement of the symbols drastically affects the interpretation.

The individual who has a language impairment should first be evaluated to determine whether or not he possesses at least these basic essentials of a functional language system. Premack (1970) and Carrier (1973) report that these language functions can be developed with visual arrays of plastic symbols placed vertically or horizontally before the child. Moores (1974) also points out that manual language can express these functions. Language (symbolic function) is usually communicated to listeners by means of a phonological system expressed as speech. Most human language users must master audible speech both as speakers and listeners. This is in contrast to Premack's system, which was used visually and tactually to map conceptual functioning. Human speech must include an array of audible phonemes, morphemes, and syntactic variations. Speakers must generate novel strings of phonological, morphological, and syntactic units to accommodate the demands of the context in which they speak and listen, and to represent abstract situations beyond sight and hearing.

In Carrier's view, special children often fail to master the intricacies of the speech-language system. They become poor communicators, meaning that they do not perform effectively when called upon to speak or to comprehend. Their discriminations are inadequate for learning how to talk in the complex interpersonal world in which they are placed.

Before we get too deep into this area, let us set out a few definitions to establish some consistency and clarity in this complex field.

Language is a set of rules and principles by which symbolic representations and meanings are correlated.

Speech is a response mode by which language becomes overt behavior—the actual behavior of individuals using language.

Communication is the system of speech events, including both gestural and verbal behavior, that is interpersonal. For instance, the system involves a special child and at least one other individual.

Perhaps a brief elaboration of each of these definitions is indicated. Carroll (1967) has explained that *language* is composed of four linguistic aspects:

   1 Phonology—the specification of the units of sound (phonemes) which go to compose words and other forms of the language.
   2 Morphology—the listing of the words and other basic meaningful forms (morphemes) of the language and the specification of the ways in which these forms may be modified when placed in meaningful contexts.
   3 Syntax—the specification of the patterns in which linguistic forms may be arranged and the ways in which these patterns may be modified or transformed in varying contexts.
   4 Semantics—the specification of the meanings of linguistic forms and syntactic patterns in relation to objects, events, processes, attributes, and relationships in human experience. [p. 43]

Although these statements clarify the principal linguistic aspects of language, they do not suggest approaches to either evaluation or intervention.

Speech behavior includes three broad categories: (1) articulation—the way sounds are formed; (2) rhythm—the time relationship between sounds in a word and words in a sentence; (3) voice—the sounds produced by the vibration of vocal folds and modified by the resonators. These three can be explicitly evaluated. A determination of *normal* or *deviate* can be made with relatively high reliability. Deviations in these categories represent the bulk of the work done by speech clinicians. Although special individuals have high incidence of deviations in these categories, speech clinics also have large numbers of children with speech deviations who have normal learning rates for most other parameters of language.

Communication as a system of interaction between two or more persons (interpersonal behavior) is also a valid way to consider the problems of special individuals. The special individual as a participant in a rapid series of language events must make a series of precise discriminations about the speech he hears and must make quick, flexible speech responses of his own. Special individuals often fall far short of the abilities of other individuals with whom they attempt to communicate.

At no point in this analysis of speech, language, and communication have we referred to the function of audition. However, it is appropriate to say at this point that with inadequate auditory functions the inputs are greatly diminished, the speech process breaks down, and learning is greatly impaired. These issues are best considered in other texts. (See Fulton (1974), Moores (1974), and Lloyd & Fulton (1972).)

Language and language disorders, when viewed within the context of a communication transaction may reveal language problems of various scopes and intensities that interfere with the process of communication. It should be recognized that language problems are but one source of communication failure. Consequently, we are also concerned with communication problems resulting from speech disorders and communication problems resulting from inappropriate speaker-listener relationships. The poor listener and the speaker who uses dialectal or substandard linguistic forms are common examples of this latter category.

LANGUAGE FORM AND FUNCTION

Language form comprises the sounds of speech (phonology), grammatical parts of speech (such as subject of sentence, nouns, verbs, adjectives, noun phrases, prepositional phrases, etc.), and morphological inflections (plural markers, verb tense markers, possessive markers, etc.).

Language function, on the other hand, refers to semantic bases underlying the communicative act. For example, a sentence of the form "subject-verb-object" typically serves the function of expressing semantic relationships existing between agents (mapped in the linguistic form as grammatical subject), action (mapped as verb form), and objects or recipients of the action (mapped as the grammatical object of the sentence). In like manner, past tense and plurality are also language functions. Their respective linguistic forms are the morphological markers *-ed* and *-s*. To express the past-tense function then, the linguistic forms map some particular function, a point too often overlooked in a description of language.

The term *function* in this context refers to linguistic effects and is part of a total theory of language. However, the term *function* is also used in communication theory to explain a language event, as in speaking of an expressive function (an act of speaking) or a listening function (discrimination of meaning or perception of phonemes). In this sense, language functions influence the child's language usage or his speech performance.

There is still another way function is used in this chapter. In behavior theory, *function* explains the relationship between stimuli and response events. Something is *functional* if it "influences" change. For instance, praise may increase study behavior. If so, praise is a functional event.

The classes of the language system referenced here are linguistic components called *phonology, semantics,* and *syntax.* The functions are the language acts and features that language users produce and comprehend. What the language teacher and clinician must do is provide instruction to synthesize the components or structures of language with their corresponding functions so that both comprehension and production of language are substantially improved. This may be done in varying degrees depending on the nature of the language problem and the characteristics of the child or adult to whom language instruction is given. For example, some children are almost completely nonverbal having, at best, a few vocal sounds and some gestures. Others may emit a few words intelligible only to a few close relatives. Such children are often called nonverbal because they have no organized linguistic system.

Other children with severely deficient language have at least the rudiments of a language code but have major gaps in their language acquisition. Their speech may not be comprehensible, or they may have a limited vocabulary or use only one- or two-word units in talking. Children with limited language may comprehend language more readily than they can express it. This can be misleading. In receptive language acts, such as following directions with motor acts (pointing and fetching), the child may use a number of situational cues to supplement his receptive language. Among the most frequent problems of the severely delayed child are unintelligibility, meager vocabulary, limited syntax, poor conceptual development, and poor comprehension.

Children with language problems do not display consistency in the severity of their various deficit features. For instance, a child with a mild problem may have considerable comprehension of language and may be able to produce a variety of relatively unintelligible language forms. Another child may possess all the tools for being a competent speaker and listener but may lack the communicative skills to comprehend or to use language appropriately in a learning environment. This is delayed language in a semantic sense. This problem will eventually restrict the child's reading and arithmetic skills.

LANGUAGE TRAINING CONSIDERATIONS

In developing a language training program the basic question is what language forms and functions to include. The ideal program would include all the forms and corresponding functions of the language in question. To develop into a competent user of that language, the learner must cope with all linguistic forms for which a specific and specifiable function can be ascribed.

A functional language training program should encompass the grammar of the adult form of the language. The adult form of the language may provide terminal goals for a language training program, but it says little or nothing about the sequence and steps to be followed in achieving the terminal goal. For this, we must turn to two guiding principles:

1 Train first those language forms and functions which have immediate utility for the child. The word "more," for example, might have some utility for the child at the one-word stage of development to express a request for reoccurrence of an event (such as "more cookie"—"more milk"). By focusing on language forms and functions having immediate utility in the child's environment, the trainer takes advantage of his readiness for acquiring such a structure and also intrinsically rewards him. This principle may not always be applicable. For instance, it is not always apparent which linguistic structure or class of structure will be of utility to a particular individual. Lacking such information, we can turn to the alternate guiding principle.

2 Normal language development data affords at least a reasonable first approximation of what to include in a language training program.

To illustrate this latter principle, let us turn to recent work by Bloom (1970) describing the form and function of the early stages of language acquisition. Language expresses relationships between particular objects and events in the real world. Bloom illustrates this in her description of her child's utterance of "mommy sock." In a strict structural description, this would be a *noun-noun* construction, with each noun serving a distinct referential function. Such a superficial description overlooks the fact that the controlling features of the environment—the events leading to the production of the utterance and, hence, the communicative intent behind the production in the first place—provide cues which enable the listener to infer more from the utterance than the oversimplified interpretation that the child has just produced a sequence of two nouns. The child's utterance "mommy sock," for example, expresses several different functions. In one case, the events indicated that a possessive function was intended. In another instance the utterance was obviously intended to convey an agentive-objective function. In the first example the child was holding up her mother's stocking. In the second instance the mother was putting the child's stocking on the child's feet. The similarity of the structural form thus obscured the fact that different functions were being expressed. In the adult form of the language, this is usually not a problem because we have distinct forms to express such functions (e.g., "mommy's sock" as opposed to "mommy is putting on my socks"). Other common language functions expressed in early child language include a negating function (expressed by some form of "no"), interrogative functions (asking questions), attributive functions (modifying nouns with adjectives), spatial and temporal location (prepositions and adverbs), nonexistence ("all gone"), and reoccurrence ("more").

The aforementioned are language functions viewed from a psycholinguistic descriptive viewpoint. These functions (and their associated forms) provide the basic content of a language training program. Table 8-1 summarizes the various communicative functions and their associated structural forms attributed to the early stages of language acquisition. Further language acquisition consists primarily of extending, modifying, and refining these elementary language forms. The functions underlying these forms remain basically the same.

The significance of Bloom's (1970) work as a model for language training is that it treats language as a system. She views the basic function of language as being semantic; that is, words refer to significant classes of events in the environment. Her view of language and language acquisition in this respect is very similar to that of Premack (1970). Bloom's work is observational and descriptive—she does not attempt to teach language to the child—but it nevertheless describes functions for language which are amenable to manipulation and training. For instance, she found that children learn notions of agent-action-

Table 8-1   Language Form and Function in Early Language Acquisition

	Language form	Language function	Example
1	Nouns (N)	Labeling objects in environment	Doggie
2	Verbs (V)	Labeling actions and states in environment	Eat, hungry
3		Express basic semantic relations:	
	(a) V + N	Action-object	Put book
	(b) N + V	Agent-action	Eve read
	(c) N + N	Agent-object	Mommy sock
4		Modifying/qualifying symbolic referent (nouns)	
	(a) adj + N	Descriptive adj + noun	Big truck
	(b) adj + N	Numerical adj + noun	Two doggies
	(c) adj + N	Possessive adj + noun	My doggies
	(d) adj + N	Demonstrative adj + noun	That book
5		Modifying/qualifying states and actions (verbs)	
	(a) V + adv	Manner adverbials	Go fast
	(b) V + N	Locative	Walk street
	N + N		Sweater chair
6		Negating an affirmative proposition	
	(a) "No" + V	Rejection	No go
	"No" + N		No cookie
	(b) "all gone" + N	Nonexistence	All gone milk
	(c) "No" + V	Denial	No break
7	"hi" + N	Notice	Hi belt
8	"more" + N	Reoccurrence	More milk
	"'nother" + N		'Nother cookie
9	N + N	Conjunction	Umbrella boot
10	Wh- + N	Interrogation	Where cookie

objects as concepts which are prelinguistic. Children interact in a world of objects, events, and relations. Their perceptual cognitive strategies suggest that their understanding of this experience includes relational notions. Subsequent learning of linguistic structure thus depends upon the prior development of certain concepts.

Bloom found that the child's actions with a referent were important to the child's learning to name it. In other words, there is a congruence between naming, stating, asking, and the actions performed with the physical reference. Of special importance in this regard were (1) existence of the referent, (2) reoccurrence of the referent, (3) action upon the referent, and (4) nonexistence where expected.

These particular conceptual functions were accordingly mapped as (1) nouns, (2) reoccurrence expressed through use of the linguistic form "more ———," (3) agent-action-object relationships expressed as subject-verb-object strings, and (4) negation.

In Bloom's view the child develops understanding of the relational features of language by perceiving the context in which it is spoken. Thus, the goal of the language training program should be to structure the environment so relational features are highlighted to teach concepts prior to the teaching of relational features as words.

Thus the data from the normal language acquisition provides us with the content and training stages for a language training program and, perhaps more importantly, with the principle that the language function and form to be trained should be developed from the child's conceptual experiences.

This is the procedure followed in the language training program outlined in the next chapter. For instance, prior to attempting to establish the symbol-reference association (e.g., naming) the child is first trained in the functional use of the object. Prior to training the use of color adjectives, for example, the child would be trained in making the necessary color discriminations and categorizations.

Before delving into the specifics of this particular language training program it might be well to review some alternative but representative language intervention procedures. Some of the procedures are geared to children exhibiting little or no language skills. Others cut across various levels of language deficits. Such a review provides the reader with language intervention alternatives to the program presented in the next chapter, as well as examples of specific procedures and materials to supplement language intervention.

THE RANGE OF LANGUAGE TRAINING APPLICATIONS

Some language intervention procedures are concerned with language enrichment. Others, such as the program described by Tawney and Hipsher (1970) are for the nonverbal, severely retarded child. Some boil down to the demonstration of a methodology to train a single linguistic rule (Guess, 1969; Baer & Guess, 1971; and Schumaker & Sherman, 1970); whereas intervention procedures such as those described by Stremel (1972) are developmental and programmatic because one stage of training is built directly upon the preceding stage.

The range of content and applicability of existing language training programs is wide indeed. Some, or portion of some, lend themselves to groups in a classroom situation. A major problem with most, however, is that the content is specific and inflexible. They are not easily adapted to individualized problems. Portions of several programs when combined may provide an effective treatment for a particular child with a particular language problem. No single program has thus far been shown to have broad applicability to the many and varied problems of all language-delayed children.

Language specialists who have published training reports and manuals are formulating a comprehensive set of strategies which can be used to teach language to children of different levels of functioning and with greatly different medical and social histories. If this trend continues, we may soon have a formal clinical methodology for language intervention. The language training program outlined in the next chapter is a step in this direction.

INTERVENTION PROCEDURES FOR CHILDREN WITH LIMITED LANGUAGE

Since 1965, many investigations with language-delayed children have been conducted. Because of methodological refinements contained in these studies (such as specification of procedures and the use of more language-related evaluation instruments), knowledge of what content should be included in a language training program has improved. A review of some of those training programs is provided in this section in order to indicate to the teacher-clinician the range of recent language training efforts. These studies demonstrate some options or supplements to the specific language training methods contained in the next chapter.

One interesting variation by Gotkin (1967) is called *Matrix Games for Young Children*. The games are sequenced pictures designed to provide practice in language concepts. The program involves short steps, active participation, and immediate feedback to the child. The goals of the program are to develop vocabulary and concepts and to teach the child to speak clearly, follow directions, and be independent. Talkington and Hall (1970) report the results of a language program based on Matrix Games. Forty Down's syndrome residents of an institution were evaluated on a language test designed by the authors. The test evaluated the amount of appropriate language usage and mastery of concepts. Half the residents were given daily language sessions based on Matrix Games and the other half were not. After 21 days of training, the experimental subjects showed greater gains in several aspects of language usage and concept mastery than the control group. Although the subjects employed in this investigation were moderately retarded, their age (average twenty-four years) indicates that they probably had some language before the training began. Hence they are not comparable to young low-functioning children who have no language at all. Thus the efficacy of Matrix Games for young, low-functioning children has not been demonstrated.

Among language training programs designed specifically for low-functioning children displaying little or no functional language skills is one developed by Tawney and Hipsher (1970). The program, called *Systematic Language Instruction* (SLI) emphasizes behavioral prerequisites to language production such as attending, motor skills, and receptive processes. The program is especially suited to low-functioning children who may need to learn behaviors such as sitting quietly or watching what the teacher does before language training begins. However, the sequencing of steps in the program has not been validated, and the program has not been tested with young, low-functioning children.

Lovaas (1968) discusses a language program employed with psychotic children. The program is based on an operant model. The two main phases of the program are the establishment of vocal behavior and the production of speech in appropriate contexts. The children involved in his study resided in a full-time facility for psychotic children. Training sessions varied from two to seven hours a day. Children were trained in verbal imitation, object labeling, prepositions, and spontaneous speech. Training was initiated with primary reinforcers, i.e., food, but after two to three months shifted to social or secondary reinforcers. The results are encouraging. Although they did not develop spontaneous language, mute psychotic children learned to imitate speech, label objects, and express simple needs.

Risley and Wolf (1968) report on a program which succeeded in training conversational speech in echolalic children. These children differ from mute children in that language is part of their behavior repertory but is not under appropriate control. Risley and Wolf employed highly structured procedures based on operant technology. Shaping, imitation training, fading, extinction, time-out, and differential reinforcement were employed in order to build new behaviors. Training began with work on eye contact, proceeded to imitation, then to naming objects and pictures, and then to phrases. Primary reinforcement, i.e., food, was used to begin training. Parents and teachers were taught to socially reinforce appropriate language behavior in order to ensure generalization. Functional verbal behavior was established with all four children included in this report.

The Lovaas (1968) and Risley and Wolf (1968) procedures have been employed by many investigators. For example, Hingtgen and Churchill (1971) used the procedures to establish imitative speech in four mute children. Sloan, Johnston, and Harris (1968) reported on a similar program for severely language-impaired children. They also trained mothers to carry out the procedures at home on a daily basis. The program emphasized skills prerequisite to language training. The moderately to severely retarded children in the study all showed increases in appropriate speech in a classroom setting. Guralnick (1972) reports the results of a language training program using undergraduate students as teachers. The program followed the Sloan, Johnston, and Harris (1968) sequence. By the end of a semester, five of the eight children had progressed to at least the next step in the program.

Longitudinal Language Training Programs

The language training programs discussed thus far have focused on establishing specific language skills in children who display little functional language. A more recent trend in language intervention studies has been to design longitudinal programs capable of accommodating a range of language deficiencies in nonverbal children with minimal syntactic problems. Sailor, Guess, and Baer (1973; see also Guess, Sailor, & Baer, 1974), have attempted, not only to design a language program that extends across much of the language-acquisition span, but also to accommodate four of the natural problems the teacher-clinician encounters.

The four problems, stated in order of increasing importance, outline what future work should include:

1   The direct comparison of the various training techniques that can be applied to the same type of language problem or deficiency.
2   Using existing behaviors of the language-deficient child to serve as predictive variables for the selection of the best training technique for the child.
3   Continuing the construction of useful training programs which are both practical in application and optimally functional for the child in his linguistic interaction with his environment.
4   The programmed transfer, or generalization, of behaviors from the controlled training setting in which (we know) they can be taught, to the child's "natural environment."

Although these problem topics are defined by language researchers and designed to guide further language research, they are important to language clinicians. They emphasize the need for alternative approaches and techniques, the importance of using language assessments for language planning, the importance of carefully designed language programs (perhaps a battery of programs) so alternative plans may be used for individual children, and the importance of extending training beyond the clinical setting. Clinicians should examine available clinical language programs, including those designed for their own clients, against these operational issues.

Stremel (1972) reports the results of a longitudinal language training program used with institutionalized, low-functioning children. The three children involved in the program were between nine and thirteen years of age. All demonstrated limited expressive vocabularies, consisting mainly of nouns, before beginning the program. The program followed a hierarchical sequence of training tasks based on the development of grammatical structures in young normal children. The three children were trained sequentially on verb production, subject-verb constructions, and subject-verb-object constructions. Training was conducted individually. All subjects showed increases in subject-verb-object constructions produced on the posttest. Two of the subjects also produced more subject-verb and subject-verb-object constructions in their spontaneous speech. The program as presented here did not include tasks which could be used with children with less-sophisticated language skills, i.e., no expressive labels and few receptive labels. The program could be extended downward to include those tasks.

Gray and Fygetakis (1968*a;* 1968*b*) presented the results of a language program based on educational programming and conditioning techniques for use with children between three and seven years of age. The program involves 40 subprograms designed to teach 55 grammatical skills. The program is designed for classrooms of about six children. Structured sessions are conducted each day. In addition, classroom time is used to encourage the use of language acquired in the structured session. The results were encouraging for the children involved, but the program as it is described is not appropriate for low-functioning, language-handicapped children. Although the children involved in the program were at least one year behind in language skills, the skills with which the children entered the program were quite sophisticated, and the program served to remediate problems in existing language structures rather than to build new structures. The authors contend that the program could be extended downward to involve children with less-sophisticated language development, but this has not been verified.

Kent, Klein, Faulk, Guenther (1972) presents a language program which was designed for institutionalized, severely retarded nonverbal children from five to twenty years of age. The program is developmental in nature, follows a structured hierarchical sequence of skills, and is based on operant conditioning principles. One segment of the program is devoted to language production prerequisites such as attending, motor imitation, and structured group play. These prerequisite skills are particularly applicable to young low-functioning children who may need considerable training before language training can begin. Once the child has mastered the prerequisite tasks, he is moved into the second phase of the program. The second phase concentrates on the development of verbal skills. The child moves from training in simple receptive skills, to more complex receptive skills, to simple expressive skills, and finally to complex expressive skills. The techniques employed in the program and the content of the program are both adequately described. The authors recognize that language training should be extended from one-to-one highly structured laboratory sessions to the child's more natural environment. No formal data on the success of the program were presented.

Language intervention with language-deficient children can be successful. Programs such as those presented by Stremel (1972), Kent et al. (1972), W. Bricker and D. Bricker (1970), and Gray and Fygetakis (1968) indicate the utility of using operant procedures in a structured, step-by-step sequenced program. Unfortunately most were developed with older language-deficient children within institutions. There is a need for more work with young children living in their own homes and who are deficient in language. This effort should concentrate on processes that are prerequisite to formal language. In addition, there are many children who have receptive language but who are unable to learn vocal speech codes. Some may need an alternate method of communication. Two possibilities involve the use of manual signs and/or tangible markers or symbols.

Nonverbal Approaches to Language Intervention

Imitative sign training was used by Bricker (1972) to teach word-object associations to a group of young, institutionalized, retarded children. The children were first taught to imitate a motor movement such as pouring. They were then taught to produce the motor movement in the presence of a specific word, e.g., pitcher. The final step was to teach an association between the word and the object. This technique facilitated word-object association and suggested that signing or motor imitation is a useful training procedure for children who demonstrate difficulty in learning names of objects.

A second approach has been to teach communication through visual symbols. Marshall and Hegrenes (1972) reported on a "written functional communication system" used with an autistic child with severely limited expressive skills. The program had three phases: (1) establishing a functional vocabulary with words printed on cards, (2) learning to sequence the word cards appropriately, and (3) transferring from word cards to written communication. Cards were labeled with food names and the child was required to match the card with the appropriate food. Other word cards were added so the child has to generate grammatical sentences to request food. Finally, the child was required to write his own word cards in order to communicate his needs. The investigators report that this program has given a noncommunicative child an effective system for communication. It should be considered for use with other children having severe expressive problems.

Carrier (1973) has developed language training programs utilizing the visual/motor medium of message transmission in place of the auditory/verbal mode. His plastic symbol system has certain advantages for language training with handicapped children. It allows communication from a child who may not have speech apparatus or writing skills, and it does not place a heavy load on memory. Unlike speech, the sentence produced is durable rather than transitory.

The plastic symbol system has one severe limitation for teaching retarded children. It has little functional value for communication outside the training situation. Carrier assumes that the complex nature of the speech response system often interferes with language acquisition. Therefore, he substitutes a nonspeech response mode for speech. In this mode, geometric forms function as linguistic constituents. The child has only to select and correctly arrange forms appropriate to the meaning to be conveyed. At least one other intervention procedure based on plastic symbols has appeared in the literature. McLean (1972) attempted to train three nonverbal disturbed children to use the plastic chips to generate three element sentences. Although only two of the subjects learned the task, and many trails were necessary for them to reach criterion performance, this approach merits more exploration with the population of language-deficient children.

Speech Disorders

Many children have specific speech problems which do not seriously affect their language functioning. A child may not have problems related to language form and/or function but may have verbal expressions which are objectionable to listeners and which interfere with adequate message reception and processing by listeners. This objectionable speech behavior is often subtle. The problem calls for minimal, but important, behavioral changes. The areas of concern may include specific articulation defects, for instance substituting a /w/ for an /r/, voice disorders involving breathiness, harshness, nasality, or hestitations in speech production referred to as *stuttering*. Speech clinicians devote more than 80 percent of their time to these speech defects. Articulation defects, that is, problems in the production of specific phonemes of a language, constitute the largest single category of speech disorders and hence should be discussed in some detail, particularly since they frequently occur in conjunction with language disorders. (Detailed discussions of evaluation and treatment for voice and stuttering problems are beyond the scope of this chapter. For such information the reader is referred to specific speech pathology literature such as Van Riper (1972) and Travis (1971).)

Articulation disorders may be categorized in four general ideological types:

1 Functional articulation disorders (those articulation disorders for which no other causative factors other than developmental delay can be attributed).
2 Articulation problems due to physical impairment of the speech musculature (speech disorders due to facial paralysis or cerebral palsied speech are examples of this category).
3 Articulation problems due to regional dialect differences (a person with a Southern dialect may be treated for articulation disorders if attending school in the East or Midwest, for example, and vice versa).
4 Related to articulation disorders due to dialect problems are those resulting from acquiring English as a second language (the foreign dialect problem) as well as articulation differences due to culturally different speech codes such as found in the phonology of black English and Mexican-American English.

For purposes of treating articulation disorders the etiologic or causative factors may be irrelevant. Most articulation evaluations, for example, describe articulation disorders in terms of either substitutions of one sound for another, omission of specific phonemes, and/or distortions in the production of specific phonemes. In theory, such characterizations ignore the underlying causes of the articulation defect. In practice, however, the underlying causes probably do affect the therapeutic approach, at least insofar as there are different approaches to treating a child who has articulation disorders as a result of speech musculature impairment than are used with the so-called functional articulation disorders in which such underlying speech musculature involvement is not apparent.

Misarticulations are frequent among younger children and children with delays in language acquisition. Because of the specific nature of phonological errors, clinicians can catalog them accurately and can plan and program articulation training. The specific nature of "simple" articulation problems may lead to the assumption that they are easily and readily corrected. This assumption is sometimes borne out in clinical records; articulatory deviations more often prove to be especially difficult to modify. The problem is more complex linguistically than is often assumed (Shriner, Holloway, Daniloff, 1969). Clinical intervention to correct articulatory errors is commonly undertaken with school-age children. Articulation problems often arise with oral reading, with social conversation in school-related activities, and with evaluations of general speech effectiveness. Intelligibility is a major problem for preschool children. Consequently, stimulation training is often advocated for preschoolers. Designed activities are planned to promote discrimination training and speech "practice." The work, usually in groups, features motivational speech activities that focus on verbal interaction and include social reinforcement.

Evaluation of articulatory errors is important to clinical planning and to the eventual outcome of therapy. It is very often the teacher who first notices that the child has poor speech intelligibility due to articulation disorders. A formal articulation evaluation is generally required to determine the nature and scope of this articulation problem. There are a number of commercially available articulation tests. The McDonald Deep Test of Articulation (McDonald, 1964) and the Goldman-Fristoe Test of Articulation (Goldman & Fristoe 1972) are two examples of widely used clinical diagnostic articulation tests. The teacher-clinician can quickly add to his inventory of commercially available articulation tests by obtaining current catalogs from publishing houses specializing in test and measurement materials. The issue is not which specific articulation test is used. It is more important that the child's inventory of correctly articulated phonemes, as well as his misarticulations, be appropriately catalogued in order to begin an articulation therapy program.

Utility and developmental sequence play a large part in determining training sequences for articulation therapy. It is usually more appropriate to begin articulation training with the /t/ or the /s/ phoneme, for instance (which occur relatively frequently in spontaneous speech) in contrast to the phoneme such as /ʒ/ (the final sound in the word rouge), which occurs infrequently. Again, lacking guidelines about which phoneme is of immediate utility to the child, the best procedure is to train missing or distorted phonemes in the order in which they are normally acquired. Sanders (1972) made a rather complete summary of the developmental sequence of acquisition of the phonemes of English. That work may serve as a guide to planning a developmental training sequence.

There are a number of commercially available programs for specific procedures involved in articulation training. Some articulation programs are general, consisting primarily of speech-stimulation games.

For programs designed to train a particular phoneme in a step-by-step sequence, the reader is referred to the discussion by Winitz (1969).

Baker and Ryan (1971) have published a *Programmed Conditioning for Articulation,* Mowrer (1971), has also developed and published a highly programmatic sequence for training specific phonemes such as the /s/ and the /r/.

Southwest Regional Laboratories (1973) in a similar fashion published a series of speech-articulation kits, each a specific and programatic procedure for training a particular phoneme. These are merely examples of articulation programs. Publishers catalogs contain comprehensive listings of available articulation programs.

Once the articulation program has proceeded beyond the initial stages of training, the clinician encounters the problem of transfer of training. Transfer in articulation therapy is commonly referred to as carry-over. Mowrer (1971) describes the process of transfer in five stages of articulation therapy:

1 Discrimination training
2 Sounds in isolation
3 Transfer among words
4 Sentences
5 Spontaneous conversational speech

Mowrer suggests that there are two instructional procedures that can maximize transfer of training:

1 Management of speaking situations outside the clinical setting
2 The use of carefully sequenced instructional programs

McLean and Raymore (1972) describe a program designed to effect generalization, or carryover, to all situations in which the child might speak. Their system emphasizes discrimination training, response development, and stimulus generalization. The last is a transfer of training to other responses for the same class, but of a different form or configuration.

Griffiths and Craighead (1972) extended the work of McLean and Raymore by adding intratherapy, generalization procedures. Although they also probe for effects of the multistimulus procedure and carry their assessment beyond a clinical study. Their conclusion is that generalization training is effective, but that extension procedures (to new settings) are necessary to get the optimal extratherapy effects.

PROBLEMS RELATED TO COMMUNICATION AND/OR LANGUAGE USAGE

Communication problems related to inappropriate or inadequate language form or function (that is, problems related to the linguistic code), or problems related to the process of speaking (problems of articulation, voice, and fluency) may be caused by the lack of tools for communication. However, we frequently encounter a child in the school system with communication problems who apparently has all the tools necessary to be an effective communicator. Language tests sometimes indicate that the child "knows" particular linguistic rules and forms. Speech testing reveals no problems in articulation, voice, or fluency which might interfere with the communication process, and yet these individuals have difficulty communicating. This is a common problem with a child who utilizes dialectal forms considered to be inappropriate in social communication outside the dialect community. This problem is frequently referred to as one of language usage. Language usage may also be a problem for a child who completes a language training program. He may demonstrate a knowledge and use of the linguistic forms in the training environment but be incapable of extending this behavior to other environments.

This problem is basically one of effective listening and speaking in a range of learning and social situations. An intriguing way to illustrate the usage problem of a preschool or kindergarten child is to place him at a table opposite another child of the same age. Place an opaque screen between the two children. Instruct one of them to be the messenger and the other to be the listener. The task of the messenger is to describe an odd-shaped piece of plastic to the listener so that the listener can select a facsimile object for an array of objects placed in front of him. The instructions to the messenger include giving (to the other child) any information about the object that will help the other child recognize the object being described. The listener is instructed to ask questions and to suggest how the messenger can provide better information.

It is probable that the success of the speaker/listener team is affected by the abstractness of the task. Given simpler materials, perhaps the child-child team could be effective. In a more general sense, it is likely that the child's use of language is influenced by the difficulty of the language task. If language tasks are graduated in difficulty, a program can be devised to provide a range of successful experiences.

A second important point is that an adult-child team (when the adult is the messenger) can handle more complex tasks. This may be a function of experience—experience for the adult as a speaker and experience for the child as a listener. Many children need experience in both listening and speaking. Even if the child has the language necessary for understanding, describing, narrating, and discussing experiences or contexts, he may still not perform unless he has had a variety of experiences with the communicative tasks required. Language enrichment programs such as DISTAR (Englemann, Osborn, & Englemann, 1969) are a step in this direction. More than likely, however, this is a challenge facing the teacher-clinician—to find or create situations and communication transactions that provide practice and experiences which enable the child to use the content of the language training program. With such an approach it is possible to establish a functional language repertory and to develop an effective communicator.

GENERAL ANALYSIS OF A LANGUAGE PROGRAM

When a clinician-teacher begins to develop a language program, the emphasis should be upon the procedures used in planning and maintaining the program. The best strategy comprises four parts:

1   Initial evaluation
2   Continuing evaluation
3   Language program
4   Program maintenance

Initial evaluation presents ways for measuring the child's current level of language functioning. This is the basis for determining the language training activities relevant to him. In a behavioral sense, the *initial evaluation* should provide a baseline for planning and comparing the child's initial performance with subsequent stages of development. The *continuing evaluation* model is a systematic way to include both intermediate probes of the child's performance and long-term evaluations. The probes are brief measures to determine if specific improvements are occurring as a function of the instructional activities. The long-term evaluations measure the more general areas of progress expected as a consequence of instruction and are then used as guides for determining the need for overall redesigns of the program. *Language program* refers to the language curriculum necessary for the child to reach the projected level of language functioning. Finally, *program maintenance* includes the selection and arrangement of the stimulus materials and the training environment, the system of reinforcement that will motivate the child to perform, the criterion performance levels to be used in each phase, and the related aspects of language affected by the specific training.

The four-part strategy helps the instructor prepare programs for individual children and for general strategies of language instruction. The system is also useful in organizing the mounting volume of information on the language acquisition and language training now available to the teacher-clinician. The sections are interrelated, but each serves to emphasize an important and natural aspect of the total program.

Initial Evaluation and Planning

The initial evaluation provides the instructor with planning information for the language training program. Limited reference is made to the efforts of many competent diagnostic clinics and clinical scientists studying physical impairments of basic speech mechanisms, and the neurology of central language processes. Such efforts contribute to the process dysfunctions discussed in other sources. The reader is encouraged to read *Brain Mechanisms Underlying Speech and Language* (Millikan & Darley, 1967), a section on "Disabilities in Children Viewed Etiologically" in *Principles of Childhood Language Disabilities* (Irwin & Marge, Eds., 1972) and *Biological Foundations of Language* (Lenneberg, 1967).

Auditory testing may provide process information important to language instruction. There is an obvious connection between poor hearing and poor language acquisition. The reduced auditory input of the hearing-impaired child may result in impoverished language stimulation. Improvements in hearing testing techniques make accurate evaluations possible for all children with whatever level of functioning (Lloyd & Fulton, 1972; Fulton, 1972). Early detection and diagnosis may lead to a special preschool language program for deaf and hard-of-hearing children. Training programs are now available for multiply handicapped deaf children (Berger, 1972). Since receptive processes are obviously involved in the child's communication, the teacher should give careful attention to auditory data in the child's case report. Hearing losses may also indicate the need for a special program of auditory training prior to or as a part of corrective speech activities for children throughout the school years.

The child's level of functioning in other areas is also important in language training. These include visual attending, sitting in a chair for reasonable periods of time, and motor imitation. These processes are directly related to instructional problems. Their assessment and modification are described in more detail in the next chapter.

More specific approaches to language assessment may be undertaken at three levels:

1 Informal assessments
2 Formal assessments
3 Continuing assessments

The first two levels relate to initial assessments; the latter with assessment at various phases of the language training program. Informal language assessment can be broken down into two general types. The simplest is the parent's or teacher's report of the child's language capacity in their overall impressions of the child's language problem. Such informal reports can be very informative and can save time for the clinician or teacher who is evaluating the child's level of language functioning. Those reports help narrow the range of possible speech and language deficits and allow the clinician or teacher to develop a preliminary test battery leading to more formal assessments. The second informal assessment procedure is somewhat more structured. It consists primarily of obtaining spontaneous speech samples taken from the child's interactions with peers, parents, and teachers.

Elicited speech samples (such as samples obtained from directions, "tell me the story of The Three Bears," or "tell me a story about this picture") help in assessing or planning a language training program for individual youngsters. Lee and Cantor (1971) describe an analysis of a child's level of linguistic functioning obtained from free spontaneous speech samples as well as from elicited spontaneous speech samples. Such assessments of the child's level of language functioning are tenuous, but they can help the clinician or teacher pinpoint the language problem well enough to allow selection of an initial test battery for a more formal language assessment.

The second level of language assessment consists of testing for comprehension and production of specific linguistic behaviors. Such assessment procedures may contain tests for verbal imitation, comprehension, or production of specific lexical or grammatical behaviors. The Parsons Language Sample (Spradlin, 1963) is an example of a formal assessment tool which includes evaluations of such behaviors as (1) imitations of verbal and nonverbal models, (2) imitation of gestures, (3) naming, (4) comprehension of verbal and nonverbal commands, and (5) performance in terms of verbal or gestural expression.

The Utah Test of Language Development (Mecham, Jex, & Jones, 1967), is another formal assessment procedure for children who display little or no verbal behavior. Another assessment procedure for nonverbal children is provided by W. Bricker and D. Bricker (1970). Such tests may provide information regarding prelinguistic behaviors or prerequisite skills, but the relationships of many of these behaviors to the language training program per se are either not specified or their relationship to language or language training programs is not clear. That is not to say that such tests have no place in the language-assessment phase of the language training program. It means that much of the behavior contained in such preverbal, prelinguistic testing represents levels of prerequisite behavior or behaviors which may be necessary for a functional interaction between the clinician and the child in the process of language training.

Cazden (1971) presents a comprehensive treatment of the language evaluation of preschool and primary school children. She provides a table covering objectives in early language development. In the table she includes a vertical list of content areas—sounds, words, grammar, objects, events, ideas, reality (discussion), fantasy (dramatic play), and thought. In the horizontal dimension she presents *behaviors* under subheadings of cognitive and affective. The ten broad, functional performance classes listed include: understand and produce simple language forms; understand and produce elaborated language (describe); understand and produce elaborated language (narrative); understand and produce elaborated language (generalize, explain, and predict); use language effectively for specific purposes to others (communication); use language effectively for specific purposes (cognition); operate on language (analyze); operate on language (transform and translate); operate on language (evaluate); and demonstrate the use of language frequently and with enjoyment.

She relates language tests and evaluation systems to her chart so that the reader can place the test in the context of specific contents and behaviors. In this way the teacher can soon learn which test procedure contains items which can be used for certain language activities. This procedure assists the teacher in developing practical testing operations and evaluative skills.

Cazden also combines cognitive, linguistic, and behavioral functions in her language-evaluation discussion. The focus of her discussion is preschool education and, by implication, language skills required by the public schools. The information is especially valuable to a teacher who has responsibility for teaching language and for teaching other language-related skills or the applications of language structures and functions.

Carrow (1972) provides another comprehensive discussion of speech and language assessment in children. Included in her presentation is a taxonomy of language functions. Her classification is divided into receptive channels, receptive processes, receptive-expressive association processes, expressive processes, and expressive channels. She also separates language functions into three levels. Under receptive processes she lists Level I, sensation; Level II, perception; and Level III, language comprehension. Under expressive processes she lists: Level I, reflective sound utterances; Level II, automatic speech; and Level III, language formulation. It is interesting that she places language competence under receptive-expressive association processes and at Level III.

Like Cazden, Carrow explains tests and evaluation procedures so the reader can equate the test with its appropriate language function(s). Carrow is strongly influenced by the psycholinguistic system utilized in the Illinois Test of Psycholinguistic Abilities (ITPA) (Kirk, McCarthy, & Kirk, 1968). However, unlike the ITPA, Carrow gives careful attention to transformational grammar. Tests that merit special mention in this linguistic area are by Lee, (1969); Carrow (1973); and Bellugi-Klima (1968). These are tests of language comprehension and may establish the probable level of a child's functional language.

Lee's test features a series of model sentences presented to the child as he is shown an array of three pictures. He is asked to point to the picture which matches the sentence. Carrow has devised a similar test to measure comprehension of specific language structures. Bellugi-Klima's procedure also may be regarded as comprehension testing.although she includes a set of manipulation tasks to test comprehension of syntactic functions. The Bellugi-Klima procedure also may be regarded as comprehension testing, although she includes a set of manipulation tasks to test comprehension of syntactic functions. The Bellugi-Klima test has the advantage of providing more stimulation and motivation because the child manipulates objects. The object-manipulation procedure also reduces the probability that the visual stimuli of the picture comprehension procedure may not adequately depict the linguistic contrasts of the test. Thus, the Bellugi-Klima test may give a more accurate picture of the child's language comprehension abilities than do those tests involving picture stimuli. This observation still lacks empirical support at this time.

Comprehension tests utilizing the multiple-choice, visual-picture stimuli may not adequately reflect the child's linguistic competence. This has been noted in several recent studies. Goodglass, Gleason, and Hyde (1970) found that a picture-language comprehension test depicted the child's knowledge of grammatical structure differently than did a comprehension-testing procedure in which the child was presented with a single picture and given a choice of two verbal stimuli (sentences) and asked which of the two sentences he preferred for the particular picture. This preference procedure and its applicability in assessing comprehension in specific linguistic structures has been demonstrated in studies by Waryas and Ruder (1974).

They found that the more traditional picture-comprehension test tended to underestimate the child's knowledge of a particular linguistic rule, in comparison to results obtained from the preference procedure. Considerable research remains to be done on the preference procedure, but the preliminary data indicate that this is a simple and effective way to assess a child's knowledge of linguistic rules and structures.

Of all the formal tests designed to sample some aspect of language behavior, probably the most common and most frequently used are those which test vocabulary comprehension. Tests such as the Peabody Picture Vocabulary Test (Dunn, 1965) and Ammons Full-range Picture Vocabulary Test (Ammons and Ammons, 1968) are representative. These tests present a verbal stimulus (word), and the child is asked to point to the appropriate visual stimulus (picture from a multiple-choice array) which best depicts the stimulus word. Such tests assess the child's receptive vocabulary. Aram and Nation (1972) have recently adapted the comprehension form of the Peabody Picture Vocabulary Test to be utilized as a test of vocabulary usage, e.g., a production vocabulary test.

These tests indicate only whether or not a child uses such structures or is capable of using such structures in his everyday functional communication. Outside the language-training situation or the language-assessment environment (under most conditons) communication involves an extremely complex exchange between a speaker and a listener. Although the child many have been trained to use a particular linguistic structure in the more controlled environment of the language training or assessment situation, this "knowledge" does not ensure that the child knows when to use such structures. This is a common problem in (so-called) language-enrichment programs. The number of such language enrichment programs is increasing, but methods of assessing functional communicative skills are still in a primitive stage.

Rosenberg (1972) described a paradigm used to empirically study the interpersonal communication process. The paradigm consists of two individuals, one designated as the speaker and the other designated as the listener. Both the speaker and the listener have identical sets of materials in front of them. It is the task of the speaker to communicate to his partner across a visual barrier so that his partner can correctly select which item is being described at a particular time. In such a paradigm, the speaker's responsibility is clearly defined by the description task. The effectiveness of the communication transaction can also be quantified in terms of the listener's accuracy in selecting the correct items in response to his partner's descriptions. Another measure obtained from such a controlled interpersonal communication paradigm is an analysis of the specific characteristics of the utterances between the speaker and the listener. The analysis may consist of a precise description of the particular linguistic structures being used (such as one might find in writing a grammar). On the other hand, the analysis may consist of noting whether a particular linguistic form, such as negation or question-asking behavior, was used. This analysis of the interpersonal communication transaction is extremely limited. However, its potential for assessing knowledge of particular structures and a child's functional use of language is obvious. A further discussion of this paradigm applied to training functions was presented earlier in the section on Problems Related to Communication and/or Language Usage. The problems of assessment are tied inextricably to program content and training sequences. As such, assessment procedures should be considered in broader perspective. Assessment should place the child in the program in the proper sequence and also should provide the clinician or researcher with feedback concerning the relevance of the training sequence and the prerequisite behaviors required to enter particular stages of the program. If a particular terminal behavior can be reached without going through an intervening prerequisite stage, it is not necessary to include that stage in the training sequence. The assessment procedure should also provide the clinician with data which aid in deciding which is most effective in achieving a particular terminal goal. These issues are analyzed more fully in the following discussion of continuing evaluation.

Continuing Evaluation

Evaluation is used to determine initial baseline levels of functioning and initial language planning and to obtain feedback on the short-term progress of the child, on the effectiveness of contingencies, and on the rate of correct responding (relative to criteria). Subtle changes in strategy are dependent upon immediate feedback. Clinical hunches are useful, but hunches do not provide objective, direct information about the effects of antecedent and subsequent events.

Simple, reliable procedures have been developed for charting and graphing behavior and for maintaining a cumulative record. Graphing the progress reveals differences in performance dimensions under various "experimental" conditions. Appropriate methods and examples of graphing are presented by McLean (1970), McReynolds (1970), and Mowrer (1969). Along with procedures for recording behavior, strategies for using recorders have emerged. Parents, teaching aides, older children, and even children themselves have been trained to record behavior.

Continuous language probes are being used with greater frequency in language maintenance to sample a child's level of performance in specific parameters of the program. The clinician usually samples the child's performance before training for the unit is begun. The probe provides a specific baseline before proceeding with the unit. A probe can also be used to check performance maintenance for completed phases. Probes may show a need to recycle to an earlier training phase to reestablish a performance until that has been lost. At other times there may need to be a probe of the effects of a contingency system to see if it is functional. These procedures are demonstrated in a film *Shift of Stimulus Control* (McLean, 1970).

A typical probe involves sampling several words or phonemic units in a class of responses that have been taught or are soon to be taught. The responses are charted and reviewed in relation to criteria or to anticipated baselines. Probes are usually minireplications of the same stimulus-response (antecedent–subsequent event) units that have been or will be taught.

Feedback derived from data describing short-term effects makes the clinician-teacher an experimental agent because the information aids in refining and improving procedures. It is not sufficient to develop procedures that result in progress. The aim should be to develop an efficient system which results in maximum progress within a given period of time. Procedures developed in this way can be defined and built into subsequent programming.

Data from long-term evaluation are also extremely useful. Data may include tabulations of short-term measurements, serial probe evaluations, and periodic broader samplings of performance which may be compared to data derived in the initial evaluation. These data enable the clinician to develop major changes in the program and to validate the long-range design.

Language Program

A language program should be built on information developed from the initial language evaluation. Several basic factors will influence the design of the program. The first is that language is acquired (learned) in a series of phases or stages which the instructor can set down in a predicted sequential system of language units. The system is a practical curriculum which includes a goal in addition to the sequential series of phases. For instance, we might use a lattice system (a form of outlining) to show developmental steps for a hypothetical young, handicapped child. The goal is language competence comparable to a normal preschool child. The individual in this hypothetical program may not be a child in the three- to four-year-old range, but the language curriculum is generally applicable to any small child who receives informal assistance from parents, other children, or friends of the family in a natural environment.

The ways in which language should be taught to the child are also important. There are two subgoals: prelinguistic training and linguistic training. Prelinguistic training implies that there are no linguistic rules or no strings of words (learned during this phase) for which syntactic rules apply.

Prelinguistic training includes *entry behaviors, motor* and *verbal imitation, naming* and *labeling,* and the *symbolic functions of agent, action,* and *object.* Each phase can be comprehensively programmed by adding small steps leading up to the completion of the behavioral unit. All these skills are usually acquired by a normal child by eighteen or nineteen months of age.

This general language program is described in the following chapter. The suggested steps are antecedent to other more complex language learning phases and should be carefully built into the developmental plan:

1 To prepare the child attentionally (to watch carefully the actions of the instructor and to listen to the verbal events); to teach the child to assume appropriate sitting posture during instruction and to handle the objects used in instruction in an appropriate functional way.

2 To learn to imitate gestures and vocal signs and to demonstrate a generalized imitative skill.

3 To learn the symbolic relationship between a spoken word and an object and the naming of several such objects.

4 To learn the words for the agent who participates with the child, the actions that are performed interpersonally, and the objects that are physically present.

Individual words learned at this stage are presumably combined later into word strings to two, three, or more units. The individual (holophrastic) word phrase is important in the child's mapping of the orienting relationship between people (agents), objects (physical world), and actions (functional movements) in which he participates. Piaget (1970) speculates that a child develops a conceptual (representational) system during these early motoric and symbolic experiences to serve as the basis for subsequent language learning.

Linguistic training includes two-word phrases, three-word constructions, expanded constructions, negative constructions, and interrogatives. Again, each phase can be divided into subprograms with as many operational steps as necessary. For instance, Sailor, Guess, and Baer (1973; see also Guess, Sailor, & Baer, 1974) have worked out a program of 61 phases leading to language performances required for prereading activities. Each phase in the sequence can be further subdivided. In the following chapter the instruction program for the five phases shown in Figure 8-1 is also detailed programmatically. The five linguistic phases suggest that

1 *Two-word phrases* are extensions of the naming and the one-word agent, action, object phrases (usually agent + object, agent + action, or action + object).
2 *Three-word phrases* represent further expansions to include, usually, agent + action + object strings.
3 *Expansions* include adjectives, adverbs, and prepositions.
4 *Negative constructions* including denial and nonexistence.
5 *Interrogatives* including "Wh" forms, reversals (Is he running?), and tag questions (He is running, right?).

The following chapter shows how each of these phases of language acquisition can be functionally taught as receptive or expressive processes. Chapter 9 presents the linguistic form first as an imitative operation, next as a receptive operation, and finally as an expressive operation. These are assumed to represent the order of difficulty and also the sequence which allows the teacher to use antecedent operations most effectively.

Maintenance Strategies

Maintenance strategies are instructional procedures that aid the teacher-clinician in carrying the program through from start to finish. The maintenance program has two subparts: behavioral management and language training. Two principal features of behavioral management are treated here—the application and alteration of contingencies and the use of training extensions and environments. The maintenance features under language training are scheduling, materials selection, and criteria.

Contingencies of Reinforcement   Contingencies are applied by the clinician-teacher to increase desired behaviors and to decrease undesired behaviors. A discussion of contingencies is provided by McReynolds (1970) under the heading of Contingencies and Consequences in Speech Therapy. In her discus-

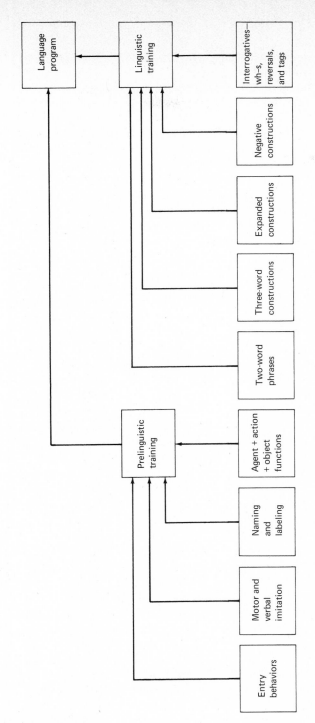

Figure 8-1

sion a contingency is a consequent event used with antecedent events (stimuli) to increase the efficiency of training.

The consequence most frequently used by clinicians is a positive reinforcer. The reinforcer is an event subsequent to the response of the child which increases the child's rate of responding. It is combined as a teaching strategy with carefully programmed antecedent events (stimuli) which have shaping properties for the child's speech patterns. For instance, when the clinician presents a word or a phonemic unit to the child, it also may have a direct subsequent effect upon the child's speech. The skillful utilization of antecedent and subsequent events constitutes the primary basis of language instruction.

Natural environmental control, especially social responses to the child's language, are the most desirable reinforcement. However, some behaviors (such as verbal imitation and symbolic match-to-sample performances) necessary for productive language cannot be easily generated through natural consequences. Tangible consequences such as ice cream, soft drinks, cheese, raisins, and sugared cereals may then be used to "pay" the child to work in a difficult developmental area. They are used with the belief (and supporting data) that repertory development in verbal behavior will make the child intelligible in the natural environment and will make verbal production a socially effective behavior without sustained extrinsic or arbitrary reinforcement.

That is why, in language training sessions, teacher attention and selective social approval are the primary bases for contingency management. However, as McReynolds (1970) explains, using tokens and allowing the child to select a desired backup reinforcer (after the session or periodically during the training sessions), stimulates greater rates of responding. The teacher should study the child and use both antecedent and subsequent events compatible with the child's already acquired interests and his social history. Emphasizing contingency management as a part of the maintenance strategy provides precision and efficiency for any teacher-clinician who is analyzing the response events of a nonresponding child.

Both the stimulus features of antecedent events and the response-supporting features of subsequent events become part of the child's semantic orientations in learning language. This is suggested by the work of Bloom (1972), Broen (1972), and Farwell (1973) in studying children in natural environments. The cue to the child's semantic acquisitions is the intimate way in which the child and adult respond to each other (the agents) and to the objects and actions in their shared environment. In the naturally occurring, reciprocal chain of events, the participants serve as each other's antecedent and reciprocal events. In responding to the adult's visual and vocal acts the child receives double exposure to his own receptive and expressive language functions; that is, he perceives language events, initiates language events, and receives reinforcing confirmations for both. The child's awareness is that the mother's speech is important to him and his is important to mother. Both events in the chain have orienting and reinforcing effects.

Contingency management can be used by any teacher-clinician who responds discriminately to children. Several well-designed and simply written publications are available. Included among them are *Changing Children's Behavior* by Krumboltz and Krumboltz (1972) and a series of practical manuals on *Managing Behavior* by Hall (1971). Instructions on the management of children in speech and language sessions are presented by McReynolds (1970), Girardeau and Spradlin (1970), and McLean, Yoder and Schiefelbusch (1972).

An interesting issue on response contingencies is raised by Spradlin (1973). He suggests that a single reinforcer applied to many different linguistic responses may be inefficient. He points out that in children's language in the natural environment there is a congruence between verbal response and the reinforcer. For example, if a child says "ice cream," "milk," "toast," or "kitty" as a request, there is likely to be a different reinforcer associated with each of those responses. Spradlin speculates that this congruence associated with each response helps keep the child from confusing responses.

Training Extensions and Environments   A training extension is a carryover or transfer (in time or location) beyond the context of the training session. McLean (1970) provides a precise method for achieving carryover for articulation training. He demonstrates that the child's responding can be evoked by stimuli (initially adult speech modeling) and can then be shifted to picture stimuli, words, and intraverbal events.

> Once a correct response can be evoked by one stimulus (for example as an echoic response to the spoken word), it can be brought under the control of other stimuli by stimulus control extension procedures. By securing the response under echoic conditions and then shifting it to textual control, the clinician increases the conditions in which the response is functional. Theoretically, if the response becomes functional under a wide range of stimulus conditions, it tends to become functional under similar conditions through a process of generalization. This process of shifting control of responses to several different stimuli seems to be the basic methodology by which the clinician seeks carryover. [McLean, 1970, p. 25]

Another extension may be achieved by training the parent to respond selectively to the speech of the child. In the simplest terms, the mother and the home become extensions of the language training of the teacher-clinician. The home can become an extension of the contexts established in the language sessions at the clinic. The extensions of practice are also extensions of function and can result in increased experience in receptive and expressive processes. The intervention effects of the formal program can thus be combined with on-going events in the child's natural environment.

Guess, Sailor, and Baer (1974) have developed an interesting procedure for effecting self-extended control. They reason that, as the child with limited language learns to control his immediate environment with word units at his command, he finds a need for other units. He does not know labels for all the things, actions, and actions-with-things he wishes to use. That is why it is important to extend the child's referents by teaching him to request further specific instruction. This is taught in the form of questions, such as "What that?" in response to unknown things and "What (are) you doing?" in response to unknown actions. "In effect the child learns to request further, specific training inputs, based on discriminating what he does not know from what he does know. This can be conceptualized as two simple chains controlled by two complex discriminative stimulus classes. Previously trained events produce labels, whereas not-previously-trained-events produce questions."

Two operational issues apply to this strategy. First, the child must be taught question-asking as a response class or he must already have this behavior prior to the instruction series. The other issue is the possibility of teaching broad classes of behavior as strategies for the development of still other classes. Instead of reinforcing individual units (only) as a strategy of instruction, the instructor should select and reinforce broad classes that can become a functional part of the child's learning history.

Language Maintenance   The maintenance features which support the on-going language program are in many respects like those just discussed. Effective scheduling, selection of materials, and use of criteria also play an important part in the programmatic effectiveness of language training. Recording behavior is equally important.

It is unnecessary to tell any parent or teacher that a child is variable, but it is important to record systematic variations in the child's daily cycles. If the child's behavior is stable and appropriate in the language training session, recording may seem unimportant. However, if the child is regularly unresponsive or hyperactive, simple charting procedures may be used in scheduling training sessions.

Materials' selection is a critical part of the total stimulus program for any child. A number of commercial kits are available—for example, the Peabody Language Development Kit (PLDK); see Dunn and Smith (1967) and DISTAR (Englemann, Osborne, & Englemann, 1969). These and similar materials provide artistically attractive and functional pictures and objects. Teachers should plan individual programs for each child using available materials and rationales which fit into the programs, including homespun strategies teachers can employ. Teachers should have a wide-range of materials and training contexts to give children added dimensions of meaning and usage. A characteristic noted in some poorly planned language programs is a unidimensional use of stimulus materials. The interest levels of both child and teacher are usually not maintained when the language "games" become limited and bleak.

Performance criteria can be used to plan and maintain a schedule of events over an extended period of time. Language training should progress systematically through identified phases and performance levels to be attained by each child before the program is moved to the next phase. In language training, the term *criterion* means simply that the child attained the required number of, or correct percentage of, responses during the session. The use of prescribed criteria is a strategy to provide data on each child and is used as the bases for moving the child through the program.

SUMMARY

Language can be taught, and indeed *is* taught, in both natural and planned environments. The mother or teacher-clinician may use a simple transaction system. This system, whether it is informally employed or carefully designed, involves improvisational features to enable the adult to teach language. In this context, *to teach* means that the adult helps the child map out the relationships between symbols and environmental events, that is, agent + action + object relationships. The child learns to affix labels to events he has learned to conceptualize. The teaching process then is limited at all times to the range of the child's semantic functions. The language curriculum of the professional instructor should be geared to this. The range of experience in language training contributes to the range of semantic functions while at the same time mapping the symbolic features that eventually become a linguistic code. Although semantic functions have not been as well cataloged as linguistic events, they can often be inferred from the child's play, from sensorimotor tests, and from informal language tests.

Important sources of information for planning language programs include functional analysis of behavior, psycholinguistics, and cognitive structure. The last is important in determining the relationships between cognitive and linguistic structures.

Language is a complex, generative system. Instructions in key units of language may generate other units. Instructions in key strategies may also stimulate new language acquisition. Deeper knowledge about teaching language to children will no doubt lead to selected interventions that will key other desired changes.

Language and communication problems may not be confined to syntactic forms and their underlying functions. Speech disorders (particularly articulation problems) frequently occur in conjunction with specific disorders related to language form and function and, even when not accompanied by concomitant language problems, speech disorders can seriously impede communication. Since speech disorders comprise the largest single category of specific detriments to effective communication for preschool and school-age children, teacher-clinicians should be prepared to cope with these problems.

Finally, the teacher-clinician must cope with the child who has no problems in either speech or language and yet has difficulty communicating. These communication problems are language-usage problems or problems related to the communication interaction itself. It is the task of the teacher-clinician to provide training and experiences which emphasize appropriate and effective use of speech and language in communicative transactions. The challenge facing the teacher-clinician, in this regard, is to provide the experiences required to develop the language-handicapped child into a functional, effective, speaker and listener in a variety of communicative transactions.

The transactions maintained should extend into both planned and natural environments, the latter figuring actively in the control, extension, and integration phases of the language-acquisition process.

DISCUSSION TOPICS

Training Strategies for Language-deficient Children: An Overview

Objective   This chapter develops the basic point that language is a complex, generative system which *is taught* in normal environments to normal children—and which *can be taught* to language-deficient children.

Exercises

1   Differentiate between and relate to curricular intervention
   a   Speech problems
   b   Language problems
   c   Communications problems
2   Should a classroom teacher of special children be able to recognize and make discriminations among the "linguistic aspects" labeled in this chapter as phonological functions, morphological functions, syntactic functions, and semantic functions? Why?
3   Could you defend the statement that Ronny Rightson displayed a *receptive* language problem?
4   Schiefelbusch et al. point out in this chapter that many language-stimulation studies have not resulted in useful programming. What are the characteristics of language studies which result (or *could result*) in valid instructional programs and/or materials?

An Intervention Strategy for Language-Deficient Children

Diane D. Bricker
Mailman Center for Child Development, University of Miami

Kenneth F. Ruder
Bureau of Child Research, University of Kansas

Lisbeth Vincent
Department of Studies in Behavioral Disabilities, University of Wisconsin

INTRODUCTION

A functional analysis of language intervention, with particular emphasis on the systematic aspects of communication in language intervention programs, was presented in the preceding chapter. For many years, authors of textbooks in special education have described the language problems of various groups of handicapped children, but they do not recommend or delineate particular remediation procedures. Limited use of language by moderately and severely retarded children, for instance, seemed inevitable and unalterable. Until recently, language-training materials or methods for severely impaired children were difficult to find. This is not a malicious oversight on the part of textbook writers. It is a recognition that little is known about how children acquire language and what intervention procedures stimulate language learning.

Language is learned very early by most children. Even two-year-old children use language. Language is a form of behavior that children "bring with them" to kindergarten or the first grade. Verbal communication is the basic tool teachers use in every area of instruction. Consequently, most teachers are not trained to teach nonverbal children, much less to teach nonverbal children how to talk. The absence of language or a severe deficiency in the use of language is a primary condition that differentiates the "educable" child from one who is "trainable." Research during the past few years (Schiefelbusch, 1972; McLean, Yoder, & Schiefelbusch, 1972) indicates that the language of children whose verbal performances are seriously deficient can be improved even when the students are adolescents (MacAulay, 1968). However, we also know that language instruction works best before the child is six years old. To be most effective, instruction should be given as soon as language delays are detected. This chapter focuses on younger children and on teaching teachers both the content and the procedures of an early language-intervention program.

The Normal Acquisition Model

Miller and Yoder (1974) suggest that the content for language training programs should be taken from data available on language development in normal children and that this content should be taught in a similar sequence. Implicit in this viewpoint are two assumptions. First, language-deficient children follow the same sequence of language development as normal children, but the rate of acquisition is slower (Lyle, 1961; Newfield & Schlanger, 1968; Lackner, 1968). Second, the developmental sequence for acquiring particular linguistic structures is not arbitrary but moves from simple to more complex structures expressing similar communicative functions.

These assumptions form the basis for many language training programs (Stremel, 1972; Miller & Yoder, 1974). However, Guess, Sailor, and Baer (1974) point out that linguists and psycholinguists, in describing the particular structures which the child has acquired, have been unable to determine a particular acquisition sequence. For instance, although data presented by Bloom (1972), Bowerman (1973), and Brown (1973) describe normal acquisition, they have not demonstrated that one set of skills precedes another, or that skills must be taught and learned in any particular order. Gray and Ryan (1973) developed a language training program in which 40 linguistic structures can be trained in any order. In a pragmatic sense, such a claim may be no more meaningful for the language interventionists than one which proposes adherence to a particular developmental sequence since neither strategy has yet empirically demonstrated that it is the most efficient and effective way to train a particular language structure. The language program described by Stremel (1972) and Stremel and Waryas (1974) exemplifies a more moderate approach in that this program adheres to the general premise that the content and the sequence for language training is based on the normal acquisition model only when it is effective in achieving functional use of a targeted linguistic structure.

Data from normal language acquisition can be useful in developing a language training program. However, to rely exclusively on the normal language development model as the basis for remedial language training may eventually be shown to be inefficient. Unfortunately, few other models on which to structure a language training program currently exist.

Intervention Strategies

The intervention program presented in this chapter is different because the teacher is given greater responsibility for determining the specific forms of instruction in terms of content and process. Specific procedures following a carefully defined daily schedule of activities are not found in this program. The teacher need not purchase special materials in order to implement the program, yet the program involves principles and strategies that are invaluable in training language skills with a wide range of language-delayed children.

Daily lesson plans imply that each child in a group should progress at the same rate. This is a naïve and unrealistic assumption. On the other hand, a fixed set of materials for use in a language-training program is possible only if children have the same interests and recognize objects and events in the same way. An individualized form of instruction demands that the teacher recognize the individual interests and capabilities of her students and select materials and motivational techniques which are effective in each situation. The purpose of the language training program in this chapter is to provide a framework and procedures for individual or small-group language training.

Normal Language Acquisition

Currently we believe the most satisfactory way to select the content and training sequence for language intervention is to draw on data provided by normal children. Language acquisition by the normally developing child and the developmental sequence for the acquisition of specific skills are presented here on the basis of group norms. Interpolation for the individual child should be done carefully, since there are differences in both the developmental sequence and the approximate age of acquisition.

Language does not develop as an isolated form of behavior but is interrelated with and dependent upon other complex skills such as sensorimotor intelligence, motor development, and concept acquisition. A normal child demonstrates many skills before he emits his first word. Piaget and Inhelder (1969), Sinclair-de-Zwart (1969), and W. Bricker and D. Bricker (1974) have pointed out the importance of earlier forms of behavior for language development.

Piaget and Inhelder, for example, posit that before a child can manipulate symbols (language being a form of symbolic behavior), he must be able to see himself as separate from objects and to manipulate the objects represented by the symbols in relevant ways. The infant's early interaction with his environment (in which he moves from waving, banging, mouthing, or throwing all objects to responding differentially to various objects) is the basis for later language development. With the language-deficient child, preliminary or prerequisite skills may need to be taught before language instruction can begin.

Another basis for language development includes the imitative skills generally acquired during infancy. These imitative skills focus the infant's attention on the language aspects of his environment. Complex motor control is necessary for the production of words. The young child apparently learns this control through early babbling and vocal play. Language does not develop in a vacuum. It develops as a consequence of continuing interaction with the physical and social aspects of the environment.

The vocal responses produced during the first several months of life are varied and unpredictable. The infant sometimes produces noises and sounds that an adult would have difficulty imitating. Between the third and fourth months, the infant begins to produce sounds which approximate those made by others in his language environment. During this phase of language development (the babbling phase), the baby learns to reproduce the same sound repeatedly. This is a frequent form of elementary verbal behavior and is easy to recognize. Babbling consists of producing long strings of sounds such as ba-ba-ba, ma-ma-ma, or pa-pa-pa.

The relevance of early babbling to later stages of language acquisition is the source of considerable controversy. One side says that children are reinforced for their babbling by having babbling imitated by their caregivers, parents, and siblings. Parental imitation of babbling is a form of shaping which leads the child to more advanced and more adultlike phonetic productions.

Many linguists and psycholinguists, such as McNeill (1970), take another view, claiming that these early forms of verbalization have no relationship to later forms of linguistic development. We do not ascribe to this viewpoint. Data on children in institutions and in isolated environments indicate that early babbling plays an important role in language acquisition (Hunt, 1961). The importance of earlier forms of behavior for subsequent development for many skill areas has been documented. For example, though not all children crawl before walking, the majority do begin with scooting, creeping, or wriggling behavior that approximates crawling before they develop the vertical position and bilateral stepping. Most children also engage in babbling prior to producing intelligible wordlike utterances. The fact that most children engage in such verbal behavior may attest to the importance of babbling as one of the early mechanisms for acquiring language.

Babbling provides the opportunity for most children to acquire several skills. First, the child learns to develop more precise control over his articulators. Second, the environment generally responds favorably to the child's babbling. If babbling occurs at the appropriate stage of development, the child is encouraged to continue to produce sounds which more closely approximate those sounds most often used in his language or those which produce the greatest effect in his social environment. For example, "mama" is one of the first consistent sounds emitted by many babies. In most cases it originates in the early babbling behavior of the infant. That particular sound is more apt to get the mother's attention than other sound combinations. The responsiveness of a mother to "mama" leads to more frequent and consistent use. This transaction is an example of the initial stages of the child using verbal behavior to manipulate his social environment. Babbling serves an important function in the language-acquisition process and should be viewed as a behavior to be encouraged.

Another early language behavior demonstrated by children includes prosodic features or the "force, quality, and pitch" characteristics of human language. Acquisition of early forms of the prosodic features coincides developmentally with the acquisition of phonemic units (Reese & Lipsitt, 1970). These prosodic features constitute the melody while the phonemes provide the lyrics of language. This aspect of speech may, according to Menyuk (1964), assist children in segmenting the stream of speech, helping them acquire the concept of "sentence." Listening to a young child who has only a few words but nevertheless produces long phonemic sequences is revealing because the child is producing nonmeaningful syllables which often closely approximate the adult inflectional pattern. For example, toddlers produce sound sequences such as "gu baba wa da?" in which the inflectional pattern rises on "da," indicating that the child has learned to produce the inflectional pattern marking the utterance as a question. Ruder and Smith (1972) observe that children's utilization of the prosodic features of speech are basic behaviors. Children, from the time of the acquisition of their first word to the time they are producing adultlike sentences, utilize subtle features of pitch as part of their communicative behavior. For example, in the 1972 study the authors noted that the child, in communicating with the mother, spoke in a significantly higher pitch than when speaking with the father. As is the case with the role of babbling in language acquisition, the relationship of early use of prosodic features with later stages of acquisition is not understood. Such features dominate the early verbal behavior of all but the most unusual children. To understand the importance of prosodic features, one has only to listen to the speech of the deaf which is characterized by a monotone production.

At approximately twelve to fifteen months of age, most babies reach two developmental milestones: they take their first step and they speak their first word. The acquisition of the first word is a milestone in regard to psycholinguistic theories concerning language acquisition. The first word marks the first stage of true linguistic development. Verbal behavior prior to acquisition of the first word is often termed a "prelinguistic stage of development." In the child's early linguistic development, receptive understanding of speech precedes production (Berry, 1969; Fraser, Bellugi, & Brown, 1963; and Winitz, 1973). However, receptive processes in children have received little attention (Friedlander, 1970). Before a baby utters his first word, he probably already understands many words or phrases spoken by adults. Between fifteen and eighteen months, the child's ability to understand or comprehend more complex verbal utterances increases. The child begins producing single words, which, although not necessarily articulated with complete accuracy, are recognizable as specific words and are used discriminatively by the child. A set of phonemes is not considered a word until the child uses them consistently in the presence of a specific object or situation.

For example, if a toddler says, "ba," when referring to ball, cat, daddy, and apple, "ba" is not considered a word since it has no consistent referent. However, if the child only uses "ba" to refer to round objects, it may be considered a word because the utterance is restricted to a specific class of objects or events (e.g., the verbal utterance "ba" maps a particular underlying concept, in this case round objects).

How the child acquires this first word (and subsequent words) is a controversial issue (Reese & Lipsitt, 1970; Creelman, 1966). Palermo's (1971) description of what motivates and moves a child from stage to stage in the language acquisition process is a reasonable description of this process, albeit a general and not universally accepted one.

> I believe that the acquisition of language may be much like the process which Skinner has called shaping, in the sense that initially the parent will accept any efforts the child makes, and, as the child shows progress, the requirements for communication become more and more stringent. The motivated child wishes to communicate more precisely, and the parent wishes him to do so. It is not a matter of the adult dropping pellets for each correct utterance, it is a matter of achieving a goal of mutual intelligibility. [Palermo, 1971, p. 47]

Around eighteen months, most toddlers begin putting words together. This phase of language development has been referred to as *telegraphic speech* (Brown & Bellugi, 1964; Ruder, Bricker, & Ruder, 1974). The child communicates with a limited number of words. For example, by holding up an empty cup and saying, "more milk," a toddler conveys the message "I want you to put more milk in my cup." The toddler generally uses content words (e.g., nouns and verbs) to the exclusion of articles and prepositions.

Production of two-word utterances is the initial stage of syntactic development. Putting two words together indicates that the child has developed a rudimentary organizational system that allows him to sequence words according to rules. Rules enable him to convey his intentions so he is understood by members of his language community. Bellugi (1972) and others argue that young children do, indeed, produce sentences on the basis of generative rules. Several investigators (Bloom, 1972; Bowerman, 1973, Brown, 1973) have demonstrated that initial sentence production by young children can be categorized in stages of development based on mean length of utterance. For example, the *mean length of utterance* (MLU) for stage one is approximately 1.5 to 2.0 words (morphemes). During this time, children begin producing two-word strings which depict semantic relations expressing an agent-action-object function. "Baby go" for instance depicts the semantic relation of agent (baby) and action (go), whereas the two-word string "play boat" is representative of the semantic relation action-object. Thus, in two-word utterances the child uses structures reflecting the underlying semantic relations of agent, action, and object (relationships between three discrete semantic/grammatical functions although still limited to productions no more than two words in length). Bloom (1970 & 1972), Bowerman (1973), and Brown (1973) describe these early two-word strings as expressing underlying semantic relations such as possession, reoccurrence (more milk), location (ball here), and negation (no drink). When the mean utterance length approaches two- to three-word constructions, the functions previously expressed in two-word strings, such as the "play boat" example, now appear in three-word strings which express the agent-action-object relations ("boy play boat," for example). Ruder and Smith (1974) characterize this early stage of syntactic development as the process of acquiring the means to express basic semantic relations. Other semantic functions expressed by similar-looking, two-word utterances, such as negation, reoccurrence, and question are characterized as operations modifying the basic content of the underlying agent-action-object proposition. Verb-adverb sequences (run fast) and adjective-noun sequences are operations performed on elements of the proposition and do not basically alter the communicative intent expressed by the underlying semantic relations. For example, negating the string "boy hit ball" to produce the equivalent of "boy didn't hit ball" has a greater effect on the intent of the proposition as a whole than an operation which simply modifies the agent-noun to produce a string such as "big boy hit ball."

In the characterization of the language-acquisition process presented by Ruder and Smith (1974) the acquisition of later more complex linguistic structure consists of operations on the basic proposition as a whole or operations on elements within the proposition. Although this may oversimplify the process, it does present the acquisition of a linguistic structure as sequential stages in the refinement of an operation. The same semantic functions endure throughout the stages of development and ultimately results in the adult form of the structure. For example, the acquisition of negation begins with a nonverbal marker accompanying a single-word utterance, such as a headshake when saying the word "milk" to indicate "I don't want milk." When the child begins producing two-word strings, the verbal negation marker expresses the same function (no milk). At this stage, both the nonverbal negative marker and the verbal negative marker function similarly. Both are operations on the proposition as a whole and both are structurally external to the proposition. The next step consists of acquiring the adult form of the verbal marker and moving the marker from an external to an internal position in the sentence. The result is the transformation of such primitive forms of negation as "No drink milk," to "I don't want milk."

In this characterization of the acquisition of syntax, the basic semantic relationships involved in expressing an affirmative proposition are those of agent, action, and object. Likewise, in terms of semantic function, negation, question, attribution, and location are used by the child in very early stages of language development. Over 90 percent of the utterances in everyday verbal communication transactions are simple, active, affirmative, declarative sentences.

The early language behavior of children includes the same units used by adults in most of their communication. The remainder of the language-acquisition process consists of refining the structural distinctions between forms used to express functions which modify either the proposition or elements of the proposition as discussed above. This refinement of structures applies to the acquisition of morphological inflections as well. The acquisition of past tense is an operation which modifies the verb element of the basic proposition and also has an effect on the proposition as a whole. In fact, the early form of the past-tense marker is structurally similar to that of negation. Both appear in some of the early manifestations in a position external to the sentence. In the case of past tense, the use of a marker such as "yesterday" appropriately modifies the statement, "yesterday I go." As with negation, later stages of the acquisition of past tense shift the marker to an internal position in the sentence and apply the appropriate morphological marker. The acquisition of past tense follows a consistent pattern across the few children who have been studied. Initially, the irregular forms such as "make" or "do" are used appropriately. Then the regular endings such as /ed/ are acquired and used appropriately. During this latter stage either morphological overgeneralization or undifferentiation often occurs so that formerly correctly produced irregular forms are made regular such as "do-doed," "make-maked," "see-seed" (Cazden, 1968). Thus, as far as morphological development is concerned, there is a definite tendency for the child to look for the rules and regularities in the language to which he is exposed. Only later do less-common irregulars and unusual forms appear, although common irregular forms may be used correctly (albeit imitatively) at an early age (Rebelsky, Starr, & Luria, 1967). The information on linguistic development at these later stages is limited. Data are available to show that most normal children quickly acquire morphological and transformational "rules" which allow the generation of an infinite number of novel, grammatically correct sentences. Menyuk (1964) has reported that the major transformations used by adults were present in her populations of first graders. For additional language development data, the reader is referred to Bellugi (1972); Berry (1969); Reese & Lipsitt (1970); Rebelsky, Starr, & Luria (1967); Ruder, Bricker, & Ruder (1974).

FORMAT FOR A LANGUAGE-TRAINING PROGRAM

The language-training program outlined below is the outgrowth of ten years of research with language-deficient children (W. Bricker & D. Bricker, 1974; Ruder & Smith, 1974). Several years ago a language-training lattice was generated. It has been discussed in detail elsewhere (W. Bricker, 1972). This lattice began with establishing behavior control and terminated with the production of meaningful sentences:

> In developing a language training model we synthesized what we could from linguistic and psycholinguistic theory and data from past research using the operant approach. We then put together, much like an engineer, a system of training events sufficient to facilitate the development of language. We defined a series of terminal

states or sub-terminal states which represent a developmental hierarchy. [W. Bricker, 1972, p. 75]

For several years specific areas within this lattice were studied in isolation using an institutionalized population available for brief periods each day. During the past five years we have been associated with a community classroom program for young, developmentally delayed, language-deficient children which has allowed us to work with the children daily on a longitudinal basis. (D. Bricker & W. Bricker, 1971, 1972, 1973; W. Bricker & D. Bricker, 1974). The shift from an institutional population allowed us to implement the language-training lattice in a longitudinal, programmatic manner. Although the original language lattice has proved extremely useful for research and model-building purposes, our experience over these last three years has documented the difficulty of asking teachers to generate daily classroom activities based on the lattice. Consequently, we generated a new lattice (W. Bricker & D. Bricker, 1974) and structured a language-training program derived from this lattice that is directly applicable to the classroom setting and for use by a classroom teacher or parent.

As discussed in the preceding review of normal language acquisition, agent-action-object semantic relations underlie early linguistic structures. The development of these semantic relations is the pivotal aspect of our language-intervention program. The inclusion of this agent-action-object expression is a necessary component of any language program.

If one considers agent-action-object structural relations as the pivotal structure in language training, then two types of training are necessary: initial training on verbal behavior for expression of propositions containing the agent-action-object relation, and subsequent training on modification of the basic proposition learned during the initial phase of the training program. The first part of the program moves the child from functional classification of objects and the comprehension of object labels to production of three-word basic agent-action-object utterances.

The second part of the program teaches the child to perform operations on these basic agent-action-object utterances. These operations are on the entire proposition (e.g., negation, question, tense) or on elements within the proposition (modification of nouns and verbs of the basic propositions). For example, a child using one-word responses designating agentive or object functions may modify this basic proposition by adding a negative marker to the verbal expression (such as the addition of the word "no," "all gone," or a simple headshake). The same operation would apply to a longer string, such as a three-word, agent-action-object string, which could be negated or could be made into a question through the use of rising terminal intonation. Operations on elements within the proposition differ because they are confined to portions of the proposition rather than the whole proposition. For example, using an adjectival modifier with the agentive noun, such as "big dog eat food," is a modification of the agentive noun with the basic communicative intent of the proposition remaining the same. The preceding examples illustrate the direction of training in phases 15 through 43 of this program. The basic semantic relations of agent-action-object serve as a pivotal structure which provides the impetus and direction in the early phases of language training. Later training phases build upon this basic structure.

It is very important to develop the necessary prerequisite skills before teaching language (W. Bricker & D. Bricker, 1974). A child should not be asked to imitate the sound /da/ if he cannot imitate gross motor activities. A child should not be asked to understand a receptive label for an object if he does not know the object's functional use. A child should not be asked to produce a verbal label for an object if he cannot discriminate that object from other environmental stimuli. Most important, the child must be under some form of stimulus or consequence control before the teacher attempts to add a new skill to the child's repertoire. Language training most often fails probably because the teacher does not establish behavior control in the initial stage of the program. The teacher should assure herself that each child is under behavior control.

In Part One of this language-training program three critical components are trained: verbal imitation, comprehension, and production. Verbal imitation is the imitation of vocal sounds produced by a model. Verbal imitation ranges from imitation of a single sound such as /a/ to the production of a sequence of several words. Comprehension refers to the control of behavior by either verbal or nonverbal stimuli. Production (as used in this program) is the ability to spontaneously emit appropriate verbal behavior. These components are presented in Figure 9-1 in a hierarchical order of our best estimate of the appropriate developmental sequence for each component. The training program is presented in this manner so the reader can follow the developmental sequence of verbal imitation, comprehension, and production as well as the relationships between the various phases of these three components. In Part Two, verbal imitation is not specifically indicated as a part of the training sequence. However, an imitation procedure may be necessary in the early phases of training. The clinician-teacher must judge whether imitation training is necessary at any point in the training sequence.

Inherent in the early phases of this training program are several important features based on our last five years of work with young, language-deficient children. First, assessment of the child's repertoire in a specific area is necessary before beginning training; otherwise, evaluating the effects of training is impossible. Second, before moving to more complex behavior the teacher should be certain that the prerequisite behavior has been acquired. Third, the training stimuli employed should be useful to the child. Fourth, training should occur in a situation that provides maximum generalization. Fifth, children should be trained in small groups to ensure efficient use of the teacher's time and to allow the children to provide each other stimulation.

The program begins in the comprehension component with Phase One, which involves training the functional use of common environmental objects such as cup, spoon, and pan. In an earlier language training program, comprehension of object names was taught in a rote manner which did not allow the

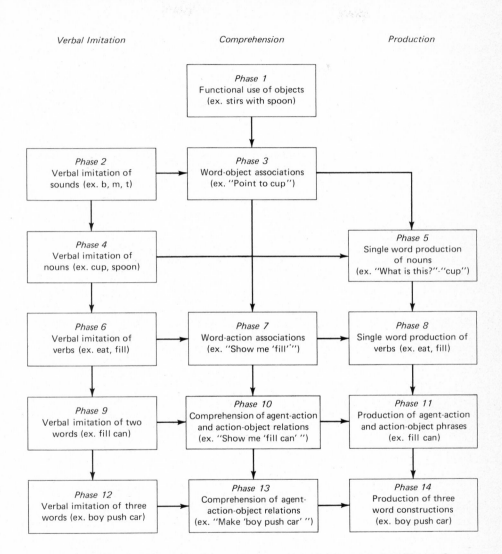

Figure 9-1 Language Program (Part I): Training of Initial Agent-Action-Object Constructions.

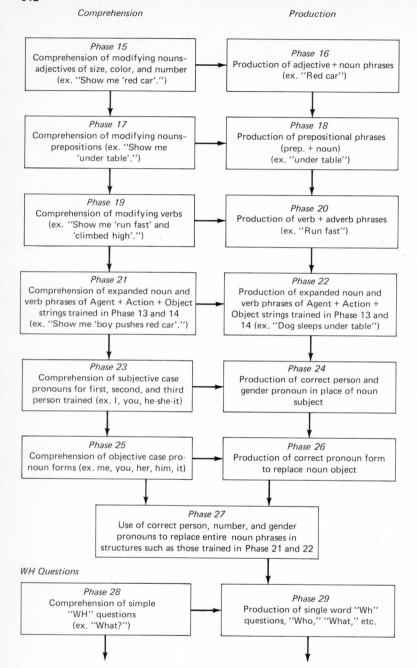

Figure 9-1 Part II: Modification of agent-action-object constructions.

Comprehension   Production

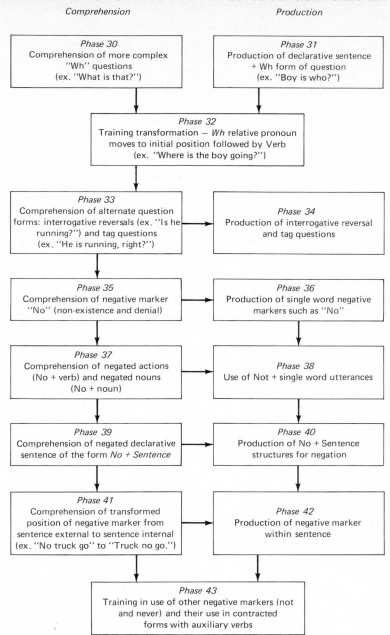

Figure 9-1 Part II *(continued).*

child to handle or use the objects. This approach produced relatively little comprehension of object names by the low-functioning children included in at least two investigations (W. Bricker & D. Bricker, 1970; Vincent-Smith & D. Bricker, 1972). Observations of the same children in another investigation revealed that although many of these children were not under the control of the object name, they could functionally classify and use the objects (W. Bricker & D. Bricker, 1974). The functional use of an object seems to be a precursor to comprehension of that object's name and, consequently, maybe a cue for learning the object's name (W. Bricker & D. Bricker, 1974). In this phase, children are taught to drink and pour from a cup and to stir and eat with a spoon with no attempt to have the child produce any verbal behavior.

When the child reaches criterion on Phase 1, the verbal imitation component is introduced (Phase 2) in which verbal imitation of sounds are trained. The training sounds selected from the training stimuli in Phase 1 are simple to produce and are presented in isolation. Phase 3 can be begun simultaneously with Phase 2 and is the second step in the comprehension component. In Phase 3, training is shifted to comprehension of object names. The stimulus objects are those used in the functional training of Phase 1. In this phase the child is told to touch or point to the named object. Since the child already has in his repertoire the functional use of the object, this functional movement can be used to help the child associate the verbal label with the appropriate object. For example, the drinking movement may be used to help the child associate the cup with its verbal label.

Phase 4 moves into verbal imitation training of the words used in Phases 1 and 3. The child has already been trained in Phase 2 to produce the sounds that comprise the training words. The child's task during Phase 4 is to learn to sequence sounds into word-length units. Completion of this phase results in a child who can imitate the training words as well as point to the appropriate object when named.

In Phase 5 the child learns to combine the skills he has acquired in Phases 3 and 4. The ability to imitate a word combined with comprehension of that word should result in the verbal production of that word in the presence of the object.

Phases 6 through 14 expand the responses to be learned in both length and complexity. For example, in Phase 9, the child is asked to imitate two-word sequences. In Phase 10 he is required to comprehend two-word utterances which should lead to Phase 11—the production of two words. These two-word utterances are agent-action and action-object phrases which describe activities that the child learned to engage in during functional-use training. In other words, knowing how to use objects in a functional manner may give the child a basis for early syntactic constructions, such as "boy eats" and "fill cup." After the child learns to imitate, comprehend, and produce two-word phrases, the agent-action and action-object phrases are expanded to include all three elements (agent, action, and object) in a single phrase such as "boy eats apple."

Throughout the language program, the teacher should administer regular probes. A probe is a test of the child's ability in a specific area. Probes are administered individually. The teacher should not give cues, prompts, or assistance during the presentation of a probe. For example, before training functional use of objects in Phase 1, the teacher should observe and record what each child does as he plays with the training objects. If he does not show at least two instances of functionally appropriate activities with each object, he should be trained on functional ways to use the objects. After this training, the teacher should again observe what the child does with the objects in a test situation. If the child demonstrates functional use of the objects, he should be moved on to the next phase of training.

Probes are given on imitation, comprehension, and production before each training phase is begun and at regular intervals during the training period. Administering brief probes enables the teacher to determine objectively whether or not the child has learned the responses.

When criterion is reached, the child is moved on to the next phase of training in the program. Sample data sheets for basic training on verbal imitation, comprehension and production are presented in Tables 9-3, 9-4, and 9-5.

All teachers, parents, or child-workers should not implement the program exactly as outlined here because children, teachers, and settings vary. There is nothing magic about the program. Teachers are free to use the program as it is, modify it, or incorporate it into on-going programs. Beginning at Phase 1 and following it without deviation to Phase 43 is not necessary. The key to success is in the hands of the teacher and in her ability to select, vary and apply materials to her children. We hope the detailed presentation here will help teachers grasp the nature of the program and eliminate much of the ambiguity found in many such program descriptions. A second reason for such detail is that the training sounds, objects, and settings were selected for specific reasons. First, the order of teaching the sounds follows a developmental sequence. That is, the sounds in the initial training groups are generally easier to produce than sounds found in later training groups. Second, common environmental objects were selected to be useful to young children. The language-deficient child's initial vocabulary should be of great utility. Third, the settings were chosen to facilitate generalization outside the classroom. For example, most children frequently encounter kitchens, consequently the words and actions learned in the classroom provide them with a functional repertoire in kitchens.

LANGUAGE TRAINING PROGRAM: PART I   TRAINING AGENT-ACTION-OBJECT STRUCTURES

Behavior-control Stage

This stage requires three basic responses from the child: (1) sitting quietly in a chair, (2) looking at the teacher's face, and (3) performing simple imitative behavior on command. Without establishing these basic prerequisite skills, training more complex skills is usually an exercise in frustration.

Sitting quietly in a chair can be shaped by placing the child in a chair and preventing him from leaving. In the beginning, appropriate sitting for even short periods should be reinforced. As the length of sitting behavior increases, physical constraints should be reduced until the child is sitting quietly for brief periods. The second goal is to have the child look into the teacher's face when told, "Look at me." If the child does not do this spontaneously, the teacher should place the child's face between her hands and direct his gaze at her while saying, "Look at me." Brief periods of looking should be reinforced. The teacher gradually reduces physical prompts and simultaneously reinforces longer periods of looking behavior. The child is ready for the third step when he looks at the teacher's face on command without physical prompts. The third step is to train simple imitative responses using gross motor behavior. The child should be seated in a chair and told to "Look at me." A simple behavior such as ringing a bell is then modeled by the teacher while she says, "Do this." If the child does not imitate the response, the teacher should physically prompt the behavior. The teacher gradually fades the prompts and consistently reinforces all appropriate behavior. When the first response is imitated on command, the teacher should introduce a second behavior such as beating a drum. The same training procedure is followed as for ringing the bell. This sequence is repeated until the child imitates ten simple motor acts chosen by the teacher. For a more detailed discussion of shaping procedures see Metz (1965) and Sloan and MacAuley (1968).

Phase 1   Training Functional Use of Objects

Setting and Objects   The first setting for the language-training program is the kitchen area. Object Group 1, which is composed of *spoon, cup, baby,* and *pan* is used. Table 9-1 contains suggested setting, words, and sounds for each phase of the program. There should be one set of objects for the teacher and one for each child in the group.

Children   The number of children in the group varies depending on their competence and manageability. The teacher should compose her groups carefully, keeping in mind the level of functioning as well as the behavior problems of each child.

Baseline Probe   Before beginning training, the teacher should take each child *individually* to the kitchen area and place a set of training items on the table in front of the child. If he begins to play with the items spontaneously, the teacher should record his responses on a probe sheet like the one illustrated in Table 9-2. Appropriate functional use of the items includes drinking from the cup, pouring from the pan, stirring with the spoon. Functionally inadequate use includes banging the objects on the table, putting the baby in the pan, and throwing objects on the floor. If the child does not use each item spontaneously, the teacher should hand the child the object and try to elicit responses by asking, "What can you do with this?" Three attempts are made to elicit a response for each item. Criterion is two instances of functional use of each item. If the child reaches criterion, he should be moved on to Phases 2 and 3. If

Table 9-1   Settings, Objects, and Sounds Used in Phases 1–14

Object group 1 (Used in phases 1, 2, 3, 4, 5)

    Setting: kitchen

    Objects: cup, pan, baby, spoon

Sounds: /k/ in *c*ups /p/ in *p*an /b/ in *b*oy; /n/ in *n*et; /u/ in spoo*n*; /æ/ in p*a*n; /el/ in m*ay*; /ʌ/ in c*u*p; /i/ in *ea*t

Object group 2 (Used in phases 1, 2, 3, 4, 5)

    Setting: self-help area

    Objects: hat, shoe, comb, soap, boy

Sounds: /h/ in *h*at; /t/ in *t*oo; /s/ in *s*oap; /m/ in *m*an; /o/ in s*oa*p; /ɔl/ in b*oy*

Object group 3 (Used in phases 6, 7, 8)

    Setting: picnic area

    Objects: wagon, man, cookie, dog, boat

    Action words: eat, ride

Sounds: /w/ in *w*agon; /g/ in *g*o; /d/ in *d*uck; /r/ in *r*ide; /al/ in r*i*de; /ɔ/ in j*aw*; /U/ in c*oo*k

Object group 4 (Used in phases 9, 10, 11)

    Setting: sand table

    Objects: can, sack, truck, car

    Action words: push, pull, fill, hide

Sounds: /ʃ/ in pu*sh*; /a/ in c*o*t; /l/ in fi*ll*; /f/ in *f*ood

Object group 5 (Used in phases 12, 13, 14)

    Setting: dollhouse

    Objects: man, lady, chair, door, window, bed

    Action words: sleep, sit, open, shut

Sounds: /ɛ/ in b*e*d; /tʃ/ in *ch*air; /l/ in *l*ady

he does not reach criterion, training should begin with the functional use of objects.

Training   To train functional use of this set of objects, the teacher takes the group of children to the kitchen area and has them sit around the table. Each child should have a set of objects in front of him. The teacher demonstrates functional use of the cup by drinking from the cup and having the children imitate. If they do not drink, the teacher physically prompts the response. If difficulty is encountered in eliciting imitative responses, it may be necessary to return to the behavior-control stage. Praise should be given for appropriate responses. The teacher demonstrates other possible uses of the cup (pouring into the pan, etc.) and uses of the other items. She varies the use of the objects in as many appropriate ways as possible, prompting the children to do the same. She also talks about the objects in simple language while demonstrating their uses, labeling them frequently for the children but not requiring the children to learn the words either receptively or expressively at this phase.

Table 9-2   Sample Data Sheet for Probes on Functional Use of Objects (Phase 1)

A. Cup
  Appropriate functional use (describe briefly)
    1.
    2.
  Functionally inadequate responses (describe briefly)

B. Spoon
  Appropriate functional use (describe briefly)
    1.
    2.
  Functionally inadequate responses (describe briefly)

C. Pan
  Appropriate functional use (describe briefly)
    1.
    2.
  Functionally inadequate responses (describe briefly)

D. Baby
  Appropriate functional use (describe briefly)
    1.
    2.
  Functionally inadequate responses (describe briefly)

Data   Although the teacher may not be able to record each child's response during training sessions, some indication of the length of training time can be obtained from the number and duration of training sessions.

Training Probe   When a child begins to demonstrate appropriate behavior without prompting, a probe in an individual session should be administered. This probe will show whether the child is learning the functional use of the objects or simply imitating the teacher and the other children. This probe is administered the same as the baseline probe. The same recording form is used.

Generalization Training   Apart from the specific training periods, the teacher should use every opportunity during the day to generalize responses learned in the training session to other activities and environments. Daily plans should include opportunities to highlight these new skills. The following series of suggested activities are designed to help children generalize the functional use of the trained objects to new situations.

Group time
  a   The children are all given an exemplar of the object used in training. The teacher or one of the children demonstrates a functional use, such as drinking from the cup, and the children are encouraged to imitate either one at a time or all together.
  b   Using two different objects, the teacher encourages interaction

between the children. For example, every other child is given a spoon and the remaining children a baby doll. One child holds the doll, while the other child feeds it. The objects are then switched.

c Each child has an exemplar of an object, and a facilitating object can either be passed around the group or the teacher or another child can walk around demonstrating the functional use. For example, each child may have a cup, and the teacher or another child walks around the group with a teapot "pouring" into the cups.

Snack time

This is an ideal time to demonstrate the functional use of the items in this object group.

a The children each have a cup. The teacher pours water from a teapot into her own cup and then prompts the children to imitate. A teaspoonful of Kool-Aid is dropped into each cup and the children are encouraged to stir the liquid until the powder dissolves. All children then drink the liquid from the cup. Eventually the children are taught the entire act of pouring the water, spooning the Kool-Aid, stirring and then drinking.

b The children may be prompted to give another child (an infant, perhaps) a drink from the cup or a bite from a spoon.

c Snacks such as raisins or pineapple chunks may be placed in a pan with a lid on it. Before the child can obtain the food, he must remove the lid, spoon out the contents into his own dish, and then replace the lid.

Outdoor play

Areas such as the water table and the sandbox should contain items from the object group. While playing in the sand or the water, the children are encouraged to engage in activities such as spooning sand into a pan, stirring the contents, replacing the lid, and then "cooking" the sand on a pretend stove. Needless to say, they should be discouraged from eating their creations.

Story time

The teacher makes up a story about a person in the kitchen fixing something to eat, or the story of Goldilocks and the Three Bears can be used. As the story person is engaged in different activities, the children demonstrate these activities with the object group items. For example, as Goldilocks eats the porridge, the children demonstrate eating porridge with their spoons and pans.

Music time

A short song may be composed to describe the different functional uses of the items in the object group. Each child has different items on the floor. They then pick out the appropriate item and demonstrate the functional use in accordance with the words of the song. For example, the song, "This is the way we . . ." can be used to demonstrate " . . . drink our milk"; " . . . stir our tea"; " . . . open the lid"; etc.

Free play

The teacher encourages the children to play house, make dinner, and eat in small groups, with as little adult intervention as possible.

Children in the later stages of the language program who have completed Phase 1 can model the appropriate behavior in a natural play situation.

Phase 2   Training Verbal Imitation of Sounds

Settings and Sounds   The setting will again be the kitchen area. Sounds to be trained are /k/, /p/, /b/, /n/, /u/, /ʌ/, /æ/, /i/, and /eɪ/ (see Table 9-1). These sounds are necessary for the production of the object names used in Phases 3, 4, and 5.

Baseline Probe   Each child should be tested individually before training is begun on verbal imitation. See Table 9-3 for the recording form for this probe. The teacher first gets the child's attention. She then presents the sound to be imitated by asking the child to "Say (*sound*)." The sounds are presented in a random order as they appear on the recording form. If the child produces the sound or some reasonably close approximation, the teacher should record the sound under (+). If he gives an unacceptable response, the sound is recorded under (−). If he makes no response within 15 seconds, a check is placed in the (NR) column. Criterion is two acceptable (+) imitations of each sound. If the child does not reach criterion, he should be trained on verbal imitation of sounds. If he does meet criterion, he goes on to receptive training.

Training   The teacher and the child should sit facing a large mirror in which they can see themselves and each other. The teacher starts with a sound which the child produced correctly on the pretest or another sound she thinks would be easy for the child to produce. Vowels are usually easier than consonants, but /b/ is an easy sound for many children. The child is asked to say the first training sound selected. If the child produces the sound correctly or makes a close approximation, he is reinforced. If he produces a sound that does not approximate the one presented, the same sound is repeated. If he still gives an incorrect response, the teacher looks into the mirror with her head beside his and again asks him to say the sound. This may help the child see how what he is doing with his own mouth differs from what the teacher is doing with hers. The teacher may want to go back to motor imitation if the child is still not improving. She could have him press his lips together as if producing a /p/ or /b/ or open his mouth as when producing vowels. He is again asked to imitate the sound while looking in the mirror. The teacher alternates among children. If a child does not respond at all, she should work with other children a few moments and reinforce them, briefly ignoring the nonresponsive child. Then she can try again to get a response from the nonresponsive child. The nonresponsive child is not allowed to play or get up and wander off while the teacher is working with other children. The verbal imitation portion of training is likely to be the most difficult for the children (and the teacher). The teacher should always have an effective reinforcer available for each child.

Table 9-3 Probe on Verbal Imitation of Sounds (Phases 2, 4, 6, 9, 12)

RESPONSE

Sound	+	−	NR
1 /u/ in cool			
2 /ʌ/ in cut			
3 /k/ in cat			
4 /n/ in no			
5 /b/ in ball			
6 /æ/ in fat			
7 /i/ in beet			
8 /p/ in pig			
9 /el/ in may			
10 /b/ in ball			
11 /el/ in may			
12 /n/ in no			
13 /ʌ/ in cut			
14 /æ/ in fat			
15 /i/ in beet			
16 /p/ in pig			
17 /k/ in cat			
18 /u/ in cool			
19 /æ/ in fat			
20 /b/ in ball			
21 /el/ in may			
22 /k/ in cat			
23 /p/ in pig			
24 /n/ in no			
25 /i/ in beet			
26 /ʌ/ in cut			
27 /u/ in cool			

Data As in Phase 1, data should be kept on the number and duration of training sessions required for each child to reach criterion. This practice should be extended to all subsequent training phases.

Training Probes This probe is a repetition of the baseline probe and should be administered individually to each child. This procedure should be extended to all subsequent training phases.

Generalization Training The teacher should use every opportunity to elicit and reinforce specific responses being trained in other activities and settings.

Group time

   a   The teacher presents the stimulus sound in group time and each child in turn imitates her. This procedure is combined with motor imitation to produce a sound game. For example, if the sound /n/ is being trained, the teacher combines the auditory stimulus /n/ with a discrete arbitrary motor response such as touching the lips or nose. The sound /k/ may be combined with a clap or touching the throat.

   b   The teacher introduces new words which begin with the sound being trained. The words are introduced by presenting pictures or objects during group time. The children repeat the initial sound. The teacher may also introduce the grapheme (letter) which represents the sound.

Snack time

     The children should learn to recognize and verbalize the names of the foods and drinks which are commonly used for snacks. The teacher uses a food and/or drink which contains the sound being trained. For example, if the sound /k/ is being trained, snacks consist of Kool-Aid, milk, cookies, or cake.

Story time

     The teacher makes up a story in which the target sound occurs frequently and in a context which encourages the children to imitate. For example, the story about the sound /k/ might contain a crow that says "caw-caw" and a mouse that says "eek-eek."

Music time

     When working on vowel sounds the children are encouraged to sing along using the vowel sound instead of saying the words.

Phase 3   Training Comprehension of Nouns

Setting and Object   The same setting and object as in Phase 1.

Baseline and Training Probes   Prior to initiating training on comprehension of the object labels, a probe is given and each child's responses are recorded on a form similar to the one presented in Table 9-4. The teacher administers the probe to each child individually by placing the four test objects in front of the child and saying, "Give me (show me, point to, touch, etc.) the (object name)." The teacher requests each of the four objects three times in a random order as listed on the recording form. If the child selects the labeled object, the teacher checks the (+) column. If he selects an incorrect object, the teachers check the (−) column. Failure to respond within 15 seconds is indicated by a check in the (NR) column. Criterion performance on the probe is the correct selection of each object two times. If the child reaches this criterion, he moves to training on verbal imitation of words (Phase 4). Otherwise, he is trained on this phase.

Training   The children are seated around the table with their objects in front of them. The teacher asks them to select the objects one at a time, varying her requests to include such phrases as "touch," "point to," "show me,"

Table 9-4   Sample Data Sheet for Probes on Comprehension (Phases 3, 7, 10, 13)

	Response		
Stimuli	+	−	NR
1 Baby			
2 Cup			
3 Spoon			
4 Pan			
5 Cup			
6 Spoon			
7 Baby			
8 Pan			
9 Baby			
10 Spoon			
11 Cup			
12 Pan			

"get," "take," "give me," or "find." She may begin teaching a new word-object association by placing only one item in front of each child and asking the child to touch the object. Imitation and physical prompts are used as necessary. When the children are touching the first training object on command, a second object is placed on the table so the children must make a choice between two objects. This procedure is continued until all objects are displayed. The children should be encouraged to play with the objects after they have selected each object correctly. They should also be encouraged to continue to label the items as they play with them. If a child has difficulty learning the association between the object and its name, he should be allowed to use the object functionally while the teacher names the object.

Generalization Training   Many suggestions for generalization training given in Phase 1 are also appropriate for training generalized comprehension. Once a child has learned to attach a verbal label to an object, the teacher can begin to expand the class of objects encompassed by that label. For example, if the object used to train "cup" has been a white coffee cup, other cups of varying size, shape and color should be used to broaden the concept of cup.

Group time
- a   Each child is given two different objects (e.g., cup and spoon). The teacher asks everyone to hold up the cup. She demonstrates drinking from the cup. She gradually discontinues the demonstration and uses only verbal cues.
- b   The children are given different objects from the same object group.

The teacher asks all children holding a particular object to stand up or go to the table. This activity is used to get the children to the table for snacks.

Snack time

The children are required to take their own cup and spoon off a tray as the teacher names the objects.

Outdoor play

A game of running is used to generalize comprehension of object names. The objects are placed in different parts of the play area within sight of the children. The children run to get them on request.

Phase 4 Training Verbal Imitation of Nouns

Setting and Words This training takes place in the kitchen area or a corner of the classroom with a mirror. The words represent the training objects in Group 1.

Baseline and Training Probes Replicate the procedure used in Phase 2, substituting words for the sounds (see Table 9-3).

Training Replicate the procedure in Phase 2 with the noted additions. If the teacher cannot elicit a reasonable approximation to the word she is training in several trials, she may try dividing the word into units. For instance, for the word "cup," she might have the child say /k∧/ first, and then /p/. After the child imitates two response units consistently, the time between the presentations of the stimuli is shortened until the two become a single unit /k∧p/. Or, the child may be taught to say /∧p/ first and then go on to /k/–/∧p/ to /k∧p/. The goal is not perfect imitation, but a reasonably close approximation (e.g., "poon" for "spoon) to the word being trained.

Generalization Training Some activities presented in Phase 2 are also appropriate for this training phase.

Phase 5 Training Single-Word Production of Nouns

Setting and Words The setting and words are the same as in Phase 4.

Baseline and Training Probes The probe recording form is presented in Table 9-5. Each child is tested individually. The teacher holds the object up and asks, "What's this?" A correct label or acceptable approximation to the correct response is scored as (+); incorrect responses as (−); and failure to respond in 15 seconds as (NR). Criterion is an acceptable response two of the three times each item is presented.

Training The teacher holds up one object and asks, "Who knows what this is?" or "Michael, what is this?" Children who make no response or an incorrect response are prompted by having them imitate the correct label. After the children have labeled the object, the comprehension and functional-use phases of training are reviewed by having the children pick up each object and play with it in an appropriate manner. The children do not have to produce the word perfectly, but they should produce reasonably intelligible approximations.

Generalization Training   The teacher should use every opportunity throughout the day to ask the children the names of the objects being trained. Most activities suggested in earlier phases are also appropriate for this phase.

Recycle Training with Object Group 2

Using the setting, objects, and sounds given in Table 9-1 for the second object group, the teacher should repeat the training specified in Phases 1 through 5. The time needed to train this second group of objects should be less than with the first object group. The setting for Object Group 2 is the self-help area and the objects are *hat, shoe, soap, comb,* and *boy.* The sounds for this group are: /h/,/t/,/s/,m/, /o/, and /ɔI/.

Phase 6   Training Verbal Imitation of Verbs

Setting and Words   The third object group (see Table 9-1) is used in this phase. The setting is the picnic area and the training objects are *wagon, man, cookie, dog,* and *boat.* The action words are "eat" and "ride." Training sounds are /w/, /g/, /d/, /r/, /aI/, /ɔ/, and /ʊ/. Before beginning training on Phase 6, children should be taught to produce the nouns used in this object group (see Phases 1 through 5).

Baseline and Training Probes   The probe procedure is the same as in Phase 4 except for the stimulus items. The teacher records responses on the form in Table 9-3, testing verbs instead of nouns.

Training   Follow the procedure described in Phase 4.

Generalization Training   The teacher should use every opportunity to have the children imitate the training words. Other words of similar phonetic content should be introduced, and the child should be encouraged to imitate these words. This will help him learn to say the same sounds in new combinations. Mirror training may be valuable during this phase.

Phase 7   Training Comprehension of Verbs

Setting and Words   The setting and words are the same as in Phase 6.

Baseline and Training Probes   A probe is given on the comprehension of action words "eat" and "ride." The cookie, boat, and wagon are placed on the table and the child is given either the dog or the man. The teacher then says, "Make it eat," or "Make him ride." Each verb is tested three times with the order of the verbs and agents presented at random. The data are recorded on a form similar to the one shown in Table 9-4. If the child does not demonstrate each verb action correctly three times, he should be trained on verb comprehension.

Training   The training is a replication of Phases 1 and 3 using motor imitation and physical prompts until the child demonstrates that he discriminates between "eat" and "ride" by manipulating the toys according to the teacher's verbal command.

Generalization Training   The teacher should extend the child's learning by having alternative training stimuli available in the classroom (e.g., other dogs and boats). By having these stimuli (both in the form of objects and pictures) available, opportunities arise for the teacher to ask a child to get the "apple," point to the "boat," or bring her the "wagon." The children should collect pictures of people and animals eating different foods and riding in different vehicles. The children can be taught to discriminate between the actions. When they have learned to make this discrimination, group time can be used to generalize the concepts. For example, each child may hold one picture which depicts eating and another which depicts riding. The teacher may request that the children hold up the picture of eating or riding. Each child holds up the appropriate picture depending on the teacher's verbal cue. Another game includes placing all the pictures in a pile on the floor. The teacher requests a child to find a picture of "eat." The child picks an appropriate picture and places it on a felt board.

Phase 8   Training Production of Verbs

Setting and Words   The setting and words are the same as Phases 6 and 7.

Baseline and Training Probes   The teacher probes the child's skill by demonstrating an activity (e.g., the dog eating the cookie) and asking the child, "What's he doing?" The child should respond with some form of the correct verb such as "eating," "eat," or "eats." Each verb is tested three times through random presentation. The child's responses are recorded on a form similar to that found in Table 9-5. If the child does not give at least two appropriate responses for each verb, he is trained on this phase.

Training   Training is similar to Phase 5. The teacher demonstrates an activity with the objects or has one child do so, and then asks, "What's it doing?" or "What's going on?" Children who do not give appropriate responses are asked to imitate the response. The imitative cues are gradually faded.

Generalization Training   Generalization of responses learned in a special training session to other settings is a major concern of this program. When the

Table 9-5 Sample Data Sheet for Probes on Production (Phases 5, 8, 11, 14)

	Response		
Words	**+**	**−**	**NR**
1 Cup			
2 Pan			
3 Spoon			
4 Baby			
5 Cup			
6 Baby			
7 Spoon			
8 Pan			
9 Baby			
10 Cup			
11 Spoon			
12 Pan			

child produces the correct label for an object without prompting, the next step is to help him generalize the use of the label to other objects of the same class in other environments. The teacher should make use of all opportunities for the child to express his wants. In other words, the child should be given a reason to talk.

Phase 9 Training Imitation of Two-word Phrases

Setting and Words The setting, objects, and action words from the fourth object group (see Table 9-1) are used in Phases 9, 10, and 11. The setting is the sandbox area and the objects are *car, truck, can,* and *sack.* The action words are "fill," "hide," "push," and "pull." Training sounds are / ʃ /, /f/, /a/, and /I/ Before beginning training on Phase 9, children should be taught to produce the nouns and verbs as single-word utterances (see Phases 1 through 8) if necessary.

Baseline and Training Probes The probe procedure is the same as in Phases 4 and 6 except for the stimulus items. The teacher should not combine each verb with each object because that makes the probe unnecessarily long. Only those items which make sense ("pull car" or "fill can") should be combined. Two exemplars of each verb are presented in combination three times in a random order. The child's responses are recorded on a form similar to the one found in Table 9-3. Criterion performance is two out of three correct trials per item.

Training The procedure is the same as in Phase 4. Children should be able to imitate each word separately (Phases 4 and 6); however, articulation skills may break down when the child attempts to imitate a two-word utterance. If this occurs, the response should be divided into two units. For example, the phrase "hide car" can be given one word at a time. When the child imitates these two response units consistently, the length of time between the presentation of the stimuli is shortened until they are imitated consecutively.

Generalization Training   Imitation of the teacher's utterances should be encouraged in the classroom situation. If the child spontaneously imitates a word, the teacher should immediately repeat his word and use other simple words to expand the utterance. This training should be related to some ongoing activity so the phrase has meaning to the child.

Teacher: "Okay children, time to drink your juice."
Children: "Juice."
Teacher: "Juice, yes. Drink juice. Say "drink juice."

Phase10   Training Comprehension of Two-word Phrases

Setting and Words   The setting and words are the same as Phase 9.

Baseline and Training Probe   A probe is administered on the comprehension of the verb plus object phrases. The teacher places the four objects on the table and says "Fill truck" (beans, rice, or sand should be available) or "Hide can." Each of the four verbs is combined with two objects three times in random order. This results in a probe composed of 24 stimulus items. The child's responses are recorded on the form similar to that illustrated in Table 9-4. Criterion is two out of three correct for each item.

Training   The teacher gives a child one object (i.e., truck) and says "Fill truck." She gives another child the can and says "Fill can." The children trade objects and alternate "filling" the two objects. A child is then given two objects (i.e., truck and sack). The teacher asks him to fill one of the objects (i.e., "Fill sack"). She prompts him if necessary. When he can correctly choose the object to fill based on the verbal direction, she introduces a third object. The child then makes a choice among three objects to fill. The procedure is repeated with another verb. The child is given a car and instructed to "Push car." Another child is given a truck and instructed to "Push truck." Each child is then given two objects (car and truck) and the teacher says either "Push car" or "Push truck." Responses are prompted if neccessary. Training discrimination between two objects is completed before going on to "Push can." The child eventually makes a choice among four objects.

The teacher alternates commands and she prompts correct responses when necessary. "Hide" and "pull" are taught in the same way as "fill" and "push." The child eventually chooses from the four objects to follow any of the verb commands.

Generalization Training Generalizing comprehension of two-word, action-object phases should be part of the daily classroom and home routine. In both group time and snack time, children should be given simple instructions. For example, a child can be asked to demonstrate "roll ball," or "hide bus." Older children can be used to demonstrate or give commands. When the children are outside, a game of follow-the-leader or Simon says can be used to demonstrate outdoor activities such as "empty pail" or "push bike."

Phase 11   Training Production of Two-word Phrases

Setting and Words   The setting and words are the same as in Phases 9 and 10.

Baseline and Training Probes   Probe procedures are the same as in Phases 5 and 8, except for the stimulus items. Each verb is combined with each object three times in a random order. The teacher demonstrates an activity (filling truck) and then asks the child, "What am I doing?" or "What's happening?" The child's response should be some form of the correct verb combined with the correct object (i.e., "fills truck," "filling truck," or "fill truck"). The child's responses should be recorded on a form similar to the one shown in Table 9-5. If the child does not give at least two appropriate reponses for each verb and object combination, he is trained on this phase.

Training   The teacher demonstrates the activity and asks the children "What am I doing?" Children who do not respond correctly are asked to imitate the verb and object phrase (i.e., fill can). Each child demonstrates the action with the same object and asks the other children what he is doing. The teacher prompts appropriate responses. She begins with one object and one verb, then goes to one object and two verbs and so on. She then introduces another object with one verb, two verbs, etc., and alternates the two objects with the four verbs. The third and fourth objects are trained in the same manner until children can identify any of the four objects with any of the four verbs.

Generalization Training   Children must be taught to generalize production of two-word responses to the classroom and to other environments. One advantage of the two-word, action-object phrase is that it is a command which can be reinforced. At group time the teacher may choose one child to be a leader for the day in a game in which the other children follow his requests. Toys and snacks are given only to children who verbalize their wants. If a child is unable to do so, the teacher provides appropriate verbal stimuli for him to imitate, then she gradually fades the verbal prompts.

Phase 12   Training Imitation of Three-word Phrases

Setting and Words   The setting, objects, and action words from the fifth object group (see Table 9-1) are used in Phases 12, 13, and 14. The setting is the doll house and the objects are *man, lady, chair, window, bed,* and *door.* The sounds to be trained are: /l/, /tʃ/, and /ɛ/. The action words are "sit," "sleep," "open," and "shut." Children should be given training with this object group on Phases 1 through 11 before beginning Phase 12. When training two-word phrases with this object group, the teacher uses both action-object phrases (e.g., "sit bed," "open window") and agent-action phrases (e.g., "man sleep," "lady sit," "lady shut," etc.).

Baseline and Training Probes The probe procedure is the same as in Phases 2, 4, 6, and 9. The stimulus items are three-word phrases. A probe which combines each agent with each action and object is unnecessarily long, and some of the action-object combinations do not make sense ("man open chair"). Therefore, using only those combinations which make sense, the teacher picks two exemplars of each verb, combines them with different agents and objects and presents them three times in random order. For example, the stimulus items for the verb "sit" might be "man sit chair," "lady sit bed;" the stimulus items for the verb "sleep" would be "man sleep bed," "lady sleep bed" (the verb "sleep" is most appropriate for the object "bed"). The child's responses are recorded on the form illustrated in Table 9-3. Criterion performance is tow out of three correct trials per training item.

Training The training is the same as previous imitation training, except three-word phrases are used. Articulation skills may break down, as well as memory skills (i.e., the children may forget one or two of the words in the sequence). This may necessitate breaking the longer responses into shorter units until the child can imitate them consistently, and then gradually combining them again into the longer verbal units.

Generalization Training Generalization procedures described in previous imitation phases may be used. The teacher should take every opportunity to let children act as teachers for other children.

Phase 13 Training Comprehension of Three-word Phrases

Setting and Words The setting and words are the same as in Phase 12.

Baseline and Training Probes Probes are administered on the comprehension of the agent-action-object phrases. All objects are placed on the table in front of the child and the child is asked to demonstrate the phrases described in Phase 12. The child's responses are recorded on a form similar to that found in Table 9-4. Criterion is two out of three correct, per item.

Training Beginning with *lady, man, chair,* the teacher says, "Make lady sit chair." She prompts responses if necessary, alternating "lady sit chair" and "man sit chair." When the child responds correctly without prompts three times, she repeats the procedure with "Lady sleep bed" and "Man sleep bed," then alternates "Lady sit chair," "Man sleep bed," etc.

The teacher repeats the process using *window* and *door* and saying "Lady open window," as she gives the lady to the child and points to the closed window. She then alternates the "lady" with "Man open window," then "Lady (or man) shut window." She alternates commands to open and shut window and repeats the training with opening and closing door. The teacher then alternates all commands, offering *lady,* or *man* with the *bed, chair, window,* and *door.*

Generalization Training   Most activities described earlier for generalization of comprehension are appropriate for three-word phrases.

Phase 14   Training Production of Three-word Phrases

Setting and Words   The setting and words are the same as in Phases 12 and 13.

Baseline and Training Probes   Probe procedures are the same as in Phases 5, 8, and 11 except for the stimulus items. Using the phrases from Phase 12 and 13, the teacher demonstrates the activity for the child and asks, "What am I doing?" or "What's going on?" The child responds with the correct agent, a form of the correct action (e.g., sit, sits, or sitting) and the correct object. The items are presented three times in random order, and the child's responses are recorded on a form like that found in Table 9-5. Criterion is two out of three correct for each item.

Training   Training proceeds as in Phase 11 beginning with two subject agents ("lady" and "man"), one verb and one object ("lady sit chair" or "man sit chair"). The teacher performs the activity and asks the children, "What's going on?" She repeats the procedure, alternating "lady" and "man" with "sleep bed," then alternates "sleep bed" and "sit chair." That is followed with "open window," then "shut window," then "open door," then "shut door." The teacher continues to alternative activities using all objects. If the child is unable to produce a phrase spontaneously, she helps him imitate the three-word phrase, gradually fading verbal cues.

Generalization Training   Every opportunity in the classroom and at home should be used to encourage the child to verbalize. The three-word phrases are descriptions of everyday occurrences. Teachers and parents should point out actions in picture books, on television, and in the home and classroom and ask the child, "What's happening?" "What's he doing?" and other appropriate eliciting phrases. Children should be encouraged to talk to the other children in the program and to siblings.

PART II   TRAINING MODIFICATIONS OF THE AGENT-ACTION-OBJECT STRUCTURES

The first 14 phases of training establish the use of linguistic structures expressing agent-action-object relations. These underlying semantic relations are directly related to the basic "subject-verb-object" (S-V-O) string of English, frequently referred to as a simple, active, affirmative, declarative sentence. This basic English sentence form accounts for approximately 90% of all the utterances used by adult speakers of English in daily communication transactions. A child speaking in three-word strings of the agent-action-object form (e.g., "Boy drink milk") is not speaking in the adult style. This utterance is not completely formed, although it contains all the basic elements necessary (S-V-O) for communication. This type of utterance is referred to as telegraphic speech in that it resembles the language of a telegram where nonessential function words and modifiers such as articles, adjectives, and adverbs are omitted.

A child who successfully completes the first 14 phases of the program has the basic elements of frequently used adult sentence structures. However, this verbal production is still deficient because adults do not speak in telegraphic sentences. The goal of Phases 15 through 43 is to modify the child's structure for expressing the basic semantic relations of agent, action, and/or object to include the linguistic forms and semantic functions necessary for the child's speech to be similar to adult speech. Teaching more sophisticated linguistic behavior requires two operations on the agent-action-object structure. First, operations which affect only individual elements (nouns and/or verbs) comprising the verbal propositions. Second, operations modifying the communicative intent of the proposition as a whole, for example, changing an affirmative statement to a negative statement.

Phase 15   Training in Comprehension of Modified Nouns

Setting and Words   The settings and nouns in this phase of training are the same as in the preceding levels. The modifying adjectives are the colors red, blue, green, and yellow. Adjectives of size and shape can be trained using identical procedures. Whether training begins with color, shape, or size adjectives is arbitrary.

Baseline and Training Probes

Discrimination Probe   Although not specifically indicated on the training sequences found in Figure 9-1, verbal labels for adjectives of size, color, and number, as well as the prepositions and adverbial modifiers, require training of the sort indicated in the early word-referent association (Phases 1 through 8). Rather than training functional use of objects as in Phase 1, the phase of training preceding the verbal labeling of size, shape, or color, consists of discrimination training to establish the conceptual base (color, shape, or size) to be mapped by the adjective label. Training should progress from gross to successively finer discriminations.

Two types of probes can be used. The first consists of nonverbal color (or shape or size) discrimination probes utilizing a match-to-sample format. Using the objects to be modified (nouns trained previously), the teacher presents four choice objects differing from each other only in the attribute to be discriminated (say, for example, four cars identical in every respect except color). The teacher then shows the child a fifth object (e.g., car) which is the same color as one of the choice objects and says: "Show me the car like this." If the child does not make a correct match on two of three trials on each color (size or shape) tested, discrimination training is conducted before color-naming training.

Color Names   Comprehension of color names is tested using the same match-to-auditory-sample procedure used in training and testing comprehension of nouns (Phase 3). The child is presented the same four items used in the color discrimination probes and is instructed to "Show me (*red*)" (or other color name). Criterion performance is two of three correct color identifications for each color tested.

Training   Training in discrimination and comprehension of color names follows the basic procedures outlined in Phase 3 (comprehension of nouns). Establishing nonverbal discrimination may be easier if the stimuli differ only by the attribute to be discriminated. The teacher should not train color discrimination using two objects different in both color and size. This involves more complex discriminations which should be trained later. When discriminations are trained and the verbal labels established, the teacher-clinician should combine modifying words with previously trained nouns (in the case of adjective modifiers) or verbs (in the case of adverbial modifiers). The transfer model described by Spradlin in this volume is effective in training comprehension and production of two-word responses. In initial training, a single adjective is paired with five or six previously learned nouns. To respond correctly, the child must use the modifier and the noun to which it applies. Upon completion of the single adjective–multiple noun training (comprehension or production), the procedure is reversed and a single noun is selected (from the group of five or six) to be modified by four different adjectives (preferably of the same size or color). Table 9-6 illustrates the training and probe sequence for modifying nouns with adjectives of color. Two of three correct responses to every combination trained in the first step (T_1—single adjective with four nouns). After criterion is reached in step T_2, single noun paired with four adjectives are probed (P_3). If criterion (two of three correct responses) is reached on the probes, the program is terminated. If not, further training (T_4 and T_5) is required, followed by probe six (P_6) to see if transfer to untrained combinations has occurred. This cycle continues until criterion performance is achieved on all adjective-noun combinations. This training demonstrates to the child that a single object (noun) can have different modifying attributes and the same modifying attributes can be used with a variety of nouns such as red car, red apple, etc. This transfer model is explained in more detail in a preceding chapter by Spradlin.

Table 9-6   Training and Probe Sequence for Adjective-Noun Structures[1]

	Nouns			
Adjectives	**Can**	**Sack**	**Truck**	**Car**
Red	T_1	T_1	T_1	T_1
Green	T_2	P_3/T_4	P_3/T_4	P_3/T_4
Blue	T_2	P_3/T_5	P_3/P_6	P_3/P_6
Yellow	T_2	P_3/T_5	P_3/P_6	P_3/P_6

[1]"T" refers to adjective-noun combinations trained; "P" refers to the combinations probed but not trained. The subscripts refer to the training/probe sequence.

Generalization Training   Procedures described in Phases 13 and 14 should be used to get the child to use descriptive noun phrases in his everyday communication. The child should also learn to use adjectives to modify new nouns as he acquires them.

Phase 16: Production of Adjective + Noun Phrases

Setting and Words   The setting and words are the same as in Phase 15.

Baseline and Training Probes   The probe procedures are basically the same as in Phase 11 (training production of agent-action combinations) except that the stimulus items are the adjective-noun combinations trained in Phase 15. The teacher should test first for color, shape, or size name (e.g., "What color is this?") in isolation to be sure the child knows color names before requiring him to produce them in combination with nouns. If the child does not produce the color names at the criterion level of two of three correct responses for each color tested, then color names should be trained to criterion using the procedures for training production of nouns in Phase 5.

When the child produces the color names correctly, production of the adjective-noun combinations trained in Phase 15 are tested.

Training   Training adjective + noun combination proceeds like the training of agent-action and action-object combinations of Phase 11. The training probe sequence follows training comprehension of adjective-noun combinations. The transfer model in Table 9-6 summarizes the training and probe sequence for both comprehension and production training.

Phases 17 and 18   Noun Modification Through Use of Prepositions

Setting and Words   Prepositions such as in, on, under, and beside, in combination with previously trained nouns, should be used in Phases 17 and 18.

Phase 17 focuses on comprehension of prepositional noun phrases and Phase 18 is concerned with production of prepositional noun phrases.

Probes and Training   The procedures for training prepositions are similar to those used in Phases 15 and 16 for training comprehension and production of adjective-noun constructions. The training probe sequence presented in Table 9-6 is also applicable during these phases.

Phases 19 and 20   Modification of Verbs

Setting and Words   For the initial training of verb-adverb constructions the words and setting of object Group 4 should be used. In addition, a wagon and tricycle should be included. The action words (verbs) "push," "pull," and "fill" should be paired with the adverbs "fast" and "slow."

Baseline and Training Probes   Probes should be given on the comprehension of each verb-adverb combination to be included in training. The teacher should give the child a truck and say "Push fast." After recording the child's response, the contrasting command, "Push slow," should be given. If the child pushes the truck appropriately slower or faster on command two out of three times across objects, criterion is met. If there is no observable difference in speed or force of the push, the teacher scores the response "−," if the child pushed faster than when responding to the initial command, the teacher also scores it "−." No response is scored "NR." Criterion responding is two of three correct on each item of the contrasting pair for each of the three verbs.

On production probes, the behavior representing "fast" and "slow" contrasts should be modeled by the teacher for each verb and the child should be asked to describe the modified action. "Fast" and "slow" can be modeled using two discriminable objects such as a car and a truck. The teacher can demonstrate "push fast" with a truck and "push slow" with a car. "Push fast" can then be demonstrated again, and the teacher asks the child "What is happening with the truck?" The fast-slow contrast should be tested with the verbs "fill" and "pull" also. Other adverb contrasts such as up-down and high-low can be tested in a similar manner with other verbs. The order of presentation should be randomized for both comprehension and production probes. Criterion performance is two of three correct responses for each verb-adverb combination.

Training   The training procedure should follow those used in Phases 7 and 8 for the comprehension and production training of isolated verbs except that "fast" and "slow" or other adverbs should be trained as contrasts with each verb prior to moving to the next verb. The basic training paradigm should be similar to that used in the probes except that the desired comprehension or production responses are modeled when the child makes an error. Feedback and reinforcement procedures are used in the training condition but not in the probe condition. Table 9-7 contains the training-probe sequence for both

**Table 9-7 Sequence of
Training and Probe Steps
for Training Verb-Adverb
Combinations[1]**

	Adverbs	
	------------	-----------
Verbs	Fast	Slow
Push	T_1	T_1
Pull	P_2/T_3	P_2/T_3
Fill	P_2/P_4	P_2/P_4

[1]T refers to verb-adverb combinations trained; P refers to verb-adverb combinations probed but not trained; subscripts refer to training-probe sequence.

comprehension and production of verb-adverb combinations; generalization
testing and training can be conducted using (*a*) untrained verbs with the trained
adverb contrasts such as "fast" and "slow," and (*b*) new adverb contrasts
such as "here" and "there" in combination with trained verbs.

Phases 21 and 22 Expanding Agent-Action-Object Constructions Using Modified Nouns and Verbs

Although training in modification of nouns and verbs is discussed as occurring
after the child has been trained to use three-word agent-action-object strings,
modification training can take place concurrently with Phases 9 through 11 which
focus on training two-word agent-action and action-object strings. The exact
sequence of training should depend on a child's needs; however, Phases 21 and
22 depend on previously trained structures. The two basic prerequisites for
beginning training on Phases 21 and 22 are (1) functional use of agent-action-
object strings and (2) use of modified nouns and verbs in two-word phrases. The
purpose of Phase 21 and 22 is to train a child to use the modifiers trained in
Phases 15 through 20 with the nouns and verbs previously trained in the three-
word agent-action-object structures of Phases 13 and 14.

Setting and Words The setting and words should be similar to those used
in training the agent-action-object structure and the modification training of
nouns and verbs.

Baseline and Training Probes These probes should be a combination of
those used in the agent-action-object proposition training and the noun and
verb modification training. The probe procedures should be similar to those of
Phases 13 and 14 with the addition that one of the basic elements be appropriately modified as trained in Phases 15 through 20. For example, in the agent-
action-object string "boy push truck," modification of the object-noun "truck"

to "red truck" requires that the child select or produce the appropriate agent (boy), action (push), and object (red truck) from a variety of different colored trucks. Initial probes in the use of expanded sentences should focus on the modification of a single element, either the agent, action, or object of the basic proposition. There are at least five stages of expansion which can be probed and subsequently trained. These stages are presented in Table 9-8.

Training Training content and sequence should follow that of the initial probes and procedurally should be similar to Phases 13 and 14. The initial training should focus on expanding the three word agent-action-object sentence to a four-word sentence as shown in stages 1, 2, and 3 of Table 9-8. From here, expansion should move to five-word sentences as in stage 4 and finally to six-word strings of the type described in stage 5. Transfer probes and training should use previously untrained modifiers as well as trained modifiers in new combinations. Finally, the child should be taught to use these expanded sentences in environments outside the training situation. The generalization training procedures for Phases 13 and 14 are appropriate for this phase of the language training program.

Phases 23 through 27   Establishing Functional Use of Pronouns

Setting and Words The items used in these phases should be the same as those used in Phases 13, 14, 21, and 22 with the addition of the first, second, and third person singular pronouns.

Probes and Training Since the same basic procedures should apply to training of first and second person singular pronouns, and all plural pronouns, only the third person singular pronoun training is outlined.

The function of pronouns, as viewed from the perspective of this training program, is to replace nouns and modified nouns. Preliminary work by Waryas (1973) on training pronouns identifies three important syntactic distinctions:

Table 9-8   Five Stages of Expanding the Agent-Action-Object Proposition

Stages	Expansions	Example
1	Modification of object-nouns	Boy push *red* truck.
2	Modification of agent-nouns	*Big* boy push truck.
3	Modification of action-verbs	Boy push truck *slow.*
4	Modification of both agent- and object-nouns	*Big* boy push *red* truck.
5	Modification of both noun and verb elements	*Big* boy push *red* truck *slow.*

1 Case: Subjective (e.g., I, she, they)
                      Objective (e.g., me, her, them)
2 Person: First (e.g., I, we)
                      Second (e.g., you)
                      Third (e.g., he, them)
3 Number: Singular (e.g., I, he)
                      Plural (e.g., we, they)

For the third person singular pronouns an additional marking is necessary:

4 Gender: Masculine (e.g., he)
                      Feminine (e.g., her)
                      Neuter (e.g., it)

Initial probes and training for the third person singular pronouns should focus on gender distinction. Case, person, and number should be held constant while the gender distinction is manipulated. For example, the previously learned string "boy push car" should be used to test and train replacing "he" for "boy" to produce an equivalent string, "he push car." A procedure for accomplishing this replacement function is to present the child with three possible agents: a boy, a girl, and a truck. In comprehension training the teacher-clinician should ask the child to "Show me, boy pushes car." After the child responds to this previously learned command, the teacher-clinician should immediately follow with, "Show me he pushes car," which requires an identical response. If the child does not respond appropriately to the pronominalized command, the response should be modeled by the teacher-clinician and the sequence "boy pushes car–he pushes car" should be repeated. The "boy-he" equivalence should be trained with at least four other agent-action-object combinations. A probe should be administered for each of the five pronominalized commands. Correct performance on four of five items probed should constitute criterion for moving to training "girl-she" equivalence and "truck-it" equivalence. Following criterion performance on the training probes for the neuter pronoun "it," the three pronoun forms "he," "she" and "it" should be trained in successive two-way contrasts until the child responds at an acceptable level of accuracy. Production of the subject pronoun forms should be trained following the same sequence and contrast as used in the comprehension training. Verbal prompts and modeling may be necessary in the early stage of pronoun production training to get the child to produce the pronoun form rather than the previously learned noun form. Once the third person subject pronouns have been trained as replacements for single nouns, training should progress to substituting the appropriate pronoun form ("he," "she," or "it") for an entire noun phrase.

Phases 28 through 34   Modification of the Basic Proposition Using Interrogatives

The training program outlined in Phases 28 through 34 is aimed toward shaping question-asking responses through a series of sequential steps. It is important to note that although the training program shapes a different linguistic form, the function of question-asking remains the same. The sequential steps in the training of interrogatives are outlines in Figure 9-1. The probe and training procedures should be similar to those detailed in Phases 13 through 22 with the content shifting from adjective, adverb, and preposition training to interrogative-form training. Consequently, the specifics of the training procedure need not be duplicated here. The procedure can be constructed by replacing the content and training sequence of the previously discussed modifier program with the content and training sequence for interrogatives as outlined in Figure 9-1.

Phases 35 through 43   Modification of the Basic Proposition Using Negation

Negation training outlined in Phases 35 through 43 should follow procedures similar to those for training the interrogative form. Negation training should begin with an external marker used to change the basic agent-action-object string from an affirmative to a negative statement. For example, the addition of "no" to "boy push truck" would change the affirmative proposition to a negative statement of the form, "no, boy push truck." Later stages of training should focus on shifting the negative marker to an internal position in the sentence as in "boy no push truck." The final step should be shaping the form of the negative marker from elementary markers to adult forms such as "boy is not pushing truck." Although the specific verbal markers change through the course of training, the function of negating an affirmative statement remains constant.

SUMMARY OF THE LANGUAGE TRAINING PROGRAM

The framework for the language training program presented here is based on normal language acquisition and is adaptable enough to allow an individualized approach. In the process of developing and presenting a rationale for the language training program, views concerning the make-up of a functional language training program have been presented. Several of these views bear reiteration to provide a summary of aspects to consider in selecting or evaluating a language training program.

The format of a language training program should be flexible and hence allow for modifications to meet the needs of a variety of children. A language training program should provide a set of principles and strategies, amply illustrated, which can be tailored by the teacher-clinician to include the specific forms of instruction in terms of content and process which are best suited to the training situation and the child's needs.

Concurrent training on forms expressing different functions is recommended, however; a consecutive training sequence for a particular structure is a necessity if one adheres to the principle that early training is prerequisite for the acquisition of later and more complex forms of behavior. Phases 1 through 14 are consecutive steps toward establishing the agent-action-object structure. Simple forms of negation and interrogation may be taught concurrently with establishing the agent-action-object sturcture, but within each of these functions there is a definite developmental (consecutive) training sequence expressed, beginning with the simple form (external to the basic statement) and progressing sequentially to the adult forms of negation and question asking. To be effective and efficient, a language training program probably should employ some mixture of concurrent and consecutive training. The exact nature of this mixture should be determined by each child's capacity and immediate communication needs.

The language program presented in this chapter is based on the assumption that language is a mapping process. Linguistic structures are viewed as ways in which the child expresses particular semantic-conceptual functions. For example, agent-action-object strings map the semantic relationships between various agents, actions, and objects in the child's environment. From this perspective, language training must become an integral part of an ongoing educational program and take place during the child's natural interaction with his environment. The goal of the program is to provide the child with both the forms and functions necessary for communication.

The major thrust of this program is to provide the language-deficient child with forms and functions necessary for verbal interchanges in his daily environment. The program is geared to the child who lacks language or uses inappropriate linguistic forms. To reiterate a point mentioned in the previous chapter, mere "knowledge" of the form and function of certain linguistic structures is not sufficient. A child may go through an entire language-intervention program and not become a more effective communicator. Thus the teacher-clinician who trains the child in the use of linguistic structures along the lines suggested has done only a partial job. The child may also have to be taught when and where it is appropriate to use such structures. Only when the child utilizes his language tools in an appropriate and effective manner in his communicative transactions can the language intervention process be said to be complete. In utilizing a *communication-oriented* approach such as emphasized in this and the preceding chapter, the outlook is optimistic for achieving the goal of not only establishing a functional language repertoire but also in achieving the ultimate terminal goal of the language intervention process—effective and functional communication. The challenge is monumental, but the first tentative steps in developing programs and procedures applicable to the attainment of this goal have been made.

ACKNOWLEDGMENTS

Part I (Phases 1 through 14) of the language training program discussed in this chapter was developed by Diane Bricker, Laura Dennison, Linda Watson, and Lisbeth Vincent as the language curriculum for the Infant, Toddler, and Preschool Research and Intervention Project and was supported in part by NICHHD Grants No. HD00043, HD000973, HD04510 and the Joseph P. Kennedy, Jr. Foundation.

Part II (Phases 15 through 43) of the language training program is an outgrowth of several years of research (Communication Research with Retarded

Children, supported by Grant No. HD00870 from NICHHD to the Bureau of Child Research, University of Kansas) by Kenneth Ruder, Joseph Spradlin, Kathleen Stremel, and Carol Waryas. Preparation of the manuscript was supported in part by Grants No. HD00870 from NICHHD and NS10468 from NINDS to the Bureau of Child Research, University of Kansas.

DISCUSSION TOPICS

An Intervention Strategy for Language-deficient Children

Objective This chapter presents a paradigm of intervention for language-deficient young children based on a *communication-oriented* approach which emphasizes that language programming should supply the child with a functional language repertoire.

Exercises

1 This chapter and the preceding one point out that normal children learn language and its "rules" in a developmental pattern. Should language intervention programs, then, be based on this pattern that linguists have described?

2 Would Lovitt and D. Bricker et al. differ in their use of perspective toward group norms? Why might they?

3 Return to Exercise 2 in Chapter 8 and rewrite (or at least rethink) your response now that you have studied Chapter 9.

4 Study the training model (Figure 9-1) carefully and write and substitute your own original examples for each box. (Be sure your items are environmentally related *and* interrelated.)

5 Which is "better": concurrent or consecutive language training? Under what conditions?

6 Why would the word "ring" be an unlikely choice for a training word in an early sequence of the Bricker program?

7 Briefly describe how you would know a subject has demonstrated
    a comprehension
    b generalization
    c attending
    d imitation

(Using examples—not necessarily language-intervention examples—would be a good method for responding to Exercise 7.)

Chapter 10

Putting It all Together: Super School[1]

B. L. Hopkins
Department of Human Development and Bureau of Child Research,
University of Kansas

R. J. Conard
Bureau of Child Research,
University of Kansas

INTRODUCTION

Two strong currents are converging in today's classrooms. One is a general insistence that we have better, more humane, but not necessarily more expensive education for all children (Silberman, 1968). The other is a refreshing trend toward integrating exceptional children into regular educational environments (Dunn, 1968). Both demand new instructional methods to enable a teacher to simultaneously work more effectively with normal children and to handle a myriad of special problems.

By the fall of 1971 a variety of behavioral technologies for education had been described in the research literature. There were evaluated demonstrations of the effects of teacher attention or praise on children's work behaviors (Hall, Lund, & Jackson, 1968), in teaching following instructions (Schutte & Hopkins, 1970), and in improving cooperation (Thomas, Becker, & Armstrong, 1968). Other research demonstrated how to eliminate common behavior problems such as social isolation (Allen, Hart, Buell, Harris, & Wolf, 1964) and arguing and talking out (Hall, Fox, Willard, Goldsmith, Emerson, Owen, Davis, & Porcia, 1971). Moreover, there were indications that many problems encountered by teachers were the result of ineffective use of teacher attention (Madsen, Becker, & Thomas, 1968). Several more specialized techniques such as token economies (Wolf, Giles, & Hall, 1968) and access to play areas (Hopkins, Schutte, & Garton, 1971) had been developed and proved to be effective in dealing with learning or achievement problems.

An optimistic reader might review this literature and assume that it is simple to train teachers to incorporate all these procedures into their teaching methods. Teachers could then efficiently handle and productively modify the diversity of problem behaviors, teach their students more academic skills than is ordinarily the case, and at the same time help their students develop improved social behaviors. However, in 1971, there was no classroom anywhere in which a single teacher, working with an economically feasible program, was using the new technology comprehensively.

That year, an arrangement was developed between the University of Kansas and the Lawrence, Kansas Unified School District No. 497 to establish a satellite demonstration class in which classroom behavior management procedures could be put to test.[2] Volunteer students were solicited from two local public schools, one in a suburban area with professional and middle-income families and the other in an older section of Lawrence where there were more relatively poor families. This satellite class was named "Super School" by the children who were students there. Super School began as a third grade in 1971–72. It expanded to include both third and fourth grades during 1972–73. This is a description of the methodology which made up Super School and the results it produced. It deals primarily with the third grade, taught by Cynthia Jacobson (Cindy), who helped to develop and test the methodology.

RATIONALE OF APPROACH

There was one overriding educational philosophy and three methodological strategies which formed the game plan for Super School. The philosophy was that "the children are always right." This does not mean that Super School teachers approved of everything their students did or acquiesced to every demand. Rather, our attitude was that there is a valid reason for everything children do. If a child is an aggressive bully, it is because he has learned to behave that way and the teacher's job is to help him to learn to behave more appropriately. If a child enters the third grade unable to read an "A" from an "I," it does not necessarily mean that the child is incapable of reading and should be thrown on a scrap heap in a special class. The school's responsibility is to find a way to teach him to read. Therefore, whenever students failed to learn and persisted in wrecking well-laid plans, we assumed that we were not teaching correctly.

The most basic educational strategy was that teaching methods built on behavioral technology would be the primary tools. A fundamental condition was that only positive methods would be used. Moreover, since it was desirable to demonstrate that one teacher with only ordinary training could operate an unusually effective classroom, the Super School teacher would use simple behavioral procedures and she would be constrained by the usual economic considerations and lack of professional support staff experienced by most teachers.

Second, materials for individualization of instruction would be used in basic subjects such as reading, math, and spelling. These materials were to be commercially available and not prohibitively expensive. Attempts to individualize instruction would be forced on the project by the wide range of skills and deficits presented by the children.

A final strategy was that data systems would be developed to provide feedback to the teacher, to allow her to make decisions about how and what to teach individual children and, if necessary, about more global changes in teaching methods and curriculum.

This philosophy and these strategies were worked into the educational program described below. The most general objectives of this program were that the average progress of the children would be at least twice the national average and that every child would advance at least one grade level per year. Attempts would be made to alleviate every behavior and social problem. Last, but perhaps most important, the children would enjoy school and their parents would approve of both the methods used and the results produced.

SELECTION AND DESCRIPTION OF STUDENTS

Before the school year began, all parents who would have children in the third grades of the two selected attendance centers were sent a letter explaining the goals and methods of the program. They were invited to attend a meeting at which questions would be answered. The children of these parents represented a diversity of academic skills, cultural backgrounds, and academic and social problems. During both years of the program, the distributions of achievement test scores at the beginning of the school year were roughly bimodal, with a proportion of children clustering at the higher end of a scale of percentiles on national norms and an equally large or perhaps even larger proportion on the lower end of the scale. However, the higher and lower clusters by no means corresponded perfectly to the middle class and economically poorer homes.

From a different perspective, the teacher had to deal with a wide range of skills. On the Paragraph Meaning subtest of the Stanford Achievement Test, grade-level scores ranged all the way from 1.0 to 6.9. The ranges were from 1.4 to 6.3 for Spelling and from 1.7 to 4.4 on the Math Computation subtest of the Metropolitan Achievement Test. The teacher, Cindy, had no inclination to ask for diagnostic work-ups because of the likelihood that some children would be terminally placed in special education programs. Nevertheless, it was estimated that three of the children could have been diagnosed as educably mentally retarded or learning disabled.

Eight of the children had very short attention spans as measured by the amount of time they stayed on task during seatwork assignments. One child had a number of disruptive classroom behaviors such as skillfully cursing the teacher, provoking fights with other children, or jumping from the top of one desk to another while shouting loudly. Another child who stayed alone during most social situations had a habit about once per day of walking quietly across the room during work periods and stabbing someone with a pencil, marking on their clothing with a pen, violently pulling someone's hair, or stealing something from an unoccupied desk. Two of the children were black, two were Mexican-Americans, three were native Americans, two had one foreign-born parent, and eleven were of those mixed, unknown, and varied backgrounds collectively called "Caucasian."

At the beginning of the second year, achievement test scores were even more widely distributed with Paragraph Meaning Scores ranging from grade level 1.0 to grade level 7.5, Spelling scores ranging from off the scale to 5.7, and Math Computation from 1.0 to 4.9. The distributions of percentile scores were again at least bimodal with more children scoring at the extremes of the distributions than in the middle. As had been the case during the first year, two children had very minimal academic skills and could have easily been placed in special education programs. Ten children had relatively limited attention spans. Two children were relatively disruptive in the classroom because of cursing, fighting, verbally refusing to comply with the teacher's instructions, and frequent facial gestures that were variously described as "sulking," "pouting," "hate looks," and "being swelled-up mad." Two children were very shy, never volunteering to talk in class and sometimes simply not responding to the teacher's questions. Fifteen of the children were Caucasian, four black, one native American, and two had one foreign-born parent.

DESCRIPTION OF PROGRAM
Teaching Methods

One of the principal goals of Super School was to determine if the behavioral technology which had been successfully employed for specific problems could be comprehensively used for a complete classroom program for a heterogeneous group of children. The general teaching methods were made up of many specific techniques, and each technique was selected or evaluated for its probable value as a motivator or reinforcer.

Moving   Picture the following scene: The teacher is seated at her desk, while the students are doing a seatwork assignment. The room is quiet. No child is being disruptive. A closer look reveals that although the students are at their stations they are less than excited about it. A few whisper back and forth about plans for recess. Others stare blankly out the window. One is actually asleep. None are involved with their work for more than a few seconds at a time.

Change the scene. The teacher is moving continually about the classroom. She stops to look at a child's work, talks with him briefly about it, and then moves on to another child. Even though desks and chairs are crowded together, there is enough space between stations so she can squeeze through to get to a child in the next row. Her movements are not predictable. She may move from one child to another child on the far side of the room. She is interacting with as many as four children a minute. The children do not have to quit work to go talk to her about something. She will always soon be there to see what they are doing.

Cindy Jacobson, third-grade teacher in Super School, had her desk removed from the room to leave more space for activities. Her supplies were kept in a wall cabinet. Moving around helped her see the good work the children were doing rather than sitting and waiting for problems to come to her, and it helped Cindy spread her attention more evenly around the classroom.

Praising Students Who Are Working   If a teacher is moving around and interacting with students about their good work, it is not difficult for her to carefully and consistently praise them for that work. This became the core of the Super School teaching methods. Many of the more specialized methods were simple variations on this theme. The praise reinforced or strengthened whatever a child was doing when it occurred. The procedure helped Cindy concentrate on the good things the children were doing instead of emphasizing their mistakes and shortcomings.

"Way to hustle, Pamela!"

"Fantastic, Kenny!"

"Chris is already on the second page of his assignment!"

Cindy geared her praises to the activity at hand. For example, if the students were doing a cursive writing assignment, Cindy's praises would be something like these:

"Very neat, Katie."

"Wow, those are nice, straight lines, Sabah!" Regardless of the activity, there were always things which Cindy could praise:

"Gee, you're working fast and accurately, Lori!"

"I haven't heard a peep out of you all morning, Deon!"

When Cindy saw the students doing good things, she was quick to point them out. That way, the students were more likely to know just which things she liked to see. At the beginning of the year, Cindy tried hard to praise as many of the students' good behaviors as she possibly could, regardless of how trivial they might seem:

"Thank you for waiting quietly, Suzanne."

"I like the way Lyndell has his hand up when he needs help."

Each student needed to be evaluated individually as to whether he deserved praise or not. It hardly made sense to expect all to be performing at the same level, so it would not have been reasonable to set absolute criteria for praising them. One student might be required to get nearly all of the problems on a page correct before she praised him, while another student might deserve praise after doing only one or two problems. In either case, it depended upon that child's skills. The rule about considering the student's previous performance also applies to social behaviors. Some students could be expected to remain at their work for long periods with little attention. Others needed to be praised every few minutes for staying at work. It was always easy to earn the teacher's praise, just by doing a little better than before:

"Nice try, Tommy. You attempted every spelling word."

"Great Patricia, that's much neater."

"You've really been courteous today, Sally."

Another example or two might be useful. If Jimmy had been goofing off most of the period, and then began to work, the teacher would praise him for working for only a few seconds. If he usually goofed off for the entire period, any work at all was an improvement. If Tommy, who had trouble spelling, usually refused even to attempt to spell the words the teacher gave him, then by attempting even a few words, he made some improvement and deserved the teacher's praise.

Descriptive Praise Some persons are annoyed by teachers who employ some behavior modification procedures and use shallow and repetitious praises such as "good" and "good boy." This is not only unimaginative, it does not really help the children. Whenever Cindy saw the students working or behaving well, she tried to name their good behaviors as she praised:

"Nice cursive, Hiram."

"You're really working fast today, Bobba!"

"Greg has already answered six problems, and they look correct, too!"

This helped let the student being praised know exactly what the teacher liked about him or his work and helped him understand how he could continue to earn her attention. It also helped let other students know what things they could do to earn the teacher's approval.

Special Problems from Praise Praising children a lot can produce problems. Suppose you are moving around the room, look over Tommy's shoulder and say,

"Fantastic, Tommy! Beautiful work!"

You will surely reinforce Tommy's work behaviors, but until he becomes used to it, you may also momentarily distract him. He turns to you and begins to carry on a conversation. What do you do? You are interested in what he has to say but it is not time for sharing and you do not want Tommy to be distracted by every little praise.

Cindy would walk away from Tommy, spot another child who was working and stop to note good things he was doing. As she continued, she would watch Tommy out of the corner of her eye. After he had returned to work, she would say,

"I see Tommy's hard at work over there!"

Later, if Cindy stopped to look at Tommy's work and he did not become distracted by her attention, she would linger a little longer with him and point out several things he was doing well. Tommy soon learned to keep right on working.

Consider another occasional problem: Cindy is moving around the room while the class is doing a math assignment. Some of the assignments are pretty tough, so Cindy is focusing her praise upon persistence and completion:

"Cynthia's really got her nose to the grindstone!"

"Wow, Jack already has five problems finished!" Another student, Tommy, hearing Cindy praise Jack for completing five problems, calls out, "Hey, teacher, I have six problems done already." Of course Cindy is pleased that he is working well, but if she praises him at that time, she will be reinforcing not his good work, but rather his solicitation of her praise. Cindy ignored his talking out. She did not praise him for his work at that time, nor did she remind him to be quiet. She simply went on to interact with another student who was working. After a few minutes, when Tommy was back at work, Cindy went over to his desk and praised him at that time for his good work. Had Cindy praised Tommy when he called out to her, she would soon have the entire class calling out to her.

Yet another problem which initially occurred was this: Cindy is moving around the room, praising students who are working hard. The students are in their seats, working well. Cindy notices that Mary is almost finished with her assignment:

"Beautiful, Mary, you've almost finished the whole job!"

Suddenly, from somewhere in the room, a little voice mimics, "Beautiful, Mary, you've almost finished the whole job." A few other students snicker. The student who mocked Cindy has obviously already caught the attention of some of his peers, so she certainly wants to avoid calling even more attention to him by scolding him in front of the class. Yet she wants the class to realize that her praises to students are sincere, and not to be taken lightly. What should she do? Cindy did two things to handle this problem. First, she completely ignored the student who mocked her, as well as the students who were snickering. Then, she looked around the class and selected a few students who were not attending to the mimic and praised them for staying at work:

"Wow, look at Janine go over there. Nothing distracts her!"

"Way to stick with your work, Anita."

Later, after the student who had mocked her had returned to work, Cindy was quick to praise him for working quietly. The other students learned that they could get more attention from the teacher by staying at work than by paying attention to the smart aleck.

Praise across the Room   Even if a teacher is doing a good job of moving around and pointing out the good work children are doing, there is a tendency for children on the other side of the room to not work as well as the children nearby. In addition, every teacher will have some children who have work spans so short that she has trouble visiting them often enough to keep them involved. How can you get students to work hard even when you are not nearby? This problem was solved in Super School by Cindy extending her praise to include children who were not near her:

"You're doing a nice job of staying busy over there, Charles."

"Way to hang in there, Mark!"

"Katie, you're really working over there in the corner!"

By praising from a distance, Cindy helped the students, regardless of where they were, to remember that she was interested in what they were doing. Although she could not actually see their work, and thus could not specifically praise it for its academic quality, she could certainly see that the students were at work, staying in their seats, and not bothering others. She praised students from a distance almost as often as she praised those who were near her—and, like regular praise, she was careful to praise immediately as the good behaviors occurred.

Praise While Helping A very common teaching problem occurs whenever a teacher must interrupt her normal routine to give individual instruction to one student. If the instruction is prolonged, many other students quit working. Suppose Dawn needs help with long division. After you have been helping her for thirty seconds you realize that you are one-by-one losing the other children and Dawn has not begun to catch on. By the time you have been helping one child for three minutes, half your class may be distracted from their work. Once you have lost that many of your group, it is difficult to get them working again. You cannot ignore Dawn's need for help and neither can you afford to have the rest of the class fall apart while you are teaching one child.

The solution is to alternate between helping one child and looking up to praise other children who continue with their work. Cindy helped a student no more than ten or fifteen seconds, then she would glance around the room, pick out a child or two staying at work, and praise them:

"Thanks for staying busy, Kathy, I'll be over to help you in just a minute."

"Jonathan and Sarah are hanging in there!"

As long as she remained with that student, she allowed no more than fifteen seconds to pass without looking up to praise other students for continuing to work. This was a little difficult to do at first. It meant that Cindy had to stay tuned in to what the rest of the class was doing while she concentrated on the problem the student was trying to solve. With a little practice, she quickly learned to divide her attention. Sometimes, initially, when Cindy was working with a student and looked up to praise other students, the student she was helping would become unhappy at the loss of her attention. Cindy did two things to handle this problem. Just as she removed her attention from the student she was helping, she would place her hand upon his head or shoulder while she praised other students who were continuing to work. This helped to reassure the student that she had not forgotten him. However, if the student still fussed or complained about her temporary removal of attention, Cindy simply walked away to help another student. Later, after he had returned to work, Cindy would go back to that student and again offer her help. If the student did not balk when she removed her attention to praise others, Cindy praised him for waiting politely.

Touches   There are many other things a teacher can do to let her students know that she appreciates their good work or conduct. The first of these is to lovingly touch the students as they work. Children enjoy quite a variety of touches, sometimes a pat on the head or shoulder, sometimes a gentle squeeze of an arm, or sometimes even a big hug. Just as with praising, Cindy was careful to give her touches only to students as they were working or behaving appropriately. This practice, like praising, was not without its problems, as in the following example: Cindy looks over Richard's paper and sees that he has been doing his work well. She praises him, and puts her hand upon his shoulder, but Richard pulls away from her hand, as though he did not like to be touched. She wants Richard to know that her touch is only meant as a gesture of affection in appreciation for his good work, but she does not want to call extra attention to him while he is squirming. How should she handle it? The best thing to do is to walk away and not say anything about it. The next time Cindy saw Richard working well, she again praised him for his work, and gave him a quick pat on the shoulder. This time, however, she was careful to make the pat very light and very brief. If he again fussed about being touched, she again walked away to another student. The next time she stopped to look at his work, Cindy again praised him and gave him a pat on the shoulder, this time a little more firmly. Very gradually, over a period of several weeks, Cindy increased the intensity and duration of her touches to Richard. Before long, Richard, just like the other students, enjoyed being praised and touched by the teacher.

Different forms of touches were appropriate for different students. Some students, especially the younger ones, liked big juicy hugs, and other students preferred more casual, subtle touches, like quick pats to the arm or shoulder, or gentle squeezes to the neck or arm.

Privileges   "Sabah, since you've been working so hard, you may line up first for lunch."

Since someone has to be at the front of any line, it makes more sense to give that honor to someone who deserves it instead of simply giving it to anyone. The way students can earn such a privilege is by behaving appropriately. The third-grade classroom provided a wealth of potential privileges. There was a rule of thumb which stated that if it were likely that a student would enjoy doing a particular thing, then that activity could be used as a privilege, to be given to a student who was working well or behaving appropriately. Whenever Cindy had anything which needed to be done, such as passing out or picking up papers or pencils, turning on or off the lights, carrying materials, taking notes to the office, helping other students, or the like, she was careful to select someone whose behavior at that time warranted such a privilege:

"Since you finished so quickly, Bobba, you may pick up the papers."

"Wow, you've really been working hard, Mark, why don't you take a break and go get a drink of water."

"Lyndell, since you've already finished your assignment, you may go over and help Janine with the bulletin board."

Cindy tried to never give anything which might be considered a privilege by the students to anyone unless they were working or behaving well, and she was careful to never use such privileges to try to get children to quit goofing off.

Marks on Papers Another effective reinforcement method is to put approving marks on children's papers. Cindy did this by first looking around the classroom to find someone who was really working well. Then she would go over to that student, perhaps pat him on the back, and praise him for being a good worker. While she was with that student, she would look at his work and praise specific good answers. Then she would write or draw something nice on his paper. Sometimes she would write out a praise comment like "Good spelling," "Great answer," or "Very neat," and sometimes she would draw something like a happy-face, or a star, or even just a "C" to note that an answer was correct. These approving marks helped the students know which papers or answers were particularly well done.

"Beautiful paper, Kathy, I'm going to give you a little happy-face right up here on top!"

"Super neat, Mark, that's a two-star answer if I every saw one!"

As with praising, Cindy was careful to evaluate each student's progress individually. When she looked at a student's paper, she compared his performance not to all the other students, but to his own previous performances.

Pointed Praise Suppose the class is working on an art project and you are moving around helping children and praising their good work. You notice that Jim is out of his seat, talking to other students. Not wanting to risk reinforcing him by calling attention to him by telling him to get back to his seat, you decide to ignore him until he returns to his seat. Several minutes later, however, Jim has still not returned to his seat. You cannot ignore him any longer, yet you still do not want to give him attention for being out of his seat. What can you do?

A particular praise technique, called pointed or suggestive praising is very useful for such situations. When Cindy saw that Jim was out of his seat, she quickly looked around the room and picked out a couple of children who were staying in their seats, working.

"Mr. Charles, you're just fantastic. You're really sticking with your work."

"Cynthia, I really like the way you've stayed at your seat and gotten so much work done!"

Usually, Jim got the message without Cindy having to attend to him directly. And Charles and Cynthia got some well-deserved praise at the same time.

Look at another example: As the class is reading library books, Cindy sees Karen and Sue talking instead of reading silently as instructed. She ignores them, hoping they will soon get back on task so she may praise them for working appropriately, but after a few minutes, they are still talking. What to do? Again, Cindy uses pointed praise:

"Beautiful, Katie, you're working so nice and quietly!"

"Wow, I don't even hear a peep out of Suzanne, she's working so hard!"

As the class lines up to go to recess, Cindy notices that a couple of the students are dawdling. If she simply ignores them, they will hold up the entire group. Here again, pointed praise is the answer:

"Looks like Kathy and Hi are ready."

"Thank you for getting in line so quickly, Mike."

Pointed praise proved to be effective when used sincerely and not negatively. Cindy almost always used it whenever she saw students behaving inappropriately. It allowed her to let the misbehaving students know what she wanted, without calling direct attention to them. At the same time, it provided an opportunity for her to praise students who were being good.

The pointed praise is like an instruction, it tells the child what you want him to do. Unlike a direct instruction, the pointed praise avoids attending to the child and possibly reinforcing whatever he is doing. At the same time, it reinforces the productive behaviors of the few children you use it for. Therefore, it helps maintain the cooperation or work of the rest of the children while getting the one who is talking, dawdling, or not following instructions back to the task.

It may also be used on academics. Suppose you see that Don has forgotten to put his name on his paper.

"Tina and Rosalyn both have their names on their papers. Good girls!"

You glance down and notice that Dick is forgetting to carry to the 10s column in addition.

"Mikelan is remembering to carry the 1 when the result is greater than 9. Great, Mike!"

Ignoring Students' Inappropriate Behaviors   Suppose Cindy is praising and moving around the classroom as the students are doing a seatwork assignment. All students are supposed to be working at their desks. Cindy notices that Tommy is walking around the room. What should she do, and why? Suppose the students are working quietly at their seats on a math assignment. Cindy sees that Jim and Bob are talking together instead of doing their work. What should she do?

She should use pointed praise for children who are at their stations working instead of talking or who are working instead of playing. It is not wise to tell the children to sit down, be quiet, or get back to work. Do that only as a last resort. Ignore misbehaviors and use pointed praise for other children instead. Too many children are reinforced by an adult telling them to stop doing something.

In each case, Cindy kept each student in the corner of her eye. As soon as she saw that he had worked for a few seconds, she quickly went over and praised him. By doing this, Cindy created a very clear contrast in consequences for the students. When they were behaving inappropriately, they received no attention from the teacher, but when they were working well, they were sure to be noticed and praised.

The same rules applied when working with academic behaviors. Suppose the class is practicing cursive writing at their seats. Cindy is moving around, praising students who are working quietly and quickly, and occasionally stopping to look over students' papers. Timothy is doing a good job of staying busy, keeping his eyes on his paper, so Cindy interacts with him. "I sure like the way you've been working this morning, Tim." As Cindy looks over Tim's paper, she notices that he is having a little trouble getting his *l*'s to stand up straight. Instead of pointing out the ones he has done incorrectly, she circles two that he has done relatively well.

"Boy, I really like this one and this one. They're so straight and tall."

By pointing out his good examples, Cindy lets Tim know what she wants him to do, without discouraging him. Another way to do the same thing is to use pointed praise. Cindy might have noticed Tim's problem, said nothing to him at the time, and then, when working with other students, given pointed praise to let the class (and Tim) know what she liked. The praise would have gone like this:

"Hey, Bobby, that's what I like to see. Nice, straight, tall *l*'s!"

In either case, she would avoid criticizing the way Tim was writing the *l*'s. The criticism would either have been reinforcing, making it more likely that Tim would continue writing poorly, or if it were punishing, there would be the risk that he would quit trying to do a good job and perhaps eventually even come to dislike writing.

A Simple Punishment System   Suppose most of the children have finished reading and are playing or working quietly in the play area. Sally and Patricia begin to argue over a toy.

"Denise and Kathy are playing well together!"

Cindy is careful to ignore the two children who are arguing. However, the girls become louder and more angry.

"Sarah and Seana are being quiet in the play area. Thanks girls!"

Still, Patricia and Sally become more heated and it looks like there will be blows unless Cindy intervenes quickly. If she tries to gently persuade the girls to cool down, she runs the risk of reinforcing them both for arguing and becoming mad. If she steps in and bawls them out or delivers a lecture she may be adding fuel to an already unpleasant fire. Super School developed a simple and unemotional punishment procedure to handle situations for which ignoring and pointed praise were not effective.

Whenever a student did something which could not be ignored, Cindy calmly asked that student to put his name and a point on the blackboard. Before she ever initiated the punishment system, Cindy drew up a clear, short list of the rules she felt were necessary to make the class function smoothly. These rules included things like "Walk in the hallways"; "talk to other students during free time or when given permission"; and "be courteous to others." If a student broke any of these rules, Cindy asked that student to put a point on the board.

For each point a student acquired he lost five minutes of recess time. When the class went out to recess, those students with points had to remain inside at their desks for the amount of time they had lost. If no one was available to stay in with the students, Cindy would take them outside with the rest of the class, but they sat at the edge of the play yard for the amount of time they had lost.

Whenever Cindy had to give points to anyone, she was careful not to appear angry or emotional. Losing recess time was enough punishment, so it was unnecessary for her to be angry with the student, and punishing a student did not stop Cindy (a minute or two later) from praising that same student if he were once again working or playing well.

When using the punishment system, it is very important to punish undesirable behaviors as soon as they occur. If not punished immediately, the student may not be sure of what he has done that was inappropriate. Cindy made it a policy never to lecture the students or to remind them of the rules. This only removed (from the students) the responsibility to remember the rules. When rules were broken, Cindy tried to punish them every time. To be inconsistent would have confused the students and been unfair. Cindy's punishment was always immediate, consistent, and delivered nonemotionally.

Even though it was basically fair and sometimes necessary, the punishment system was used only as a last resort. Before she used punishment, Cindy would check herself to see if she was doing a good job of praising the students for good behaviors and whether she was using enough descriptive or pointed praise.

Transitions   One problem detected early in the first year was that a great deal of time was lost while students switched from one activity to another. By the time students passed in papers, exchanged books, or came back into the room and found their seats, many minutes would elapse. It seemed that there should be a way to shorten the time lost between activities, using the techniques which had proven so effective during the academic periods. Cindy started using descriptive praise to specifically name the things she liked to see during transitions:

"Great! Charles already has his book out!"

"Pamela is already back in her seat, ready to go."

"Jack didn't waste any time. He's already started."

During the first minute or two of the new activity, Cindy used a great deal of praise for students who were already at work. Once everyone had settled down to work, she began devoting more time to overseeing the academic activity, helping students and praising good and consistent workers. The same technique was useful for other types of transitions, such as filing into or out of the classroom, going back to work after free time, and other things the class did as a group.

"Beautiful, Debbie, you're standing in line really nicely."

"Thank you for lining up so quickly, Amal."

"I sure like the way Kieru got back into her seat so quickly!"

"Wally is in line now, not bothering anyone."

"Look at Rosalyn, staying in line, being so quiet."

To facilitate the transitions, Cindy employed a signal, a large card, one side of which was white and the other yellow. This card was placed where it was easy for all the students to see.

"Charles, would you put the card on white please."

This was the signal for the students to clean up their desks or free-play area. Cindy still used much descriptive praise at the same time.

"Thank you, Miss Katie, for picking up so quickly."

"Nice job of cleaning up, Tony."

Then, after a minute:

"Kerry, would you please turn the card to yellow."

This meant that the students were to get into their seats as quickly as possible, and wait quietly for the next activity to begin. Again, Cindy would praise those students who complied quickly. If a student refused to comply, Cindy would calmy ask that student to put a point on the board.

The transition card provided a clear signal for the students, both through its easy visibility and by Cindy's request to have it changed from one color to another.

Grading Papers　Whenever a student puts anything down on his paper, it is at least an effort. Regardless of how poor the effort may be, it is important not to discourage it. This is why Cindy always tried to point out correct work on student papers instead of pointing out errors. The absence of *C*'s or stars by some answers shows which answers did not earn the approving marks. It is not necessary to punish a child by pointing out mistakes. Similarly, Cindy gave scores to papers by marking the number correct rather than the number wrong. It is far better to let a student miss a few questions than it is to make him feel discouraged or afraid to try. As long as you keep him trying, you can help him improve.

No matter how poor the paper, Cindy always found something nice to say about it to let the student know that she was glad he was trying. Each student's work was compared to his own previous work, not to the work of his peers. Very gradually, she expected more and more from a student before he earned his praise, but she was always careful to keep the students trying. Every graded paper was liberally sprinkled with written marks like "*C*," "Right!," "Good job!," "Excellent!," "Much Improved," "Super!"

Using a Free-time Area　One of the most effective tools in motivating students to work more rapidly was the free-play area. This area was nothing more than the back third of the classroom. Creation of the play area meant that the desks had to be crowded a little more toward the front of the room, but no one seemed to mind. There was nothing fancy about the free-time area— it was just another part of the regular classroom—but it was supplied with things the students enjoyed playing with. Initially, many educational games were placed within the free-time area, but the students showed little lasting interest in these games. Instead, they preferred things they could use to make their own toys and games, such as cardboard boxes, glue, scissors, string, colored paper, and the like. The free-time area also had a small record player, books, pencils, and paper.

Students were not automatically privileged to play in the free-time area. They had to earn that privilege by completing assignments. Since most of the students' assignments were individualized, Cindy could easily estimate the amount of work each student should do within the class period. Once a student had finished his work, he was instructed to raise his hand. Cindy went to the student's desk and looked over his work. Although she could not take time to check every problem or answer, it was easy to spot-check the work. She checked to see that the student had answered every problem. If her spot-check showed that the student had answered most of the problems correctly, she invited him to go to the free-time area. If a student skipped some of his assigned work or did work that was poor in comparison to what he usually did, he was quietly asked to complete his assignment or redo part or all of the work. Occasionally, the students became a little rowdy in the free-play area. Whenever this happened, Cindy instructed the disruptive child or children to return to their seats.

Lecturing   One of the most difficult situations to handle was the problem of maintaining interest during lecture situations. At times, there was new material which needed to be presented, and the only feasible way to present it was through a lecture. Cindy did many things to help the students get the most out of her lectures. First, she lectured for only a sentence or two, rather than for several minutes at a time. After she had spoken briefly, she would stop and ask questions about what she had just said. This gave the children a chance to use the information they had just learned while it was still fresh in their minds. After asking two or three questions, Cindy would then lecture for another sentence or two. By asking many questions throughout the lecture, Cindy was able to keep the children tuned to the lecture. To help keep everyone involved, Cindy often asked questions of students who did not have their hands up, as well as those who did. This allowed her to distribute the questions more evenly and brought responses from several students who might have remained reluctant to volunteer answers.

The basic classroom motivation techniques were also used during lectures. Cindy used praise and pointed praise right along with her lecture:

"I can see that Maria is listening carefully."

"Boy, Robbie is paying good attention over there."

"I sure like the way Charles sits there quietly."

Whenever a student answered a question incorrectly, or failed to answer it at all, Cindy did not prompt him or repeat the question. Instead, she went right on to another student with the same question. Had she repeated the question for the student, she would only have risked reinforcing him for not paying attention or being reticent. After another student gave the correct answer to the question, Cindy would go back to the child who had missed it, and ask him the same question a second time. Then, when he answered it correctly, Cindy would praise him for listening and for giving the correct answer. Sometimes, especially at the beginning of the year, she found it necessary to repeat this process a few times before the students would respond. Cindy very often repeated questions, even though a student had given the correct answer, to allow other students to answer, and to ensure that everyone had heard the answer. Review quesitons were thrown in often, to help students remember material from previous lectures.

"Good answer, Debbie. You've remembered the lesson from yesterday very well."

"How about that! I can tell that Wayne was listening earlier."

Lecturing presented its own special problems. One was teaching children to answer questions only when called upon. Some students would occasionally become excited and call out the answer to Cindy's questions without being called upon. When this happened, Cindy ignored the student who called out. She asked the questions of a student who was sitting quietly, as though she had not heard the other student at all. When the student called upon gave the correct answer, Cindy quickly praised it, like all correct answers. She also used pointed praise.

"Thank you Amal, for waiting until I called on you."

A few students were reluctant to answer the teacher's questions, even when they knew the answers. Cindy did several things to help them. First, she asked the student a question she was sure he could answer. If the student did not answer, she did not give him any extra attention by trying to persuade him. Instead, she went on to another student with the same question. When another student answered the question, Cindy used pointed praise:

"I'm glad you tried to answer that question, Tommy, even though you weren't sure of the answer."

Then she returned to the first child and asked the question again. When he answered, even if he answered incorrectly, Cindy praised him for trying. Gradually, as the student began to try to answer more questions, Cindy required his attempts to be more correct before she praised his answers.

Sometimes children became a little too excited and waved their arms wildly about in an attempt to get Cindy's attention. When her children did this, Cindy ignored them and called on others who were sitting quietly, praising them for raising their hands properly.

"I think I'll let Kieru answer this one. She has her hand up nicely." Later, though, if the child who had been overexcited began sitting properly, Cindy called upon him to answer, and praised him for his good behavior.

Very gradually, over the entire school year, Cindy increased the number of sentences of lecturing before asking questions and decreased the number of questions she asked. This helped students learn to listen attentively for longer periods of time.

Directions, Announcements, and Rules Whenever Cindy had information to share with the class, such as giving directions for assignments, making announcements or establishing rules, she gave the information only once. To repeat the information each time a student requested it would only have caused the students to listen less attentively. For example, when giving an assignment, Cindy told the students which pages to do and how the problems were to be worked. She then instructed the students to begin working. If a student had questions regarding his own particular assignment, he was instructed to wait until the class had begun working, and then raise his hand for help. However, if a student asked for a repeat of the assignment, Cindy did not repeat the assignment or instructions. She did not reprimand him for not listening, but simply ignored his request. The same was true of rules. If a student broke a rule, Cindy did not lecture or scold him. She simply punished him with no further explanation. To have repeated rules or assignments for the students would have removed the responsibility for listening to the assignment. The same policy was used for announcements. Cindy was careful to give announcements when the class was able to hear her clearly.

When rules were established, Cindy went over them just once. She announced the rule, allowed the class to discuss it, especially as to why it should be necessary, and from then on did not repeat it. If a student broke a rule, he was punished. The rule was not repeated. Although this practice may seem a little harsh, it helped them in the long run. By presenting information only once, and requiring the students to hear it the first time, Cindy helped them become better listeners and more responsible workers.

Reducing Support   For the first portion of the school year, Cindy praised almost everything she liked. She often praised students at an overall rate of 5 to 10 times each minute. The actual amount of praise each student needed to keep working varied greatly, depending upon the student's independent work skills. Some students would remain on task for an entire period, with only occasional praise for good work. Others required praise every minute or two.

During the latter half of the school year, the amount of praise given each student was gradually decreased in order to prepare the students for reentry into regular public schools where they might not receive such a concentrated amount of praise. By doing this gradually, the teacher helped the students maintain their good work habits. The important thing was to never decrease the amount of praise a student received until he stopped working. If a student were being praised an average of 20 times during a thirty-minute work period, the teacher might lower the number of times during a week to 17 or 18, then the next week to 15 or 16. At any point that the teacher felt the student was not maintaining his good work habits, she stopped decreasing her praise and increased it a little, if necessary, until his good work habits were reestablished.

In summary, the process is basically to (1) praise a student for all of his good work behaviors, until he is working to the best of his ability, and (2) after his good work habits are well established, very, very gradually decrease the amount of praise, until the student is able to work independently.

Teaching Methods for Special Problems

Most special problems were remedied by employing several general teaching methods. A few examples of these and how they were handled will clarify how other teachers may deal with similar problems.

Sally was the child who cursed, climbed on desks during class periods, and got in fights with other children. The cursing might be directed at the teacher whenever Sally was given some relatively direct order such as "Please hang up your coat in the back of the room." Cursing and fighting were also directed at other children, both boys and girls, whenever they disputed Sally on the playground or in the classroom or refused to let her have her way. Sally would climb on desks and jump from one to another during classroom work periods. Likely reinforcement for all these behaviors were the reactions of both adults and peers whenever the behaviors occurred. Therefore, these sources of reinforcement had to be eliminated and reinforcers programmed for more appropriate behaviors.

Jumping on desks was the first behavior to be satisfactorily modified. Picture this situation. Part way through a reading period, Sally quit working and started trying to talk to one of her neighbors. The neighbor kept working, probably because of Cindy's use of pointed praise:

"Lori, you are doing a good job of sticking to your work."

"Thank you for not bothering your neighbors, Deon."

"Sally sat and looked around for a minute or two, then climbed atop her desk and began jumping from desk to desk. Cindy, in a few seconds, used several methods to deal with this problem. Immediately, she said:

"Sally, put a point on the board."

Otherwise, she ignored Sally's actions. When Sally did not go to the board to write her name and a point, Cindy wrote in two points for her. As soon as Sally climbed onto her desk, Cindy began using praise and pointed praise for the rest of the children to help them ignore Sally's antics.

"That's the way to keep your eyes on your work, Jack."

"Way to not be bothered, Bobba."

"Nice job, Diane."

After a few instances of table jumping the children learned to ignore Sally even if they got their books stepped on during an episode. Sally finally climbed down from a desk and returned to her seat and work. After a few seconds of work, Cindy walked to her, placed an arm around her shoulders:

"Look at the good work Sally is doing. This one is correct and this one. Great job!"

To keep Sally working, a behavior incompatible with jumping on desks, Cindy frequently glanced in her direction to see if she was at work. If she was, Cindy might say:

"Way to hang in there Sally."

And perhaps a minute later there was praise for Sally while Cindy was helping another child.

"It looks like Sally will soon be through."

At the end of periods when Sally had not jumped on desks there was special recognition.

"Sally, you're really having a good day! (Perhaps this was accompanied by a hug.) Would you like to go get the milk for lunch?" After an especially good day, Cindy would take a few seconds to single out Sally:

"You've really had a super day. I don't think we've had a run-in all day. That's great! Keep up the good work."

Cursing and fighting were handled in similar manners. Once Sally attacked another child in the classroom with little or no provocation. Cindy, with little emotion, said, "Put a point on the board, Sally," and moved quickly to attend to the child who had been attacked, praising this child for not crying and not reacting to Sally. Sally let go with a chain of expletives:

"You white bitch! Bitch! You don't care about what happened to me. Mother fucker! . . ."

Cindy simultaneously put two points on the board for Sally and began praising other children for not attending to her.

"Way to hang in there Greg, Mark and Lyndell!"

"Good job of ignoring, Janine!"

The result of all of this was that Sally received virtually no attention from anyone for her outburst except when Cindy briefly gave her the points. The initial victim of Sally's attack was reinforced for remaining unemotional. All the children learned a little more to not reinforce Sally under the wrong circumstances.

After an outburst began, Sally might not settle down again for ten minutes. Throughout this time, Cindy stayed busy reinforcing the other children for not attending to Sally. A few seconds after Sally returned to work:

"Let's see how you are coming along, Sally. Good Job! You have every problem worked correctly so far. Keep trucking!"

As before, there were special praises whenever Sally passed up opportunities to fight or curse.

"That's the way to keep cool, Sally! Nice job!"

"Sally, you haven't been in a fight all week. Come here and let me tell you how well you have been doing."

"When I gave you that point this morning, you didn't get mad at me. I just wanted you to know how much I appreciated that. You are really beginning to grow up."

Patricia was the child who was frequently socially isolated and occasionally hurt other children or stole things when no one was looking. Cindy's work on social isolation included the usual attention and praise for both Patricia and other children whenever they played and worked together:

"You girls look like you are having a good time. Would you like to get out the record player?"

"Thank you Suzanne for helping Patricia with her spelling."

In addition, Cindy was careful to avoid interacting with Patricia whenever she went off to work by herself instead of working in a group or whenever she avoided peers during recess and simply sat alone.

The stealthy stealing and hurting other children was more difficult to modify. Stealing might go undetected so that if Cindy tried to reinforce Patricia for not stealing, she never knew if there may have been an occasion of stealing only a few minutes before. Similarly, Patricia was subtle enough about hurting others that they usually did not complain immediately. These circumstances led Cindy to employ the only physical punishment used during the course of the project.

Both Cindy and the senior author talked to Patricia's parents telling them about the nature of the problem (they were already aware of it) and the proposed method for dealing with it. For the next few days, Cindy made a special effort to reinforce Patricia for getting along with other children. She also tried to keep an eye on Patricia when Patricia was perhaps not aware of it. One day, she saw Patricia slip a box of crayons from a neighbor's desk and place them in her dress pocket. Immediately, Cindy took Patricia by the arm, led her from the classroom, found a convenient witness, and sternly said,

"Do not steal things! Do not try to hurt other children!"

Cindy turned Patricia over her knee and spanked her on the bottom about four times with the tips of her fingers and told her to remain there for a few minutes. This entire sequence took probably no more than 15 seconds. When Cindy returned for Patricia, she had quit crying and Cindy simply asked her to return to work. Cindy continued to work very hard to reinforce Patricia for getting along well with the other children and not taking things from them. When other children were not near enough to hear, she might put her arm around Patricia and say,

"I don't believe you have hurt anyone all day. I appreciate that and I'm sure they do too!"

or,

"Patricia, we haven't had anything stolen in a week. Thanks for your help."

Lenny was an example of a special problem which required no special methodology, but responded to the regular Super School teaching methods. Early one morning the senior author walked into the observation room for the fourth grade to take a work-check. On the fifth cycle of counting the number of children who were on task, he realized that he had never before seen the boy sitting in a corner desk. Sherrill Bushell, the fourth-grade teacher, did not know him either, but had assumed that he was some new student and had put him to work in a math book. He said his name was Lenny. Investigation revealed that he had just been enrolled in a learning-disabilities classroom in the same building as Super School. He had been the terror of his home school and had a reputation for consistently disputing anything an adult asked him to do while never participating in any academic exercises. Surprisingly, he had immediately responded to the teaching methods in use and had been at work on four of the five work-checks made before his presence was discovered.

Steve Kurz, the teacher in the learning-disabilities classroom in which Lenny was enrolled, then modeled his methods after the third grade of Super School. Although Lenny continued to have run-ins with adults, particularly in his home school, his belligerence and lack of work quickly disappeared in Steve's room. Lenny was soon moved into the third grade for a part of his school day and was always a good and cooperative worker. Joan Daniels, Steve's supervisor commented, "I don't think there is such a thing as a learning-disabled child. There are only teachers who don't know how to work with some children."

Wendell had fewer academic skills than any other child enrolled in Super School. He did not correctly spell a single word on the spelling subtest of the achievement tests given at the beginning of the school year. His reading skills were almost nonexistent, and he was 1.6 years behind grade level on the Math Computation subtest. He cursed a bit and was occasionally aggressive, but did not émit either of these behaviors as often as Sally. Cindy used the same procedures she had used for Sally. However, Wendell's biggest problem was a behavioral deficit—he almost never engaged in any of the academic assignments. He was occasionally a bit disruptive in the classroom, but more often he just sat looking around the room or resting his head on his desk as though asleep. During lecture or discussion activities, he never volunteered to participate and rarely responded when called on. It was no wonder he had learned little in school. No one had ever taught him to engage in activities from which he might learn.

Cindy used pointed praise to first get Wendell to work on assignments: "Spanky is hard at work!"
"I see Chris is giving his math a try!"
"Tina has her name on her paper!"
These would all be children who sat near Wendell. If Wendell so much as looked at his paper or wrote the first letter of his name at the top of it, she was quick to use praise across the room:
"Wendell! That's the way to go!"
"Wendell is getting to work!"
It was immediately obvious that Wendell's work span would be so short that it was necessary to reinforce his work once a minute to keep him at it. Cindy made it a habit for several weeks to glance at Wendell every few seconds. Whenever she saw him at work, she praised him regardless of where she was or what she was doing:
"Way to hang in over there, Wendell!"
"Pardon me Kathy. Way to keep working, Wendell!"
Frequently, when she would see Wendell at work, she would go to him to point out and praise the improvements he was making and point out good things he had done:
"Boy, you are really working, Wendell! You already have five problems completed. This one's correct and this one and this one. And you are writing your numbers neatly too! That's the way to go."
During this interchange, Cindy probably placed her hand gently on Wen-

dell's shoulder and gave him a gentle pat or squeeze as she left. Whenever Wendell sat daydreaming, she simply ignored him until he returned to work.

As Wendell became a more reliable worker, Cindy very gradually reduced the frequency of across-the-room praise for him and did not visit him quite as often. Even by the end of his third-grade year, Wendell was reinforced for working and for doing relatively good jobs much more than other children who had by then learned to work independently for very long periods of time. Cindy was still careful to go over his papers at the end of work periods to provide reinforcement for long sequences of work:

"Let's see your workbook, Wendell. You know you are really getting a lot done now. I saw you really hanging in there today. You are sure getting to be a hard worker. Everything on this paper is correct! Very, very nice writing, too!" Cindy used the procedures described above under lecturing to get Wendell to participate in lectures and discussions:

"What's the function of hemoglobin?"

Several hands go up, but not Wendell's.

> "Denise?"
> "It's the red pigment in the blood that carries gases like oxygen to our cells."
> "Good answer!"
> "Who remembers the name of the organ that pumps the blood throughout our bodies? Wendell?"
> "The heart."
> "Great! Good remembering!"

If Cindy misjudged how difficult a question Wendell could or would answer, she would frequently give him a chance to recover.

> "What would you do then if you felt like you were going to faint or pass out, Wendell?"
> "I don't know."
> "Mikelan?"
> "Lie down and prop my feet up on something."
> "Good thinking! Why would that help?"
> "It would keep blood and oxygen going to my brain."
> "Great! Wendell, what would you do if your little sister passed out?"
> "Prop her feet up on something so the blood would go to her head."
> "Right! That would be a way to help her."

Wendell was never put down, scolded, or even told he was wrong if he volunteered a poor answer.

> "Who can figure out what the third power of three is?"
> "Good! I see a lot of hands. Wendell's hand is up. Tell us what you think."
> "Nine?"

"Good try! I bet I know how you got that. Good try! What do you say Heather?''

Tommy was representative of many children who followed instructions and classroom rules poorly. Pointed praise, praise for following instructions, and occasional points and loss of recess time were primary tools for helping these children.

"Clear everything off of your desks and we will work on art projects.''

Most of the children quickly complied, but Tommy still has books and papers piled on his desk.

"Wayne has his desk cleared!''

"It looks like Maria is ready to start!''

"Thank you for clearing your desk, Chris.''

Finally, Tommy takes the hints and clears his desk.

"Good, Tommy!''

Occasionally, of course, even early in the year, Tommy would carry out instructions. Whenever Cindy noticed this, she was quick to let Tommy know she appreciated it:

"Tommy, you sure were quick to get to work!''

or,

"Hey! Tommy has his envelope addressed correctly. Good listening!''

Some of Tommy's failures to follow instructions were flagrant. Suppose Cindy has just asked a child to place the signal card on yellow to indicate that it is time for the children to move from the play area back to some academic period. All the children except Tommy quickly move to their desks. Tommy is still playing with a pile of cardboard boxes in the corner.

"Good Spanky!''

"Way to hustle Christine!''

Tommy still doesn't budge.

"Tommy put a point on the board.''

At the next recess period, Tommy either remained at his seat for five minutes or accompanied the children to the playground, but sat and watched the others for five minutes. Nothing more is said about his dawdling in the play area.

To keep the use of these procedures in perspective, it should be mentioned that praise and pointed praise were probably used a hundred times more often than points and loss of recess time.

Data Management

A number of crucial decisions during the two years of the program were based on systematic data. The following is a brief description of the various data systems and how they were used.

Achievement Testing Program   Several subtests of various achievement tests were administered at the beginning of the school year and at the end of each quarter during the first year. These included the Paragraph Meaning,

Word Meaning, and Spelling subtests of the Stanford Achievement Test (Kelley, Madden, Gardner, and Rudman, 1964) and the Mathematics Computation and Mathematics Concepts subtests of the Metropolitan Achievement Test (Durost, Bixler, Wrightstone, Prescott, and Balow, 1970). In addition, all subtests of the Iowa Test of Basic Skills (Lindquist and Hieronymus, 1964) were given to the students in October as part of the public school district's testing program. However, the ITBS scores were not used in management decisions.

First, the test data were employed to place the children in the individualized instructional programs. The tests were employed in this way at the first of the year for all children. Subsequent achievement testing was employed in three ways: (1) to provide an overall evaluation of the program; (2) to evaluate the programs in the specific areas of instruction; (3) to diagnostically evaluate the academic progress of individual children.

At the end of each quarter, the mean progress of the children was determined as a way to assess the adequacy of the classroom work in particular curriculum areas. In one instance this led to a major revision of the curriculum. During the first year, the mean grade-level score on the spelling subtest was 3.1 at the beginning of the year when the children began working on the Behavior Research Laboratories (BRL) spelling program (see Figure 10-3). By the end of the first quarter, the mean grade-level had decreased to 2.9. This caused some concern, but no great amount of activity. It is not unusual for grade-level scores to fluctuate widely from one testing to another only a few days later. Perhaps the second testing produces a number of downward fluctuations for several children. Perhaps we had placed some of the better spellers too low in the program so they were working on words they already knew. At any rate, the children were continued on the BRL spelling program the second quarter.

Testing at the end of the first semester indicated that the mean grade level of the class had continued to decrease to 2.8. Moreover, there was no systematic relationship between the absolute level of the grade-level scores which the children attained and the progress in grade-level scores during the two quarters. The spelling activity was summarily changed. A homemade spelling program in which children simply practiced spelling lists of words and then took tests over them was substituted for the BRL. Achievement test progress was much more acceptable during the third quarter of the year (See Figure 10-4).

No other sweeping changes in curriculum or teaching methods were dictated by analyses of achievement test results. However, one wonders how many thousands of classroom teachers each year spend time with curriculum materials and methods which are not producing desired results. Further, they may have no way of discovering the shortcomings because there are no systematic evaluation provisions. Achievement testing is by no means a panacea. In fact, such tests may not measure important behaviors. Scores for small groups of children can fluctuate widely. Giving and scoring the tests takes time. However, the test results can provide at least a piece in the evaluation puzzle.

Achievement test progress of individual children was carefully scrutinized by Cindy at the end of each quarter. Scores were difficult to evaluate because they fluctuated widely. On several occasions, she noted that a child's grade-level score had decreased substantially in some academic area. She retested these children on an alternate form of the same subtest during the next day. More often than not the newly obtained grade-level score was more in line with reasonable progress. However, if the second testing produced results consistent with the first, curriculum or teaching methods might be altered for a single child. A change was made if the testing results were consistent with data from weekly report cards or work-checks.

Weekly Report Cards   During the first year of the program, children took weekly report cards home to their parents. These were constructed by projecting the goals for a year's work in the Sullivan reading program and the Singer math program onto a sheet of graph paper. Figure 10-1 is an example of a weekly reading report for Brad. The vertical axis counts the number of pages worked since the beginning of the year. The horizontal axis marks the dates of the end of the school weeks. The dashed line indicates the rate at which the child must progress to complete the desired 2,000 pages in the program by the end of the school year. Daily assignments were always dated in the workbooks.

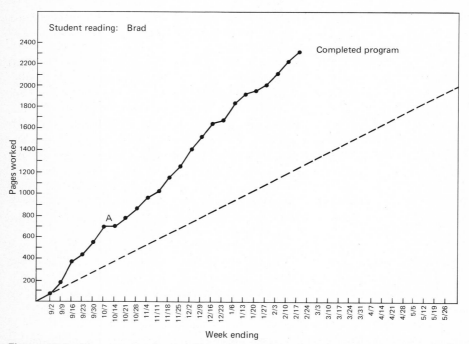

Figure 10-1 An example of a weekly report card to show a student's progress in the programmed reading series. The broken line defines the minimum rate of progress desired, the solid line, the student's actual progress.

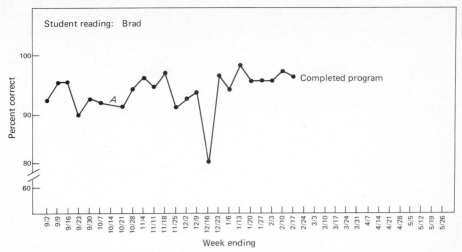

Figure 10-2 A weekly report card showing the percent of frames worked correctly in the programmed reading series.

Therefore, it was a simple matter to count the number of pages worked from the end of one week to the next. Brad had worked 540 pages by September 30. He worked about 160 pages during the next week. He completed the Sullivan program the week of February 17, having worked just over 2,300 pages since the beginning of the school year.

Initially, there was no indication of the accuracy of the work. We assumed that accuracy would always be maintained at 90 percent or higher in reading and 80 percent or higher in mathematics. The assumption was wrong. Parents indicated they wanted feedback on the accuracy of their children's work and the accuracy data were being kept anyway. Therefore, graphs showing the average weekly percent correct for both math and reading were added to the weekly report cards. Figure 10-2 is an example of one of the weekly accuracy graphs for reading.

Brad remained above the goal of at least 90 percent of the frames worked correctly every week except the one ending on December 16, when his weekly average fell to almost 80 percent. The A entered for the week ending on October 14 indicates that Brad was absent that week.

The weekly records were kept during the second year of the program. They were used by the teacher but were not sent home with the children. The records were often discussed during parent-teacher conferences, and they formed a partial basis for report card grades and for many important management decisions.

Brad's weekly reports illustrate how one type of information assisted in making decisions. During the week ending December 16, Brad completed almost 200 pages in the reading program, but the percent of frames he worked correctly decreased from a weekly average of 93 to just above 80. Rate of work and quality of work sometimes seesawed so that as one increased the other decreased. Perhaps Brad had worked rapidly, but relatively carelessly during that week. With this information, Cindy took care to reinforce correct work and perhaps put less emphasis on working rapidly, completing assignments, and finishing problems. Yes! Within wide limits, a teacher can easily cause children to be more careful or careless, faster or slower. If the speed and accuracy of academic work tend to offset each other, the teacher must be careful to maintain a balance between the two.

Careless speeding was a common problem at one time or another for about 30 percent of the children. There were fewer children whose work was very slow and highly accurate. It would hardly be functional to be 100 percent accurate, but complete only one page a day. If this threatened, Cindy was quick to reinforce fast work a bit more and accurate work a bit less.

The first books in the reading program were so carefully developed that a child could probably work a large proportion of the frames correctly by responding to contextual cues such as the pictures, while ignoring the words of the text. Therefore, Cindy was careful to give children reading in the lower books frequent brief opportunities to read frames orally. She, of course, differentially praised good reading and improvements in reading. Nevertheless, the weekly reports sometimes revealed steady work rates with sudden drops in accuracy when a child had progressed to about Book 6. This was about the point that children could no longer work the frames correctly by responding to contextual cues alone. If this occurred, Cindy checked to see if the child could correctly read the material. If he could, his accuracy problem was handled by simply reinforcing correct work. If the child could not orally read the material at that level in the program, she quickly checked back through the pages with him until his oral reading became acceptable. She would have him start reading at that point and would be careful to frequently reinforce correct work during the next few days.

Difficulties too numerous to detail were encountered in the math program. The hardback math books were duplicated so the children could work in them like workbooks. This change produced an immediate increase in the work rates on the weekly report cards. Most specific problems with math were probably detected on a daily basis as the papers were graded or when children asked for help. Occasional difficulties went undetected until the weekly reports were examined. A brief inspection of the weekly reports helped detect gradually developing trends such as an almost imperceptible slowdown over a period of three or four weeks.

Work-check Data   A special adaptation of the pla-check procedure (Risley and Cataldo, in press) was employed in the initial training of the teacher, in working out some of the teacher training methods and occasionally in troubleshooting specific problems. This data collection procedure was originally developed to be used as a theory-free evaluation device for Head Start, day care, and preschool programs. It is simple and easily learned. The basic idea is to simply count at some objectively determined time the number of children who are engaged in the planned activity. In the third-grade classroom, during seatwork assignments, for example, we might count the number of children seated, and oriented towards their work each time the sweep second hand of the stopwatch reaches 60. If we systematically look up one row and down the next, counting as rapidly as possible those children who are working, we are not likely to bias the data by waiting until Sammy at the back of the third row gets back to work. This procedure does not indicate if a child is doing a good job or actually accomplishing some work, but it shows that there is some chance that work is occurring. The number of children counted as being on task during each sweep can be divided by the number of children present to give a percentage independent of children leaving the classroom to go to the bathroom or leaving the work area to go to the free-time area.

A few examples of work-check data follow: Table 10-1 work-check data were taken during the first ten minutes of reading on September 2, early in the school year. Notice that the children do not get to work quickly and that there are never more than 65 percent at work at the same time.

Table 10-1 Work-check Data— Reading

Minute	Percent children working
1	30
2	45
3	40
4	65
5	60
6	60
7	35
8	40
9	55
10	65

A few weeks later, after Cindy had worked hard to teach the children to stick to their assignments and not be distracted by each other and by her frequent praise statements, the data in Table 10-2 were obtained. At this time, Cindy was doing a much better job getting a large percentage of the children on task because of her increased use of descriptive praise, praise across the room and praise while helping. Still, the children are not quick to get to work. A large percentage of them still were not working even five minutes into the period.

The noted slowness in getting to work prompted the development of the specialized reinforcement procedures to help children make transitions from one activity to another much more rapidly. After these transition procedures were in effect, the work-check data in Table 10-3 were taken at the beginning of a reading period. By the end of the first minute, 74 percent of the children are on task and the percentage remained high throughout the time the sample was taken.

To give you something to aim for as you begin to practice the teaching

**Table 10-2   Work-check Data—
Reading**

Minute	Percent children working
1	38
2	33
3	48
4	43
5	62
6	81
7	86
8	76
9	86
10	86

methods described above, the data in Table 10-4 represent the work behavior during an entire forty-minute reading period in the second year of the program. The data for minutes seven through twenty-nine are deleted because the percentage is always above 75. The percentage began to vary more widely during the last ten minutes because children were finishing assignments and causing some distractions as they moved from the work area to the play area. Moreover, the teacher was grading papers and was probably doing a less effective job of praising children for sticking to their work. At the end of the thirty-eighth minute, only six children remained in the work area, and only three of them were working. Data on work checks during math and spelling periods were generally less impressive than those taken during reading. In math there were many more times when a child needed the teacher's help before working ahead. This caused that child to go off task momentarily and it probably kept the teacher from working as effectively with the rest of the children. In addition, we suspected that reading was more intrinsically rewarding than math. In spelling, after the

**Table 10-3   Work-check Data—
Reading**

Minute	Percent children working
1	74
2	79
3	95
4	84
5	79
6	89
7	89
8	79
9	100
10	84

Table 10-4   Work-check Data—Reading

Minute	Percent children working
1	60
2	85
3	70
4	90
5	90
6	85
.	.
.	.
.	.
30	73
31	89
32	81
33	75
34	100
35	81
36	57
37	67
38	50
39	100
40	100

homemade spelling program was adopted, the children who were calling out words or waiting for the teacher to give them a test had relatively little to occupy their time.

The basic work-check data were primarily used then to evaluate the effectiveness of the teaching procedures and as a means of providing an approximate overall evaluation of an academic period.

Slight variations on this procedure can provide more detailed information on the work performance of a particular child. For example, if a child's weekly report card indicates that a child is not working at a desirable rate, a work-check on him alone will quickly reveal if he is staying on task but working slowly, or if he is perhaps dawdling or daydreaming a considerable part of the time. In the first case, the teacher should start praising his working fast, completing pages of his work, etc. In the latter case, she should frequently glance at the daydreamer or dawdler and praise him from across the room when he is on task. The section on teaching methods gives more detail on how each of these methods can be used.

Data systems can provide an evaluation of procedures used to solve specific behavior problems of individual children. Examples of such systems are dealt with extensively in other chapters and need not be treated here.

Daily Schedule   Every teacher knows that there is no such thing as a daily schedule which applies to all days. Schedules are constantly modified to accommodate heavy snowfalls, trips to have school pictures made, half-days necessitated by parent-teacher conferences, the regular school parties, and the student who becomes very ill just as music is about to begin. A typical day might be:

8:30–8:40	Attendance, milk money
8:40–9:40	Mathematics
9:40–10:00	Writing
10:00–10:20	Recess
10:20–10:50	Spelling
10:50–11:20	Social studies
11:20–11:45	Multiplication drill
11:45–12:15	Lunch
12:15–12:45	Lunch recess
12:45–1:30	Science
1:30–2:00	Composition
2:00–2:20	Recess
2:20–2:30	Music
2:30–3:20	Reading

Fifty-minute reading and one-hour math periods were somehow included in the schedule every day even if a day was shortened by a field trip or parent-teacher conferences. What may be misleading about the schedule is that these times for starting a period were really followed. In some classrooms, starting reading at 2:30 might mean that the teacher begins to try to get the children in their seats at 2:30, assignments are given out at 2:38, and a few children still do not begin until 2:45. In Super School, because of the teaching methods used, it took 10 to 20 seconds to get all children from one activity (returning from recess) to another (being ready to begin reading). Assignments usually required less than a minute. After assignments were made, 80 percent of the children would be working on them after only one or two minutes.

RESULTS

Achievement Tests

The major academic evaluation of Super School is quite straightforward. The quarterly achievement test progress in reading is shown in Figure 10-3. At the beginning of the year, the class average on the Paragraph Meaning subtest was a bit less than the 3.0 expected on the basis of national norms. According to the norm data of the achievement tests, the progress to be expected during a school year is about 0.8 grade levels. (It is surprising to some people that the expected rate of progress during the summer months is apparently only slightly lower than the rate expected during the school year.) Therefore, according to national averages, the third-grade children would be expected to progress to about the 3.8 to 3.9 grade level by the end of the year. The goal set for the project was to have the children progress at a rate twice that of the national average. Progress in reading exceeded this goal by a comfortable margin.

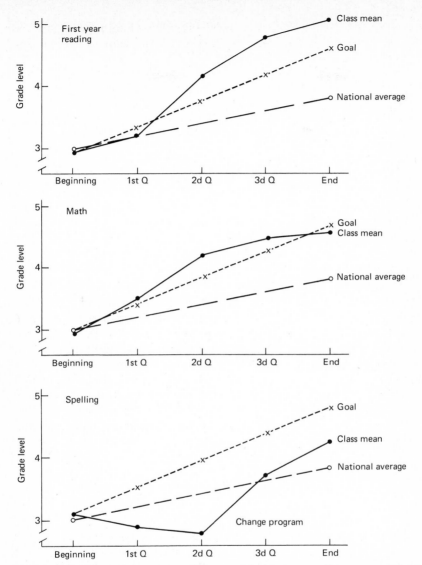

Figure 10-3 Plots of the mean achievement test scores on the paragraph meaning, math computation, and spelling subtests at the beginning of the school year and at the end of each quarter during the first year of the third grade.

Progress in achievement test scores on the Metropolitan's Mathematics Computation subtest was slightly less than had been set by the goal. Progress in spelling was uneven. The average score became worse through the first two quarters and then improved markedly during the last two quarters after the spelling program was changed. Still, overall progress fell short of the goal by about 0.5 grade levels. Progress on the other subtests, the Stanford Word

Meaning and Metropolitan Mathematics Concepts tests, given throughout the year was closely correlated with the results shown.

Results of the second year were similar to these obtained during the first year. At the beginning of the second year the mean grade level of the class was 3.71 on paragraph meaning and increased 1.83 grade levels to 5.54 at the end of the school year. The mean spelling-achievement test score increased from the 3.24 grade level to 5.10 for an increase of 1.86 grade levels. The mean of the math scores increased 2.26 grade levels from 2.96 at the first of the year to 5.22 at the end of the year.

A different perspective of progress can be obtained by comparing the distribution of percentile scores at the beginning of the year to the distribution of percentiles at the end of the year. This comparison can be made for the second year by inspecting Figure 10-4. The entire distribution of reading percentile scores is moved toward the higher end of the scale during the school year. Of particular interest to the special educator is the fact that the entire lower end of the distribution is displaced upward. The four children scoring in the first decile at the beginning of the year moved into the second and third deciles by the end of the year. With continuing improvement in percentile scores, the distribution must become progressively more negatively skewed as fewer children score at the lower end of the scale and more and more children pile up at the top of the distribution. The distributions for math and spelling for the second year and all distributions for first year reading, math, and spelling were qualitatively similar.

Parent Feedback

At the end of the second school year, but unfortunately not at the end of both years, the parents of all children in the third grade were sent questionnaires

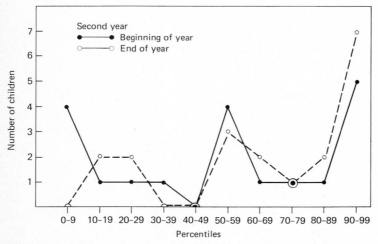

Figure 10-4 Distribution of percentile scores on the paragraph meaning subtest at the beginning and end of the second year of the third grade.

and asked to mail them back anonymously. Samples of a few questions asked and the percent of respondents giving various answers are listed in Table 10-5 (p. 376). In response to a request for suggestions on ways the program could be improved, many parents simply left that section of the questionnaire blank. Three responded that they were "satisfied" or "couldn't be happier." Two suggested that there be more emphasis on artistic and musical creativity. One indicated that he would like more frequent feedback on his child's school activities and progress. One suggested that his child needed more experience in praising to enable him to be complimentary in a more sincere way. One simply requested that the program be continued for another year.

A similar questionnaire was given to the children by the senior author at the end of the school year. Table 10-6 (p. 378) gives sample questions and the percent of children giving various responses.

In an informal discussion with the senior author after the questionnaire had been completed, the children were not too articulate in making specific suggestions to improve the program. However, they named a number of things they did or did not like. Three boys indicated they did not like the "point system," which was about the only punishment procedure used in the class. Several said the school year was too long. A few said it was too short. Three girls said they did not like gym. Several said they thought the fourth graders tried to act too big. There were many positive comments about Cindy's teaching methods and a recent field trip to Robbie Green's grandfather's farm. Several said they liked having carpeting in the classroom and being able to take off their shoes during academic periods. Two children volunteered amid giggles that Mr. Finkbinder, some imaginary principal whose role was occasionally played by the senior author, "wasn't very mean."

Specific Problems

There is no efficient way to detail the many positive changes in classroom and problem behaviors which occurred during both school years. All but a very few children who were excellent students to begin with became better workers. This was reflected both in work-check data and in the weekly report cards. The relatively distractible children who would be labeled as having poor attention spans had generally developed very satisfactory rates of work by the end of the third or fourth weeks of school. Sally was gradually taught to not jump from desk to desk. Her episodic cursing was largely eliminated by Christmas of her third-grade year. By the end of her fourth-grade year, she was a model of mature serenity. Patricia was abruptly taught to not stab and steal, and she was gradually integrated into social activities with the other children. Pouting gradually died out as children found that it did not pay off as well as some more socially agreeable reactions to life's adversities.

Some of the program's most rewarding results were those complex behaviors we call happiness and other attitudes which are so difficult to measure that we never bother to try. The children's and parents' questionnaire responses are partial information. However, they do not reflect the complexity of behavior we

Table 10-5 Questions Asked Parents at the End of the School Year, and the Percent of Respondents Giving the Indicated Answers

Overall, in comparison to other schools my child has attended, we think Haworth Hall has been:

	Worse						Better
	1	2	3	4	5	6	7
Percent:	0	0	0	0	8	25	67

In each of the following areas, how much do you think your child has benefited from Haworth Hall in comparison to other schools he has attended:

		Worse						Better
		1	2	3	4	5	6	7
Reading	Percent:	0	0	0	0	17	17	67
Math	Percent:	0	0	0	8	8	8	75
Spelling	Percent:	0	0	0	0	8	0	92
Science	Percent:	0	0	0	0	8	8	83
Social studies	Percent:	0	0	0	0	8	42	50
Art	Percent:	0	0	25	25	17	17	17
Music	Percent:	0	8	25	17	25	0	25
Cursive writing	Percent:	0	0	0	25	0	25	50
Grammar	Percent:	0	0	0	17	25	25	33
Writing composition	Percent:	0	0	8	0	42	8	42
Development of social skills	Percent:	0	8	0	17	0	42	33
Handling of special problems	Percent:	0	0	0	17	0	42	42
Development of a good attitude	Percent:	0	0	0	8	0	17	75

How happy is your child with school?

	Unhappy						Happy
	1	2	3	4	5	6	7
Percent:	0	0	0	8	0	8	83

How happy are you with your child's teacher?

	Unhappy						Happy
	1	2	3	4	5	6	7
Percent:	0	0	0	8	8	8	75

If your child could relive this school year, do you think he would again want to attend school at Haworth Hall?

	No						Yes
	1	2	3	4	5	6	7
Percent:	0	0	0	0	0	0	100

If you could relive this school year, would you again send your child to Haworth Hall?

	No						Yes
	1	2	3	4	5	6	7
Percent:	0	0	0	0	0	0	100

Table 10-5 (continued)

We encourage our teachers to encourage their students with positive comments. In this respect, do you think the teacher has used too many or too few positive comments for your child?	Too few			About right			Too many
	1	2	3	4	5	6	7
Percent:	0	0	0	75	8	17	0

We encourage our teachers to use very little criticism of their students. In this respect, do you think the teacher has used too much or too little criticism for your child?	Too little			About right			Too much
	1	2	3	4	5	6	7
Percent:	0	0	0	100	0	0	0

If our teachers feel they must use criticism with their students, we encourage them to generally deliver the criticism as unemotionally as possible. In this respect, do you think your child's teacher has been too unemotional or too emotional?	Too unemotional			About right			Too emotional
	1	2	3	4	5	6	7
Percent:	0	0	0	92	8	0	0

With respect to classroom discipline, do you think your child's teacher has been too strict or too lax?	Too strict			About right			Too lax
	1	2	3	4	5	6	7
Percent:	0	0	0	92	8	0	0

call happiness. The children learned to respond more appropriately to each other's desirable behaviors and they developed some skills in not responding to inappropriate behaviors. They were admittedly self-conscious and insincere sounding when these skills first began to develop. During the fall of the second year, the senior author overheard a conversation in the hallway which went something like this, "I like the way you are walking on the right side of the hall, Rosalyn." There were a few giggles, "Well, I like the way you are praising me for walking on the right side, Mikelan." More giggles, "Well, I like the way you are praising me for praising you for . . . !"

The project staff received many informal reports from parents that the children were becoming much more positive in social situations at home. Several said that our third graders had become more cooperative and effective in interacting with other children than were the parents themselves. One mother commented that she did not like the way her son had learned to ignore her when she was trying to get him to do something. Around school there were many instances in which the children used their behavioral skills very effectively, like

Table 10-6   Questions Asked Children at the End of the School Year, and the Percent of Children Giving the Indicated Answers

		No	Some	Very happy
Are you happy you came to school at Haworth Hall?		1	2	3
	Percent:	0	14	86

		Not much	Some	A lot
How much do you like your teacher?		1	2	3
	Percent:	0	0	100

		Not much	Some	A lot
How encouraging is your teacher in helping you to want to do your work?		1	2	3
	Percent:	0	21	79

		Not often	Some	A lot
How often does your teacher say nice things to you?		1	2	3
	Percent:	21	7	72

		Not often	Some	A lot
How often does your teacher criticize you?		1	2	3
	Percent:	7	21	72

the day the frequently belligerent and easily provoked Sally walked away from an opportunity to fight and three children immediately began bragging about it. Every child in the third grade during the second year could assume the teacher's duties and run a very effective work period for up to twenty minutes with no assistance.

RETROSPECTIONS

Hindsight is infallible. There are always thousands of rational sounding second guesses for even relatively rewarding projects. The following are a few we would like to share with teachers who might try to duplicate the program.

There is so much guesswork involved in selecting curriculum materials that it is surprising that children are as successful in school as they are. Teachers do not have time or resources to thoroughly test materials they are currently using or to investigate those they are considering. Perhaps they should use a periodic achievement test program to determine if their materials and methods are performing as intended. If these data are not satisfactory, about the only thing a teacher can do is change her materials, methods, or both.

When Super School began, some project staff believed that even poor materials are good enough if a teacher has sufficiently effective teaching methods to cause the children to become interested in what they are doing and diligent in their work. This opinion still exists. Nevertheless it must at least be tempered. If the things children are working on do not teach them what we want them to learn, good teaching and motivation methods are limited. In addition, materials in which concepts and skills are well organized and well presented can make the teachers' jobs much easier and help children experience a great deal more success. Finally, there is constant talk among curriculum experts that materials must be intrinsically interesting or rewarding. We would agree. However, writers and publishers often take the easy way out on this issue and do little more than splash a little color on pages.

Educators are at the mercy of publishers. They can only use what publishers sell. Publishers are not responsible for educating children, but for making money by selling books and materials. Their major responsibility is to sell whatever makes the most money. If school districts began to seriously evaluate the materials they use and refuse to buy those which do not fulfill their purported purposes, publishers might become more interested in educating children and making teachers' jobs easier.

The teaching methods worked as they were designed to work. If we made an error with them, it was only in not using them more aggressively than we did. We sometimes have a tendency, when problems arise, to wait and hope they go away. Sometimes they do go away. However, the odds are that they will remain. It is a much better strategy to have the teacher begin to work with problems as soon as they are noticed. Dozens of times Cindy noted that a child was becoming more careless with his work or a bit of a bully on the playground. Many such situations were corrected without any special intervention. However, if the problems did not disappear in a week or two, some intervention was required and the problem was then probably slower to get corrected than if it had been dealt with when it was first noticed.

The goals of achievement test progress twice the national norm now seem quite arbitrary. It would probably require no real overextension of the teaching methods to produce gains three or four times the national norms. There were many free minutes that could have been devoted to more reading or math during every school day. From the beginning of an academic period to the end of it, the Super School third graders probably devoted much less time to academics, particularly in the case of reading, than children do in most public schools. However, it is difficult to believe that children need to learn more than Super School third graders were learning.

When the program began, we hoped that individualization of instruction and powerful teaching methods would serve to narrow the gap between the advanced students and those who were academically much less skillful. The speculation was that the advanced students would continue to make good progress and the less skillful would make even more progress until the distribution of skills was narrowed. We guessed that the slower children had simply never learned to work or follow instructions and that they would begin to catch up with good teaching methods. Figure 10-4, which shows the changes in the distribution of percentile scores during one year, could be interpreted as confirming this expectation. However, it should be remembered that there is a ceiling at the ninety-ninth percentile so that once a child has reached this point, further improvement on achievement test scores cannot be reflected in the distribution.

From a different viewpoint, the advanced children benefited from the program more than their less-advanced classmates. The average grade levels of progress of children in the top half of the distributions were always greater than the progress of children in the lower half of the distributions. Perhaps the advanced students had been averaging 1.5 grade levels of progress each year before they entered the third grade where their progress quickly increased to 2.0 or 2.5 grade levels per year. A less advanced student may have been making only 0.5 grade levels per year and increased to 1.2 grade levels per year. His percentage gain was greater than that made by his more skillful classmates. However, he was at a disadvantage to begin with and his absolute gain in grade levels is still less than that of some of his classmates. Therefore, at the end of the school year there is a greater gap between the top and bottom of the distribution than at the beginning.

There is a real possibility that every improvement in educational practice will benefit relatively skillful children more than their less fortunate classmates. If this is the case, the special or compensatory educator who would improve the lot of his students may face a never-ending task. If he can produce technical improvements that will immediately help his children learn more, these same improvements are likely to benefit bright students even more.

TEACHER-TRAINING METHODS

The school psychologist, special education coordinator, or teacher who might wish to duplicate the third grade teaching methods will encounter one difficulty. How do you learn or teach someone else to carry out all the complex procedures in a smooth fashion so that they become a natural part of teachers' styles of working with children?

Research on teaching (Gage, 1963) has been devoted more to describing teaching and analyzing characteristics of teachers than to finding ways to teach more effectively. Nonetheless, there are a few reliable cornerstones. Modeling may be an effective procedure to communicate to teachers the complex methods involved in effective teaching (McDonald & Allen, 1967). Independent of the method by which instruction is given to teachers, some form of feedback regarding their performance apparently helps them reach established goals (McDonald & Allen, 1967; Thomas, 1971; Cossairt, Hall, & Hopkins, 1973). There is evidence that objective criteria for specific teaching methods facilitate acquisition and maintenance of those methods (Saudargas, 1972; Vazquez & Hopkins, 1973).

By integrating modeling, objective criteria, and immediate feedback into a basic training package, the combined advantages suggest that many of the seemingly complex teaching methods employed in Super School can, in fact, be duplicated by other teachers in many different teaching situations. The authors are currently refining and further evaluating this training program.

Selecting and Sequencing Teaching Methods

The first step in the development of the training program was to select and specify as objectively as possible the methods to be taught to teachers. The methods employed in Super School and described under "Teaching Methods" became the core of the program. Two guides were followed in determining the order in which these methods would be taught before those that are more complex or difficult; 1) methods which are prerequisites for others should be taught first; and 2) whenever possible, those methods which will help teachers and their students most should be taught first. The final order corresponds to the order in which the skills are described under "Teaching Methods."

Modeling

Rather than using master teachers modeling the methods for teachers in training, the program employs video tapes of teachers demonstrating the various procedures. The use of video tapes provides a number of advantages over live models. The tapes can be easily transported and used at the convenience of the teacher trainees. By narration and editing it is possible to focus a particular video taped sequence on one or a few teaching skills rather than having a master teacher demonstrate a bewildering array of methods. Video tapes allow convenient staging of particular critical incidents which occur infrequently in a live teaching situation. The methods are presented in eighteen, four- to eight-minute video tapes. These tapes provide the models for each of the 18 lessons of the program.

Lesson Criteria

Specific behavioral objectives have been written for each lesson. These are generally quantitative and specify how often a teacher is to use the methods described in particular lessons. For example, Lesson One is concerned with moving about the classroom. The criteria for it are that the teacher trainee will move in an unpredictable pattern and interact with at least 20 children per five minutes of time. To some extent the criteria are cumulative over lessons so that for Lesson Three, a teacher must meet the objectives for Lesson One, Two, and Three.

Feedback to Teachers

After a teacher has watched a video tape for a particular lesson and has had a few days to practice the skills specified for that lesson, she is visited by a member of the training staff who gives her a check-out over the lesson. These check-outs are at least five minutes long. An observation code and recording procedures help the training staff accurately record the teachers' frequency of use of the various methods. This record becomes the primary source of feedback to the teachers.

Passing and Recycling

If the feedback record indicates that a teacher has met or exceeded the criteria for a given lesson, she automatically passes that lesson. She can, in fact, immediately ask for a check-out over the next lesson if she has already seen the corresponding video tape. If a teacher does not meet the criteria on a given check-out, it is not treated as a failure. Instead, the teacher is given a copy of the record which indicates the ways in which her performance was different from the criteria. She then can immediately take a new check-out over that lesson or wait, watch the video tape again, and take another check-out during the next staff visit to her classroom. This means that a teacher never fails a lesson. She eventually masters every method of the program. In addition, the program is individualized so that teachers may work through the eighteen lessons as rapidly or as slowly as their interest, schedules, and skills allow. Each may progress at a comfortable rate.

SUMMARY

The technology is available to make drastic improvements in the quality of education received by all children whether they are normal, accelerated, or members of various arbitrary special groups. Moreover, children like the Super School form of education and it is generally approved by their parents. Finally, teachers or persons about to become teachers can easily learn to use the methods, and instructors, school administrators, or consultants have the technology available to allow them to train teachers to carry out the methods.

Formal evaluations of new programs are necessary to keep us honest—to help us use only those innovations which benefit children. However, more subjective and emotional forms of feedback are often our strongest reinforcers. The children's attitudes toward Super School were reflected in ways other than through their positive comments on the questionnaires. Two parents reported that their children had frequently whined and tried to avoid going to school in the morning while they were in the second grade and that these problems completely disappeared in Super School. Toward the end of the second school year, the children began asking if they could continue in Super School the next year. They were told that the prospects were poor because the grants which had partially supported the third and fourth grades were expiring and the school district had given no indication that it would support the program. At that same time, a local radio station was conducting a treasure hunt by giving out daily clues about where $1,000 had been hidden. As a late spring afternoon recess ended, a group of girls ran up to the senior author and handed him a hastily written note which read:

Dear Mr. Finkbinder,
        During the thousand dollar hunt, some of us girls in the third grade were hunting. We were going to give it to you so there could be a fourth and fifth grade. We are very sorry that we didn't find it.

Love,

Katie	Amal
Mikelan	Denise
Loretta	Christine
Kathy	Maria

DISCUSSION TOPICS

Putting It All Together: Super School

Objective   This chapter is a description of a model classroom which incorporates behavior modification techniques in dealing with learning or achievement problems. In describing the Super School program, it offers model suggestions to the student in the areas of:

1   Effective teaching methods
2   Data management
3   Selection of curriculum
4   Implementation of methodology

Exercises   Assuming you were implementing the methods outlined in this chapter in your own "super" classroom, write a brief description of how you would react in each of the following situations:

1   Joe has trouble in math. When time comes to work on math, he refuses to even attempt to work the problems.
2   When you "lecture," Mary Sue takes out her purse and starts playing with its contents.
3   Each time you praise Kim, she runs over to you and hugs you.
4   Each time you praise another student, Paula goes to that student's desk to look at what she has done.
5   Kelly has trouble in spelling. As you walk around the room, he looks at other students' papers for the correct answers. Most of the time you see him, but once you did not and praised him for a correct answer.
6   Keith makes a big show and brags when he has to put a point beside his name on the blackboard.
7   Paula needs long periods of help in her science work. She will work as long as you are standing by her desk and helping her. When you walk away or praise some other student, she quits working.
8   Because of a water shortage at the school, your school day is reduced to three hours a day, from 8:30 to 11:30 a.m., for a week. You must change the schedule to fit this condition.
9   Sally hits you each time you touch her.
10   Tommy acts out often in class. He prefers staying alone in the classroom or sitting on the side during recess.
11   You have allowed 10 minutes for the class to work on individual art projects. Beth hurriedly and inaccurately has finished hers after three minutes and is staring out the window.

12   Matt does not like to sit at his desk. He quietly and accurately does all of his work while standing behind his desk.

13   Whenever Art addresses you, he calls you "Teach."

14   Kelly has a broken arm and it will be in a cast for six weeks. It is not his preferred arm so he can still do his assignments. However, he whines and complains that his arm hurts whenever he is asked to do any work.

15   Joel does not like for you to put any marks on his papers and pushes your hand away whenever you try.

16   Karen is a model student during classroom work. However, when she is allowed to go to the free-time area, she wanders from student to student—hitting them and disrupting their activities.

17   When you begin reducing the amount of praise for Sally's work, she begins crying and complaining that you do not like her anymore.

18   Whenever she thinks you are not looking, Stacy pinches the student nearest her.

19   John's achievement test at the end of the first quarter shows a marked decrease in his spelling scores.

20   Lenny's parents call you every Friday evening and talk for nearly an hour, generally complaining about the progress of their child. You are not sure they understand that Lenny is making progress.

21   Carol had a kidney infection for two weeks and had to be given permission to go to the bathroom several times a day. The infection is gone, but she still asks to go to the bathroom just as frequently.

22   Most of your class seems to be working at their social studies assignment. Your principal has asked you to tell him what percentage is attending to their work.

23   Curt's report card shows that he is not working at a rate as high as you think he should. You are not sure if he is working slowly or if he is daydreaming and wasting work time.

24   You are asked by your principal to set up guidelines for a curriculum selection. These need to be *principles* for selection rather than specific names of programs.

25   The spelling book you want to use for several students is no longer available. No other material fills the needs of the students as well.

NOTES

1   This work was supported in part by the U.S. Office of Education through a grant, OEG-0-70-1820(725) Training Teachers of Teachers in Behavior Modification in Early Childhood Education, and in part by a grant from the National Institute of Child Health and Development, HD-02528. Preparation of the manuscript was partially supported by Social and Rehabilitative Services grant, 59-P-35116/7. Many persons provided consultation and assistance in setting up the classroom. Particular thanks are due to Karen Blase, George Semb, and Brian Jacobson, graduate students at the time the project was carried out and especially to Cynthia Jacobson and Sherrill Bushell, teachers.

2   Mr. Robert Taylor, Elementary Coordinator, Dr. David Kendall, Assistant Superintendent for Instruction, and Dr. Karl Knox, Superintendent, were helpful in making the initial arrangements. Mr. Donald Sheppard, Mr. Robert Lowther, Mr. Michael Carpino, Dr. Ray Miller, Mrs. Helen Norwood, Mr. Garry Stouffer and Mrs. Betty Fields helped us to attend to may details of busing, getting school pictures made, keeping up with school records, etc., which were not unique aspects of the program, but were essential to the well-being and happiness of our children.

REFERENCES

Abeson, A. *A continuing summary of pending and completed litigation regarding the education of handicapped children*. Arlington, Va.: Council for Exceptional Children, 1973.

Adelman, H. S. Remedial classroom instruction revisited. *The Journal of Special Education,* 1971, **5,** 311–322.

Allen, K. E., Hart, B. M., Buell, J. S., Harris, F. R., & Wolf, M. M. Effects of social reinforcement on isolate behavior of a nursery school child. *Child Development,* 1964, **35,** 511–518.

Ammons, R. B. & Ammons, H. The full-range picture vocabulary test, Missoula, Montana: *Psychological Reports,* 1968.

Anderson, R. L., & Bancroft, T. A. *Statistical Theory in Research,* McGraw-Hill, 1955.

Aram, D. & Nation, J. *Developmental language disorders: Patterns of language behavior*. Paper presented at the American Speech and Hearing Association Convention, San Francisco, 1972.

Ausubel, D. *Reading in school learning*. New York: Holt, Rinehart and Winston, 1969.

Azrin, N. H., Bugle, C. P., & O'Brien, F. Behavioral engineering: Two apparatuses for toilet training retarded children. *Journal of Applied Behavior Analysis,* 1971, **4,** 249–253.

Azrin, N. H., & Lindsley, O. R. The reinforcement of cooperation between children. *Journal of Abnormal and Social Psychology,* 1956, **52,** 100–102.

Baer, D. M., and Guess, D. Receptive training of adjective inflections in mental retardates. *Journal of Applied Behavior Analysis,* 1971, **4,** 129–139.

Baer, D. M., Peterson, R. F., & Sherman, J. A. The development of imitation by reinforcing behavioral similarity to a model. *Journal of Experimental Analysis of Behavior,* 1967, **10,** 405–416.

Baer, D. M., & Sherman, J. A. Reinforcement control of generalized imitation in young children. *Journal of Experimental Child Psychology,* 1964, **1,** 37–49.

Baer, D. M., Wolf, M. M., & Risley, T. R. Some current dimensions of applied behavior analysis. *Journal of Applied Behavior Analysis,* 1968, **1,** 91–97.

Baker, R., & Ryan, B. *Programmed conditioning for articulation.* Behavior Sciences Institute, Monterey, Calif., 1971.

Ball, T. A. *Itard, Seguin & Kephart: Sensory education—A learning interpretation.* Columbus, Ohio: Merrill, 1971.

Barton, E. S., Guess, D., Garcia, E., & Baer, D. M. Improvements of retardates' mealtime behaviors by timeout procedures using multiple baseline techniques. *Journal of Applied Behavior Analysis,* 1970, **3,** 77–84.

Baumeister, A. A., & Klosowski, R. An attempt to group toilet train severely retarded patients. *Mental Retardation,* 1965, **3,** 24–26.

Becker, W. C., Englemann, S., & Thomas D. R. *Teaching: A course in applied psychology.* Chicago: Science Research Associates, Inc., 1971.

Becker, W. C., Madsen, C. H., Jr., Arnold, C., & Thomas, D. R. The contingent use of teacher attention and praise in reducing classroom behavior problems. *Journal of Special Education,* 1967, **1,** 287–307.

Bellugi, U. Development of language in the normal child. In J. E. McLean, D. E. Yoder, & R. L. Schiefelbusch (Eds.), *Language intervention with the retarded.* Baltimore: University Park Press, 1972.

Bellugi-Klima, U. *Evaluating the young child's language competence.* National Laboratory on Early Childhood Education, Washington, D.C.: Educational Resource Information Center (ERIC), 1968.

Bensberg, G. J. *Teaching the mentally retarded.* Atlanta: Southern Regional Educational Board, 1965.

Berger, S. L. A clinical program for developing multimodal language with atypical deaf children. In J. E. McLean, E. E. Yoder, & R. L. Schiefelbusch (Eds.), *Language intervention with the retarded.* Baltimore: University Park Press, 1972, **10,** 212–235.

Berry, M. F. *Language disorders of children: The bases and diagnoses.* New York: Appleton-Century-Crofts, 1969.

Bijou, S. Application of experimental analysis of behavior principles in teaching academic tool subjects to retarded children. In N. Haring and R. Whelan (Eds.), *The Learning Environment: Relationship to behavior modification and implications for special education.* Lawrence, Kansas: University of Kansas Press, 1966.

Billingsley, F. F., & Smelser, S. J. *A group contingency system: An analysis of group component effects.* Unpublished manuscript, Experimental Education Unit, Seattle, 1973.

Billingsley, F. F., & Smelser, S. J. A group approach to classroom management: The behavior game. *Teaching Exceptional Children,* 1974, **7:**1, 30–33.

Birnbrauer, J. S., Wolf, M. M., Kidder, J. D., & Tague, C. E. Classroom behavior of retarded pupils with token reinforcement. *Journal of Experimental Child Psychology,* 1965, **2,** 219–235.

Bloom, B. S., Hastings, J. T., & Madaus, G. F. *Handbook on formative and summative evaluation of student learning.* New York: McGraw-Hill, 1971.

Bloom, L. *Language development: Form and function in emerging grammars.* Cambridge, Mass.: The M.I.T. Press, 1970.

Bloom, L. Semantic features in language development. In R. L. Schiefelbusch (Ed.), *Language of the mentally retarded.* Baltimore: University Park Press, 1972, 19–34.

Bowerman, M. *Learning to talk: A cross-linguistic comparison of early syntactic developments, with special reference to Finnish.* London: Cambridge University Press, 1973.

Bowers, C. A. Accountability from a humanist point of view. *Educational Forum,* 1971, **35,** 479–486.

Breland, M. Application of method. In G. J. Bensberg (Ed.), *Teaching mentally retarded children.* Atlanta: Southern Regional Educational Board, 1965.

Bricker, D. D. Imitative sign training as a facilitator of word-object association with low-functioning children. *American Journal of Mental Deficiency,* 1972, **76,** 509–516.

Bricker, W. A. A systematic approach to language training. In R. L. Schiefelbusch (Ed.), *Language of the mentally retarded.* Baltimore: University Park Press, 1972.

Bricker, D. D., & Bricker, W. A. Toddler research and intervention project report: Year I. *IMRID Behavioral Science Monograph No. 20, Institute on Mental Retardation and Intellectual Development.* Nashville: George Peabody College, 1971.

Bricker, D. D., & Bricker, W. A. Toddler research and intervention project report: Year II. *IMRID Behavioral Science Monograph No. 21, Institute on Mental Retardation and Intellectual Development.* Nashville: George Peabody College, 1972.

Bricker, D. D., & Bricker, W. A. Toddler research and intervention project report: Year III. *IMRID Behavioral Science Monograph No. 23, Institute on Mental Retardation and Intellectual Development.* Nashville: George Peabody College, 1973.

Bricker, W. A., & Bricker, D. D. Development of receptive vocabulary in severely retarded children. *American Journal of Mental Deficiency,* 1970, **74,** 599–607. (a)

Bricker, W. A., & Bricker, D. D. A program of language training for the severely language handicapped child. *Exceptional Children,* 1970, **37,** 101–111. (b)

Bricker, W. A., & Bricker, D. D. An early language training strategy. In R. L. Schiefelbusch & L. L. Lloyd (Eds.), *Language perspectives: Acquisition, retardation, and intervention.* Baltimore: University Park Press, 1974.

Brigham, T. A., Graubard, P. S., & Stans, A. Analysis of the effects of sequential reinforcement contingencies on aspects of composition. *Journal of Applied Behavior Analysis,* 1972, **5,** 421–429.

Broden, M., Hall, R. V., Dunlap, A., & Clark, R. Effects of teacher attention and a token reinforcement system in a junior high school special education class. *Exceptional Children,* 1970, **36,** 341–349.

Broen, P. A. The verbal environment of the language-learning child. *ASHA Monograph No. 17,* 1972.

Brown, M. C., & Devine, P. *A reorganization plan for enhancing normalization of institutionalized mentally retarded residents.* (Parsons University Affiliated Facility and Parsons Research Center Working Paper 295). Parsons, Kansas: Parsons State Hospital and Training Center, 1973.

Brown, R. *Psycholinguistics.* New York: Free Press, 1970.

Brown, R. *A first language: The early stages.* Cambridge, Mass.: Harvard University Press, 1973.

Brown, R., Copeland, R., & Hall, R. V. The school principal as a behavior modifier. *Journal of Educational Research,* 1972, **66,** 175–180.

Brown, R. W., & Bellugi, U. Three processes in the child's acquisition of syntax. *Harvard Educational Review,* 1964, **34,** 133–151.

Bruner, J. S., Goodnow, J. J., & Austin, G. A. *A study of thinking.* New York: Wiley, 1956.

Buchanan, C. D. *Spelling: A Sullivan Associates Program.* Palo Alto: Behavioral Research Laboratories, 1967.

Cain, L. F., & Levine, S. *A study of the effects of community and institutional school classes for trainable mentally retarded children.* San Francisco: San Francisco State College, 1961.

Cain, L. F., Levine, S. D., & Elzey, F. I. *Manual for the Cain-Levine Social Competency Scale.* Palo Alto: Consulting Psychologists Press, 1963.

Carrier, J. K. Application of functional analysis and a non-speech response mode to teaching language. (Parsons [Kansas] Research Center Report No. 7). Parsons, Kansas: Parsons State Hospital and Training Center, 1973.

Carroll, J. B. Psycholinguistics in the study of mental retardation. In R. L. Schiefelbusch, R. H. Copeland, and J. O. Smith (Eds.), *Language and mental retardation.* New York: Holt, Rinehart and Winston, 1967, 39–53.

Carrow, E. Assessment of speech and language in children. In J. E. McLean, D. E. Yoder, & R. L. Schiefelbusch (Eds.), *Language intervention with the retarded.* Baltimore: University Park Press, 1972, 52–88.

Carrow, E. *Test for auditory comprehension of language.* Austin, Texas: Learning Concepts, 1973.

Cazden, C. The acquisition of noun and verb inflections. *Child Development,* 1968, **39,** 433–448.

Cazden, C. B. Evaluation of learning in preschool education: Early language development. In B. S. Bloom, J. T. Hastings, & G. T. Madaus (Eds.), *Handbook on formative and summative evaluation of student learning.* New York: McGraw-Hill, 1971.

Chavez, A. L. *An evaluation of the applicability of a responsive teaching workshop replicated in a Latin American country.* Unpublished Masters Thesis, University of Kansas, Lawrence, Kansas, 1973.

Christopoles, F., & Renz, P. A. A critical examination of special education programs. *Journal of Special Education,* 1969, **3,** 371–379.

Clark, M., & Hall, R. V. *Parents as modifiers of behavior in preschool children,* Manuscript submitted to *Child Development,* 1973.

Clark, M., & Hall, R. V. *Behavior Modification of problem behaviors by parents using a responsive teaching approach.* Manuscript submitted for publication, 1974.

Clark, M., Lachowicz, J., & Wolf, M. A pilot basic education system for school dropouts incorporating a token reinforcement system. *Behaviour Research and Therapy,* 1968, **6,** 183–188.

Conlon, M. F., Hall, C., & Hanley, E. M. The effects of a peer procedure on the arithmetic accuracy for two elementary school children. In G. Semb (Ed.), *Behavior analysis and education, 1972.* Lawrence, Kansas: University of Kansas Press, 1972.

Copeland, R., Brown, R., Axelrod, S., & Hall, R. V. Effects of a school principal praising parents for student attendance. *Educational Technology,* 1972, **12,** 56–59.

Copeland, R., Brown, R., & Hall, R. V. School phobia: Effects of behavior modification treatment applied by an elementary school principal. *Child Study Journal,* 1974, **4,** No. 3, 125–133.

Cossairt, A., Hall, R. V., & Hopkins, B. L. The effects of experimenter's instructions, feedback and praise on teacher praise and student attending behavior. *Journal of Applied Behavior Analysis,* 1973, **6,** 89–100.

Creelman, M. *The experimental investigation of meaning.* New York: Springer, 1966.

Cruickshank, W. M., & Johnson, G. O. (Eds.), *Education of exceptional children and youth* (2d ed.) Englewood Cliffs, N.J.: Prentice-Hall, 1967.

Dayon, M. Toilet training retarded children in a state residential institution. *Mental Retardation,* 1964, **2,** 116–117.

DeCecco, J. P. *The psychology of learning and instruction: Educational psychology.* Englewood Cliffs, N.J.: Prentice-Hall, 1968.

Dixon, L. *Training an "in front" spatial discrimination using a programmed stimulus series.* Unpublished Doctoral Dissertation, University of Kansas, 1972.

Doll, E. A. A survey and program for special types of education in Trenton, N.J. *White House conference on child health and protection,* Sec. 3. Washington, D.C., 1931.

Doll, E. A. *Vineland Social Maturity Scale.* Nashville: Educational Test Bureau, 1947.

Drucker, P. F. *The age of discontinuity.* New York: Harper & Row, 1969.

Dunn, L. M. *Peabody Picture Vocabulary Test.* Minneapolis: American Guidance Service, 1965.

Dunn, L. M. Special education for the mildly retarded: Is much of it justifiable? *Exceptional Children,* 1968, **35,** 5–22.

Dunn, L. M. (Ed.), *Exceptional children in the schools* (2d Ed.). New York: Holt, Rinehart and Winston, 1973.

Dunn, L. M., & Smith, J. O. *Peabody Language Development Kit.* Circle Pines, Minn.: American Guidance Service, 1967.

Durost, W. N., Bixler, H. H., Wrightstone, J. W., Prescott, G. A., & Balow, I. H. *Metropolitan Achievement Tests,* New York: Harcourt, Brace, Jovanovitch, 1970.

Dwyer, P. S. *Linear computations.* New York: John Wiley & Sons, Inc., 1951.

Dybwad, R. F. The international scene: Patterns of organization and development in member associations of the international league of societies for the mentally handicapped. *Mental Retardation,* 1973, **2**(1), 3–5.

Eaton, M. D. *Applied behavior analysis of certain reading skills of seven boys with learning disabilities.* Unpublished doctoral dissertation, University of Washington, Seattle, 1972.

Eaton, M., & Feldman, A. The influence of self-directed and teacher-directed flashcard drill on performance in basic add facts. In N. G. Haring (Project Director) *A program project for the investigation and application of procedures of analysis and modification of behavior of handicapped children.* Annual report for grant OEG-0-70-3916 (607) Washington, D.C.: U.S. Dept. of Health, Education, and Welfare, 1973.

Eaton, M., & Swenson, A. *An investigation of the difference in maintenance rates of addition probes of pupils held to criteria for one, two, or three days.* (Working Paper No. 7, Experimental Education Unit), University of Washington, 1973.

Ellis, D., & Prelander, J. *A program sequence of phonetic skills.* Annual report for a Program Project for investigation and application of procedures of analysis and modification of behavior of handicapped children. OEG-0-70-3916(607), University of Washington, Experimental Education Unit, 1973.

ENCOR Annual Progress Report (1972–1973), Central Services, 116 South 42nd Street, Omaha, Nebraska 68131.

Englemann, T., Osborn, J., & Engelmann, T. *Distar language: An instructional system.* Chicago: Science Research Associates, Inc., 1969.

Farwell, C. B. The language spoken to children. *Committee on linguistics papers and reports on child language development,* Vols. 5 & 6. Palo Alto: Stanford University, 1973.

Ferritor, D. E., Buckholdt, D., Hamblin, R. L., & Smith, L. The noneffects of contingent reinforcement for attending behavior on work accomplished, *Journal of Applied Analysis of Behavior,* 1972, **5,** 7–17.

Ferster, C. B., & Perrott, M. C. *Behavior principles.* New York: New Century, 1968.

Ferster, C. B., & Skinner, B. F. *Schedules of reinforcement.* New York: Appleton-Century-Crofts, 1957.

Forness, S. The mildly retarded as casualties of the educational system. *Journal of School Psychology,* 1972, **10,** 117–126.

Forness, S., & MacMillan, D. Reinforcement overkill: Implications for education of the retarded. *Journal of Special Education,* 1972, **6,** 221–230.

Fox, R., Copeland, R., Harris, J., Rieth, H. J., & Hall, R. V. *A computerized system for selecting responsive teaching studies catalogued along twenty-eight important dimensions.* In Ramp, E. (Ed.), *Behavior Analysis in Education.* New York: Appleton-Century-Crofts, 1975.

Foxx, R. M., & Azrin, N. H. The elimination of autistic self-stimulation behavior by overcorrection. *Journal of Applied Behavior Analysis,* 1973, **6,** 1–14.

Fraser, C., Bellugi, U., & Brown, R. Control of grammar in imitation, comprehension, and production. *Journal of Verbal Learning and Verbal Behavior,* 1963, **2,** 121–135.

Friedlander, B. L. Receptive language development in infancy: Issues and problems. *Merrill-Palmer Quarterly,* 1970, **16,** 7–51.

Fulton, R. T. *Auditory stimulus—response control.* Baltimore: University Park Press, 1974.

Fulton, R. T. A program of developmental research in audiologic procedures. In R. L. Schiefelbusch (Ed.), *Language of the mentally retarded.* Baltimore: University Park Press, 1972, p. 169–188.

Gage, N. L. (Ed.) *Handbook of research on teaching.* Chicago: Rand McNally, 1963.

Garber, N. B. Operant procedures to eliminate drooling behavior in a cerebral palsied adolescent. *Developmental Medicine and Child Neurology,* 1971, **13,** 641–644.

Gardner, W. I. *Behavior modification in mental retardation.* Chicago: Aldine Atherton, 1971.

Gentry, N. D., Gardebring, M.,& Eaton, M. The influence of oral reading rate on drill on all words in a passage. In N. G. Haring (Project Director) *A Program Project for the Investigation and Application of Procedures of Analysis and Modification of Behavior of Handicapped Children.* Annual report for grant OEG-0-70-3916(607) Washington, D.C.: U.S. Dept. of Health, Education and Welfare, 1973.

Giles, D. K., & Wolf, M. M. Toilet training institutionalized, severe retardates: An application of operant behavior modification techniques. *American Journal of Mental Deficiency,* 1966, **70,** 766–780.

Girardeau, F. L., & Spradlin, J. E. A functional analysis approach to speech and language. *ASHA Monograph No. 14,* 1970.

Glass, G. V., & Stanley, J. C. *Statistical methods in education and Psychology.* Englewood Cliffs, N.J.: Prentice-Hall, 1972.

Gold, M. W. The acquisition of a complex assembly task by retarded adolescents. *Final Report* Project No. 8-8060, University of Illinois, Champaign-Urbana Library, May 1969.

Goldman-Fristoe test of articulation. Circle Pines, Minn.: American Guidance, 1972.

Goldberg, I. I., & Cruickshank, W. M. Trainable but non-educable. *National Educational Association Journal,* 1958, **47,** 622–623.

Goodglass, H., Gleason, J. B., & Hyde, M. Some dimensions of auditory language comprehension in aphasia. *Journal of Speech and Hearing Research,* 1970, **13,** 595–606.

Gotkin, L. *Manual for matrix games.* New York: Appleton-Century-Crofts, 1967.

Gray, B. B., & Fygetakis, L. The development of language as a function of programmed conditioning. *Behaviour Research and Therapy,* 1968, **6,** 455–460. (a)

Gray, B. B., & Fygetakis, L. Mediated language acquisition for dysphasic children. *Behaviour Research and Therapy,* 1968, **6,** 263–280. (b)

Gray, B., & Ryan, B. *A language program for the non-language child.* Champaign, Ill.: Research Press, 1973.

Griffiths, H., & Craighead, W. E. Generalization in operant speech therapy for misarticulation. *Journal of Speech and Hearing Disorders,* 1972, **37,** 485–494.

Grossman, H. J., et al. (Eds.) [for] American Association on Mental Deficiency. *Manual on terminology and classification in mental retardation.* American Association on Mental Deficiency/Special Publication No. 2, 1973.

Guess, D. A functional analysis of receptive language and productive speech: Acquisition of the plural morpheme. *Journal of Applied Behavior Analysis,* 1969, **2,** 55–64.

Guess, D., Sailor, W., & Baer, D. M. To teach language to retarded children. In R. L. Schiefelbusch and L. L. Lloyd (Eds.), *Language perspectives: Acquisition, retardation, and intervention.* Baltimore: University Park Press, 1974.

Guralnick, M. J. A language development program for severely handicapped children. *Exceptional Children,* 1972, **39,** 45–49.

Hall, R. V. *Managing behavior, Part 1: Behavior modification: The measurement of behavior.* Lawrence, Kansas: H & H Enterprises, Inc., 1971. (a)

Hall, R. V. *Managing behavior: Part II: Basic principles.* Lawrence, Kansas: H & H Enterprises, Inc., 1971. (b)

Hall, R. V. *Managing behavior: Part III: Applications in school and home.* Lawrence, Kansas: H & H Enterprises, Inc., 1971. (c)

Hall, R. V. Responsive Teaching: Focus on measurement and research in the classroom and the home. *Focus on Exceptional Children,* 1971, **3,** Love Publishing Company, 1–7. (d)

Hall, R. V. Training teachers in classroom use of contingency management. *Educational Technology,* 1971, **9,** 33–38. (e)

Hall, R. V., Axelrod, S., Foundopolous, M., Shellman, J., Campbell, R., & Cranston, S. The effective use of punishment to modify behavior in the classroom, *Educational Technology,* 1971, **11,** 24–26.

Hall, R. V., Axelrod, S., Tyler, L., Grief, E., Jones, F., & Robertson, L. Modification of behavior problems in the home with parent as observer and experimenter. *Journal of Applied Behavior Analysis,* 1972, **5,** 53–64.

Hall, R. V., Ayala, H., Copeland, R., Cossairt, A., Freeman, J., & Harris, J. Responsive teaching: An approach for training teachers in applied behavior analysis techniques. In E. A. Ramp and B. L. Hopkins (Eds.) *A new direction for education: Behavior analysis, 1971.* The University of Kansas Support and Development Center for Follow Through, Department of Human Development, 1971, 127–157.

Hall, R. V., & Broden, M. Behavior changes in brain-injured children through social reinforcement. *Journal of Experimental Child Psychology,* 1967, **5,** 463–479.

Hall, R. V., & Copeland, R. The responsive teaching model: A first step in shaping school personnel as behavior modification specialists. In F. Clark, D. Evans, L. Hammerlynck (Eds.) *Implementing behavioral programs for schools and clinics*. Champaign, Ill.: Research Press, 1972, 125–150.

Hall, R. V., Cossairt, A., & Crowder, J. Responsive teaching: A practical behavior modification approach for schools. *Challenge,* 1973, **2**, 4–5.

Hall, R. V., Cristler, C., Cranston, S., & Tucker, B. Teachers and parents as researchers using multiple baseline designs. *Journal of Applied Behavior Analysis,* 1970, **3**, 247–255.

Hall, R. V., & Fox, R. *Responsive Teaching Model Transparency Kit*. Lawrence, Kansas: H & H Enterprises, Inc., 1973.

Hall, R. V., Fox, R., Willard, D., Goldsmith, D., Emerson, M., Owen, M., Davis, F., & Porcia, E. The teacher as observer and experimenter in the modification of disputing and talking-out behaviors. *Journal of Applied Behavior Analysis,* 1971, **4**, 141–149.

Hall, R. V., Lund, D. & Jackson, D. Effects of teacher attention on study behavior. *Journal of Applied Behavior Analysis,* 1968, **1,** 1–12.

Hall, R. V., Panyan, M., Rabon, D., & Broden, M. Instructing beginning teachers in reinforcement procedures which improve classroom control. *Journal of Applied Behavior Analysis,* 1968, **1,** 315–322.

Hamblin, R. L., Buckholdt, D., Ferritor, D., Kozloff, M., & Blackwell, L. *The humanization processes: Social, behavioral analysis of children's problems*. New York: John Wiley & Sons, Inc., 1971.

Haring, N. G. *A project to provide additional education for experienced teachers to improve learning conditions for handicapped children in regular classrooms*. (Final Report Project No. 577001) OEG-0-9-577001-558(725), 1969–1971.

Haring, N. G., Hayden, A. H., & Allen, K. E. Programs and projects: Intervention in early childhood. *Educational Technology,* 1971, **11**, 52–60.

Haring, N. G., & Kunzelmann, H. The Finer Focus of Therapeutic Behavioral Management. In J. Hellmuth (Ed.) *Educational therapy Vol. I*. Seattle: Special Child Publications, Inc., 1966.

Haring, N. G., & Lovitt, T. C. Operant methodology and educational technology in special education. In N. G. Haring & R. L. Schiefelbusch (Eds.), *Methods in special education*. New York: McGraw-Hill, 1967, 12–48.

Haring, N. G.,& Phillips, E. L. *Analysis and modification of classroom behavior*. Englewood Cliffs, N.J.,: Prentice-Hall, 1972.

Haring, N. G., & Schiefelbusch, R. L. *Methods in special education*. New York: McGraw-Hill, 1967.

Harris, F. R., Wolf, M. M., & Baer, D. M. Effects of adult social reinforcement on child behavior. *Young Children,* 1964, **20,** 8–17.

Haughton, E. Aims—growing and sharing. In J. B. Jordon and L. S. Robbins (Eds.) *Let's try doing something else kind of thing*. Arlington, Virginia: The Council for Exceptional Children, 1972.

Health, Education and Welfare, Department of. *Mental retardation source book*. Washington, D.C., 1972.

Henderson, H. H., Clise, M., & Silverton, B. *Modification of reading behavior: A phonetic program utilizing rate acceleration*. Ellensburg, Wash: H. H. Henderson, 1971.

Henricksen, K., & Doughty, R. Decelerating undesired mealtime behavior in a group of profoundly retarded boys. *American Journal of Mental Deficiency,* 1967, **72**, 40–44.

Hewett, F. M. The engineered classroom: An innovative approach to the education of children with learning problems. In U.S. Department of Health, Education and Welfare. *Innovation in special education.* Washington, D.C.: U.S. Government Printing Office, 1972.

Hewett, F. M., Taylor, F. D., & Arturo, A. P. The engineered classroom: An innovative approach to education of children with learning problems. In R. H. Bradfield (Ed.), *Behavior modification: The human effort.* San Rafael, Calif.: Dimensions Publishing Co., 1970.

Hillman, B. W. The effect of knowledge or results and token reinforcement on arithmetic achievement of elementary school children. *Arithmetic Teacher,* 1970, **17**, 676–682.

Hingtgen, J. N., & Churchill, D. W. Differential effects of behavior modification in four mute autistic boys. In D. W. Churchill, G. D. Alpern, & M. K. DeMeyer (Eds.), *Infantile autism.* Springfield, Ill.: Charles C. Thomas, 1971.

Hollis, J. H. Solution of bent-wire problems by severely retarded children. *American Journal of Mental Deficiency,* 1962, **67,** 673.

Hollis, J. H. Development of perceptual motor skills in a profoundly retarded child: Part I, prosthesis. *American Journal of Mental Deficiency,* 1967, **71,** 941–952 (a)

Hollis, J. H. Development of perceptual motor skills in a profoundly retarded child: Part II, consequence change and transfer. *American Journal of Mental Deficiency,* 1967, **71,** 953–963. (b)

Hollis, J. H. *Direct measurement of the effects of drugs and alternative activity on stereotyped behavior.* (Parsons Working Paper #168), Parsons State Hospital and Training Center, Parsons, Kansas, 1967. (c)

Hollis, J. H., & Gorton, C. E. Training severely and profoundly developmentally retarded children. *Mental Retardation,* 1967, **5,** 20–24.

Holt, J. *How children fail.* New York: Holt, Rinehart & Winston, 1968.

Homme, L. *How to use contingency contracting in the classroom.* Champaign, Ill.: Research Press, 1970.

Homme, L., deBaca, P. C., Cottingham, L., & Homme, A. What behavioral engineering is. *The Psychological Record,* 1968, **18,** 425–434.

Homme, L. E., deBaca, P. C., Devine, J. V., Steinhorst, R., & Rickert, E. J. Use of the Premack principle in controlling the behavior of nursery school children. *Journal of the Experimental Analysis of Behavior,* 1963, **6,** 544.

Hopkins, B. L., Schutte, R. C., & Garton, K. L. The effects of access to a playroom on the rate and quality of printing and writing of first and second grade students. *Journal of Applied Behavior Analysis,* 1971, **4,** 77–87.

Horner, R. D. Establishing use of crutches by a mentally retarded *spina bifida* child. *Journal of Applied Behavior Analysis,* 1971, **4,** 77–87.

Hunt, J. McV. *Intelligence and experience.* New York: Ronald Press, 1961.

Hunziak, M. M., Maurer, R. A., & Watson, L. S. Operant conditioning in toilet training of severely mentally retarded boys. *American Journal of Mental Deficiency,* 1965, **70,** 120–124.

Iano, R. P. Shall we disband special classes? *The Journal of Special Education,* 1972, **6,** 167–177.

Irwin, J. V., & Marge, M. *Principles of Childhood Language Disabilities.* New York: Appleton-Century-Crofts, 1972.

Jackson, P. W. *Life in classrooms.* New York: Holt, Rinehart & Winston, 1968.

Johnson, G. O. *Training program for severely mentally retarded children.* Albany: New York State Interdepartmental Health Resources Board, 1958.

Johnson, G. O., & Capobianco, R. J. *Research project on severely retarded children.* Albany: New York State Interdepartmental Health Resources Board, 1958.

Johnson, W. Clinical point of view in education, Chap. II in W. Johnson, S. Brown, J. Curtis, C. Edney, and J. Keaster (Eds.), *Speech Handicapped School Children.* New York: Harper & Row, 1967.

Jones, R. Behavioral change: Methodology concepts and practice. In E. J. Hammerlynck and L. C. Hamly (Eds.), *The fourth Banff international conference on behavior modification.* Champaign, Ill.: Research Press, 1973.

Jones, R. L. Labels and stigmas in special education. *Exceptional Children,* 1972, **38,** 553–564.

Kanfer, F. H. Behavior Modification—An Overview. In C. E. Thoresen (Ed.) *Behavior modification in education: The yearbook of the national society for the study of education.* Chicago: University of Chicago Press, 1972.

Kapfer, M. B. *Behavioral objectives in curriculum development: Selected readings.* Englewood Cliffs, N.J.: Educational Technology, 1972.

Kelley, T. L., Madden, R., Gardner, E. F., & Rudman, H. C. *Stanford achievement test.* New York: Harcourt, Brace and World, 1964.

Kendall, M. G. *A course in multivatiate analysis.* Hafner Publishing Co., 1957, Chap. 3.

Kent, L. R., Klein, D., Falk, A., & Guenther, H. A language acquisition program for the retarded. In J. E. McLean, D. E. Yoder, & R. L. Schiefelbusch (Eds.), *Language intervention with the retarded.* Baltimore: University Park Press, 1972, 151–190.

Kirk, R. E. *Experimental design: Procedures for the behavioral sciences.* Belmont: Brooks and Cole, 1969.

Kirk, S. A. *Educating exceptional children.* Boston: Houghton Mifflin, 1962.

Kirk, S. A. *Educating exceptional children* (2d ed.). Boston: Houghton Mifflin, 1972.

Kirk, S. A., McCarthy, J. J., & Kirk, W. D. *The Illinois Test of Psycholinguistic Ability.* (Rev. ed.). Urbana, Ill.: University of Illinois Press, 1968.

Kirk, S. A., & Johnson, G. O. *Educating the retarded child.* Boston: Houghton Mifflin, 1951.

Koenig, C. H. Charting the future course of behavior. Unpublished doctoral dissertation. University of Kansas, 1972.

Krumboltz, J. D., & Krumboltz, H. B. *Changing children's behavior.* Englewood Cliffs, N.J.: Prentice-Hall, 1972.

Lackner, J. A developmental study of language behavior in retarded children. *Neuropsychologia,* 1968, **6,** 301–320.

Lee, L. L. *Northwestern Syntax Screening Test.* Evanston, Ill.: Northwestern University Press, 1969.

Lee, L. L., & Cantor, S. M. Developmental sentence scoring: A clinical procedure for estimating syntactic development in children's spontaneous speech. *Journal of Speech and Hearing Disorders,* 1971, **36,** 315–340.

Lenneberg, E. H. *Biological foundations of language.* New York: Wiley, 1967.

Lent, J. R. *Reduction of negative social behaviors in a workshop setting.* Paper presented at the 89th Annual American Association on Mental Deficiency Convention, Miami Beach: June 1965.

Lent, J. R. Mimosa Cottage: Experiment in hope. *Psychology Today,* 1968, **2,** 51–58.

Lent, J. R. *A demonstration program for intensive training of institutionalized mentally retarded girls:* Detailed progress report (Five-year Summary, June 1965 through July

1970). U.S. Department of Health, Education and Welfare, Public Health Service Grant MR 1 801 069, Bureau of Child Research, University of Kansas. Parsons, Kansas: Media Support Services, Project MORE, 1970.

Lent, J. R., Dixon, M. H., Schiefelbusch, R. L., & McLean, B. The Hansons: A retarded couple in the community. In B. B. Hauch & M. F. Freehill (Eds.), *The mentally retarded—Case Studies*. Dubuque, Iowa: Wm. C. Brown, 1972.

Lent, J. R., LeBlanc, J. & Spradlin, J. E. Designing a rehabilitation culture for moderately retarded, adolescent girls. In R. Ulrich, T. Stachnik, & J. Mabry (Eds.), *Control of human behavior*, Vol. 2. Glenview, Ill.: Scott Foresman, 1971.

Lilly, M. S. Special education: A teapot in a tempest. *Exceptional Children*, 1970, **37**, 43–48.

Lilly, M. S. A training based model for special education. *Exceptional Children*, 1971, **37**, 745–750.

Lindquist, E. F., & Hieronymus, A. N. *Iowa Test of Basic Skills*. Boston: Allyn and Bacon, 1964.

Lindsley, O. R. Direct measurement and prosthesis of retarded children. *Journal of Education*, 1964, **147**, 62–81.

Lippman, L., & Goldberg, I. I. *Right to education: Anatomy of the Pennsylvania case and its implications for exceptional children*. New York: Teachers College Press, Columbia University, 1973.

Lloyd, L. L., & Fulton, R. T. Audiology's contribution to communications programming with the retarded. In J. E. McLean, D. E. Yoder, & R. L. Schiefelbusch (Eds.), *Language intervention with the retarded*. Baltimore: University Park Press, 1972.

Louttit, C. M. *Clinical psychology of exceptional children (3rd ed.)*. New York: Harper, 1957.

Lovaas, O. I. A program for the establishment of speech in psychotic children. In H. Sloane & B. MacAulay (Eds.), *Operant procedures in remedial speech and language training*. Boston: Houghton-Mifflin, 1968.

Lovaas, O. I., Freitag, G., Kinder, M. I., Rubenstein, B. D., Schaeffer, B., & Simmons, J. Q. Establishment of social reinforcers in two schizophrenic children on the basis of food. *Journal of Experimental Child Psychology*, 1966, **4**, 109–125.

Lovaas, O. I., Freitag, L., Nelson, K., & Whalen, C. The establishment of imitation and its use for the establishment of complex behavior in schizophrenic children. *Behavior Research and Therapy*, 1967, **5**, 171–181.

Lovaas, O. I., Koegel, R., Simmons, J. Q., & Long, J. S. Some generalizations and follow-up measures on autistic children in behavior therapy. *Journal of Applied Behavior Analysis*, 1973, **6**, 131–165.

Lovaas, O. I., Litrownik, A., & Mann, R. Response latencies to auditory stimuli in autistic children engaged in self-stimulatory behavior. *Behaviour Research and Therapy*, 1971, **9**, 39–49.

Lovaas, O. I., & Simmons, J. Q. Manipulation of self-destruction in three retarded children. *Journal of Applied Behavior Analysis*, 1969, **2**, 143–159.

Lovitt, T. C., Guppy, T. C., & Blattner, J. E. The use of a free-time contingency with fourth graders to increase spelling accuracy. *Behaviour Research and Therapy*, 1969, **7**, 151–156.

Lovitt, T. C., & Hansen, C. L. Round one: Placing a child in the right reader. *Journal of Learning Disabilities*, in press.

Lyle, J. G. A comparison of the language of normal and imbecile children. *Journal of Mental Deficiency Research*, 1961, **5,** 40–51.

MacAulay, B. D. A program for teaching speech and beginning reading to nonverbal retardates. In H. N. Sloane & B. D. MacAulay (Eds.), *Operant procedures in remedial speech and language training*. Boston: Houghton-Mifflin, 1968.

Madsen, C. H., Jr., Becker, W. C., & Thomas, D. R. Rules, praise and ignoring: elements of elementary classroom control. *Journal of Applied Behavior Analysis,* 1968, **1,** 139–150.

Mager, R. F. *Preparing instructional objectives.* Palo Alto: Fearon Publications, 1962.

Mager, R. F. *Goal Analysis.* Belmont, Calif. Fearon Publishers, 1972.

Mahoney, K., Van Wagenen, R. K., & Meyerson, L. Toilet training of normal and retarded children. *Journal of Applied Behavior Analysis,* 1971, **4,** 173–183.

Marquesen, V. *The effects of mild physical restraint upon problem behavior in a severely retarded boy.* Unpublished master's Thesis, University of Kansas, 1972.

Marshall, N. R., & Hegrenes, J. The use of written language as a communication system for an autistic child. *Journal of Speech and Hearing Disorders,* 1972, **37,** 258–261.

McCracken, R. A. *The teaching of reading, a primer.* Klamath Falls, Ore.: Klamath Printing Co., 1971.

McDonald, E. *A deep test of articulation* (Picture and sentence forms). Pittsburgh: Stanwix House, 1964.

McDonald, F. J. Behavior modification in teacher education. In C. E. Thoresen (Ed.) *Behavior modification in education: The yearbook of the national society for the study of education.* Chicago: University of Chicago Press, 1972.

McDonald, F. J., & Allen, D. W. *Training effects of feedback and modeling procedures on teacher performance.* (Technical Report No. 3). Stanford Center for Research and Development in Teaching, Palo Alto, 1967.

McKenzie, H. S., Egner, H. A., Knight, M., Perelman, P. K., Schneider, B. M., & Garvin, J. S. Training consulting teachers to assist elementary teachers in the management and education of handicapped children, Experiment I. *Exceptional Children,* 1970, **37,** 137–143.

McLean, J. E. Extending stimulus control of phoneme articulation by operant techniques. In F. L. Girardeau, & J. E. Spradlin (Eds.), *A functional approach to speech and language.* ASHA Monograph No. 14, 1970, 24–47.

McLean, J. E. Shift of stimulus control: A clinical procedure in articulation therapy. Produced by the Bureau of Child Research, University of Kansas (37 min. 16 mm color), 1970.

McLean, J. E., & Raymore, S. L. *Programmatic research on a systematic articulation therapy program: Carry-over on phoneme responses to untrained situations for normal-learning public school children.* (Parsons Research Center Report No. 6) Parsons, Kansas: Kansas Center for Mental Retardation and Human Development, 1972.

McLean, J. E., Yoder, D. E., & Schiefelbusch, R. L. (Eds.), *Language intervention with the retarded.* Baltimore: University Park Press, 1972.

McNeill, D. *The acquisition of language: The study of developmental psycholinguistics.* New York: Harper & Row, 1970.

McReynolds, L. V. Contingencies and consequences in speech therapy. *Journal of Speech and Hearing Disorders,* 1970, **35,** 12–24.

Mecham, M. J., Jex, J. L., & Jones, J. D. *Utah test of Language Development.* Salt Lake City: Communication Research Associates, Box 11012, 1967.

Menyuk, P. Syntactic rules used by children from preschool through first grade. *Child Development,* 1964, **35,** 533–546.

Metz, J. R. Conditioning generalized imitation in autistic children. *Journal of Experimental Child Psychology,* 1965, **2,** 389–399.

Meyerson, L., Kerr, N., & Michael, J. L. Behavior modification in rehabilitation. In S. W. Bijou & D. M. Baer (Eds.), *Child development: Readings in experimental analysis.* New York: Appleton-Century-Crofts, 1967.

Miller, G. A., Galanter, E., & Pribram, K. H. *Plans and the structure of behavior.* New York: Holt, Rinehart and Winston, 1960.

Miller, J., & Yoder, D. Teaching language to retardates: A format, not a receipt. In R. L. Schiefelbusch & L. L. Lloyd (Eds.), *Language perspectives: Acquisition, retardation and intervention.* Baltimore: University Park Press, 1974.

Miller, K. L. Principles of everyday behavior analysis. Belmont, Calif.: Wadsworth, 1974.

Millikan, C. H. & Darley, F. L. *Brain mechanisms underlying speech and language.* New York: Grune & Stratton, 1967.

Montessori, M. *Montessori Method* (translated by Anne E. George). Philadelphia: Stokes, 1912.

Moores, D. F. Nonvocal systems of verbal behavior. In R. L. Schiefelbusch and L. L. Lloyd (Eds.), *Language perspectives: Acquisition, retardation, and intervention.* Baltimore: University Park Press, 1974.

Mowrer, D. E. Evaluating speech therapy through precision recording. *Journal of Speech and Hearing Disorders,* 1969, **35,** 239–244.

Mowrer, D. E. Transfer of training in articulation therapy. *Journal of Speech and Hearing Disorders,* 1971, **36,** 427–446.

National Association for Retarded Citizens. *Residential programming for mentally retarded persons: Developmental programming in the residential facility.* Arlington, Texas, 1972.

Newfield, M. U., & Schlanger, B. B. The acquisition of English morphology by normal and educable mentally retarded children. *Journal of Speech and Hearing Research,* 1968, **11,** 639–706.

Nihira, K., Foster, R., Shallhaas, M., & Leland, H. *AAMD adaptive behavior scales* (Rev. ed.). Washington, D.C.: American Association of Mental Deficiency, 1970.

O'Brien, F., & Azrin, N. H. Developing proper mealtime behaviors of the institutional retarded. *Journal of Applied Behavior Analysis,* 1972, **5,** 389–400.

O'Brien, F., Bugle, C., & Azrin, N. H. Training and maintaining a retarded child's proper eating. *Journal of Applied Behavior Analysis,* 1972, **5,** 67–73.

O'Leary, K. D., & Becker, W. C. Behavior modification of an adjustment class: A token reinforcement program. *Exceptional Children,* 1967, **33,** 637–642.

O'Leary, K. D., Kaufman, K. F., Kass, R. E., & Drabman, R. S. The effects of loud and soft reprimands on the behavior of disruptive students. *Exceptional Children,* 1970, **37,** 145–155.

Palermo, D. S. On learning to talk: Are principles derived from the learning laboratory applicable? In D. I. Slobin (Ed.), *The ontogenesis of grammar.* New York: Academic Press, 1971.

Panyan, M. C. *Managing behavior, Part 4, Behavior modification: New ways to teach new skills.* Lawrence, Kansas: H & H Enterprises, Inc., 1972.

Patterson, G. R. An application of conditioning techniques to the control of a hyperactive child. In L. P. Ullman and L. Krasner (Eds.), *Case Studies in Behavior Modification.* New York: Holt, Rinehart and Winston, Inc., 1966, 370–375.

Patterson, G. R., & Reid, J. B. Reciprocity and coercion: Two facets of social systems. In C. Neuringer and J. L. Michael (Eds.), *Behavior modification in clinical psychology.* New York: Appleton-Century-Crofts, 1970.

Piaget, J. Piaget's theory. In P. Mussen (Ed.), *Carmichael's manual of child psychology.* New York: Wiley, 1970.

Piaget, J., & Inhelder, B. *The psychology of the child.* New York: Basic Books, 1969.

Postman, N., & Weingartner, C. *Teaching as a subversive activity.* New York: Delacorte Press, 1969.

Premack, D. Toward Empirical Behavior Laws: 1. Positive Reinforcement. *Psychological Review,* 1959, **66,** 219–233.

Premack, D. A. A functional analysis of language. *Journal of the Experimental Analysis of Behavior,* 1970, **14,** 107–125.

Pribram, K. H. *Language of the brain: Experimental paradoxes and principles in neuropsychology.* Engelwood Cliffs, N.J.: Prentice-Hall, 1971.

Quay, H. C. Special education: Assumptions, techniques, and evaluative criteria. *Exceptional Children,* 1973, **40,** 165–170.

Rao, C. R. *Advanced statistical methods in biometric research.* New York: Wiley, 1962.

Rarick, G. L., Widdop, J. H., & Broadhead, G. D. The physical fitness and motor performance of educable mentally retarded children. *Exceptional Children,* 1970, **36,** 509–524.

Rebelsky, F. G., Starr, R. H., & Luria, Z. Language development: The first four years. In Y. Brackbill (Ed.), *Infancy and early childhood.* New York: The Free Press, 1967.

Reese, H. W., & Lipsitt, L. P. *Experimental child psychology.* New York: Academic Press, 1970.

Reynolds, M. C., & Balow, B. Categories and variables in special education. *Exceptional Children,* 1972, **38,** 357–366.

Rieth, H. J., & Hall, R. V. *Responsive teaching model readings in applied behavior analysis,* Lawrence, Kansas: H & H Enterprises, Inc., 1974.

Risley, T. R., & Cataldo, M. F. Evaluation of planned activities: the pla-check measure of classroom participation. In Davidson, Clark, & Hammerlynck (Eds.), *Evaluation of social programs in community, residential and school settings.* Champaign, Ill.: Research Press, (in press).

Risley, T. R., & Wolf, M. M. Establishing functional speech in echolalic children. *Behaviour Research and Therapy,* 1967, **5,** 73–88.

Risley, T., & Wolf, M. Establishing functional speech in echolalic children. In H. Sloane & B. MacAulay (Eds.), *Operant procedures in remedial speech and language training.* Boston: Houghton-Mifflin; 1968.

Ritter, E. L., & Wilmarth, A. L. *Rural school methods.* New York: Scribner, 1925.

Roa, C. R. *Linear statistical inference and its applications.* New York: Wiley, 1965.

Rogers, D. C., Ort, L., and Serra, M. D. *My Word Book Spelling Program.* Pasadena: Lyons and Carnahan, 1970.

Rosenberg, S. The development of referential skills in children. In R. L. Schiefelbusch (Ed.), *Language of the Mentally Retarded,* Baltimore: University Park Press, 1972.

Rothstein, J. H. California's program for the severely retarded child. *Exceptional Children,* 1953, **19,** 172.

Rothstein, J. H. (Ed.) *Mental retardation readings and resources.* New York: Holt, Rinehart and Winston, 1971.

Ruder, K., & Smith, M. *Children's imitations of parents' speaking fundamental frequency.* (Bureau of Child Research Working Paper), University of Kansas, 1972.

Ruder, K., & Smith, M. Issues in language training. In R. L. Schiefelbusch and L. L. Lloyd (Eds.), *Language perspectives: Acquisition, retardation, and intervention*. Baltimore: University Park Press, 1974.

Ruder, K., Bricker, W., & Ruder, C. Recent psycholinguistic research on the language acquisition process. In J. Gallagher (Ed.), *Review of research on exceptional children*. Washington, D.C.: Council on Exceptional Children, 1975.

Sabatino, D. A. Resource rooms: The renaissance in special education. *The Journal of Special Education*, 1972, **6**, 335–348.

Sailor, W., Guess, D., & Baer, D. M. Functional language for verbally deficient children: An experimental program. *Mental Retardation*, 1973, **11**, 27–35.

Sanders, E. When are speech sounds learned? *Journal of Speech and Hearing Disorders*, 1972, **37**, 55–63.

Saudargas, R. A. Setting criterion rates of teacher praise: The effects of video tape feedback in a behavior analysis follow through classroom. In G. Semb (Ed.), *Behavior Analysis and Education*. Lawrence, Kansas: Support and Development Center for Follow Through, 1972.

Schiefelbusch, R. L. Introduction. In N. G. Haring & R. L. Schiefelbusch (Eds.), *Methods in special education*. New York: McGraw-Hill, 1967.

Schiefelbusch, R. L. (Ed.). *Language of the mentally retarded*. Baltimore: University Park Press, 1972.

Schumaker, J., & Sherman, J. A. Training generative verb usage by imitation and reinforcement procedures. *Journal of Applied Behavior Analysis*. 1970, **3**, 273–287.

Schutte, R. C., & Hopkins, B. L. The effects of teacher attention on following instructions in a kindergarten class. *Journal of Applied Behavior Analysis*, 1970, **3**, 117–122.

Senter, R. J. *Analysis of data: Introductory statistics for the behavioral sciences*. Palo Alto: Scott, Foresman, 1969.

Shriner, T. H., Holloway, M., & Daniloff, R. G. The relationship between articulatory deficits and syntax in speech defective children. *Journal of Speech and Hearing Research*, 1969, **12**, 319–325.

Sidman, M., & Stoddard, L. The effectiveness of fading in programming a simultaneous form discrimination for retarded children. *Journal of the Experimental Analysis of Behavior*, 1967, **10**, 3–15.

Silberman, C. *Crisis in the classroom: The remaking of American education*. New York: McGraw-Hill, 1968.

Silverman, R. E. Two kinds of technology. *Educational Technology*, 1968, **8**, 1–10.

Sinclair-de-Zwart, H. Developmental psycholinguistics. In D. Elking & J. H. Flavell (Eds.), *Studies in cognitive development*. New York: Oxford, 1969.

Skinner, B. F. *The technology of teaching*. New York: Appleton-Century-Crofts, 1968.

Sloane, H. N., Johnston, M. K., & Harris, F. R. Remedial procedures for teaching verbal behavior to speech deficient or defective young children. In H. N. Sloane & B. D. MacAulay (Eds.), *Operant procedures in remedial speech and language training*. Boston: Houghton-Mifflin, 1968.

Sloane, H. N., & MacAulay, B. D. (Eds.). *Operant procedures in remedial speech and language training*. Boston: Houghton Mifflin, 1968.

Smith, D. D. *The influence of instructions, feedback and reinforcement contingencies on children's abilities to acquire and become proficient at computational arithmetic skills*. Unpublished doctoral dissertation, University of Washington, 1973.

Spradlin, J. E. The Parsons Language Sample. In R. L. Schiefelbusch (Ed.), Language

Studies of Mentally Retarded Children, *Journal of Speech and Hearing Disorders,* January Monograph Supplement, 1963, **10.**

Spradlin, J. E. *The Premack hypothesis and self-feeding by profoundly retarded children: A case report.* (Parsons Working Paper No. 79), Parsons, Kansas: Parsons State Hospital and Training Center, 1964.

Spradlin, J. E. *Psycholinguistic training with retarded children.* Speech given at a symposium, "Psycholinguistic Development in Children: Implications for Children with Developmental Disabilities," sponsored by the Department of Health Rehabilitation Services, Division of Retardation, Tampa, Florida, 1973.

Spradlin, J. E., Girardeau, F. L., & Corte, E. Fixed ratio and fixed interval behavior of severely and profoundly retarded subjects. *Journal of Experimental Child Psychology,* 1966, **2,** 340–353.

Staats, A. W., & Butterfield, W. H. Treatment of nonreading in a culturally deprived juvenile delinquent: An application of reinforcement principles. *Child Development,* 1965, **4,** 925–942.

Staats, A. W., Finley, J. R., Minke, K. A., & Wolf, M. M. Reinforcement variables in the control of unit reading responses. *Journal of the Experimental Analysis of Behavior,* 1964, **7,** 139–149.

Staats, A. W., Staats, C. K., Schultz, R. E., & Wolf, M. M. The conditioning of textual responses using "extrinsic" reinforcers. *Journal of the Experimental Analysis of Behavior,* 1962, **5,** 33–40.

Stanberry, M., & Harris, J. Reduction of tardy behavior in junior high school pupils. *Managing behavior, Part III, Behavior modification: Applications in school and home.* Lawrence, Kansas: H & H Enterprises, Inc., 1971.

Starlin, C. M. Evaluating progress toward reading proficiency. In B. Bateman (Ed.) *Learning disorders, Vol. 4; Reading.* Seattle: Special Child Publications, Inc., 1971.

Starlin, C. M., & Starlin, A. *Guides to decision making in spelling.* Bemidji, Minnesota: Unique Curriculums Unlimited, 1973. (a)

Starlin, C. M., & Starlin, A. *Guides to decision making in computational math.* Bemidji, Minnesota: Unique Curriculums Unlimited, 1973. (b)

Starlin, C. M., & Starlin, A. *Guides to decision making in oral reading.* Bemidji, Minnesota: Unique Curriculums Unlimited, 1973. (c)

Stevens, J. C., & Savin, H. B. On the form of learning curves. *Journal of Experimental Analysis of Behavior,* 1962, **5,** 15.

Stremel, K. Language training: A program for retarded children. *Mental Retardation,* 1972, **10,** 47–49.

Stremel, K., & Waryas, C. A behavioral-psycholinguistic approach to language training. In L. V. McReynolds (Ed.), *Procedures for the modification of children's language behavior.* ASHA Monograph, 1974.

Striefel, S. Television as a language training medium with retarded children. *Mental Retardation,* 1972, **10,** 27–29.

Striefel, S., Bryan, K., & Aikens, D. Transfer of stimulus control from motor to verbal stimuli. (Parsons Research Center Working Paper No. 293), Parsons State Hospital and Training Center, Parsons, Kansas: 1973.

Striefel, S., & Eberl, D. Imitation of live and videotaped models. (Parsons Research Center Working Paper No. 288), Parsons State Hospital and Training Center, Parsons, Kansas: 1973.

Striefel, S., & Weatherby, B. Instruction-following behavior of a retarded child and its controlling stimuli. *Journal of Applied Behavior Analysis,* 1973, **6,** 663–670.

Suppes, P., and Suppes, J. *Sets and Numbers*. New York: L. W. Singer Co., 1968.

Surratt, P. R., Ulrich, R. E., & Hawkins, R. P. An elementary student as a behavioral engineer. *Journal of Applied Behavior Analysis,* 1970, **2,** 85–93.

Swenson, C. R., & Billingsley, F. F. Behavior Games—Project Report XI-C. In N. G. Haring (Project Director) *A Program Project for the Investigation and Application of Procedures of Analysis and Modification of Behavior of Handicapped Children.* Annual report for grant OEG-0-70-3916(607). Washington, D.C.: Department of Health, Education and Welfare, 1973.

Talkington, L. W., & Hall, S. M. Matrix language program with mongoloids. *American Journal of Mental Deficiency,* 1970, **75,** 88–91.

Tawney, J. W., & Hipsher, L. W. *Systematic instruction for retarded children: The Illinois program. Part II: Systematic language instruction.* (Project No. 71205), U.S. Department of Health, Education and Welfare Grant No. OEG-0-8-001025(032), University of Illinois, 1970.

Taylor, W. F. *The effects of praise upon the quality and quantity of creative writing.* Unpublished master's thesis, University of Akron, 1965.

Terrace, H. S. Errorless transfer of discrimination across two continui. *Journal of the Experimental Analysis of Behavior,* 1963, **6,** 223–232.

Thomas, D. R. Preliminary findings on self-monitoring for modifying teaching behaviors. In E. A. Ramp & B. L. Hopkins (Eds.), *A new direction for education: Behavior analysis.* Lawrence, Kansas: Support and Development Center for Follow Through, 1971.

Thomas, D. R., Becker, W. C., & Armstrong, J. M. Production and elimination of disruptive classroom behavior by systematically varying teacher's behavior. *Journal of Applied Behavior Analysis,* 1968, **1,** 35–45.

Thorndike, E. L. *Animal intelligence.* New York: Macmillan, 1911.

Touchette, P. E. Transfer of stimulus control: Measuring the moment of transfer. *Journal of the Experimental Analysis of Behavior,* 1971, **15,** 347–354.

Travis, L. *Handbook of speech pathology and audiology.* New York: Appleton-Century-Crofts, 1971.

Van Riper, C. *Speech correction principles and methods.* Englewood Cliffs, N.J.: Prentice-Hall, 1972.

Vazquez, G. F. & Hopkins, B. L. Effectos de un paquet de entrenamiento para maestros. In G. F. Vazquez & B. L. Hopkins (Eds.), *Education para ninõs: aportaciones humanisticas de la ciencia y la tecnologia conductual.* Mexico City: Sociedad de Padres de Familia del Colegio "Walden Dos," 1973.

Vincent-Smith, L., & Bricker, D. A comparison of receptive vocabulary skills in the delayed and nondelayed toddler. In D. Bricker & W. Bricker, Toddler Research and Intervention Report: Year II. *IMRID Behavioral Science Monograph No. 21,* George Peabody College, Nashville, 1972.

Wahler, R. G., Wenkel, G. H., Peterson, R. J., & Morrison, D. C. Mothers are behavior therapists for their own children. *Behaviour Research and Therapy,* 1965, **3,** 113–124.

Waite, K. B. *The educable mentally retarded child.* Springfield, Ill.: Charles C Thomas, 1972.

Walker, H., & Buckley, N. The use of positive reinforcement in conditioning attending behavior. *Journal of Applied Behavior Analysis,* 1968, **1,** 245–252.

Wann, K. D., Vreeland, J. D., and Conklin, M. A. *Learning About Our Country.* Boston: Allyn and Bacon, 1967.

Warren, S. A. Academic achievement of trainable pupils with five or more years of schooling. *Training School Bulletin,* 1963, **60,** 75–88.

Waryas, C. Psycholinguistic research in language intervention programming: The pronoun system. *Journal of Psycholinguistic Research,* 1973, **2,** 221–237.

Waryas, C., & Ruder, K. On the limitation of language comprehension procedures and an alternative. *Journal of Speech and Hearing Disorders,* 1974, Vol. 39.

Weintraub, R. J., Abeson, A. R., & Braddock, D. L. *State law and education of handicapped children: Issues and recommendations.* Arlington, Va.: The Council for Exceptional Children, 1972.

Whalen, C. K., & Henker, B. A. Pyramid therapy in a hospital for the retarded: Methods, program evaluation and long-term effects. *American Journal of Mental Deficiency,* 1971, **75,** 414–434.

Whalen, C. K., & Henker, B. A. Creating therapeutic pyramids using mentally retarded patients. *American Journal of Mental Deficiency,* 1969, **74,** 331–337.

Wheeler, A. H., & Fox, W. L. *Managing behavior, Part V, Behavior modification: A teacher's guide to writing instructional objectives.* Lawrence, Kansas: H & H Enterprises, Inc., 1972.

White, O. R. ''A manual for the calculation and use of the median slope—A method for progress estimation and prediction in the single case'' University of Oregon: Regional Resource Center for Handicapped Children, Working Paper No. 16, 1972. (a)

White, O. R. *Methods of data analysis in intensive designs.* Paper presented at the American Educational Research Association's national convention in a symposium entitled ''The intensive approach in counseling,'' Carl E. Thoreson, organizer; John D. Drumboltz, chairman, both from Stanford University, April, 1972. (b)

White, O. R. ''The prediction of human performances in the single case: An examination of four techniques. University of Oregon: Regional Resource Center for Handicapped Children, Working Paper No. 15, 1972.

White, O. R. *Glossary of behavioral terminology.* Champaign, Ill: Research Press, 1971. (a)

White, O. R. ''The 'Split-Middle': A 'Quickie' method of trend estimation'' University of Oregon, Regional Resource Center for Handicapped Children, Working Paper No. 1, 1971. (b)

Whitman, T. L., Zaharas, M., & Chardos, S. Effects of reinforcement and guidance procedures on instruction-following behavior of severely retarded children. *Journal of Applied Behavior Analysis,* 1971, **4,** 283–290.

Whitney, L. R., & Barnard, K. E. Implications of operant learning theory for nursing care of the retarded child. *Mental Retardation,* 1966, **4,** 26–29.

Winer, B. J. *Statistical principles in experimental design.* New York: McGraw-Hill, 1962.

Winitz, H. Problem solving and the delaying of speech as strategies in the teaching of language. *ASHA,* 1973, **15,** 583–586.

Winitz, H. *Articulatory acquisition and behavior.* New York: Prentice-Hall, 1969.

Wolf, M. M., Giles, D. K., & Hall, R. V. Experiments with token reinforcement in a remedial classroom. *Behaviour Research and Therapy,* 1968, **6,** 51–64.

Wolf, M. M., Risley, T. R., & Mees, H. Application of operant conditioning procedures to the behavior problems of an autistic child. *Behaviour Research and Therapy,* 1964, **1,** 305–312.

Wolfensberger, W. Will there always be an institution? I: The impact of epidemiological trends. *Mental Retardation,* 1971, **9,** 14–38.

Zimmerman, E. H., & Zimmerman, J. The alteration of behavior in a special classroom situation. *Journal of the Experimental Analysis of Behavior,* 1962, **5,** 59–60.

Index